BEYOND THE WORD: RECONSTRUCTING SENSE IN THE JOYCE ERA OF TECHNOLOGY, CULTURE, AND COMMUNICATION

THEORY / CULTURE

General editors: Linda Hutcheon, Gary Leonard, Janet Paterson, and Paul Perron

DONALD F. THEALL

Beyond the Word: Reconstructing Sense in the Joyce Era of Technology, Culture, and Communication

UNIVERSITY OF TORONTO PRESS
Toronto Buffalo London

Toronto Buffalo London
Printed in Canada
Reprinted in 2018

ISBN 0-8020-0630-2
ISBN 978-1-4875-8504-4 (paper)

Printed on acid-free paper

Canadian Cataloguing in Publication Data

Theall, Donald F., 1928–
Beyond the word : reconstructing sense in the Joyce era of technology, culture, and communication

(Theory/culture)
Includes bibliographical references and index.
ISBN 0-8020-0630-2

1. Communication and culture. 2. Technology – Social aspects. 3. Joyce, James, 1882–1941. I. Title. II. Series.

P90.T44 1995 302.2 C95-931977-8

University of Toronto Press acknowledges the financial assistance to its publishing program of the Canada Council and the Ontario Arts Council.

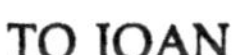
TO JOAN
'the allmaziful ... bringer of plurabilities' who made it all possible

Contents

Preface

It has been a lifelong preoccupation of mine that the study of communication has suffered by not being more directly involved with the entire spectrum of the arts of cultural production and that the study of all modes of cultural production have until recently suffered from being carried on in relative isolation from one another. *Beyond the Word* aims at demonstrating that a common productive activity is present in all cultural production from cartoons and comic strips, TV series and hypermedia, to poetry, painting, and drama. It also explains how such cultural production is a vital and intrinsic part of the development and renewal of human language and communication. While the rise of cultural studies, the academic acceptance of the importance of the history of communication, and the unquestioned recognition of film and multimedia as forms of cultural production on a par with literature, drama, and art have been positive developments, the appropriate removal of a traditional claim of privilege for the Fine Arts, including literature and poetry, has often in practice turned into a debunking of the more traditional arts and a covert privileging of popular and mass art. This extreme reversal of the past makes works such as this one even more imperative.

The first and major debts that I owe for leading my interests in this direction are to those with whom I developed these interests over four decades ago: Marshall McLuhan, Edmund Carpenter, and their associates in the early *Explorations* group at the University of Toronto; and to Richard Robinson and John Wevers, early pioneers in developing an interest in linguistics at the university. Marshall, who directed my doctoral thesis, imparted to me a spirit of trans-disciplinarity which has provided the grounding for most of my career, including this book.

There are many specific debts. Friends and colleagues who have read all or part of the manuscript at various stages and who offered advice and encouragement include Fred Flahiff, Darko Suvin, David Crowley, John Fekete, George Szanto, Ian McLachlan, Peter Ohlin, and Patrick Parrinder. Dušan Makavéjev provided many opportunities for conversations that were of inestimable value, and he has read the manuscript, but most of all he has been a warm and encouraging friend. Many other colleagues through conversations offered guidance and encouragement, including Marc Angenot, Donald Bouchard, Jacques Languirand, John Grierson, Archie Malloch, David Mitchell, Paul Heyer, Alan Orenstein, Joseph Ronsley, Lorraine Weir, David Williams, Annie Meir, and Abbott Conway. The work would not be as successful as it is without their guidance or support, but the way in which that support developed into the present work is solely my responsibility. John Unsworth's and Eyal Amiran's having published an article of mine in *Postmodern Culture* – parts of which are used in this book – reassured me of the topicality of my interests and provided a valuable sounding-board in terms of subsequent comments and contacts.

While this book is primarily about communication, culture, and technology in relation to cultural production, James Joyce's writings play a central role within it. Anyone working on any aspect of Joyce, particularly *Ulysses* and *Finnegans Wake*, is indebted to a rich, diverse, and dedicated community of scholars. A particular debt is due to those who have laboured on the *James Joyce Archives* – Michael Groden, Danis Rose, and David Hayman. Joyceans who have encouraged or reassured me about the direction of my work have included Richard Ellmann, Cheryl Herr, Brandon Kershner, Tom Staley, and Lorraine Weir. But the entire community of Joyce scholars have contributed to my understanding of Joyce and guided me in recognizing the centrality of his work to the shaping of the theoretical as well as literary direction of the twentieth century and as providing a basis for a theory of cultural production (i.e., a contemporary trans-disciplinary poetic) as an ecology of sense.

There are three other friends without whom this work would not have been possible: Richard Ogilvie and Stephen Moore, whose excellent medical care and personal encouragement over the period provided me with the energy, health, and quality of life to return to research and writing; and John Murray, whose advice and assistance contributed to arranging the freedom to execute this and other projects.

Financial aid and moral encouragement were provided by McGill University, Trent University, the Social Sciences and Humanities Research Council of Canada, and the Canadian Federation for the Humanities. Trent University was particularly generous in providing the opportunity for an extended leave following my term as its president, which enabled me to return to this work. At various points, material assistance was also provided by the National Film Board of Canada.

The personnel of Trent University's Computer Services, especially Ken Brown and George MacDougall, have provided considerable technical aid and advice. The Centre for Computing in the Humanities at the University of Toronto, through its superb software and generous technical support, made an arduous task considerably easier. Its coordinator, Willard McCarty, generously acted as a guide in my early days of learning about computing in the humanities. Personnel at the Robarts Library at the University of Toronto have generously provided helpful assistance with specific problems that arose during the process of writing. Many thanks to three of my research assistants who helped at various stages: Tim Freeborn, Ray Fritz-Nemeth, and Andrés Zelman.

Suzanne Rancourt, editor at University of Toronto Press, has been helpful and encouraging. An essential aspect to a successful book is a dedicated, informed, and sensitive copy editor; so special thanks go to Ken Lewis, who has been of inestimable aid.

Finally, a deep feeling of gratitude to my children – Thomas, Margaret, John, Larry, Harold, and Michael – who remained loyal and supportive even when the demands of combining a research and administrative career meant that there was less time for us to be together. The most essential and encouraging reader and co-researcher has been my spouse for forty-five years, Joan.

Introduction

In the 1970s when the first PCs came off the line, the last stage of the metamorphosis of the book began. The awakening of that new poetic age was first announced by Mallarmé, just before the twentieth century began. Its full implications are the major focus of James Joyce's writings, for by the eve of the Second World War a new poetic sensibility clearly had emerged, marked by the publication of *Finnegans Wake, the* major poetic achievement of the decades between the two wars. *Finnegans Wake* signalizes a whole new relationship with language, with audience, and with the everyday world. Joyce anticipated the age of the microcomputer and the micro's easy relationship with telecommunications, while also dramatizing certain developments which were and would be taking place in poetry and the arts as a result of the dramatic socio-economic, cultural, and technological changes which had started in the mid-nineteenth century.

As the twentieth century progresses towards the third millennium, one of the many transformations which has occurred is that Art with a capital *A* has now lost its privileged position. A new, broader, less elitist, more equitable conception of cultural production has emerged. As early as the late 1920s when Gilbert Seldes wrote about *The Seven Lively Arts,* this process was already well under way. Its aftermath has created a situation in which, whenever words like *art* or *poetry* are used, complex ambiguities arise. In spite of this, such traditional terms are still widely used in our discussion of the forms of cultural production.

Inventive cultural productions (which I will call *the poetic,* whether they are achieved in language, another medium, or a mixture of media) are the means by which the limits of and the boundaries between semiological systems (including those frequently called extra- or non-verbal languages) are transformed or surpassed. Humour, drama, film, comics, poetry, story-telling, and the like are essential ingredients of a process that ought to be identified as the groundwork of an ecology of communication, a process by which expressive and communicative action can accommodate socio-cultural, political, and technological change. Following Gregory Bateson, who spoke of the ecology of mind, I have called this the ecology of sense, primarily because it is through playing with signs and signifiers and their relation to people's perceptions of embodiment that the communicative repertoire is extended and deepened, permitting people to cope with changing reality and construct artificial realities.

Beyond the Word, challenging some current academic opinion to the contrary, asserts that the poet or artist in her or his practice can simultaneously be a theorist. It explores the process by which cultural productions can also be major theoretical statements through the intensity and complexity of their implications. There is a dialectic present in the very nature of expressive, communicative activity which encourages the presentation of a theoretical orientation. This is partly a function of the unavoidably pragmatic 'ecological' role of the activity. It is also a function of the situation that cultural producers who actively explore new potentialities are in that very process raising theoretical questions, and if they are self-conscious of this, they are articulating theoretical positions. James Joyce's or Federico Fellini's explorations of the creative processes of the artist with its challenges and conflicts, as discussed in this text, provide obvious examples of this reflexivity, but as the exposition will demonstrate, so do less obvious contemporary examples such as Stanley Kubrick, Dušan Makavéjev, and Paul Klee among others.

This intervention in the discussion of the relationship between media, texts, and society identifies and explores how, along with the appearance of new communication technology, an *unbinding of textuality* occurs which frees the idea of text from its original connection with manuscripts and books. To establish this it is necessary to traverse the wandering path from *symboliste* interest in coenaesthesia (the integration or orchestration of the arts) and synaesthesia (the 'transmutation of the senses') to the emergence of hypertext, cyberspace, and virtual reality (the 'electrical immersion of the senses') in the 1990s.[1] *Beyond the Word* traces the complex dialogue that occurs between poets, artists, other cultural producers, and technology that is simultaneously directed towards developing a critical, yet reconstructive, theory of techno-culture. The interest of high modernist artists in engineering (e.g., Marcel Duchamp, Paul Valéry, Sergei Eisenstein, jazz musicians) and in art and communication as social machines (e.g., Walter Gropius, Le Corbusier, Malcolm Lowry) is of central importance to understanding this dialogue.

James Joyce's *Ulysses* and *Finnegans Wake* are key texts, if not *the* key texts, for understanding this complex interaction of the new modes of technological reproducibility with cultural production. Joyce's literary practice, which shared with his contemporaries a view of the modern artist as a contemporary Leonardo, implied and encompassed a theory of culture and communication which has had, and continues to have, implications for poetic theory, social and cultural theory, and communication theory. Joyce's *Wake* is a summa or encyclopaedic culmination of the age of mechano-electrification (1880–1940) – an era which explores extensively the new culture of time and space. In *Ulysses* and *Finnegans Wake*, Joyce developed a contemporary poetic of communication with which we are still striving to catch up. His position (with a little irony) can be described as 'pre-post-modern,' since he anticipates so many insights of semiology, post-structuralism, and postmodernism long before most of these movements emerged or matured. Comedy, communication, and counter-communication (censorship) converge as topics in Joyce's final work, *Finnegans Wake*. The *Wake* must become one of the more essential documents for communication studies, along with Lewis Carroll's *Alice* books, Wittgenstein's philosophy, and Kenneth Burke's writings on rhetoric and symbolic action.

Joyce thus provides a key theoretical and poetic text throughout the discussion that follows. So it begins with an examination of the relationships between the poetic (the deconstructive and reconstructive activity of semiotic creation), people's erotic and sensory bodies, and the new techno-culture of time and space with reference to Joyce's experience as an artist and to a broad perspective of the cultural milieu in which he operated. This requires developing and refining a concept of the poetic construct as a poetic machine – a designed assemblage of expressive and communicative semiotic elements in any medium or genre. Stanley Kubrick's film *Dr Strangelove* is used as an example to explore this perspective, since for its moment in time it brought together a poetic action, the strategies of popular and mass arts, and a particular medium – film – which appealed to a wide spectrum of the public in order to satirically and comically probe one of our most anxiety-ridden social, psychological, and political problems – nuclear warfare. This satiric and critical work, cast within the practices of modernism and postmodernism, reflectively probes the destructive potential of contemporary techno-culture. Joyce's earlier, more encyclopaedic and theoretic vision of the techno-culture and the implications of that electro-chemico-mechanical world, where both the 'etym' and the atom can be transubstantiated, more clearly reveals the ecological function implicit in Kubrick's film. Both works envision a new embodiment of poetic and rhetoric in a world where people's sense of body is electro-mechanical as well as organic.

This leads to the next critical area, where the new problems of embodiment are crucially related to modernist and avant-garde interest in the harmonization of the senses and the role of the artist as an engineer. Synaesthesia and coenaesthesia both signal a trend towards intersensory inclusiveness and thus towards technologies that will enable such inclusiveness. McLuhan – using Joyce, the English-speaking modernists, and the symbolists – intuited this trend within the development of electric technologies of production, reproduction, and dissemination. McLuhan's 'the medium is the message' anticipates the present moment when the microcomputer is both the medium and the message. McLuhan, believing he was developing Thomistic proportional analogies, was actually dramatizing the differential gaps that were revealed by the analogies. The discovery of such gaps in our own understanding, or between our views and others, assists us in learning. Poetic works involved with such gaps provide models for communicating in a self-questioning manner, so that the experimental nature of the poetic work involves playing with the surface of sense, with the multiplicity of meaning and polysemy of language achieved by optimizing the structure of the poetic work as assemblage and machine, and exploiting the thrust towards the transversality of textuality.

At this stage and in a later chapter discussing the contemporary thrust to move 'beyond media,' McLuhan's work (and that of his Toronto colleague, Harold Innis) are considered. Between 1964 and 1968 McLuhan placed on the agenda a whole new vocabulary, and consequently a new conceptual structure, for the investigation of art, literature, culture, and communication. While his work very rapidly (in less than a decade) fell into academic disrepute – because of his apparent PR-oriented techniques, small *c* conservative theology and politics, and his scholarly 'inventiveness' – the agenda he advanced and the vocabulary he developed penetrated academic, artistic, popular, and official culture. Over twenty-five years later, while a few catch phrases remain identifiable, a McLuhanesque vocabulary and agenda, largely anonymous, have permeated not only cultural and communication studies, but the media and bureaucracy. That is only the beginning of the problem, for the unconsciously parodic way the concepts and ideas generated by McLuhan are often used in media and by the academic and bureaucratic establishment is completely impervious to and unaware of how he derived them or by what means he propagated them.

Explorations (1954–8), one of *the* seminal journals promoting interdisciplinarity in the human sciences, provided a cross-disciplinary collection of perspectives on the role of the arts of expression and communication in understanding the contemporary relationships between culture, communication, and technology. Its co-editors, Edmund Carpenter and Marshall McLuhan, fostered under Carpenter's influence the conceptual relationship between the practice of the artist and practice of the anthropologist. Seeing artistic works as poetic anthropology and anthropology as an interpretation of the poetic inventiveness of everyday culture, Carpenter's project complemented and supplemented that of McLuhan. In *Beyond the Word* the project of *Explorations* and its fruition in McLuhan's works are contextualized within the work of the symbolist, high modernist, and radical modernist (or postmodernist) poets and artists and with the histories of the arts of rhetoric and of poetics that constituted McLuhan's fundamental sources.

Exploring further the role of gaps in the communicative process, Lewis Carroll's 'nonsense' provides an illuminating juxtaposition with Joyce's work and with McLuhan's perverse verbal play, exploring that play with the surfaces of signs and things that is so crucial to the difference between sense and nonsense. The pragmatists, particularly John Dewey, who influenced Kenneth Burke, reveal an interest in art as experimentation that complements the experimental art of the avant-garde. Some of the most intense forms of play with sense involve people's embodiment, as in W.B. Yeats's, Joyce's, and Wyndham Lewis's involvement with the 'wild body.' A communication-oriented interpretation of Mikhail Bakhtin's theories on the carnivalesque and the dialogic and Joyce's use of the Viconian 'new science' underscore their relationship to communication and embodiment. If the 'wild body' and other play with sense and nonsense are this central, then comedy and laughter are necessarily the basis of any complex theory of communication. The laughter and comedy of the Joyce era are lustral, transgressive, and future-oriented, providing instruments for exploring the multiplexity of the changing relationships between culture, technology, and communication.

The experimentation of Laszlo Moholy-Nagy or Gyorgy Kepes is one way of seeing the unfolding development from the early avant-garde experimentation of Duchamp to the multimedia exploration of MIT's Media Lab and the various HIT (human interface technology) research programs, an unfolding which frequently acknowledges the theoretical contributions of Joyce, Eisenstein, and other modernist artist-theorists. The reassessment of Innis's and McLuhan's contribution to our understanding of communication and of the role of poetics in the latter's interpretation of Innis clarifies why McLuhan (although largely rejected by academic researchers on communication and post-structural literary theory) continued to be of genuine significance to artists, writers, and researchers interested in the techno-cultural domain.

This is supplemented by an investigation of the way in which McLuhan's popularization of the terms *media* and *orality*, while originally useful and illuminating, has inhibited the way we think about communication, technology, art, and media. As communication is more fully understood as a universe of interacting signs and as technology permits more and more inclusive and individualized media, a new multimedia parapoetics appears in the form of hypertextuality and virtual reality. The process that began at the turn of the century with the rediscovery of Leonardo as the poet-engineer has by now created an awareness that the poetic work, as an assemblage of bits, is a 'machinic' assemblage – as Deleuze and Guattari have argued.

Since *Beyond the Word* is a nomadic and transverse exploration of communication, textuality, media, literature, and the arts, the journey unfolds topically. In that process, certain theorists and theoretically oriented artists are examined in greater detail, but the actual journey is shaped along meandering paths derived from Joyce, his modernist colleagues and predecessors, and the Joycean era of post-structuralism and postmodernism. The decision to highlight certain individual figures has usually been a result of where those meandering paths lead. Some of the choices, such as Burke or Bakhtin, become obvious because of emphases in the exposition such as the comic, the grotesque, the dialogic, and the communicative. Some of them arise naturally from the area of discourse, such as Benjamin and Bataille with their interest in experimental arts, technology, laughter, communication, and the body.

McLuhan and Burke are central because of their indebtedness to Joyce; while Deleuze and Guattari are important because of the way their insights into the nomadic, the transverse, the machinic, the Oedipal, and the body provided illumination. Bateson, a figure more familiar to social scientists and communication theorists than to those concerned with the arts, is examined in detail because of his theories concerning art and cybernetics and the overlap of many of his artistic emphases with Joyce and Burke, particularly his stress on the importance of comedy and humour. His prime contribution to the argument is that his concept of the ecology of mind provides the ground for extending communication theory into the ecology of sense, thus providing a crucial role for innovative cultural production in the developing of relatively undistorted communication. Barthes, whose semioclasm – while oriented in a radically different socio-political direction – is close to McLuhan's, is a natural foil and a way of extending the issues into recent French post-structuralism.

The artists examined in the process form what may at first seem like an arbitrary mosaic, but each has been selected because of ways his or her works contribute to illuminating the argument. In the case of Stanislaw Lem,

William Gibson, or Gene Roddenberry's TV productions, the selections obviously tie in with the techno-cultural theme and relate to aspects of what I have denominated the 'Joyce era.' Alexander Pope is chosen for a historical perspective because he and his colleague Jonathan Swift wrote major poetic works about the new mechanical technologies of their time which encompass major theoretical insights. In the case of film-makers, Fellini, Makavéjev, and Kubrick in their practice all make theoretical contributions involving the body, the comic, and the communicative, which is why they are featured rather than Godard or Bergman. Particularly in Fellini's case, the Joycean context, which Fellini himself has alluded to, is an additional factor in the choice; but so are his complex reflections on the film-maker as artist. Makavéjev, I believe, has made a powerful contribution to the understanding of the ecology of sense, which ironically has been politically/socially suppressed because of its forcefulness. Furthermore, he provides an interesting counterpoint to Leni Riefenstahl, whose work is included to explore the possible ecological function of aesthetically powerful, yet ethically deplorable, works. In a brilliant analysis of *Mein Kampf*, 'Hitler's Rhetoric,' to be mentioned later, Burke has shown how even the most diabolical and objectionable of texts can contain within themselves semiological systems (rhetoric and grammar of motives or symbologies) that assist in the interpretive unmasking of the very project being advanced. While some contemporaries might unqualifiedly condemn Pauline Réage's *Histoire de l'O* (*The Story of O*) as pornographic, this book provided a generation within and outside of France with a new semiology of eroticism that has contributed to the questioning and revision of taboos in interpersonal relations and to a deepened understanding of the role of exchange and sacrifice involved, thereby contributing to the discourse that has permitted greater personal choice and liberation.

All cultural production is permeated by ambivalence, since all intersubjective human interaction is necessarily engaged in a complex dialogue about our mutual coexistence within a world of differences. Throughout his writings, Barthes again and again illustrates the ambivalence of cultural objects interpreted as texts (networks of significance) within the particular socio-cultural and historical context that produced them. He demonstrates that the legendary DS-19 Citroen, the Eiffel Tower, margarine and detergent advertising, or Charlie Chaplin can establish their own modes of multisensory re-exploration of experience. Just as the concerns of *Mythologies* are similar to those of *The Mechanical Bride* (though the theoretical orientation is different), the focus of interest at different stages of Barthes's career from *Mythologies* to *Barthes on Barthes* closely parallels McLuhan's from *The*

Mechanical Bride to *Culture Is Our Business*. It is noteworthy that some of the earliest writing of both authors concerned the history of classical rhetoric and the arts of language.

This is not primarily a book about the individuals selected, but rather about a series of thematic nodes which enlighten the understanding of the process by which poetic production contributes to the development of relatively undistorted communication. Many of these themes have been touched upon already – such as sense and nonsense, comedy and communication, and a dramatic theory of communication. Other such nodes dealt with at length include: tactility as the intrasensory and its extensions; the oral, the literate, and the tactile; memory and communication; the ambivalence of the poetic as critique exemplified in contemporary avant-garde film and SF (science fiction) in print and video; and the history of poetic as a history of communication. Terms such as *poetic* or *tactile* are used in ways that may not be considered usual, as earlier remarks have already indicated. Some of these differences, of necessity, can only be established as our exploration proceeds.

Since communication as secular communion engages the experiential panoply of the human body, the node involving tactility and the sensory is central. *Beyond the Word* explores the crucial role of tactility and the intra- and intersensory in relation to dance and the fragmented communication of the sensual and sensing person through a detailed discussion of poetic explorations of the images of the foot and the toe in relation to the surfaces of the earth and the body. The stress on synaesthesia and the accompanying conception of the integration of the arts ultimately situates tactility as central to the new poetics of communication and dramatizes the importance of the education of the senses to the project of modernism and its subsequent radical modernist transformations. The importance of tactility in relation to the electrochemical operation of the nervous system as a kind of contemporary interior common sense (*sensus communis*) entails a discussion of the sensual, sensuous, bodily basis of communicative experience as it relates to an ecology of sense and communication, the poetic activity as '*making sense*.'

The dance of the mind in the body is implicated in the electro-mechanical nature of life itself and people's new consciousness of electro-mechanization and the global city, which is manifested in radical modernist views of poetic engineering and the transverse, intertextual, 'open' text. Considering people, as Joyce did, to be 'patternminds' with 'paradigmatic' senses, memory emerges as the crux of communication. This is reflexively related to the entire discussion and leads to a critical reassessment of the role of orality, visuality, and tactility in the web of memory and their respective roles in the 'unbinding of the text.' Since such a thesis can only be sustained if it applies prior to and beyond the modernist or postmodernist, the history of the poetic – building on Vico's and Joyce's work – is established as a major aspect of the history of communication.

Beyond the Word challenges many deeply established ideas of what has been described as a postmodernist world. In fact, it challenges the very existence of a postmodernism distinct from what might better be called a radical modernism. More fundamentally, it challenges the concept that the poetic does not have an essential socio-cultural function in the processes of human communication. While demonstrating how the poetic is present in all forms of cultural production and has always challenged the existence of such categories as the fine arts, this inquiry identifies a function of the poetic in all cultural activity, which makes the poetic an ecological necessity of the relations of the human organism to the socio-cultural environment that shapes the very nature of human communication.

A Note on Acronyms and Reference Style

Joyce's works have been cited following the accepted forms used by Joyce scholars. Quotations are from *Ulysses: A Critical and Synoptic Edition*, ed. Hans Walter Gabler et al., 3 vols (New York: Garland Publishing 1986); and *Finnegans Wake* (1939; rpt, New York: Viking 1960). *Ulysses* is cited by section and line; viz. (*U*17.1523). *Finnegans Wake* is cited by page number and line; viz. (*FW*123.4). Occasionally a second method of citation is used for *Finnegans Wake*. Though Joyce chose not to use formal divisions, it has become accepted by scholars to divide the text into four books with chapters, except for Book IV. These are then cited parenthetically by Roman and Arabic numerals respectively; viz. (I,3).

The following acronyms are used throughout the text:

AI	artificial intelligence
CNS	central nervous system
CPU	central processing unit
GUI	graphic user interface
HIT	human interface technology
SF	science fiction
VR	virtual reality

A Note on Acronyms and References

BEYOND THE WORD

1

The Poetic Body in the New Culture of Time and Space: Communication, Art, and Technology in the Twentieth Century

In 1909 a struggling young writer, James Joyce, returned to his native Ireland to explore purchasing and managing a Dublin movie house. This act in itself provides a striking symbol of the way that the new media of technological reproduction occupied a central position in the modernist movement. That the same writer as he matured avidly consumed pop art forms – porn novels, penny romances, comics, newspapers, and films – is an index of how modernity had become enmeshed with popular communication. His youthful indecision, whether to adopt a career as a concert tenor singing on the Irish music room circuit or as a writer, provides another striking example of how the modernist sensibility combined the elite arts of the past and the popular arts.

A knowledge of Joyce's *Ulysses* provides fundamental insight into the role of communication in everyday life. Its action counterpoints the advertising man, Leopold Bloom, and aspiring *symboliste* poet, Stephen Dedalus; the struggle between the dominance of the English language over a colonialized culture and the metamorphosis of that language within the undervalued dialect of Anglo-Irish; the impact of popular music and story-telling in everyday Dublin and the presumed dominance of serious music (already an aspect of 'The Dead' in *Dubliners*); the impact of the then underworld of sex, violence, bodily processes, polymorphous perversion, and sensual transgression on the apparently ordered and managed world of civic and religious proprieties and pieties.

Joyce moved beyond *Ulysses* to a book about books, media, and communication. *Finnegans Wake* became the focal point of controversy over modernist indifference to communication. It is a work that encompasses all of the newly emerging mass media, the rapidly expanding world of pop cultural production, and the spectrum of the traditional arts and popular entertainment. Its very subject (the dreams of a single night in the bedroom of an Irish innkeeper and his spouse) raises the question of how people communicate with the unconscious; its technique (the crafting of a night language which still involves the rapidly changing day world of the third decade of the twentieth century) is itself an exploration of the intersecting of the conscious and unconscious in everyday communication.

This should not be surprising, for the communication revolution was well under way before the end of the first half of this century. Modernist art confronted changing patterns of time and space, an encounter dramatized in the titles of such publications as Siegfried Giedion's *Space, Time and Architecture* (1941) and Wyndham Lewis's *Time and Western Man* (1927), and in Apollinaire's identification of the new scientific-mathematical conception of space in *Cubist Painters* (1913). Examples of the transformation of spatial perception abound; for instance, Delauney's *Eiffel Tower* or Gertrude Stein's remarks on the influence of the aeroplane on the age of Picasso.[1] Since these processes of change were and still are techno-scientific, the machine, and particularly communication machines (the camera, still or moving, the printing press, the phonograph, the telegraph) and transportation machines (the locomotive, the bicycle, the automobile, the aircraft) came to be critically positioned within the new dialogue among artists. This occurred because artists and writers had always been fascinated with machines, and the art work itself could be understood in machinic terms as an assemblage.

Let's reflect for a moment on the particular historical context in which Joyce matured as an artist. Within the five years before Joyce was born, Edison developed both sound recording and the electric light. During the early years of Joyce's life, the Eiffel Tower was erected; Lumière explored moving pictures; Marie Curie discovered radium; Marconi completed the first transatlantic broadcast; the Wright brothers developed the aeroplane; Einstein expounded his theory of relativity; and Ford completed the process of mass mechanization taking command by developing the assembly line for the production of motor cars. During the fifty years prior to Joyce's birth, telegraphy, the telephone, photography, the typewriter, the rotary press, and electromagnetic power had been developed. Joyce provides a prime example of the huge impact these developments had on all of the arts. Speaking about his work, Joyce stressed the importance of mechanics, chemistry, and mathematics in his later books, especially *Finnegans Wake*. In 1929 he had organized the publication of a series of essays entitled *Our Exagmination Round His Factification for Incamination of Work in Progress* (note that his title has its own complex references to building, fortifying, producing, laying out roads, etc.) to assist readers in understanding fragments called *Work in Progress*, which were early versions of what ultimately was published as *Finnegans Wake*. After the *Exagmination* was published, he then suggested that there should be another 'book of only 4 *long* essays by 4 contributors,' the subjects of three of these essays being on the roles of mechanics, chemistry, and mathematics repectively in his *Work in Progress*.[2]

The seventy years from 1880 to 1950 mark off a period of history which experienced the development of electricity, the final closing of the world's frontiers, the discovery of atomic fission, ultra-rapid transportation, and instantaneous worldwide communication. These dramatic changes in conceptions of time, space, speed, and distance had an impact on how artists thought about communication and how professional communicators practised their craft. One result was the emergence of a new interest in the intermixing of modes and means of communication, which arose naturally from such hybrid media as silent film, then black-and-white sound film, and later technicolour. Technologies associated with the changing concepts of space and time primarily included technologies which changed the ways humans communicated and even the nature of communication itself. The relationship of communication to the flow of electricity, to the fragmentation of information, and to energy flows became evident enough that the perennial awareness that humans communicate using signs selected from a wide variety of modes of expression assumed a new importance, particularly in questioning the central role which language was supposed to occupy in human communication.

This was also a period when for the first time in centuries not only the particular primacy of the written language (especially the printed language) was challenged, but for the very first time the privileged role of language itself. The revolution of the word is more accurately a revolution from the word! This transition began in the final years of the nineteenth century and moved towards the conclusion of its first stage with the publication immediately before the Second World War of Joyce's *Finnegans Wake* (1939); during the war, of T.S. Eliot's *Four Quartets* (1943), and after the war, of Ezra Pound's *Pisan Cantos* (1948). Entirely new conceptions of what constituted human communication were developing as a result of the discovery of the new modes for producing, reproducing, and distributing communication, such as photography, phonography, and television.[3] Endless crises involving communication have occurred throughout the twentieth century, continuing on through the Cold War and the Iron Curtain up to the present information explosion with its accompanying panic concerning universal social unrest. Rapid technological change accompanied by ever-accelerating social and political change, which has by now become an almost banal refrain describing the unfolding pattern of development in both the developed and the developing worlds, came about only as a result of the multiplicity of new possibilities that emerged during this century. What happened during the period 1880–1950 is still the shaping spirit of the twentieth century as it moves towards its conclusion, and through the effects of media – both desirable and undesirable – it has become part of the inheritance of the entire world.

Changing concepts of time and space and fascination with the machine permeated the new popular arts as well, for animated films such as *The Roadrunner* series marry the cubist perspectives of Lyonel Feininger and Fernand Léger with mechanical motion. Artists, animators, creators of comic strips, and SF cover artists all explored the same language of change. The American painter Feininger, who was a member of Wassily Kandinsky's expressionistic Der Blaue Rieter (Blue Rider) group and taught at the Bauhaus, began his career as a cartoonist and illustrator. In one year (1906), Feininger produced two comic strips for the *Chicago Tribune* – the *Kin-der-Kids* and *Wee Willie Winkie's World*. Later in life, he carved small wooden figures of characters from *Kin-der-Kids* for his children and 'laid out plans of a fantastic city ("the city at the edge of the world") directly from *Wee Willie Winkie's World*.'[4] The languages of the arts – old and new, 'high' and 'low' – were interwoven early in the modernist movement, for artistic practice extended into, interacted with, was incoporated into, and often encompassed the arts of everyday life long before such extensions and interactions were more widely recognized by critics, scholars, or the public. Subsequently, the conception of art as a privileged, elite body of material began its long, slow process of decay, which is continuing today; a decay that Joyce recognized when he attributed the success of his works to the everyday creativity of people interacting.[5] *The Seven Lively Arts*, the title of a collection of essays published in 1924 by the dramatic and cultural critic Gilbert Seldes, who edited the *Dial*, clearly establishes that the collapse of the conceptual barrier represented as the institution of the 'Fine Arts' had begun.

Comics, typical of the 'lively arts,' are unquestionably a form of communication, as Maurice Horn notes in his *Encyclopedia of Comics*. The new interconnectedness of these popular modes of expression with the so-called traditional arts posed pressing questions about communication and the status of Art. In the 1920s the confrontational stance of avant-garde movements, such as Dadaism and surrealism, towards the bourgeois public (presumably differentiated from the people) further dramatized the crisis in communication. That very dramatization itself constituted an intense communication, which, through being enigmatic, complex, and difficult, challenged popular thinking, which characterized the process of communication as direct and transparent. Communication as topic, motif, or subtext pervades the writings of Joyce, Valéry, Pound, Bataille, Eliot, Proust, and others. Eliot even declared that poetry (and, in fact, all art) communicates before it is understood. So by 1928 even academic criticism began to view the problem of artistic evaluation primarily as a problem in communication. Artists and writers became engrossed in the problems of communication, massification, and technological production, reproduction, and distribution thirty or forty years before social scientists and journalists began speaking of their contemporary world as the Communication Era (which has recently been replaced by the Information Age, or the age of cyberspace marked by the conjoint effect of personal computers with telecommunications!).

New groups of professional communicators emerged into prominence – for example, advertisers, broadcasters, PR consultants, photo journalists – and their activities necessarily aped those of the artist or popular artist. As Joyce intuited in *Ulysses*, these are the modern sophistic rhetoricians who adopt the strategies of poetry for the purposes of persuasion. The growing social importance of the popular arts and mass communication led to professional academic reflection on these activities, a reflection which in the English-speaking world (with very few exceptions) dogmatically denied that understanding communication could profitably be pursued through examining art works or discourse about art works as well as through the usual methods and theories of the social sciences. In the early 1950s, Carpenter, McLuhan, and Raymond Williams stood alone as individuals prepared to explore such questions.

Today, from a perspective of historical development, there is a greater awareness of the importance of these questions, which has come about partly through increased knowledge of the work of the Frankfurt School (Adorno, Horkheimer, Benjamin, and Krauss); the development of cultural studies from the work of Raymond Williams and Stuart Hall; the development of structuralism, semiology, and post-structuralism in France within a centre of communication studies in Paris;[6] and the short but significant impact of McLuhanism. Burke, whose theory of symbolic action recognizes the role of the poetic in social ecology, the importance of drama to understanding the poetic and symbolic, and the principle that poetic theory is a basic aspect of communication theory, anticipated this later interest in communication by over twenty years.[7]

To understand the contemporary relevance of the poetic to communication theory, it is necessary to understand that there are strong historical reasons for regarding the terms *poetry* and *poetic* as being terms which are inclusive of all the arts.[8] At the inception of theorizing about poetry, drama, and other arts of presentation (e.g., dance, song), the poetic was conceptualized as an act of making or producing – a view that consequently considers the poetic work as a construct. In this book, *poetry* and *poetic* will be used *to speak about designed assemblages of expressive elements whatever the medium or genres within which they are constructed*. The term *poetic* will entail *the theoretical exploration of this act of assembling in and of itself*. All poetic assemblage naturally involves breaks and disjunctions. Modern poetry differs radically from that of past centuries in deliberately assembling poetic machines that depend upon breaks, gaps, and disjunctions which invite wandering transverse exploration of the surfaces, thereby producing ambivalence and negativity. Such constructs make the transverse connections between sharply separated moments the primary, frequently the only, ground for communication.

Stanley Kubrick's *Dr Strangelove, or How I Learned to Stop Worrying and Love the Bomb,* a useful example of the coalescence of art, popular culture, and mass communication that has been seen to characterize modern art, is a poetic work that exemplifies such radical disjunction and transverse exploration. In *Strangelove,* Kubrick constructs a semiology for exploring the military-political-diplomatic tensions of international game playing, using an assemblage that involves the documentary industrial training film tradition as applied to the operation of a B-52; the comic hall traditions of Buster Keaton and Laurel and Hardy; Vera Lynn as the popular song personality of the Second World War in hit songs such as 'We'll Meet Again'; the 'Battle Hymn of the Republic' as the 'national' anthem of the American South; the predominance of Coca-Cola and the U.S. Army as mass advertisers; Freudian and Jungian psychoanalytic concepts; and, ultimately, the mythico-social interplay of the motifs of Desire, Love, and Death. With sado-masochistic laughter, Kubrick probes the underside of technology by examining the critical breakdown of nuclear fail-safe, including the examination of the nature and character of its overseers: the generals, the politicians, and Dr Strangelove.

The episodic structure of Kubrick's film enhances the disjunctions, insists on the transversality, and amplifies the satiric effects; this deliberate structuring simultaneously distances from, and involves the viewer in, the excesses of Kubrick's vision. One pattern of motifs that contributes to this effect is found early in the film. Responding to a summons from the Pentagon involving a possible nuclear crisis, General Turgeson, just before he leaves their hotel room to go to the war room, tells his secretary to begin her erotic countdown to climax in coition upon his return. In some 'readings' of the film, this incident is later related to various other events: General Ripper's discussion of bodily fluids with his British executive officer, Major Mandrake; the love affair of the B-52 pilot, Major Kong, with his plane and subsequently his riding the nuclear bomb as it falls from the bomb bay on its mission of destruction; Dr Strangelove's meditations on the future descent of the privileged into the mine shafts to survive the fallout, which will be accompanied by obligatory polygamy to repopulate America; and, finally, the closing moments of Vera Lynn's 'We'll Meet Again' juxtaposed against the 'beautiful' cinematography of mushroom clouds.

This poetic machine, *Strangelove*, has the potential to generate a large number and variety of digressing paths, differing for each viewer, intensifying ambivalence, yet inviting an intensification of exploratory behaviour characteristic of all poetry. The very way Kubrick uses technological machinery and technological organization dramatizes the gaps inherent in people's attempt to control their biosphere. The very realism of his reconstruction of the management of a B-52 becomes a component and contributor to the satiric dance of sounds, images, words, gestures, and movements by which the machinic nature of this poetic assemblage is generated. Like other contemporary art, this film generates exploratory action by occupying the gaps that occur as the result of the increasingly overpowering activity of rhetorics of manipulation which continually appropriate the techniques, strategies, and accomplishments of immediately preceding poetry and art. It must be understood that the activities of such manipulative rhetoric do not preclude poetry from emerging within its productions, for they necessarily use the same resources as poetry, art, and everyday life. Besides, the operation of such manipulative rhetorics establishes still further gaps and disjunctions which the arts then expose and utilize.

Fellini's use of Wagner's music for the 'Ride of the Valkyries' in the spa scene of *8½* (to reveal the comic dimension of the ritual of spa visits) provides another example of the reabsorption and transformation of manipulative rhetoric, for that scene capitalizes on the exploitation of Wagner's music by advertisers, political publicists, and promoters as well as locating Wagner's music in a doubly ambivalent focus: in the immediate present, as a possession of those social groups using 'distinction' as a form of domination, and, historically, as reflecting Wagner's own fascination with the massification of myth. When Nietzsche identifies Wagner and French Romanticism as 'great discoverers in the realm of the sublime ... of the ugly and horrible, still greater discoverers in the sphere of effects and display windows,' he partly explains this ambivalence: 'On the whole, an audaciously daring, magnificently violent, high-soaring and high sweeping type of artist, they alone have taught *their* century – it is the century of the *mass* – the concept of the "artist." But *sick*.'[9] The complex use Fellini makes of such a phenomenon, like Kubrick's multifarious satire in *Strangelove*, reflects the complex nature of the high modernist world that provided the context for the work of these poetic film-makers.

The theoretical implications of Joyce's later writings provide a paradigm for understanding this complexity and, consequently, a necessary subtext for examining the relationship between communication, text, and media. *Ulysses*, a poetic work rather than a novel, deliberately turns the epic upside down, while simultaneously evolving a complex poetic language for coping with and redefining the contemporary experience characterized by urbanization, internationalization, mechanization, and alienation. Joyce designed an intricate working chart to use in writing *Ulysses*. Each of the eighteen episodes takes place in a particular location at a particular time of day and is assigned a specific technic, symbol, art, colour and bodily organ which permeate it. This structure governed the encounters of individuals, social institutions, and life-world that are revealed by taking diagonal cuts of the terrain of Dublin as a living *community*. Movements of people, sensory experience, and information, which produce Dublin's geoscape, create gaps and generate a disjunctive, labyrinthine movement across earth, air, and river, which is then retraced as the new communication flows within the *community*. This movement inscribes a mapping of networks on the surface of the city, for the social body (individual or corporate) is uninscribed (like Artaud's body-without-organs) without the operation of the poetic-dramatic machine or other semiotic machines associated with social praxis (economic, political, etc.). This, though, is the stuff of communications (the action within which the social communications of everyday life is always embedded) re-establishing movement between the gaps created in the normal or predictable flows of human life. Joyce envisages the living, moving bodies of his Dubliners as transforming the body politic of the city through its citizens' secular consciousness of the city as a machine, which provides for them an ability to participate in intensive communication (a secular communion – a sort of secularized Corpus Christi).

The symbiosis between the person and the *city* as the site of communication defines the action of *Ulysses*, just as *Ulysses* maps the territory in which people communicate. Interplaying complexly with the geography of time and space, Joyce presents what he describes in the *Wake* as 'a map of the soul's groupography.' The fragmentized, cosmopolitan conglomerates of psychological nomads who are part of the world of Joyce's Dublin, Eliot's

London, or Proust's Paris already reveal a reaction to the multifarious multitude of privatized people who live in late industrial society. For Joyce (who anticipates Ricoeur's concept of the text as meaningful action), the city itself is a text, a communicating machine, just as all the meaningful action within its precincts is also textual. Joyce examines the transformations of textuality which occur under the impact of contemporary communication technology and changing social forms by utilizing sudden moments of illumination in which everyday life is transfigured.[10] This series of transfigurations is a series of particles – particular moments or bits of existence – which are used to implode the web of fragmented meanings that characterize social life in the cosmopolis.

While *Ulysses* intricately plays with the analysis of differences that reveal those breaks and disjunctions that have characterized modernist and postmodernist arts, it subtly reappropriates the productions of the manipulative rhetorics that were originally constructed by appropriating productions, techniques, strategies, and accomplishments of immediately preceding art and poetry. Joyce materially grounds his writing within a detailed exploration of contemporary society as an extended communal body. Then he thoroughly exploits the breaks or disjunctions of the society's everyday life and reconstructively situates them within a poetic action that transforms that everyday world and opens up possibilities for liberating human potential to understand that society.

Joyce's two main characters, Leopold Bloom and Stephen Dedalus, are antithetical both in their professional pretensions and their personalities. This opposition between promotion (PR and advertising) and poetry dramatizes the problematic tension between contemporary manipulative and pragmatic rhetorics and the poetic. Furthermore, this antithesis is grounded in events that engage the characters in situations which raise questions concerning the contemporary separation and reintegration of space and time, the predominance of personal and institutional reflexivity about knowledge, and the way in which many aspects of interaction are dislocated from the immediate space in which people live. In *Ulysses* these are reflected respectively in incidents such as the following: Bloom's and Stephen's experiences in the newspaper office, where space, time, and the spatio-temporal situation provide the background of the action ('Aeolus,' episode 7); the complex, reflexive interaction of the encylopaedism of the style with the simplicity of the action when Bloom takes Stephen home ('Ithaca,' episode 17); the remote effects of global and colonial events and decisions on Irish nationalism in Dublin which surface through the satiric application of 'gigantism' (the quasi-medical term Joyce used for this technic) to the encounter between Bloom and the chauvinistic Citizen in Barney Kiernan's pub ('Cyclops,' episode 12). An investigation of the reconstructive context within which these actions take place and how they relate to everyday reality reveals the organization of socio-cultural structures that the networks of media, text, and communication reveal again and again.

By the eve of the Second World War, a new poetic sensibility clearly had emerged, marked by the publication of *Finnegans Wake*, the major poetic achievement of the decades between the two wars. This work has been wittily described as 'ante-post-modern,'[11] since it easily evades classification or periodization as modernist or postmodernist. The *Wake*, completing the project that begins with *Ulysses*, attests to a whole new relationship with language, with audience, and with the everyday world. Here Joyce anticipates the age of the microcomputer and the micro's easy relationship with telecommunications, while also dramatizing changing socio-economic, cultural, and technological patterns first explored in *Ulysses*. The 'counter-poetic' *Wake* is one of *the* key contemporary texts for a theoretical understanding of the struggle between the primacy of oral and written language and the hyperlinguistic semiotics of the new electronic media. This enigmatic book is not only a polysemic, encyclopaedic book designed to be read with the simultaneous involvement of ear and eye, but it is also a self-reflexive book about the role of the book in the electro-machinic[12] world of the new technology. The *Wake* is the most comprehensive exploration, prior to the 1960s or 1970s, of the ways in which these new modes created a dramatic crisis for the arts of language and the privileged situation of the printed book.

The *Wake* dramatizes the necessary deconstruction and reconstruction of language in a world where multi-semic grammars and rhetorics, combined with entirely new modes for organizing and transmitting information and knowledge, eventually would impose a variety of new, highly specialized roles on speech, print, and writing. As the world awakens to the full potentialities in the new electric cosmos for the construction of artefacts and processes of communication, Joyce foresees the transformation (not the death) of the book: going beyond the book as it had historically evolved. Since the action takes place in a dream world, he can produce an impressive prophetic imaginary prototype for the virtual worlds of the future. His dream world envelops the reader within an aural sphere accompanied by kinetic and gestural components that arise from effects of rhythm and intonation realized through the visual act of reading; but it also reproduces imaginarily the most complex multi-media forms and envisions how they will utilize his present, which will have become the past, to transform the future.[13]

The hero(ine) in the *Wake*, 'Here Comes Everybody,' is a communicating machine, 'This harmonic condenser enginium (the Mole)' (310.1), an electric transmission-receiver system, an ear, the human sensorium, a presence 'eclectrically filtered for all irish earths and ohmes.' Joyce envisions the person as embodied within an electro-machinopolis (an electric, pan-global, machinic environment), which becomes an extension of the human body, an interior presence, indicated by a stress on the playfulness of the whole person and on tactility as calling attention to the intersensory, intrasensory interplay of sensory information within a body's electrochemical neurological system.

Major patterns for the future direction of communication ensue from the implications of such events as the birth of TV and the monitor 'as highly charged with electrons as hophazards can effective it' (615.7–8), a process in which the evolution of the micro and its effect on the universe of signs is implicit. In a mode of technologically mediated production and distribution of communication such as TV, *'the bairdboard bombardment screen'* (the monitor) *'teleframe[s] ... the charge of a light barricade,'* and the images are *'borne by their carnier walve' 'down the photoslope in syncopanc pulses, with the bitts bugtwug their teffs'* (349.08–12). Joyce anticipated this relationship by speaking of 'bitts' in relation to TV broadcasting in this pub scene where the customers watch a fight on TV (possibly the first fictional TV bar room scene in literary history).

The TV image of two fighters, Butt and Taff, has its own metamorphic quality, closely associated through language with the newly discovered medium of television and also related to tales of a number of historic battles. TV, the electronic processing of word, image, sound, and gesture is the 'abnihilisation of the etym' (discussed below), which Joyce predicted would occur in the world of 'verbivocovisual presentements' (TV and film):

> *[In the heliotropical noughttime following a fade of transformed Tuff and, pending its viseversion, a metenergic reglow of beaming Batt, the bairdboard bombardment screen, if tastefully taut guranium satin, tends to teleframe and step up to the charge of a light barricade. Down the photoslope in syncopanc pulses, with the bitts bugtwug their teffs, the missledhropes, glitteraglatteraglutt, borne by their carnier walve. Spraygun rakes and splits them from a double focus: grenadite, damnymite, alextronite, nichilite: and the scanning firespot of the sgunners traverses the rutilanced illustred sunksundered lines Shlossh! A gaspel truce leaks out over the caseine coatings. Amid a fluorescence of spectracular mephiticism there coaculates through the inconoscope stealdily a still ...]* (349.7–19)

Terms associated with TV broadcasting and TV technology abound in this passage about the transformation and 'viseversion' (vice versa imaging) of Tuff's image. The name of the discoverer of television, John Logie Baird (in 1925, the year before Joyce began the *Wake*), is included, since the television receiver is described as 'the bairdboard bombardment screen,' which receives the composite video signal 'in syncopanc pulses' (the synchronization pulses that form part of the composite video signal), coming down the 'photoslope' on the 'carnier walve' (i.e., the carrier wave, which carries the composite video signal). The receiver is conceived as a 'light barricade' against which the charge of the light brigade (the video signal) is directed. 'Teleframe,' 'scanning,' 'spraygun,' 'caesium,' and 'double focus' all refer to some aspect of TV technology, and their use can be similarly explained. While 'bit' was not used as a technical term in communication technology at the time, it was not difficult for Joyce to think of the electrons or photons as bits of information which created the mosaic TV picture. This is reinforced by the reference to 'guranium,' a portmanteau formation from 'geranium' (suggesting strong to vivid red) and 'uranium,' for this reference links the passage about the 'charge of the light barricade' with another set of references to the same telecast introduced by the phrase 'the abnihilisation of the etym' (353.22) – a phrase which weaves together references to war, the destructive transformation of the natural world, and the transmutation of language (and, more particularly, of writing) in our super-mechanized world.

The *etym*, Joyce's imaginary unit for the true source of a word in historic terms, and the *atom*, as the basic unit of matter until 1931, when the possibility of atom smashing arose, are based on a conception of assemblages of different bits. In the case of the atom, the discovery of the presence and significance of other bits led to its potential annihilation – smashing of the atom – a process in which uranium played a significant role. For Joyce, TV's annihilating the etym is also very important, for it alters the relationship of memory with the root language. The 'etym' is a fundamental 'bit' in the Joycean world, just as the atom is in the physical world. For Joyce, TV's annihilating the 'etym' is as significant in the realm of culture as the potentiality of destroying the atom in the physical world. Since, however, neither etym nor atom disappears as a result of the contemporary challenge, the process is an *ab-nihilisation*, not actually a destruction. In all these texts there is an omnipresent insistence on the centrality of and metamorphosis of bits of difference, which nowadays Joyce would have probably extended into genetics and molecular biology.

The doubling of an element (e.g., 'atom' as 'etym') or, even more precisely, multiplexing it (e.g., 'at' + 'om,' 'et' + 'im' or *a* and *e* added respectively to 'tom' and 'tim') leads to the possibility of annihilating the element in the process of its transformations. This is further underlined by the fact that the conflict of meanings arising from the new overlayered structures which result from such multiplexing can threaten the historical basis of the 'etym,' each particular linguistic element being embedded in its established lexical meaning (cf. etymology). TV and film, by their basic strategy of infolding heretofore separate elements, represent elementary forms of such transformations.

In neither case does such a doubling destroy the original element, for the doubling is actually redoubled. Eytm replaces atom, the primary element, but is then again replaced by atom in the reader-listener's unravelling of the effect. In our particular example, neither 'atom' nor 'etym' is annihilated for each still exists as a shadow or trace of the transformative process. This leads to a still more complex deciphering of the resulting nodes, which form a semiotic web, producing still greater perplexity concerning the sense of the potential communication that results from this division of elements of speech or writing into smaller and smaller bits. Doubling within communicative texts – whether books, films, visual or auditory presentations – generates an intensity which ultimately increases intelligibility, or at the very least provides a greater impression of sense. When any atom, etym, or bit of sense is broken down, new atoms, etyms, and bits of sense arise.

Gesture provides just such a unit rooted in the body and its sensory system, for in the *Wake* it is reported of Shem, the poet figure: 'In the beginning was the gest he jousstly says for the end is with woman, flesh-without-word ... ' (468.5–6).[14] The four-part interplay of ambivalent terms – jest, gesture, *geist* (Ger., spirit), and the obvious reference to *logos*, the word of John 1: 1–2 – roots the ideal and the rational in the material and in faculties associated with the 'lesser activities' of the 'lower parts' of the body. It is an identification thoroughly consistent with the history of rhetoric, for such important documents as Quintilian's *Institutio Oratoria* and the *Rhetorica ad Herrenium* follow Demosthenes in stressing that the three most important things in oratory are: 'Delivery, delivery, delivery.' Delivery is the rhetorical action (and, for that matter, the dramatic action) which includes the body and bodily communication through gesture, articulation, demonstration, and physical presentation.[15] Gesture and voice appeal to the eye and the ear, thus rooting communication in a concurrence of processes of material elements: sound, rhythm, movement, visual appearance.

In *Stephen Hero*, the early draft of *A Portrait of the Artist as a Young Man*, Joyce has his youthful artist argue that rather than treating gesture as elocutionists do, a rejuvenated art of gesture should be developed as a theory of rhythm.[16] Later, in *Ulysses*, at Bella Cohen's whore-house during the climactic scene in Dublin's Nighttown, where Leopold Bloom and Stephen first meet face to face, the young aspiring poet declares that gesture is the universal language: 'So that gesture, not music, not odours would be a universal language, the gift of tongues rendering visible not the lay sense but the first entelechy, the structural rhythm' (*U*15.105–7). Gesture, word, and memory are closely intertwined in the Joycean universe, where, he asserts, 'Begin to forget it. It will remember itself from every sides, with all gestures, in each our word' (*FW*614.20). Partly as a result of ethno-linguistic studies and partly as a factor of how consciousness was being changed by communication technology, twentieth-century artists developed a hyper-sensitivity to the importance of gesture.

Modern dance as the rhythmic art of gesture emerged with Isadora Duncan, whose ideal was to restore dance to being 'the most noble of the arts.' She suggested it as an alternative or supplementary form of communication to speech for, 'if I could tell you what it meant there would be no point in dancing it.'[17] Defending her exposure of her body when dancing, she observed that in addition to its being 'symbolic of the freedom of woman,' it permitted her to 'use my body as a musician does his instrument, as a painter uses his palette and brush, and as a poet the images of his mind ... for am I not striving to fuse soul and body in one unified image of beauty?'[18] Artist after artist, with fundamentally different social, political, and intellectual positions, discovered the fundamental importance of gesture.

Walter Benjamin explains Bertolt Brecht's theory that his 'epic theatre is gestural' by arguing that gesture is difficult to falsify and 'has a definable beginning and a definable end.'[19] According to Benjamin, one of the epic theatre's great achievements is 'making gestures quotable,' a process achieved by interrupting someone in the process of action as in the freezing of a cinematic shot in a frame.[20] With film, photography, and television becoming realities, the complexity of kinaesthetic communication *and* its interaction with speech, writing, and other arts became pivotal. Cinematic gesture is closely associated with close-up and editing (particularly montage), which intensify the gestural quality within the flow of cinematic movement. The authority of montage and the associated assemblages within the visual arts (collage) dramatized the gestural qualities of communication, for while the nature of abstract art seemed far from the natural movements of the human body, the dialectic of structure and movement with the concomitant creation of a visual grammar and syntax promoted the relation of sign to gesture and their close association at the birth of the arts as represented by the drawings in the Altamira Caves. The 'gest' is the 'etym' of communication involving other signs beside verbal ones.

Siegfried Giedion, who treats 'gesture' as a fundamental concept in the 'beginnings of art,' discusses how bodily parts like hands and the forearm are used as magic symbols. Demonstrating how the hand and forearm were a central gesture in primitive art, he remarks, 'From the hand and the forearm it is not far to gestures of the hand: an even more expressive symbol than the hand alone. The gesture can ward off or protect.' Giedion further draws specific attention to Léger's use of hands in the stained-glass window at Augincourt as well as Picasso's in the UNESCO building in Paris and Le Corbusier's choice of them for the dominating monument in the newly founded capital of East Punjab.[21] Hands and arms intrigued modern artists fascinated by the tribal roots of human communication.

In *Ulysses* the aspiring young poet, Stephen Dedalus, demonstrates the power of such a magical gesture when he wields his ashplant (a hermetic magic wand wielded by arm and hand) to break the chandelier in Bella Cohen's brothel:

STEPHEN

Nothung!

(He lifts his ashplant high with both hands and smashes the chandelier. Time's livid final flame leaps and, in the following darkness, ruin of all space shattered glass and toppling masonry). (U15.4241–5)

While Joyce was writing *Ulysses,* Marcel Jousse, whose work demonstrated the interrelationship of rhythm, breathing, gesture and the bilateral symmetry of the human body, associated the 'verbo-motor' development of language from gesture with the emergence of the oral language. Jousse's theories, which like Joyce's preceded those of Walter Ong, Eric Havelock, Harold Innis, Albert Lord, and Milman Parry, stressed the primacy of the tactile and the kinaesthetic in communication, which led to McLuhan's later assertion that the electronic 1960s marked a return to tactility.[22]

Shem, Joyce's poet figure in *Finnegans Wake,* reflects the artistic values of this age when he speaks of the 'handtouch which is speech without words' (174.10). What then are the implications of the foundation of language in neuro-muscular movements and the concomitant gestures which associate humans and animals? Implicit in Isadora Duncan's transformation of dance, just as in photography's renaissance of the 'sublime' impact of the unclothed (the naked, realistic, as opposed to the imaginary, nude) body,[23] is that communication has a privileged relationship with the body and that relationship engenders a continuum which the evolution of communication reflects. Communication as gesture underlines this relationship.

Giambattista Vico, an important influence on Joyce and a major figure in contemporary social theory, had speculated that 'the first language in the first mute times of the nations must have begun with signs, whether gestures or physical objects, which had natural relations to ideas.'[24] Vico appears to have implicitly recognized that in communicating or expressing oneself a person must submerge her or his identity. Sharing an understanding of gesture and object implies abandoning oneself to a mediated region where each participant tries to comprehend some of the experience of the other. The *Wake* describes how Shem the poet used to 'agree to every word as soon as half uttered, command me!, your servant, good I revere you, how, my seer? be drinking that! quite truth, gratias I'm yoush, see wha'm hearing? also goods, please it, me sure?, be filling this! quiso, you said it, apasfello, muchas grassyass, is there firing-on-me?, is their girlic-on-you?, to your good self, your sulphur, and then at once focuss his whole unbalanced attention upon the next octagonist who managed to catch a listener's eye' (174.10–14).

This echoes Charles Baudelaire's aphorism describing his 'hypocrite lecteur, mon semblable, mon frère!' ('Hypocrite reader, my fellow man, my brother!'), which Joyce parodically renders 'My shemblable! My freer!' (489.28) when Shaun, the politician, describes his brother, Shem. This merging of selves (or the loss of self in another) parallels other views of communication contemporary with the *Wake*, for Georges Bataille also had described 'the flowing into one another' which constituted the process of communication, 'a play of the isolation and the dissolution of beings.'[25] As George Herbert Mead speculated on the development of language from gesture in his theory of communication as symbolic interaction, artists and poets were exploring the interactive potentialities of communicative action arising from the body itself.

Some corollaries accompany this choice of gesture as the foundation of communication, which considers speech and written language as particular components of an integrated communication system. First of all, when speaking of the poetic, it is essential to adopt a more historical sense of the term and regard the poetic as an art of assembling or constructing which may involve all modes of communication. Pound speaks of language permeated with verbal complexity – *logopoeia* – as the dance of intellect among words. T.S. Eliot, following St John Perse, discovers a need to speak of a poetry in prose, anticipating the foundation of the poetic-semiotic that was to become a central emphasis in the discussions of post-structuralists.

At the same time as these theories about gesture as the root of communication and of the poetic motive developed, the doctrine of synaesthesia assumed a new importance. Synaesthesia, which was first recognized as a poetic device about the same time as the abstract discussion of gesture in traditional rhetoric occurred, now provided film-makers, dramatists, and synthesizers of new genres – such as the Dadaists – with a further basis for an integrated poetic practice, whether in light, sound, movement, speech, writing, celluloid, pigment, assembled objects, or any combinations thereof. These new modes of artistic expression can be regarded as types of poetic practice in the same way that Coleridge and the German Romantics spoke of each of the fine arts existent in the early nineteenth century as poetry. In his essay 'On Poesy or Art,' Coleridge used the term 'poetry' in a similar, though not quite identical, way when he spoke of poetry in sounds, poetry in images, and poetry in words, all as manifestations of poetry, the art of making.[26] Such a position concerning the integration of the arts bequeathed to modernism and its aftermath a capacity for dealing with the new world of cultural production – mass produced objects, entertainment, and information.

The arena of everyday life again had begun to shape the mind of the poet and artist, just as it had for Rabelais and Shakespeare. In his *Wake,* Joyce clearly establishes the extent to which some creative acts accomplished by industry and business in the everyday world of the twentieth century had come to be used as 'gests' and 'etyms' by modern poets and artists as major components of their works. Since literally, Joyce's hero (the dreamer) is an everywoman and everyman – a 'Here Comes Everybody' – the *Wake,* consistent with a recognition of the creative activity implicit in the life of all people, derives most of its material from the everyday world. Comics, movies, radio broadcasts, newspapers, music halls, popular song, tavern life, stand-up comics, circuses, and dirty jokes occupy a place side by side with religious rituals, mythology, Dante, Shakespeare, Goethe, Baudelaire, Aquinas, Hegel, Spinoza, and Nietzsche.

Recognizing the fount of creative energy in the everyday world, Joyce suggests in a rhetorical query that 'His producers are they not his consumers?' (497.1–2). Continuing his preoccupation with the everyday world exhibited in *Ulysses,* the poet of *Finnegans Wake* explores experimentally the socio-cultural parameters of everyday life as they are revealed through the night world of the imaginary: darkness, dream, hallucination, memory. Such a poetic practice implies some theoretical understandings about cultural studies. The *Wake* utilizes the entire continuum of creative activity: first, that creativity of everyday life manifested by virtually everyone in her or his daily acts of communication and self-expression; next, the pragmatic creativity of those producers of entertainment, persuasion, or commercial artifacts; and finally, that flexible self-conscious and self-reflective creativity of the poet and artist. At the moment which marked the beginning of a decade of darkness and war, Joyce's work declares the poetic recognition of the inherent creativity of humankind.

Joyce's achievement is the culmination of a period; though, as most such culminations, it is prospective as well as retrospective, since it transcends most of the work of the period. Inventing innovative strategies for a contemporary poetic, reflecting on the period from 1880 to 1940, and critically evaluating arguments against modern art's interest in the new culture of time and space – such as those of Wyndham Lewis – his poetic practice encompasses a theory of communicative action. That practice is directed to a festive, dialogic, encyclopaedic, and bodily-oriented conception of the process of communication which moves beyond the conception of differentiated media of communication. Mallarmé had predicted that the early decades of the twentieth century would see poets move beyond literature. Eliot two decades later observed that Joyce had reduced style to zero.[27] In the 1960s Marshall McLuhan came to be for the populace the prophet of the death of the book, since many commentators transformed his observations on these problems into an unqualified prediction and endorsement of that death. What actually has been implied as taking place in this process is not the movement beyond a particular medium, such as the book or print, but a movement beyond the very idea of a unique communication medium. The appearance of new methods of technological production, reproduction, and distribution permitted the possibility of transcending traditionally recognized modes and returning to the original vision of the poetic as a concept which could simultaneously embrace various modes of communication, as in Aristotle's treatment of drama in the *Poetics*. Joyce represents a monumental movement beyond media – itself a comic commentary on McLuhan and his commentators. The explication of this phenomenon is a key to understanding the complex interrelation of comunication, media, and text as an index to the contemporary world.

2

The Micro as the Medium and the Message: Synaesthesia, the Harmonization of the Senses, and the Mechanics of Art

The poetics of modernism and its aftermath are firmly grounded in the issues of communication, technology, and culture. Since discussions within modernist poetics ranged from observations about gesture and tactility to questions of the artist's relation to neuro-chemical and neuro-electrical technologies, it is not difficult to see in the development of the modernist (and postmodernist) arts a major aspect of what might be described as the 'pre-history of cyberspace.' Ultimately, the full development of cyberspace, or virtual reality, will provide people with the capability to interact within all-encompassing environments across space and time, while simultaneously utilizing data bases of varying media mixes from many distant and disparate locations. Discrete bits and pieces of information in a wide variety of media will be assembled in these interactions, each unit conforming to its own specific scheme of organization (i.e., hypertextually, taking hypertext to include hypermedia). Workplace applications, such as remote surgery or remote job training, will radically change the practical world; intellectual and cultural applications will change cultural production and traditional liberal arts education just as radically. The poetry of artistic interactivity will produce entirely new art forms that will further contribute to producing new semiologies (grammars and rhetorics) by which people will communicate. In these metamorphoses, once again the tension between fiction and reality will reveal the principle that fiction itself is part of reality; for virtual reality, like fiction, is an assembling, making, or construction.

Our new found capability to create participatory, interactive virtual worlds through the combination of telecommunications, computers, and other electrotechnologies should entail a reassessment of McLuhan's intuitions; for McLuhan, although he never used terms such as 'cyberspace' or 'virtual reality,' flourished as international guru by being the prime prophet announcing the coming of cyberspace (which he described without cyberspace or virtual reality actually having established its existence). Natural prophecy, the medieval way of thinking about futurology, a Thomistic concept with which McLuhan was naturally familiar, occurs through a reading of history and its relation to that virtual, momentary social text, the present, which is dynamic and always undergoing change. It is only through such reading that the future existent in history can be known or come to be. McLuhan's reading of the collision of history and his present moment led him to foresee a world in which communication will be tactile, post-verbal, fully participatory, and pan-sensory.[1]

What McLuhan called 'acoustic space' – a spherical environment within which aural information is received by the central nervous system (CNS) – also embodies for him another transformation of the hermetic poetic insight that 'the universe (or nature) [or, in earlier versions, God] is an infinite sphere, the center of which is everywhere, the circumference nowhere.'[2] Today, as Jorge Luis Borges's writing has implied, virtual reality is coming to be our contemporary pre-millennial epitome of Pascal's infinite sphere, a place where each participant (rather than *the* deity) as microcosm is potentially the enigmatic centre. Here people englobed within virtual worlds find themselves interacting within complex, transverse, intertextual multimedia forms that are interlinked globally through complex, rhizomic (root-like) networks. It is not surprising then that McLuhan's works, side by side with those of Gibson, had been avidly read by early researchers in MIT's Media Lab,[3] for these researchers also anticipated the creation of VR that would be characterized as producing a cyberspace of 'acoustic spaces and involvements' that is also 'tactile, haptic, [and] proprioceptive.'[4]

Why do McLuhan's words still stand as a prophecy of this emerging VR age? Because an important part of the history of the development of cyberspace and even its pre-history are embedded in the symbolist and modernist history of semiotics, rhetoric, and poetics. McLuhan understood the implications of the histories of art, technology, and the construction of society in our century for the creation of virtual worlds and interactive participation as none of his disciples, such as Walter Ong, nor his critics, such as James Carey, did.[5] But McLuhan, as the above reference to Pascal's sphere suggests, depended for this insight on a complex set of sources. Some of those sources – late nineteenth- and twentieth-century poets, other artists, and their interpreters – are part of what constitutes the early history of VR and cyberspace. What then is the value of recognizing this? Tracing this early history is essential to interpreting and evaluating some of cyberspace's and virtual reality's potential human and socio-cultural effects.

VR, the production of virtual reality in cyberspace, while encompassing the traditional audio-visual media, offers the potential for expanding these to include the tactile, the olfactory, and intrasensory and intersensory phenomena. Cyberspace is the culmination of a series of technological developments which began to achieve critical force in the early nineteenth century. The immediate history of cyberspace's development is rooted in the discovery of how to utilize electricity through electro-mechanics, electro-chemistry, and electronics and in the development of the micro-analysis of mechanical processes with the accompanying possibilities of automation, as exemplified, for instance, by the Jacquard loom and Babbage's differential analyser.

Under the impact of electricity, electro-mechanics, and electro-chemistry, the first new modes of technological producibility, reproducibility, and dissemination of knowledge and information appeared: the telegraph and photography. That historical moment in 1837 when the telegraph was patented (by William Cooke and Charles Wheatstone),[6] followed in 1838 by Samuel Morse's invention of the Morse code and in 1839 by Daguerre's development of photography in the daguerreotype, is critically important. While the telegraph compressed space through its increased speed in disseminating codified information, photography opened up the possibility of reproducing 'virtually' actual existing objects and of spanning time by creating new visual histories. In their wake, Babbage's earlier discovery of the concept of the differential analyser that started people on the path towards automation, robotics, and 'compunications' moved closer to practical realization. The final challenge of the unique primacy of print had begun. With rapidly developing electric technologies, the world of the Gutenberg Galaxy would in a little over a century and a half give way to the Compunications Chaosmos.[7]

The rapidly accelerating process by which the relationship between technology and cultural production had changed since the 1850s invited poets, artists, and cultural producers to explore potential socio-cultural roles for the broad range of new modes of technological production, reproduction, and dissemination and frequently to predict or pioneer directions in which they would develop. By re-examining the limits of language as experienced before the onset of electric media, artists and writers have contributed to rethinking how to utilize the entire repertoire of new technological modes of communication. Their explorations have been generating many new technologically producible and reproducible art forms, including new cultural productions within popular, mass, and alternative cultures. By considering the work of these artists as an aspect of the history of communication (the exploration of the potentialities and limits of various communication paradigms), it becomes possible through some of their very astute intuitions about the future potential of electric media to perceive, retrospectively, the significance of those inventions which since the late 1830s have catapulted Western society on the path towards cyberspace.

The unfolding history of poets and artists confronting electro-mechanical techno-culture, which begins during the 1850s, reveals a gradually accelerating interest in synaesthesia and in artistic works which are syntheses, integrations, or orchestrations of the arts (i.e., cœnaesthesia). With the development of new modes of technological producibility, reproducibility, and dissemination, synaesthesia, which had always existed as a component of the practical knowledge of the artist, comes to be identified conceptually, associated with the synthesis of the arts, and assigned a central role in the new poetics. Exploring these concepts of synaesthesia and of integration is a natural supplement to the discussion of gesture and communication in the preceding chapter, for the world of modernism is a world of interplay between disjunctions, differences, and oppositions, on the one hand, and networks, connections, and trajectories, on the other.

Writers had always been aware of synaesthesia (i.e., the perception, or the description of perception, of one sense modality in terms of another) for it has a lengthy history as a rhetorical and poetic device going back to Graeco-Roman poetry, prose, and philosophy. (Examples abound, such as Donne's speaking of 'loud perfume,' Shelley of the 'music' of the hyacinth, and even Kipling of the dawn which 'comes up like thunder.') Greek literary theory not only recognized the metamorphosis of genres, but this transmutation of form that is the basis of synaesthesia. If for Greek critics poetry constituted painting which speaks, while painting or sculpture could be described as silent poetry, there was clearly some recognition of the fluidity of sensory information in the activity of human communication.

As a matter of practical consciousness, Shakespeare was quite familiar with this interplay of audio, visual, spoken, and written communication for he constantly played with these various modes of expression, in a way that was quite familiar to the Elizabethan writer and artist. Living in an alchemical world where metamorphic transformations were considered the norm of nature, Shakespeare instinctively discerned the interdependence among the arts of sensory information and readily perceived the poetic effects that could be achieved by using such transmutations. For example, in Sonnet 23:

O, let my books be then the eloquence
And dumb presagers of my speaking breast,

Who plead for love, and look for recompense
More than that tongue that more hath more express'd.
O learn to read what silent love hath writ:
To hear with eyes belongs to love's fine wit.

This interplay between the visual, the verbal, the literal, and the auditory illustrates how Shakespeare perceives the interplay of media and the impact of one medium upon another. 'Love's fine wit' speaks of that acute consciousness of the sensory which is an intrinsic part of the feelings of love and of those desires which lead to the production of aesthetic expression. Reading regarded as hearing with eyes, yet seeing beyond or behind words, renders an account of the act of reading which reveals that it has the potential of reproducing total participation in the life-world from which the writing emanates. In *As You Like It* Shakespeare's Duke speaks in this manner of the sweetness of adversity:

... this our life exempt from public haunt,
Finds tongues in trees, books in the running brooks,
Sermons in stones and good in everything. (2.1.15–17)

And his melancholy scholar, Jacques, can declare that 'All the world's a stage ...' since literary works which use language as a way of evoking the energy of kino-audio-visual images and the complexities of verbal meaning itself must be executed with an implicit, though not necessarily reflective, awareness of the continuum of communication.

Overt theoretical recognition of the concept of synaesthesia occurs in 1857 (subsequent to the discovery of telegraphy and photography) with Baudelaire's writing *Fleurs du mal,* though the word identifying this concept does not first appear in English until around 1890. Artists and writers began to intuit the future transformational power of the coming of electro-communication through theoretical rearticulation of the concept of synaesthesia and of trends towards integration of all the arts as central aspects of *symbolisme.* These synaesthetic and cœnaesthetic transformational matrices were unconsciously responding to that digitilization implicit in Morse code and telegraphy, anticipating how one of the major characteristics of cyberspace would be the capability of transforming all modes of expression into minimal discrete contrastive units – bits.

One important aspect of this overt recognition of the concept of synaesthesia is that its articulation indicates that under the impact of social and technological change, there emerged a greatly heightened consciousness that communication is a continuum of which language is only one significant component. This theoretical awareness of synaesthesia enabled artists to think more deeply about the possibilities of introducing the effects of different media within their own particular mode of art. It accelerated the breakdown of the borderlines between the usually accepted modes of artistic production. Consequently, it would become generally recognized that most newer art forms emerge from combining existing art forms with new technologies to create new potentialities, or even by combining new technologically mediated art forms to produce still other artistic possibilities, as Sergei Eisenstein observes when speaking about the orchestration of the arts through the integrative power of film.[8] (It is worth noting, however, that within a few decades after his writing this, 'film' had become a 'discipline' and had been itself hypostatized as a unique art form and/or medium distinct from other art forms such as television.)

When vowels could be imagined as generating colours and the idea of a colour organ could become a product of the imagination, the fluidity of the interaction of sound, image, sign, and gesture had come to occupy an intrinsic place in artist practice. *Poésie concrète* again became a recognized form for poets such as Guillaume Apollinaire and e.e. cummings, while in the visual arts the collage, such as those of Kurt Schwitters, embraced printed material as well as other objects. Newspapers easily found their place in cubist inner landscapes, such as Pablo Picasso's *Guernica,* since in a way the layout of the newspaper itself could be perceived as symbolist or cubistic.[9] A filmic use of such effects can be found in Orson Welles's remarkable use of sound to create imaginary visual action in *Citizen Kane*: the dramatic structure of the scene in which Kane's wife, Susan, fails to poison herself is encompassed by the difference between two sounds – the nearby gasps of Susan and the banging of Kane on the door – while a tension is established between the two poles, shockingly differentiated by the depth of focus.[10] These productions of the first half of the century are only a beginning. Possibilities of achieving a still greater potential for a concrete audio-visual, kinetic poetry developed gradually as the artistic awareness and technical resources themselves developed. Full fruition could not be achieved before the arrival of the microcomputer with its ability to provide graphics, animation, and synthetic sound in a processing unit which had dramatic economies of cost and relative friendliness to the user.

The perception that such possibilities would come to be technologically realized long preceded their actual realization in the 1970s and 1980s when the PC appeared. To the current generation of poets, inheritors of the perceptions of the high modernist era, quite naturally, the micro is the medium. So it is surprising, after the popularity of McLuhan's books, that little attention continues to be paid to how the perceptions of artists often seem to prophesy the coming of a new era of technology and social values; for they clearly provided an 'early warning system' to alert people to the implications of the newly emerged 'age of communication' which was quickly followed by 'the era of cyberspace and telematics (or compunication).' This potentiality of the poet as a future-oriented, radar-like sensor has not been widely recognized partly because such a way of regarding history has frequently been considered as granting priority to purely formalist concerns, just as McLuhan's entire project is regarded as the final flowering of that North American formalism developed by the New Critics and logical positivism.[11] But the predictive potential in McLuhan's work ought not to be read as associated with such a formalism, since the forms with which an artist works are themselves signs discovered through the artist's exploration of new factors in the changing context of her or his times.

The interpretation of Joyce's major works in the first chapter demonstrates that they provide a gauge to the metamorphoses of the arts since 1880 and envision a future which is coming to be; a future in which the synchronization or integration of modes of communication is prevalent and in which the role of verbal poetry is being transformed. Extrapolating from Joyce's immediate present and the history which had brought that moment about, *Ulysses* and *Finnegans Wake* move towards a future in which earlier purposes of the novel will now be achieved in multimedia poetic forms, such as film. This involves the creation of a malleable language in which synaesthesia, synchronicity, or the actual metamorphoses of sensory experience are enmeshed in the creation of verbal language itself – speech and printed words – such as in: 'It scenes like a landescape from Wildu Picturescu or some seem on some dimb Arras, dumb as Mum's mutyness, this mimage ...' (*FW*53.1–3); or 'odable to os across the wineless Ere no oeder nor mere eerie' (*FW*53.4); or 'if an ear aye sieze what no eye ere grieved for' (*FW*482.35). This is poetry made by a modern poet who is 'failing of that kink in his arts over sense' (*FW*490.5).

Joyce creates a comic-satiric machine for exploring distorted communication. His play with the multiplicities of sense in language – with communication – deliberately exploits gaps to force the exploration of what creating paths across those gaps will reveal about our culture and its future. Similar strategies can be used to develop anarchistic, encyclopaedic satire which probes the paradoxes of the surfaces of knowledge. Such a critique of the state of learning and culture is also a summation of bodily existence and the potential experience of society directed towards social, political, and intellectual reform. Joyce is centrally engaged in learned, yet excessive, exorbitant, and excrementitious satire like that of Rabelais, Swift, Sterne, Pope, and Wyndham Lewis.[12] He uses the carnivalesque life-force that shapes everyday life to probe the follies and ignorance of learning, power, and wealth.

This medley of the bawdy, the grotesque, parody, and commonplace laughter is transformed into one of Joyce's poetic means for exploring the ambivalence and anarchism of the modern world. His poetic construct, *Finnegans Wake,* is a communicating machine in which the filling in of gaps, as in Lewis Carroll's *Alice* books, plays with signifiers and through them with the surface of this world to reveal ambivalences and labyrinthine complexities. The metamorphic, of which the synaesthetic is a specific type, is crucial to this activity. The evolution of synaesthesia as a self-conscious poetic or artistic strategy created a set of conditions which dramatized the interaction of fluidity and gaps breaking the sensory flow. This operation of intersensory interaction further opens up potentialities for communication by permitting a greater complexity of transverse connection (e.g., intertextuality) within an individual work.

Gaps naturally create chasms or an abyss, a radical absence. Gaps first appear as theoretical preoccupations in art and philosophy in the writings of Mallarmé and Nietzsche. Modernism discovered that symbols have always been constituted of profound areas of absence: thus silence came to occupy a significant role in the contemporary arts. Evidently, while I am not exclusively speaking about gaps in quite this way, it should be apparent that there is a relationship; for a gap, to the extent it is a hiatus or incompleteness, can at least partially be filled in. In the growth of knowledge, such absences have, in fact, provided the space in which new fields of knowledge develop. Interdisciplinarity evolves as a questioning of the gaps created by existing fields. In either sense, a gap is a seduction to interpret. Symbols cry out for understanding. Understanding requires interpretation. Gaps between fields of knowledge invite explorations which involve the discovery of how and why the gap developed. This process is a discovery of the rhizome-like networks, which Joyce described as 'feelful thinkamalinks,' that proliferate on surfaces; it is like a nomadic group creating a map through their wanderings – an Odyssean periplum.

If the imaginary making of poetic signs – Joyce's dreamer as 'bilder' (*FW*62.8; 77.3; 377.26) – is achieved through everybody's participation in the everyday history of humanity, then in our century this activity immediately dramatizes some pivotal gaps. One such gap is that which emerges when aesthetics, accounting for the relation of art to expression and symbol by creating a privileged realm of high art and culture that severs art from everyday communication, is confronted by the radical interaction of art and popular culture. Another gap is exposed when the theoretical divorce of language (especially either speech or writing viewed as a privileged form by structuralists and North American deconstructionists) is challenged by the claims of the broader, yet essentially integrated, system of human communication underlined by the rise of technological producibility and reproducibility.

The arts of language (oral poetry, story-telling) and the arts of writing (novels, romance, poetry, essay writing), therefore, are doubly privileged – as arts of distinction or discrimination and as linguistic texts – and this has caused them to have a less and less central role in today's social and cultural communication. This is further reinforced by the epistemological stance which stresses that reliability can only be achieved within a delimited field of specialization, so that the study of writing or print, for example, is in itself enough of a challenge without attempting to locate it in relation to other arts, other intellectual areas, or other media of communication. Yet these gaps appear at the very time when the authority of writing is being challenged and the necessity for re-examining and redefining the nature of communication and expression has become critical.

From the earliest times, people apparently recognized that they actually can and often do communicate by using a multiplicity of means or modes of communication simultaneously. The participant in a Greek forum understood that a speaker supplemented language with the use of gesture, demonstration, visual illustration, and the modification of sound, rhythm, and movement. The arts of rhetoric, which together with the arts of grammar and logic essentially composed the traditional arts of language, were disciplines within the arts of language that included, though in a more subordinate way, extra-linguistic aspects of communication. In their poetry, as well as in rhetorical practice, the Greeks appear to have favoured language in action, for drama was considered to be the epitome of the poetic. While the ancient traditions of rhetoric had extended the art of persuasion outward into the fields of gesture, voice, tone, behaviour, and even demonstration (e.g., presentation of evidence), the even more ancient traditions of poetics had been developed on the model of the most multimedia art form of the classical world – drama – a form including song, dance, scenery, costume, gesture, and movement as well as the arts of language. This acceptance in practice of the importance of mixing media ultimately had relatively little effect on the dominance of the Word as the central distinguishing feature of human interchange until the coming of the new modernist culture of time and space.

By the end of the Renaissance, rhetorical theorists under the influence of the printing press had also extended the art of rhetoric to include writing, for rhetorical treatises began to provide more fully developed descriptions of the epistolary style (i.e., an informal style for writing letters and for use in other informal genres), and they also often included discussion of devices exclusively used in written presentations, such as orthography, typography, punctuation, and even the visual shape of the lines and stanzas of a poem as it was set out in print. With this new interest in writing, accompanied by the standardization of language, the historical roots of rhetoric as being the art of speaking directed towards the communicative and persuasive practice of an embodied person had virtually disappeared.

By the eighteenth century, Alexander Pope in his *Dunciad* could celebrate the death of the Word, owing to the impact of the improved printing press and the creation of a large popular audience. The *spoken word* had been an embodied word resilient with sense; the *printed word* was becoming a standardized, disembodied word divided from all immediate sensory experience. The machinery of the body had given way to a more abstract machine for mass producing the disembodied word; contemporary drama occupied a lesser role in the pantheon of the arts. But even Pope's world yearned for some experience that provided a kind of mixture of media and a foretaste of virtual realities. Pope's grotto with its *camera obscura* is one such precursor of serendipitous mixed media virtualities.

Just about a century later, with the beginnings of photography and telegraphy, a new re-embodying of the communicating person commenced as people thinking about the arts began to speak about an integrated and interrelated system of communication which people used in expressing their ideas, feelings, desires, and visions. The synaesthetic and cœnaesthetic refocus how sense, or the knowledge implicit in sensory activity, always emphasized gaps, for the senses formed a complex labyrinth functioning by their interaction with internal and external gaps. Discovery of the electro-mechanical body brought to awareness how sensory activity functioned within the body, since the neuro-muscular system itself depended on the on-and-off firing of bursts of electric energy.

The role of the poet in relation to 'sense' had received recognition in a major eighteenth-century philosophical work, Vico's *New Science*, which anticipated some perspectives of phenomenology and semiotics. Joyce chose the central core of this work as the scaffolding for the *Wake* – Vico's conception of 'poetic wisdom': 'Throughout this book it will be shown that only so much as the poets had first sensed of vulgar wisdom did the philosophers later understand esoteric wisdom; so that the former may be said to have been the sense and the latter the intellect of the human race.'[13] The complex role of the word *sense* (and its various equivalents in other Indo-European languages) provides a key guide to questions about the environmental or ecological aspect of communication, for it signifies a crucial historical ambivalence manifested by the ease with which it can become a complex pun: sense as *a* sense employed in processing sensory information; sense as such sensory information; and sense as 'import or signification.'

Sense, that is, the root *sens-,* is involved in the English words *sensory, sensuous, sensual,* and *sensibility. Sense* can describe a single sensory system, or in the plural ('senses') refer to the entire sensory system; it can also refer to virtual internal organs such as in 'the common sense.' Further, it can refer to a general feeling about or perception of something; and, it can also be used for the meaning or signification of a word or sign. Apparently this word embraces the gamut of perception and conception from the physical to the abstract and mental, a characteristic which is reflected in the association of *sensory* and *sensual* with the physical, and *sensuous* with the intellectual. Philosophers seem to agree that there is no connection between the physical aspect of the root *sens-* and the philosophical term 'sensuousness' (for a cognitive mental faculty) and that any attempt to connect them is merely verbal play on the ambiguities implicit in its history. Yet Herbert Marcuse has pointed out that 'in German, *sensuousness* and *sensuality* are still rendered by one and the same term: *Sinnlichkeit.* It connotes instinctual (especially sexual) gratification as well as cognitive sense-perceptiveness and representation (sensation). This double connotation is preserved in every-day as well as philosophical language, and is retained in the use of the term *Sinnlichkeit* for the foundation of aesthetics. Here the term designates the "lower" ("opaque," "confused") cognitive faculties of man *plus* the "feeling of pain and pleasure" sensations *plus* affections.'[14]

Aesthetic as the 'science of sensitive cognition,' which is the way a near contemporary of Vico's, Schiller, defined it in his *Letters on the Aesthetic Education of Man* (1795), might also be used to describe Vico's 'poetic wisdom.' Schiller in his *Letters* conceived of people remaking their civilization by virtue of the liberating force of the aesthetic function, just as Vico had argued that the 'world of human society has ... been made by men, and its principles are therefore to be found within modifications of our own human mind,' a process which begins with the development of 'poetic wisdom.' The holism that has characterized Gregory Bateson's theories about culture and communication appears quite consistent with this interrelating of the sensory (and sensual) with sensuousness.

Bateson's concept of an ecology of mind implies an ecological role for communication. That role involves what is the necessary complement to a concept such as the ecology of mind, which I will call the ecology of sense, for an ecology of sense is an obvious corollary to Bateson's 'ecology of mind' (or, as he suggests elsewhere, 'ecology of ideas'). Since the poetic act is in part both a technical (and technological) and a semiological exploration of the limits of communicative action, it is possible to speak of the 'ecology of sense,' for the poetic act in all of the arts is partly directed towards people communicating about renewing or opening up possibilities for ongoing communication.

There is an ecology of sense because the poetic is partly involved with specific types of learning: learning to intensify communication and thus learning about learning to communicate intensely and, still further, learning about the process of learning about learning to communicate intensely. This is why poetic activity has frequently been associated with children's learning through mimicry.[15] The ecology of sense arises within communication as secular communion as described by John Dewey and Burke, so that the ecology of sense functioning through the poetic act involves the spectrum of communication beyond the purely rational. It should be remembered that the poetic, while it is a feature of what has normally been described as creative writing and art, also occurs in daily communication, as Joyce suggested in his insistence on the co-participation of his audience in his poetic productions.

Speaking about 'sense' in the ecology of sense raises questions concerning how signs, images, symbols, and icons interact. What is there about certain constructions of signs which determines that they have a greater survival value for impacting on people's understanding of their world and themselves? Are there activities that involve a free play of perception as a way of permitting the exploration of the interactions between signs, images, and icons and people's minds, nervous, and sensory systems? Is Bateson's discovering an epistemological significance in the activity of play (and the accompanying message 'This is play')[16] associated with the fact that poetics and play were related together at the very inception of poetics (for example, in Aristotle's *Poetics*)? Bateson himself extended his concept of play to encompass a range for activity from humour to drama.

Implicit in such an ecology is the idea of difference – a difference that makes a difference.[17] This is the essence of Pound's aphorism 'Make it new,' which not only set forth a standard for modernist poetics, but simultaneously led to a reassessment of the history of literature and art, where such difference could be repeatedly discovered. (The history of English poetry provides one example of this with its periodic reiteration of poetic revolutions: Dryden at the beginning of neo-classicism; Wordsworth and Coleridge at the beginning of Romanticism; Pound at the beginning of modernism.) This process of differentiation is complex, since it occurs at the meeting point between the formal aspects of the physical that we normally speak about in terms of the senses, or the perceptual activity of the central nervous system (CNS). The doubleness that has been perceived in the conception of sensuousness, which is linked both to the sensual and to the sensory, underlines this bridging of the physical and the mental implicit in 'sense.'

Sense can be considered as a 'fourth dimension' – a dimension manifesting a logic of becoming. Sense is not the body or object; it is not the word; and it is not a sensitive or rational representation. It is the node where the sign and the material spasmodically and temporarily span a gap. Sense seems to embrace a doubleness; to invite verbal playfulness. That doubleness and playfulness produce complex ambivalence. The ambivalence of sense manifests itself in all poetic forms. Contemporary painting and sculpture have underlined this fact with the intrinsic role that entitlement has played in such works as Alberto Giacometti's *Invisible Object*, the complex ambivalence of which over-layers aspects of native masks, a preying mantis, a primitive stylization of a woman, a gallows-like construction, a rigid frame, a cage, and a machine at rest.[18]

Calder's *Only, Only Bird* metamorphosizes a Medaglia d'Oro coffee can into a parodic modern phoenix (or, perhaps, a peacock?); Warhol's *Campbell's Soup Can with a Can Opener* (1962) or *Four Campbell's Soup Cans* (1965) decontextualize the image of a Campbell's soup can in a poetic act which has virtually become an archetype of the transformation of the role of mass culture in the 'postmodern' world. In each such case, sense plays a complex role in which remembered sensuality, sensory experience, and sensuousness contribute to the materialized dematerialization of the art object. Some of Klee's finest magic squares take on part of their magic through the process of entitlement (e.g., *Ancient Sound* [1925]), though in all of these examples, which are characteristic of contemporary art, the phenomenon of sense plays across the surface of the work.

A predominant feature of modernist and late modernist (or postmodernist) writing is the presence of strategies associated with the 'ambiviolence' (*FW*518.2) of sense that is exemplified in such varied writers as Acker, Beckett, Borges, Joyce, Lem, Pynchon, or Rushdie. Complex polysemous figures, such as the Joycean puns and portmanteau forms, which play with sense, frequently typify this type of comic or satiric writing. Such verbal strategies are supplemented by the complex structural ambivalence that is to be found in Borges's *Labyrinths* or Lem's extended studies of imaginary future encounters with alien intelligences – *Fiasco* or *Eden* or *His Master's*

Voice. A near anarchistic ambivalence can be achieved either through the probing of schizoid inner voices, as in Beckett's novels, or by reflection on the anarchy of diversity and difference within contemporary globalized society as in Acker's *Empire of the Senseless*.

Joyce, particularly in his dream work, the *Wake*, often plays with the word *sense* in the very spirit of its duplexity or multiplexity in passages such as 'the sound sense sympol in a weedwayedwold of the firethere in the sun in his halo cast. Onmen' (612.29–30). The pun and his other portmanteau constructions are obviously natural 'sound sense sympol[s].' To understand the complexity contained in this phrase, consider the context within which it occurs. This phrase concludes a debate before the High King of Ireland between the Archdruid (a composite of the Irish philosopher Bishop Berkeley and a fifth-century Druid priest) and Saint Patrick, who has just arrived in Ireland in 432. They argue about Patrick's intention to light the Easter Vigil fire at Tara and about the nature of light and of the deity. Since this incident occurs at the conclusion of the *Wake* and therefore just before the dreamer awakes, the sun rises as the fire is lit and the effect produces a 'sound sense sympol.' Throughout the night language of the *Wake* with its 'dreamydeary' (5.26) action, the reader has been admonished to pay attention to the ratios between sound and sense: 'Can you not distinguish the sense, prain, from the sound, bray?' (522.29–30); '(here keen again and begin again to make soundsense and sensesound kin again)' (121.15).

Such strategies that play with the sense and sound of language have frequently been regarded as suspect, since they play primarily with the surface (e.g., puns or portmanteaus that utilize the sound and often the orthography). However, such devices open up rambling networks of connections (rhizomes, lianas) that generate simultaneous multiple meanings. This multiplexity typifies the operation of sense and how it establishes an ecology of sense essential to the processes of communication. These devices are not only effective, but are intrinsically integrated with those processes that generate the ongoing semiotic vitality for communication to cope with social and environmental change. This is possible because the pun and its relation to metaphor and metaphor-like devices (e.g., montage in film, collage in the visual arts, verbal juxtaposition, the layout of the newspaper page, etc.) composes an action or event inviting a general type of interpretative activity by which people make sense of their world, their society, and themselves. In this process, the immediacy of the living body's experience is joined to the abstractions of remembered intelligence.

Just as the word *sense* can be so easily played with through paronomasia, this very same wordplay that is often utilized to link together aspects of 'lower' (e.g., excremental) and 'higher' (e.g., spiritual) levels of human concerns,[19] also links a lower level of sensation, 'sound' or the materiality of letters, with higher levels of cognition. 'Sense,' then (in some of its meanings), does participate in creating Joyce's 'sound sense sympol' (sympol = symbol + simple), which is simultaneously: (1) the opposite of complex or enigmatic; (2) a synonym for a single medicinal herb, which signifies the therapeutic nature of the flowers (i.e., figures) of speech that make symbols sensible; and (3), paradoxically, a symbol, a complex sign formed from the duplex or multiplex conjunction that is a modality of textual use which is both a mode of producing a text and also a mode of interpreting every text.[20]

The realization that the pun is a 'sound sense sympol' also extends the operation of punning into realms of communication which are not solely verbal. In the incident between Patrick and the Archdruid, Patrick's liturgical invocation and the manifestation of light that create the final 'sound sense sympol' is a multi-media combination of gesture, visual presentation, and words. Verbal puns often depend on recollected images, but actual images and even non-verbal sounds themselves, as we well know, can be the ambivalent or ambiguated equivalent of puns. A filmic pun or a pun in a comic strip can easily be conceived as its own kind of 'sound sense sympol,' often involving printed words and spoken sounds as well as other symbols.

Ingmar Bergman's use of fireworks and rockets in *All Those Women* (a witty intertextual parody of Fellini) is also a witty reference to orgasm, which contributes the first literal level of such a pun. This is later elaborately worked out 'intertextually' by Dušan Makavéjev in *Manifesto* (1988), where he makes visual and verbal fun of the Bergman film as he had made fun of his own use of the pun in the animated opening titles where fireworks and rockets emerge from the name of the director. The propinquity of puns to allusions (or at least as one strategy for calling attention to allusions) is one of its natural modes of enrichment.

All such strategies are too frequently condemned as being artificial and mechanical. They play with surface effects to suggest profundity; they achieve an art of rising to the heights by skimming above the surfaces. The close association of the exercise of making sense, which involves the surfaces of bodies, of texts, and of situations, with the capability of releasing the play of the senses and the intellect has long been recognized as critical to communication, understanding, and the transfer of knowledge. Bergson noted the mechanical role on which all comic effect depends. Deleuze has associated this with the way that contemporary art as represented by Proust or Kafka operates.

Generations accustomed to the cinema and to the composition of the television image find it a natural mode for thinking of the arts in a world where mechanization has taken command and whose effects have been exponentially multiplied by electricity. But it ought to be just as natural and just as correct in such a world to identify communication itself as an electrified machine. Deleuze has clearly qualified the way that the 'machinic,' as he calls this phenomenon, is not *mechanical* in the sense of *mechanistic*. A communicating machine is an assemblage, a multiplicity which is made up of many heterogeneous terms and which establishes liaisons, relations between them, across ages, sexes and regions. This is not primarily mechanistic for 'an assemblage is never technological; if anything, it is the opposite. Tools always presuppose a machine, and the machine is always social before being technical. There is always a social machine which selects or assigns the technical elements used.'[21]

The notion that the literary work (or, at least, the contemporary literary work) is a machine becomes a recurrent feature in the work of many late nineteenth- and twentieth-century writers. Joseph Conrad, for example, spoke frequently about his work and its relation to the mechanics of nature, and he described his novel *Nostromo* as being a literary machine. Valéry's meditations on Leonardo, architecture, and on engineering and poetry all demonstrate this preoccupation with mechanization accompanied by the tendency to view the creative work as machine. Joyce described *Finnegans Wake* as a work of engineering and himself as an engineer.

A classic statement of this theme occurs in the correspondence of Malcolm Lowry – a passage which could just as easily refer to to the writings of Borges, Kafka, Lem, or Joyce, or to McLuhan's quasi-poetic meditations on the book in *The Gutenberg Galaxy*: 'It can be regarded as a kind of symphony, or in another way as a kind of opera – or even a horse opera. It is hot music, a poem, a song, a tragedy, a farce, and so forth. It is superficial profound, entertaining and boring – according to taste. It is a prophecy, a political warning, a cryptogram, a preposterous movie and a writing on the wall. It can even be regarded as a sort of a machine: it works too, believe me, as I have found out.'[22] While Deleuze, who cites this passage in a discussion of schizoanalysis and the work of art as a 'desiring machine,' correctly observes that for Lowry and many of his contemporaries, the modern work of art is a machine and functions like one, Lowry extends it much further, declaring that 'the modern work is anything it seems.'[23] In describing such a machine, Lowry also speaks about how the arts are interrelated, how the arts and popular culture have come together, how movie projection and writing merge, and how politics blend with utopian prophecies and Freudian concealment.

Such motifs also shape the very action of the dreamer's dreaming in the

Wake. This literary or artistic machine is a machine for communicating for it creates what Deleuze calls a condition of transversality; a concept relating to the discontinuity and fragmentation that confronts the artistic process in the contemporary world.[24] Arguing that an understanding of how transversality works is essential to an understanding of the relationship of the unconscious and human communication, Deleuze explains how Proust employs transverse communication in his writing:

> The narrator continues his own affair, until he reaches the *unknown country*, his own, the *unknown land*, which alone is created by his own work in progress, the *Search of lost Time 'in progress,'* functioning as a desiring-machine capable of collecting and dealing with all the indices. He goes toward these new regions where the connections are always partial and nonpersonal, the conjunctions nomadic and polyvocal, the disjunctions included, where homosexuality and heterosexuality cannot be distinguished any longer: the world of transverse communications, where finally the conquered nonhuman sex mingles with the flowers, a new earth where desire functions according to its molecular elements and flows. Such a voyage does not necessarily imply great movements in extension; it becomes immobile, in a room and on a body without organs – an intensive voyage that undoes all the lands for the benefit of the one it is creating.[25]

Using his discovery concerning how such 'transverse' communication operates by linking discontinuous fragments of artistic works to one another, Deleuze can explore transversality as an aspect of contemporary poetics ranging over a variety of media and poets: for example, Joyce, Mallarmé, Artaud, Lovecraft, Godard, Brecht, and Chaplin.

Sense and synaesthesia collaborate in developing transversality, in the work's producing within and on itself its own effects. Synaesthesia, as an archetype of the transformation achieved through the spontaneous perception of momentary connecting links between differences, also prefigures the inherent possibility within communication for the transformation from one code system to another. It is hardly surprising that nonsense, a major aspect of the stuff of dream and imagination, which plays a fundamental role for all contemporary arts in their specific encounter with the history of changing forms of communication, is crucial for understanding the operations of sense and synaesthesia. If synaesthesia is involved in playing with the transmutability of the effects of the senses resulting from the perceiving (i.e., sensing) of transient resemblances that are actually momentary connections between differences, it is concerned with the surface of meaning, the play of the signifier, which is the domain of what we describe as sense.

Sense is that which we presume as soon as we begin to speak, so that we can speak of 'good sense' and 'common sense'; but just as sensory experience is a matter of surfaces which we encounter, so when we speak of the sense of something said or written or presented, it is a matter of the encounter with the surface. As Deleuze reflecting on Bergson observes, 'you don't go from sounds to images and from images to sense: one settles right away in the sense'[26] Joyce's making 'soundsense and sensesound kin again' (*FW*121.15). In the very act of reading or listening, an unconscious acceptance of the metamorphoses on which synaesthesia takes place occurs. Playing on the multiple meanings of the word *sense* dramatizes the emergence of modernism with its simultaneous interest in synaesthesia and nonsense.

3

From Sense to Nonsense: Gesture, the Body, and Communication

Charles Dodgson, an Oxford mathematician (logician) of the Victorian age and an avid amateur photographer who, using the pseudonym Lewis Carroll, began writing the *Alice* books in 1862, is usually acknowledged as the grand master of nonsense. This poet of paradox plays with the whole spectrum of language as if it were metamorphic. Flamingoes become croquet mallets and hedgehogs, the balls. Words become whatever characters want them to mean. Language itself becomes a material which can be reshaped to create 'snarks,' 'slithy toves,' and 'frumious bandersnatches.' He not only elevates the principle behind synaesthesia to a universal semiotic strategy, he anticipates the semiotic perspective of language and the potentialities of playing with machines for coding and decoding that prefigure the appearance of the computer.

A few years ago, Hofstadter's *Gödel, Escher, Bach: An Eternal Golden Braid* achieved notoriety as *the* cult book for intellectuals interested in the arts and in modern thought. This 'metaphorical fugue on minds and machines in the spirit of Lewis Carroll' included at the conclusion of each section a poetic prose dialogue between Achilles, the Tortoise, and other such characters structured in the shadow of the *Alice* books. Hofstadter links minds, the arts, mathematical construction, and machines (particularly computers) together in a series of meditations on what he describes as his personal religion: a quest through the labyrinthine corridors of how humans try to explore the nature of their own thought processes. He parallels various series of concepts: those that necessarily overlap with or underlie AI; the productions of artists, musicians, and mathematicians; and the writings of Lewis Carroll. The juxtaposition shows how a mysterious set of labyrinthine structures identified by modern artists, philosophers, and mathematicians facilitate contemporary 'rereadings' of the complexities of Bach and Escher.

Gödel's theorem is precisely the type of paradox that would have charmed Dodgson's logical wit, and the connection of poetics with machines, especially machines which encode and decode, would have appealed to his fascination with puzzles and with verbal structure.[1]

Since the late nineteenth century, Carroll has fascinated poets, artists, philosophers, and linguists, such as Joyce, Deleuze, and Eco. Even part of Wittgenstein's philosophic interest in the horrific relevance of nonsense to the understanding of how language works has been associated with the enigmas from which Carroll constructed his nonsense work.[2] Perhaps more than any other twentieth-century poet, Joyce's later works display the same intricate interplay of logic, semantics, poetics, psychology, and social analysis which Carroll developed into the surprising fusion of structures that creates the form of his deceptively simple story-books for children and which has contributed to their ongoing fascination.

Though the whole perspective of the *Alice* books has often been described as formalist, they are very revealing about the lifestyle of a social class and are deeply enmeshed in a web of Victorian technological anticipation of the modern with its metamorphic poetics of science fiction and techno-cultural fairy tales, such as the Oz books. Problems arising from social hierarchies, prejudices, and conceptions of social role are involved in the way 'dreamland' or 'mirror land' animals regard Alice and one another. Technologies such as the railroad train, the newly developed industrialized sense of time, and optics also have a role in these books. Alice discusses with the mouse its prejudice against cats and dogs, with a sheep, the problems of train travel in a timeless dream world, and with others the White Rabbit's near hysterical concern about consulting his watch in order to be on time. A technological orientation is further evident through the ways in which a reader is conscious of the influence of Carroll's enthusiasm for photography and of his fascination for mathematics, games, puzzles, and logic that is manifested in many of the visions and transformations encountered in these imaginary worlds.

The *Alice* books, while staged in the world of dream and the imaginary, are directly involved with human communication, for dreaming is an action in which the mind-body that constitutes a person undertakes to produce a way of communicating its suppressed content to the ego of the mind-body which is the dreamer. Consequently, Alice is constantly encountering dilemmas which involve paradoxes that confuse, complicate, conceal, or inhibit communication, such as in her discussion of the poetry of Jabberwocky with Humpty Dumpty, her attempts to sort out her reactions to the chaotic communication of the Mad Hatter, the March Hare, and the Dormouse, her befuddlement with the misunderstandings of Twiddledum and Twiddledee, or her attempts to comprehend what the Red and White Queen are talking about.

Another level of communication and exchange which is involved through the transformation of the normal or expected rules of games – such as chess, croquet, or card games – contributes further complications to the structure of these dream worlds. Social rules and procedures also undergo curious transformations, exemplified in the parodies of justice dispensed by the courts. At the heart of Carroll's nonsense worlds, consumption is associated with communication, for there is an unstable equality developed throughout these works between speaking and eating, ironically foreshadowing the connections which will later become apparent (under the impact of all-pervasive mass advertising) between the motivations of communicators and the consumption of their products. Carroll's basic use of this duality of eating/speaking is associated with the psychoanalytic concept of orality and with the liberation of the mouth for expression and communication rather than consumption.

Nonsense is related to the synaesthetic. Both processes, like metaphor, depend on metamorphosis and all of them, being related to the process of making sense of the life-world, operate by skirting over the surface of existence, for sense is a matter of sliding along the surfaces of differing sequences of words or objects. The micro now being the medium further dramatizes this faculty of sliding along the surfaces, but also of breaking up flows and continuities, for it facilitates the multimedia hypertextual arranging of signs, a transverse procedure. Nonsense, metaphor, and synaesthesia prefigure this sliding and breaking. In one way or another, all of them depend on effects related to metamorphosis and the exploitation of difference. Ovid, the master of metamorphoses, used stories of transformations in his *Metamorphoses* as ways of explaining the workings of a nature permeated by gods. Ovid's cosmology begins with a description of chaos where the original conflict of cold and hot, wet and dry, soft and hard, heavy and light, is finally resolved either by a god or a kindly Nature.

Throughout the history of thought in the Western world, even in the face of heavy opposition from some Christian theologians, the fascination with Ovid's tales attested to the allegorical power of the description of radical changes of form and how easily these transgressions of nature were adopted as metaphors, transgressions of communication. Metamorphosis, like the making of sense, involves a complex spectrum of means and modes for expressing and communicating that clearly imply the ways in which a communicator is an engineer or designer who creates a machine that communicates. Francis Bacon's treatise on the ancient gods identified each god or demi-god with natural powers, so that for Bacon adapting Ovid's tales about Dædalus,[3] for example, suggests this mythical architect represents the powers of humanity to control nature.[4] Therefore, it is certainly fitting that the presiding personality of the metamorphic in the modern world is Daedalus, Ovid's 'cunning artificer.' Mallarmé clearly identified Daedalus with the subtle engineer and artist – the very same figure that Joyce connects with the youthful artist, Stephen Dedalus, in his *A Portrait of the Artist as a Young Man*.

In each of the phenomena under discussion – synaesthesia, disjunction, metaphor, and nonsense – the juxtaposition of intersecting series is essential to that transfer of meaning which is essential to the making of sense. Kipling's description of the dawn involves a series of visual effects of the colour spectrum, a series of effects of levels of sound, the clusters of meaning associated with the word and concept of thunder, and the clusters of meaning associated with dawn. In a more radical example, Rimbaud's association of vowels with colours intermingles the elements of the spectrum with effects of sound, producing one possible way of making sense of the qualitative effects of the pronunciation of vowel sounds.

As a minimum interpretation, a colour organ exhibits possible interrelations of rhythm, tone, texture, and the other components shared between the structuring of sound and of colour within the processes of expression and communication. While there is an element of nonsense involved here, since we all know sounds are sounds, and colours are colours, there is also a playing with the surfaces of bodies to construct the world anew; for from such nonsense arises a machine simulating sense, which may well be indistinguishable from sense itself, just as Alice's dream, which becomes a tale told by a tale-teller, is perceived with all the intensity of an experience of the waking world.

Dream, nonsense, metamorphosis (and it should be noted that Alice's world is as intensely metamorphic as Ovid's), metaphor, and the making of sense are interrelated processes. Carroll realized that they all involve working with 'bits' of a world by working with 'bits' of sense. Joyce, crafting his *Wake* by designing a language to deal with the night, especially dream (his 'Nichtian glossery' which is 'nat language in any sinse of the world' [83.12]), later memorialized this in speaking of the alphabet as 'allforabit' (19.2). This in a way anticipates how the conception of a 'bit' of information in digitalized form would enable the devising of processes by which sensory information, letters, visual or sound elements, etc., could be produced by a computer out of discrete 'bits' of electric signals. Playing with the word *bit* in our own way just as Joyce has done, we might speak, on one hand, about how Carroll treated these bits of sense, the bits of graphic marks or visual elements, and, on the other, about how the electrical engineer came to use the term 'bit' to designate the information signalled by turning an electric switch on or off. There is a way in which this concept of the 'bit' of information epitomizes those other differences involved in the making of sense with which Carroll is concerned. Here the Daedalian artificer as engineer comes to the forefront.

Joyce, elaborating and intensifying the characteristic interests of his era, clearly exhibits his awareness of the significance of bits (i.e., small discrete units, rather than cybernetic bits) of information in the process of making sense and of communicating. In his description of the TV scene being watched by the patrons in Here Comes Everybody's (HCE's) pub, the 'missledhropes' (*FW*349.11), the golden berries of the mistletoe – a composite of missiles, misled, missal, mistletoe, and tropes – become imaginatively the charges of light bombarding the receiver, 'glitteraglatteraglutt.' These 'missledhropes' function as 'syncopanc pulses,' missiles producing the tropes of a 'verbivocovisual' missal, since they have the 'bitts bugtwug their teffs.' The wordplay on *bit* (i.e., the bits between their teeth) evokes some of the earliest uses of this word related to biting and eating, thus creating an interplay between speaking (communicating, informing) and eating, just as in the *Alice* books. Deleuze, in commenting on Carroll's works, has outlined this relationship of speaking and eating and demonstrated its importance for contemporary schizoanalytic interpretation.[5]

Speaking in this way about bits is not a question of mere analogues. The synaesthetic, the metaphoric, and the making of sense depend on the bits from which the processes arise. Whether the bits result from the interchange of words, groups of words, or ideas; or from the interchange of different sense data; or, even, from the juxtaposition of what makes sense and what appears not to make sense, the primary process of doubling or juxtaposing (and multiplexing) series of meanings operates. These processes of playing with sense are not neutral. Bits of culture are embedded in such bits of information. In Alice's adventures, examples of such embedding are the mouse's views on cats and dogs; Alice's views about constantly undergoing sudden changes in size; her way of comprehending the relationships of eating and being eaten, or speaking and being spoken to. Social and cultural problems are inevitably implied in the process of playing with the way people make sense of their everyday world.

Joyce uses the very extensive selection of nonsense figures in the *Wake* to assist in understanding this rapidly changing world of social, technological, political, and hence communicative relationships. This enables him to create a new language, which is related to a new self-consciousness concerning the spectrum of communication. Carroll's playing with logic and with psychology grounded in his social world becomes in Joyce's *Ulysses* and *Finnegans Wake* an exploration of the unconscious assumptions of that social world itself. Just as Alice's adventures depend on such doubling and redoubling, *Finnegans Wake* as a book about communication is concerned with doubling, for it is the book of 'doublends jined' (20.16) deeply involved in the intersecting of series and the counterpointing of opposed pairs. Technology as a war on the senses and a war on sense is the result of one of those intersections fused in that imaginary presentation of a fight, which is also a bar-room brawl and a war through the medium of television which itself 'bombards' the sensorium of the viewer.

Joyce's and Carroll's use of these semiotic devices is foreshadowed in the work of earlier writers confronted with rapidly shifting social, cultural, and technical worlds. From Rabelais, Swift, Sterne, Shakespeare, and the *symbolistes* as well as from the *Alice* books, Joyce at various stages of the genesis of *Finnegans Wake* developed the range and complexity of verbal play by which he created the night language for this dream world, a machine developed for reading and recording the effects of contemporary society on the individual and the family. His presentation of 'alys' (57.28), who is 'yung and easily freudened' (115.23), situates Carroll's dreamer in the universe of psychoanalytic discourse as well as logical and semantic game-playing. Synaesthesia is at the very root of Joyce's identifying the 'proteiform' (107.8) Alice figure with a flower girl ('le lys' = lily) whose variegated reflections produce the spectrum of colour, but whose laughter produces simultaneously a spectrum of sound, the flowers of speech.

Carroll extends his metamorphoses of the logic of symbols into transformations of the logic of sense. When this complex verbal play is extended to explore realms of major power and sovereignty, it transforms self-consciousness about metamorphosis into consciousness concerning the socio-political realm itself. Alice's dreams concern the follies of kings and queens, the exploitation of commoners, and the critique of a closed social order. This is not necessarily a result of Carroll's critical awareness concerning needed social change. Rather it is a function of any of those 'sense-making' activities that break down the well-ordered surface in order to consider how people make sense of their world. Play with logic, if it uses illustrative examples, necessarily plays inadvertently with the social world in which people are embedded, just as the symbolic logician is often unconscious of the problems she or he illuminates in other spheres while employing examples of contemporary immediacy in teaching logic.

This logical play on which Carrollian nonsense is founded performs a heuristic function that arises from employing the instruments of logic to produce comedy. This particular heuristic is involved with the very foundations of human communication. A digression into Dewey's pragmatic discussion of the relation between the arts and the processes of human communication will assist in understanding why nonsense provides such a powerful model of human communication and how this is related to the problem of sense. In *Democracy and Education* Dewey unqualifiedly points out the close resemblance between communication and art: 'The experience has to be formulated in order to be communicated. To formulate requires getting outside of it, seeing it as another would see it, considering what points of contact it has with the life of another so that it may be got into such form that he can appreciate its meaning. Except in dealing with commonplaces and catch phrases one has to assimilate, imaginatively, something of another's experience in order to tell him intelligently of one's own experience. *All communication is like art*' (italics mine).[6] Nonsense which forces the exploratory intelligence to work with gaps created by grammar, logic, and mathematics produces a strong desire to derive intelligiblity from a still broader range of sensory interplay with gaps and surfaces. As self-consciousness about communication grows in the process of exploration, it brings to consciousness how the discovery of gaps and their exploration takes place through interaction with the external world, for communication can only occur by sacrificing the integral isolation of self.

Dewey, like G.H. Mead, speaks of communication in conjunction with communion as the 'sacrifice' of self in the intersubjectivity of communication that comes about through co-participation with another. The artist works to create a unique type of communication, for 'works of art are the only media of complete and unhindered communication between man and man that can occur in a world full of gulfs and walls that limit the community of existence.'[7] Dewey, in speaking about art, is speaking about the making of dedicated and intensified cultural productions that contribute to the formation of momentary human communities which arise from a sharing in common, of co-participating: 'Communication is the process of creating participation, of making common what had been isolated and singular; and part of the miracle that it achieves is that, in being communicated, the conveyance of meaning gives body and definiteness to the experience of the one who utters as well as to those who listen.'[8] Such communication is not the function or the 'intent' of art, but it is a natural consequence of the artistic activity.

Participation as an essential aspect of all artistic activity can be viewed as the aesthetic action of appropriative enjoyment (consumption), or as the artistic activity which combines operative perception with aesthetic perception (production), or as both since the consumer is also a co-producer. Participation is for Dewey the most distinctively human quality, and art is essential to bringing about the most intense forms of participation precisely because it is 'a device in experimentation carried on for the sake of education,' 'a new training in modes of perception.'[9] These ideas about the education of the senses are strongly echoed in the poetic practice and theoretical observations of many high modernist poets (e.g., Klee, Pound, Eisenstein, Moholy-Nagy). In *Experience and Nature,* Dewey clearly indicates how art in educating perception is an experimental assemblage of natural tendencies and events that can both intensify satisfaction and develop new meanings: 'Art is a continuation, by means of intelligent selection and arrangement, of natural tendencies and natural events ... In such a case, delightfully enhanced perception or esthetic appreciation is of the same nature as enjoyment of any object that is consummatory. It is the outcome of a skilled and intelligent art of dealing with natural things for the sake of intensifying, purifying, prolonging and deepening the satisfaction that they spontaneously afford. That, in this process, new meanings develop, and that these afford uniquely new traits and modes of enjoyment is but what happens everywhere in emergent growths.'[10] But if the arts (including the so-called fine arts) are experimental and educative – the highest form of communication – then, as well as contributing to the emergent growth of our discriminatory processes of communication, they ought to have a specific contribution to make to the understanding of practice. They should to have a specific role to play in the making of sense that will link appropriative enjoyment of the aesthetic activity to the operative perception of the artistic activity.

An ancillary question arises as to whether or not art is to be viewed in a broad perspective in which the traditional liberal arts, such as grammar, dialectic, or rhetoric, or other arts of discourse, can be included in the same category and on the same basis as poetry, music, film, or dance. On both these questions, the Deweyean instrumentalist and the socialist critique largely agree for in Marx's writing there is a strong relation established between art and this making of sense:

> Just as music alone awakens in man the sense of music, and just as the most beautiful music has *no* sense for the unmusical ear ... the *senses* of the social man are *other* senses than those of nonsocial man. Only through the objectively unfolded richness of man's essential being is the richness of subjective *human* sensibility (a musical ear, an eye for beauty of form – in short, *senses* capable of human grati-

fication, senses affirming themselves as essential powers of *man*) either cultivated or brought into being. For not only the five senses but also the so-called mental senses – the practical senses (will, love, etc.) – in a word, *human sense* – the human nature of the senses – comes to be by virtue of its object, by virtue of *humanized nature*. The *forming* of the five senses is a labor of the entire history of the world down to the present.[11]

Like the early Marx, Dewey stresses the process of the formation of 'human sense' as a way of making 'man's *sense human*' as well as creating the '*human sense*' corresponding to the entire wealth of human and natural substance. 'Experience,' Dewey argued, is 'the sign ... of that interaction of organism and environment which ... is a transformation of interaction in participation and communication.' The senses as instruments produce our 'sense' of this experience; that is, 'meaning so directly embodied in experience as to be its own illuminated meaning.'[12] It is just like discovering a clue that suddenly reveals how every aspect and element of some puzzling situation fits together – the whole thing suddenly 'makes sense.'[13] From this perspective, the artist as poet or maker in making a poem is 'making sense' of his experience.

At the beginning of the twentieth century, what was problematic in this way of talking, and particularly this way of thinking, about poetry or art was that sensory information was regarded as a lower form of knowledge and as deluding. Works like Yeats's 'Crazy Jane' poems are characteristic of how contemporary artists confronted this problem, for in the dramatic dialogues of these poems Yeats presents a monistic vision that embraces the poles of this duality between the more spiritual mind and the lower senses. In 'Crazy Jane Talks with the Bishop,' Crazy Jane responds to the Bishop's admonition to 'live in a heavenly mansion':

'Fair and foul are near of kin,
And fair needs foul,' I cried.
'My friends are gone, but that's a truth
Nor grave nor bed denied,
Learned in bodily lowliness
And in the heart's pride.

'A woman can be proud and stiff
When on love intent;
But love has pitched his mansion in
The place of excrement;

For nothing can be sole or whole
That has not been rent.'[14]

Crazy Jane asserts how the world that is significant for people is a world in which fair is embedded in foul; the higher qualities – love – in the baser ones – excrement. This is an insight which had been common to such classical writers as Aristophanes, Petronius, Rabelais, Pope, and Swift as well as to the modernist sensibility. The Bishop, who embraces the transcendental (as Rabelais's clerics did the scholastic-medieval world), blinds himself from realizing that people live in the immanence of excrement. The presumed hierarchy of relations between the lower and higher levels of human activity, the sensual and the intellectual, the excrementitious and the cerebral, the body and the spirit, is abrogated. Ezra Pound appealed to contemporary avant-garde attitudes when he compared the Rabelaisian spirit of Joyce's *Ulysses* to Hercules' cleaning the Augean stables, for Rabelais's world of carnivalesque excess is one of the earliest and strongest post-medieval exemplars of such learned encyclopaedic satire of cultural domination and political sovereignty.

Bakhtin's remarkable study of Rabelais, *Rabelais and His World*, first published in English in 1972, has demonstrated how Rabelais, writing at the moment of transition from the Middle Ages to the Renaissance (a moment of which a distinguishing feature was the techno-cultural revolution brought about by the discovery of the printing press), realized how these processes of playing with the logic of sense are not neutral. He analyses how the carnivalesque use of bawdiness, low comedy, farce, and blasphemy, and the general playful spirit in Rabelais's satire, contribute to his reconstruction of language, which opened up new potentialities for critique by extending the discourse of the intellectual and the theological, enabling more people to communicate about new liberatory possibilities in the Renaissance.

This Rabelaisian type of preoccupation with the so-called 'lower' parts of the body and the spectrum of *sense* (the sensual and sensuous), especially as they relate to the anal, genital, and digestive centres of the body and their gratifications, is engaged in displaying through a verbal and conceptual playfulness the depth of the relationship between the everyday operation of the aesthetic dimension and the intellectual liberation of each person's own awareness of his or her nature. Rabelais reminds us that, inherent within this playing with the entitling or naming of sense, there is a natural multiplicity of meaning; a polysemousness, depending on a series of overlayered doublings, linking concerns of instinctual gratification, cognitive sense-perceptiveness, sensation, feeling, and the activities of the intellect. He achieves this through the way that the ludic spirit (the spirit of play) functions in the carnivalesque world of *Gargantua and Pantagruel*.

Rabelais uses a wide variety of doublings and multiplicities to open up the petrified language of sixteenth-century scholasticism, in a manner suggestive of strategies Carroll and Joyce were to use. One such strategy has to do with playing with print itself. Others include the use of polyglossia[15] (playing with multiple languages); the inter-animation of words; and allowing the series of terms relating to the carnivalesque to intersect with the series of terms of philosophical-theological discourse. Bakhtin explains in detail how one of the language games used in *Gargantua* has an artistic and ideological meaning. This game, the *coq-à-l'âne* (from cock to donkey), involves a play with language and with sense that anticipates that of Joyce: 'First of all, it is a game of words, correct expressions, (proverbs and adages) and common sequences of terms deprived of their logic and meaning. It is as if words had been released from the shackles of sense, to enjoy a play period of complete freedom and establish unusual relationship among themselves. True, no new consistent links are formed in most cases, but the brief coexistence of those words, expressions and objects outside the usual logical conditions discloses their inherent ambivalence. Their multiple meanings and the potentiality that would not manifest themsleves in normal conditions are revealed.'[16]

One of Rabelais's most far-reaching strategies is the extensive exfoliation of the language of the body achieved by a contrapuntal action between the individual organs or parts of the body and the unified body as a surface unity – an imaginary body without organs.[17] Rabelais's use of this grotesque body has frequently been associated with modernist writing such as *Ulysses* and *Finnegans Wake*, where the grotesque body celebrates as equals all bodily openings – mouth, anus, vagina, penis, breasts – and their products – words, saliva, feces, urine, semen, and milk – seeing them as extensions of bodily gesture. Through the use of this wide range of grotesque and playful verbal transformations and metamorphoses that shape the text of *Gargantua*, Rabelais crafts an experimental language specifically designed to open up new liberatory possiblities for communication. The new technology of the printing press, by opening up a new sensitivity to spoken and written language, contributes to Rabelais's methods in crafting his experimental language.

Bakhtin clearly assigns Rabelais's art a functional role in communication, for *Gargantua* experiments (plays with) signs and language to develop new verbal strategies for handling experience. Rabelais's writing reveals that the moderns were not the first to discover that love exists in 'the place of excrement.' It is hardly surprising that Pound as well as Valéry and Valéry Larbaud identified Joyce's work with that of Rabelais,[18] though Joyce claimed not to have read him until a few years after he first began writing *Finnegans Wake*.[19] While many moderns (including postmoderns) appear to have Rabelaisian affinities, or, at the least, affinities with the revival of the comic grotesque (e.g., Brecht, cummings, Jarry, Wyndham Lewis, Mann, Henry Miller, Borges, Beckett, Nabokov, Neruda, Vonnegut, Lem, and Gibson), and while these affinities also characterize many film makers (e.g., Kubrick, Fellini, Kurosawa, and Makavéjev), Joyce's writings provide the closest modern analogue to Rabelais's practice.[20] Rabelaisian insights have been directly related to communication by Burke, whose theory of symbolic language roots communication in the excremental – 'thinking with the body' – and the critical – 'marvel of the negative.'[21]

Joyce's writings embody an advanced twentieth-century transformation of the comic grotesque that so fascinated Bakhtin. While radically different, the affinities of Joyce's works to Rabelais's have to do with their mutual application of laughter to the social, cultural, intellectual, and technological transformations that marked their moments in history. Some of the specific similarities they share involve utilization of themes, strategies, or techniques such as carnivalesque travesty of scriptural books; parody of scholarly wisdom; parodical liturgies; games; travestied prophecies; play with the authority of numbers; ambivalent abuse in carnivalesque intercourse; the use of *grotesque realism* in which the 'bodily element is deeply positive'; and the symbolic use of the feast of the Ass and of Easter laughter (*risus paschalis*). Some of these particular items are important since they involve concepts central to the analysis of communication: the book as medium; the process of communicating and disseminating knowledge; forms of communal participation; interactive discourse; bodily communication; and secular communion.

Comedy as critique is closely related to regenerating the processes of communication. Laughter permeates the writings of both Joyce and Rabelais, which are representative of the 'serio-comical,' or what Greek poetics described as *spoudogeloion*.[22] Joyce points out the relevance of this genre in describing the poet of the *Wake*, who speaks 'on excellent inkbottle authority, solarsystemised, seriolcosmically' (263.23–5).[23] Joyce's laughter (which plays with the encyclopaedic,[24] the temporal, and the cosmic), like Rabelais's, is intertwined with the most radical changes in the world around him. The encylopaedic, the temporal, and the cosmic are once again crucial and problematic in our modern electronic society, yet their very complexity and ambivalence can only be encompassed by the chaotic paradoxes of the serio-comic. The spatio-temporal is once again in process of transformation; the growth of knowledge has vastly expanded the encyclopaedic; and contemporary discourse has seen the return of cosmology,[25] accompanying the 're-enchantment of the world.'[26] The exploration of the resulting gaps and newly generated serendipitous networks questioning the centrality of the person in her or his life-world creates natural grotesqueries and requires a comic mode of exploration.

The central role of laughter and comedy in Joyce's work is epitomized in the *Wake*'s declaration: 'Outragedy of poetscalds! Acomedy of letters!' (425.24). Joyce indicates that this approach involves 'politicoecomedy' (540.20) and examines the 'hydrocomic establishment' (580.25), for in transforming the language and liberating it through his 'comicsongbook' (380.24), he transforms the novel, thereby preparing a new metamorphosis of this genre for the future electric age. In the spirit of Joyce's lifelong commitment to comedy as the most significant creative form, the 'Feenichts [i.e., phoenix + fairy's night] Playhouse' section of the *Wake*, which is centrally concerned with drama, children's folklore, and play, concludes, 'Loud, heap miseries upon us yet entwine our arts with laughters low!' (259.7–8).

Serio-comical laughter, carnivalesque and transgressive, characteristic of everyday life, is the crucial factor in understanding the special role of sense in works such as *Gargantua* and the *Wake* for 'the basic carnival nucleus ... does not, generally speaking, belong to the sphere of art. It belongs to the borderline between art and life. In reality, it is life itself, but shaped according to a certain pattern of play.'[27] This ambivalent laughter is festive and universal in scope, a quality which Joyce had discovered through his roots in a 'minority culture,' colonial Ireland, with its further colonialized commitment to the Roman Catholic Church. In a mutated form, the humour of the carnivalesque market-place was as applicable to Europe of the first half of the twentieth century as its earlier manifestation had been in Europe of the late sixteenth century.[28]

This type of humour not only focuses on the body and consequently sensory experience and sense, but emanates from the body and its various electrochemical systems – neurological, muscular, and circulatory. Joyce's work, commencing with the publication of *Ulysses*, is centrally concerned with the body, its orifices (the anus, the genitalia, female breasts, and the mouth), and with bodily processes associated with them – eating, drinking, copulating, masturbating, buggering, urinating, and defecating. Perennial matter for laughter, these activities of the often so-called 'lower' parts have always been the subject of 'low' (or frequently 'dirty') humour; they also are the bodily activities which, along with the tactility of the skin, emphasize the sensory nature of people.[29]

The grotesque from which such laughter arises is a phenomenon that is 'unfinished, outgrows itself, transgresses its own limits.'[30] Joyce's Finn, like Gargantua, is a giant; the feasts at his wake are orgies of excess parodying all of the sacred rituals in the world. Throughout the *Wake*, all kinds of transgression and excess occur: blasphemy, sacrilege, adultery, rape, fellatio, cunnilingus, masturbation, sado-masochism. In *Ulysses*, such explorations include Bloom sitting in the 'jakes'; his acting out his fantasies as the masturbating voyeur watching Gertie McDowell on the Strand; and his adventures with Stephen at Bella Cohen's whore-house in Nighttown. All these transgressions and excesses appear in contexts celebrating the body and life, rather than in the darkness of Artaud or de Sade.

The *Wake*, sections of which were appearing as *Work in Progress* at the same time that Bataille was writing his earliest essays exploring erotism, excess, sacrifice, and the sacred, traverses the very same 'perverse' territory. Joyce's selection of the everyday ritual of the *Wake* for the focus of his dream work chooses a setting for an examination of life, death, laughter, and communication involving ritual, excess, and the sacred. The imaginary sleeper dreaming as a living body and a dead body is the locus of sacrifice and sacrament, of tears and laughter – 'laughtears' (15.9). The symbolic action of waking the dead, characteristically contemporary with the intellectual sensibility of the era of Freud, Mauss, and Fraser, fits Joyce's purpose well, for he envisions a world of becoming in which everybody (for HCE, Here Comes Everybody, is his real hero) and everybody's body (which is ultimately not separable from each 'everybody') is also in the act of becoming – a 'becoming' that concludes with 'becoming corpse.' HCE's body, like Deleuze's 'body without organs,' is a body in the perpetual act of being formed and reformed; in the dream, he is constantly retracing the traces of transverse wanderings across the surfaces of sense.

Finnegans Wake celebrates a secularized Corpus Christi, a contemporized Rabelaisian body about which Bakhtin wrote: 'It is the people's growing and ever-victorious body that is "at home" in the cosmos. It is the cosmos' own flesh and blood possessing the same elemental force but better organized. The body is the last and best word of the cosmos, its leading force. Death holds not terror for it. The death of the individual is only one moment in the triumphant life of the people and mankind, a moment indispensable for their renewal and improvement.'[31] This body exists for Joyce in a *'chaosmos,'* because in its becoming it is becoming increasingly aware it is not at the centre of the universe. Still, it is also aware of itself as the only point of contact with which to perceive and glory in the diversity of that *'chaosmos.'* Recognition that the body is not a centre, decentres the authority of all 'spiritualizations' of the body. Laughter, as the response to that recognition, invokes sense to open up lines of communication.

Joyce's manifesto has reverberated throughout the second half of the century. Some four decades after *Ulysses,* critics have frequently commented that Fellini's film-making is Joycean in conception. When queried about the similarity of the young Guido to the young Stephen of the *Portrait,* or of his satire of the clergy and the church to Joyce's, or of the harem scene in *8 1/2* to Joyce's brothel in *Ulysses,* or just the apparent consistency of their sense of the human body or their use of humour, Fellini disavowed any specific knowledge of Joyce's work, but he asserted: 'The truth is that it isn't necessary to read a certain author – say, Joyce – if Joyce has been really important, as he has been, to contemporary culture. Then you come to know Joyce by looking at the lay-out of a magazine, speaking with people, observing how a girl is dressed.'[32] Fellini's work shares with Joyce the interest in grotesquerie, comedic transgression, excess, and laughter in films such as *La Dolce Vita, Satyricon,* and *Juliet of the Spirits.* But most of all, Fellini celebrates the body as decentred and laughter as the means for opening up lines of communication.

A symptomatic indication of this renewed importance of the body in contemporary poetry and art has been the growing recognition of the importance of Vico's *New Science,* which, by examining a series of important relationships between communication, the arts of expression, and the creative arts, develops a 'poetic' for the science of politics showing how the 'world of human society has ... been made by men, and its principles are therefore to be found within modifications of our own human mind.' Such an exploration of the communicative function of the symbolic world has been a seminal influence throughout the twentieth century. Vico explores the body as the externalization of mind in the *New Science,* where he develops the concept of communication as a concept of embodiment:

LXIII

§236 The human mind is naturally inclined by the senses to see itself externally in the body, and only with great difficulty does it come to attend to itself by means of reflection.

§237 This axiom gives us the universal principle of etymology in all languages: words are carried over from bodies and properties of bodies to express the things of the mind and spirit.[33]

Vico also sees poetry as an 'outering' (or 'uttering') of the body, for the most sublime poetry is produced by the 'deficiency of human reasoning power.'[34] The first wisdom of the gentile world began with a 'felt and imagined' metaphysic of people who 'were all robust sense and vigorous imagination':

[These] peoples, who were almost all body and no reflection, must have been all vivid sensation in perceiving particulars, strong imagination in apprehending and magnifying them, sharp wit in referring them to their imaginative genera and robust memory in retaining them. It is true these faculties appertain to the mind, but they have roots in the body and draw strength from it. Hence memory is the same as imagination, which for the reason is called *memoria* in Latin. (In Terence, for example, we find, *memorabile* in the sense of imaginable, and commonly we find *comminisci* for 'feigning,' which is proper to imagination, and thence *commentum* for a fiction.) ... Memory thus has three different aspects: memory when it remembers things, imagination when it alters or imitates them and invention when it gives them a new turn or puts them into proper arrangement and relationship. For these reasons the theological poets called Memory the mother of the Muses.[35]

The poetic faculty, submerging the whole mind in the senses, must plunge deep into particulars, so that within this 'new science,' memory is a science of particulars.

While Vico's *New Science* provides one of the major sources for the overall structural pattern of *Finnegans Wake*, in *Ulysses* Joyce also utilizes Vico's concept of the relationship between the world's body and the social body (and/or body politic). Joyce, adapting his use of Vico to his own particular poetic problems, envisions modernity as creating a new state of ignorance with which our current system of signs is unable to cope. Just as Vico undertook the search for a 'True Homer,' Joyce parodically sees himself becoming the 'new Homer,' confronting the poverty of everyday language,[36] striving to make himself understood, and attempting to interpret the newly awakening world[37] by forging the communicative potentialities of the post-Nietzschean, post-Marxist world. Such a project is necessarily involved with communication. Joyce's revolution of the word (which could actually be called the sign's second coming!) should not be written off as a 'political' failure just because its initial difficulties restrict the range of the receptivity of its communication, for he is creating what Vico calls fables in brief: vivid, anthropomorphic metaphors that are chiefly formed from the human body and its parts, and from the human senses and passions.

In the very construction of *Ulysses*, Joyce exploits this classical image of the body politic by designing a structural chart for his work in which each section of his epic is related to an organ of the body, specific human activities, a geographic area of Dublin, a poetic symbol, and to a specific time of day. Blood, for example, is the dominant organ[38] of the 'Wandering Rocks' section, in which a variety of vignettes show the movement of the major characters and a variety of other important Dublin personalities through the labyrinth of the city's streets in the mid-afternoon. *Finnegans Wake,* a dream book structured about the shape of the sleeping body, intertwines the flow of bodily fluids (as an internal river) with the stuttering on-and-off activity of the nervous system to produce the imaginary re-creation of the everyday world within the world of dream. All communication is encompassed within the body of each person, a body in which female and male, youth and age, intellect and emotion, all coexist. Communion, therefore, becomes coterminous with intensified (i.e., deepened and complex) communication.

4

The Joyce Era: Modernity and Poetics

While James Joyce is one of the major, perhaps *the* major, European poet of this century, his writings, which are also crucial to any discussion of the social role of the poetic activity and its relation to technology and communication, are still largely unrecognized as major contributions to contemporary historical and theoretical discourse. Joyce's poetic practice constitutes the most conscious exploration prior to 1960 of the limits of literature and of the relationship between literature, art, and the poetics of communication.

Decades before the writings of Barthes, Deleuze, Derrida, Eco, or McLuhan, Joyce wrote books that were pivotal for examining relationships between the body and poetic communication and for exploring aspects of such items on the contemporary intellectual agenda as orality and literacy; the importance of transverse communication in contemporary discourse; the role of transgression in communication; the role of practical consciousness in everyday life; and the relationship between the events of everyday life and their embodiment and materialization in the sensory nature of the contemporary interior monologue. Considering the deeper and more far-reaching impact of Joyce's practice and his historico-theoretical awareness, the periodization of literature and the arts of the first two-thirds of this century ought rather to be called the 'Joyce Era' than the 'Pound Era,' which would still be appropriate if the only innovations Joyce had ever introduced were those in *Ulysses*.

Remarks made by Joyce's friend and contemporary T.S. Eliot provide a substantial insight into the nature of those innovations. In 1923, one year after its publication, Eliot depicted *Ulysses* as 'the most important expression the present age has found.' He notes that the significance of the method Joyce developed lies in his having each episode parallel the *Odyssey*, and then using styles and symbols appropriate to each episode.[1] The parallel with the *Odyssey*, according to Eliot, is one specific aspect of a more fundamental method which 'has the importance of a scientific discovery,' for 'no one else has built a novel upon such a foundation before, [since] it has never before been necessary.' Thus, 'in using the myth, in manipulating a continuous parallel between contemporaneity and antiquity, Mr. Joyce is using a method others must pursue after him. They will not be imitators any more than the scientist who uses the discoveries of an Einstein in pursuing his own, independent further investigations.'[2]

This strategy, which had first been introduced into *symboliste* poetry with Baudelaire's transgressive, wandering exploration of the streets and enclaves of the city in his visions of Paris in *Fleurs du mal*, is strikingly described by Eliot from the perspective of official art as 'introducing something new and something universal in modern life ... not merely in the use of imagery of common life, not merely in the use of imagery of the sordid life of a great metropolis, but in the elevation of such imagery to the *first intensity*.'[3] Elsewhere Eliot observed that he first learned from Baudelaire 'a precedent for the poetical possibilities never developed by a poet writing in my own language, of the possibility of the fusion between the sordidly realistic and the phantasmagoric, the possibility of juxtaposition of the matter of fact and the fantastic.'[4]

Ulysses' method represents a considerable expansion of this paralleling of the phantasmagoric and sordidly realistic. Furthermore, Joyce's metamorphoses (and, for that matter, Baudelaire's) are not achieved simply by seeing contemporaneity as only 'sordidly realistic' and juxtaposed against the phantasmagoria of a mythic or heroic past. Joyce is aware that the past also has its sordid aspects and the present, its redeeming qualities, which can be phantasmagoric and the gateway towards a necessarily imaginary, phantasmagoric future. 'Phantasmagoria,' in its earlier sense of a magic lantern show, and later as applied to the haphazard associativeness of dream sequences or hallucination, is thus a proto-cinematic term which is best illustrated in the fifteenth episode, 'Circe' or Nighttown.

The use of parallelism that Eliot noted in *Ulysses* is combined by Joyce with a methodical development of differentiated styles, techniques, and symbols associated with the specific action that takes place in each of the eighteen episodes, with the specific hour of the day at which the action occurs, with a particular organ of the body, with a particular art or science, and with a dominant colour or combination of colours. This strategy, outlined by Joyce in (a) structural plan(s) of *Ulysses*,[5] redoubles Baudelaire's doubling and then redoubles the redoubling, creating that peculiarly dense multiplexity which is characteristic of the 'open' works of contemporary poetry and art. This structural method is a method for producing difference rather than resemblances, since the contemporary world is permeated by so many clear breaks with its past.

The third major method employed in *Ulysses* is the stream of consciousness or interior monologue, the importance of which Joyce stressed by specifically singling it out when commenting to friends about his work. He told Frank Budgen that he first discovered the interior monologue in Edouard Dujardin's *Les Lauriers sont coupées* ('We'll to the Woods No More'), which he had purchased in 1903: 'I try to give the unspoken, unacted thoughts of people in the way they occur. But I'm not the first one to do it. I took it from Dujardin. You don't know Dujardin? You should.'[6] In his adaptation of Dujardin's 'stream of consciousness' method to a more complex and comprehensive technique for exploring the drama of the inner life, he critiques and expands the Freudian-Jungian conception of the 'unconscious,' demonstrating how Freud's version of the unconscious, in spite of its extensive examination of 'the psychopathology of everyday life,' failed to deal with many significant roles of the unconscious in the ordinary daily social life of people (those activities which demonstrate that there is a 'practical unconscious' just as there is practical consciousness).[7]

While this statement might at first seem problematic, since the Freudian unconscious is so immersed in certain aspects of 'everyday life,' Bateson, commenting on the Freudian view of the unconscious, explains how early Freudian theory was upside down:

> Classical Freudian theory assumed dreams were a *secondary* product, created by 'dream work.' Material unacceptable to conscious thought was supposedly translated into the metaphoric idiom of primary process to avoid waking the dreamer. And this may be true of those items of information which are held in the unconscious by the process of repression. As we have seen, however, many sorts of information are inaccessible to conscious inspection, including most of the premises of mammalian interaction. It would seem to me sensible to think of these items as existing *primarily* in the idiom of the primary process only with difficulty to be translated into rational terms. In other words, I believe that much of early Freudian theory was upside down.[8]

In his construction of the interior monologues of Stephen, Molly, and Bloom, Joyce combines aspects of the repressed content of the Freudian unconscious (well identified by the critical tradition) and of the idiom of primary processes involved in mammalian interaction, such as the varieties of signals associated with hunger in the 'Lestrygonians' episode (peristaltic rhythm, gastro-intestinal rumblings, preoccupation with smells, obsession with food) or with exhaustion in the 'Eumaeus' episode. In any given episode, the combination of material identified with primary processes can be quite complex, such as in the 'Ithaca' or the 'Penelope' episodes where such strategies as recollection and sudden recognition by association combine with mammalian instincts and repressed sexual associations (e.g., the scene of Bloom and Stephen urinating together in the backyard, which involves astronomy, astrology, ritual, animality, potential voyeurism, physiological need, etc.). In the dream vision of the *Wake*, the dream encompasses both the repressed material and the material inaccessible to conscious inspection in the idiom of the primary processes, for a dream itself constitutes both a ground and a series of communicative figures through which to communicate with the primary processes and of necessity includes the entire, embodied person.

This Joycean adaptation of the stream of consciousness is characterized by three essential developments which anticipate Bateson's critique of Freud. First, he presents and illustrates in action the role that 'unspoken words, unacted thoughts,' play as part of the formation of the practical consciousness by which people live in the everyday world. Second, he materializes, despiritualizes, and embodies the interior monologue, for this inner speech is intimately intertwined with the CNS (brain and nervous system), as Bloom's noon hour stroll through Dublin in the 'Lestrygonians' episode demonstrates. Thirdly, in the act of so doing, he merges the internal and external, the dialogic and the monologic, into a medley of intertwining and interactive voices.

All three of his 'methods' (the continuous parallel between antiquity and contemporancity; the appropriate synchronizing of style, structure, action, time, and bodily organs; and the Joycean 'stream of consciousness' as embodied practical consciousness) are critical for understanding the contemporary transformation of the poetic and its relation with everyday culture. Instead of being a return to the classical mode, as Eliot apparently assumed, these methods provide the very means for bringing about a new metamorphosis of the novel. Eliot did recognize that Joyce, by reducing style to zero through his use of a multiplicity of styles, announced the death of the novel as it had come to be.[9] But that zero results from a plenitude, an excess, a transgression, not a regression or reaction in the direction of a conservative conception of the classical. Each of the three methods Joyce employs in *Ulysses* contributes to his project of creating a new language, which is itself related to a new self-consciousness about the spectrum of communication.

Since laughter and the inter-animation of words and verbal units are essential aspects of this project, it is consistent that from his earliest days as an artist, Joyce held the comic form of poetry to be the most advanced.[10] Joyce's conception of laughter evolved in his later works, becoming more dynamic, more dependent on transgression and excess in the symbolic action and its execution, and therefore more capable of dealing with the contemporary urban landscape and its complexities of communication. Just as Shem, the 'alshemist' poet of the *Wake*, is a 'sham and a low sham,' Joyce's comic laughter is 'low,' playing with 'litter(s)' through play with 'letters.'

Ulysses and the *Wake* celebrate the lowly world of bodily parts, eating, drinking, copulating, urinating, and defecating and the lowly materials of everyday life, counterpointing them against the serious business of the hegemonic forces of society – the 'bourse and politicoecomedy' (540.20), as the *Wake* puts it. *Finnegans Wake* is a book that is a 'comicalbottom copsjute' (110.26) in which the 'APOTHEOSIS OF THE LUSTRAL PRINCIPIUM' (286.R2) was to be accomplished through 'comic cuts'(286.8)[11] (comic strips, film, burlesque, etc.) and 'series exerxeses'(286.8) (comic lists and nonsense based on play with serial forms). The insight that schizoid laughter[12] facilitates profound communication arises among early contemporary avant-garde artists (e.g., Chaplin, the Dadaists, Jarry, Joyce, and Proust). The comic, as a dissociating and disassembling energy, expedites and intensifies the cultural analysis and critique characteristic of modern ways of exploring the cultural text. Burke stressed the importance of the comic, of the grotesque, of perspective by incongruity, for a theory of communication. Burke's insight was further developed by Hugh Duncan, who regarded the comic as a form of sanctioned doubt essential to social change and social integration.[13]

Later, Bateson specifically related poetry, drama, laughter, and humour to the understanding of schizophrenia and the disentangling of distorted communication. Nevertheless, poetry and art still remain largely untapped resources for theory and analysis. Strategies of decontextualization through the creation of comic recontextualization – which are applied to cultural objects such as ads, consumer products, sports, media stars, and newspapers in Barthes's semioclastic *Mythologies* or in McLuhan's iconoclastic *Mechanical Bride* – just begin to explore this potential.[14] Not only had Wyndham Lewis satirically analysed such objects a quarter of a century earlier, but Joyce had also demonstrated the integration of the comic with methods of multiplexity in a poetic work that presents an alternative way of exploring communication in action. So *Ulysses*, probably intentionally, is virtual ethnography.

Polysemia and polyglossia, the other essential ingredients of Joyce's strategy, evolve from the relatively simple wordplay of *A Portrait of the Artist as a Young Man,* through the very complex polysemic use of language in *Ulysses,* to the crafting of the dense polyglot 'Nichtian glossery' (83.10) of the *Wake.* At each stage, the evolving polyglossia and polysemia intertwine with comic laughter, a combination that permits Joyce to construct his works within the vital world of everyday experience. Joyce's awareness of the importance of this everyday world results in his conscious exposition of the communication process through which his audience as consumer plays a role in producing the author as articulator (speaker and writer): 'His producers are they not his consumers? Your exagmination around his factification for incamination of a warping process. Declaim!' (497.1–2).

In an early discussion of the *Wake,* Joyce had told a close friend, Eugene Jolas, how everybody participated in co-creating his books: 'Really it is not I who am writing this crazy book. It is you, and you, and you, and that man over there and that girl at the next table.'[15] The degree to which this has become a significant aspect of modern writing is measured by the increasing self-reflection of artists and poets on their poetic experience and by their greater recognition of the collective nature of the communication process. Drama represents the living symbol of this collectivity to the extent that each audience changes a play, just as each group of auditors changed the dramatic recitation of an epic by a poet in an oral culture.

The intrinsic connection between these modes of the poetic, the dramatic, and everyday life provides Joyce with a means for decontextualizing and recontextualizing the world of commercial objects, of mediated forms of human communication, and of mechanized life in order to examine them as they exist in the everyday world. In the first decade of this century, a very young Joyce described one of his prime methods as 'vivisective,' attributing to it the qualities of a radical modernity:

> The modern spirit is vivisective. Vivisection itself is the most modern process one can conceive. The ancient spirit accepted phenomena with a bad grace. The ancient method investigated law with the lantern of justice, morality with the lantern of revelation, art with the lantern of tradition. But all these lanterns have magical properties: they transform and disfigure. The modern method examines its territory by the light of day ... All modern political and religious criticism dispenses with presumptive States, presumptive Redeemers and Churches. It examines the entire community in action and reconstructs the spectacle of redemption. If you were an aesthetic philosopher you would take note of all my vagaries because here you have the spectacle of the aesthetic instinct in action.[16]

Joyce adopted, and thus anticipated in principle but more complexly and comprehensively, the same practice of decontextualization and recontextualization as that of Barthes and McLuhan, which he jestingly describes in the *Wake* as 'mortisection or vivisuture, splitten up or recompounded' (253.34). He employs 'vivisuture' to *epiphanize* (i.e., clearly and intensely display and expose) everyday events, images, and phrases. This term, 'epiphany,'[17] which Joyce contributed to critical discourse, appears as an individual word in the *Wake* only once, in the climax (III,3),[18] when a dream character exclaims: 'How culious an epiphany!' (508.11). *Culus* is 'fundament' in Latin, and one of Hercules' labours was the cleaning of the Augean stables.

This passage illustrates that both 'epiphany' and 'vivisection' ultimately reveal how experimental poetic play – by involving the lower, more excremental, and more fundamental or basic aspects of the everyday world – illuminates the workings of 'the entire community in action.' The 'mortisection or vivisuture' characteristic of Joycean comedy is primarily directed towards exhibiting a complex blending of delight and sorrow in material existence that uses the comic epiphany as its foundation. Epiphany metamorphosizes the cloacal occurrences of everyday life by making manifest the complexities and contradictions implicit in words, images, and processes that are present in all human communicative action. Since these poetic strategies of vivisection and epiphany characterize the practice of a wide spectrum of modern artists and writers, identifying, defining, and describing them contributes to understanding contemporary poetic theory and practice.

Other aspects of Joyce's method are also typically contemporary. Joyce's materialistic, embodied, interior monologue or 'stream of consciousness' differs from earlier instances by being multi-dialogic; the internal entails the external, while through multiplexity of style and allusion, the external encompasses the internal. The exterior is explored as it is recorded within the interior world, yet this is a doubled and redoubled exploration, for the external always already includes the internal which has been exteriorized, for 'There are sordidly tales within tales, you clearly understand that?'(522.2–4). This type of 'monologue' is a modernist realization of one of Pascal's techniques in *Pensées* – the painting of thought in action (*le peinture de la pensée*) – but this design is achieved by Joyce and his contemporaries through 'thinking with the body' where 'thought' is not dualistically divorced from the body in action.

Since mass-mediated modes of living, expressing, and communicating have composed a major proportion of every person's life-world in this century, this conception of an interior landscape, which is actually inscribed on the surfaces, permits Joyce's poetry to confront directly (as other literature was beginning to do indirectly) the phenomenon of the ongoing transformation of the everyday life-world marked by (1) the mass urbanization of people; (2) growing internationalism; (3) new technologies for coping with mass urbanization and globalization; (4) intensified commodification of intellectual and emotional experience; and (5) an acceptance of a pervasive sense of permanent dislocation and disorientation. The carnivalesque culture of the traditional market-place was being transformed into an urban technologized circus, an image which was to preoccupy the sensibility of contemporary artists as exemplified in works such as Fellini's various films about Rome (*La Dolce Vita, 8½, Roma,* and *The Clowns*).

Contemporary 'metanovels,' particularly Joyce's *Ulysses* and Proust's *Recherches,* occupy a highly contradictory or paradoxical position as regards art's relationship with communication. These works, which were crucially involved in the broad struggle to overcome the demand for relative transparency in literature as a medium of communication, foster the transformation of the traditional Romantic, the alliance of privileged creativity and art as spiritual communion, into a new alliance of that creativity implicit in all human existence with art as secular, sensory, sensual communion of people in action. While *all* creative work, including that which has been hypostatized as *A*rt (in the sense of Fine Art), has always involved communication, in the modern era the problem of communication has been consciously reflected upon and the relevance and role of art to communication queried. In earlier periods, whether those engrossed with the classical mirror (of mimesis, representation, and reflection) or with the Romantic lamp (of expression, inner experience, or native genius), art works communicated, even if their producers' intentions had not consciously included this goal.

While from time to time throughout the history of literature writers have specifically reflected on aspects of the communication process (as Rabelais, Swift, Pope, Pascal, and Bacon did), they seldom reflected on the role of communication itself as problematic. The doctrine of art for art's sake that denied any relevance to communication, or any mode of utility to art works, surfaced towards the closing decades of the nineteenth century, just when communication became problematic and the means of producing, reproducing, and distributing communication were changing radically. Paradoxically, some artists simultaneously became aware of the essential inventive and innovative role of the poetics of artistic production in transforming the means, modes, and expressive repertoire of communication; that is, poetry's role within the ecology of sense. Formulae, such as 'the poet purifies the dialect of the tribe,' or the painter opens up new possibilities of vision, presuppose a role that creative production has in developing the ability of people to interact by expanding the resources through which they communicate.

This modern poetic imagination, operating on multiple levels, probes the complexity of communication through comic, satiric, and parodic techniques that are nomadic and transgressive, strategies the nature of which pose major difficulties for a transparent communication. Yet the very proponents of the new arts' particular concept of the material body that involved this transgressive, therefore complex, and often obscure approach also stressed strongly the communicative role of the poetic – for example, Bataille, Joyce, and Pound.[19] The concept of transgression has a long, historic association with poetics. Some Renaissance rhetorical and poetical theorists defined the figures of speech as 'transgressions' of speech – deviations which either intensified stylistic effect or made the meaning more precise or complex. The stress on the concept of 'shock' among avant-garde artists (1910–20) invoked deviations from the expected (transgressions) to achieve a poetic effect that re-evaluated the normal and the expected. In the process, their modes of shock were directed often simultaneously both at the sensual and sensory aspects of the body and the cognitive structure of the mind.

Pound's formulae for 'making it new' (1920s) employed such transgressions to increase poetic precision, particularly with respect to meaning. Bataille, through association with ethnographers and sociologists, could broaden the concept by envisioning the symbolic ceremonies of gift-giving, such as the Haida potlatch ceremonies, as a communicative action in which the transgressions of use value (the conspicuous and destructive display of largesse in outstripping one's neighbours in generosity) carried messages about status, power, and community (1930s). Using this model of the sacrifice, he establishes the basis for the communicative relationship in the modern arts between the polymorphously perverse eroticism and the socio-political embodiment of people. Following the articulation of information theory (1946–50), a variety of scholars such as Jakobson(1950s) and Eco (1960s) have asssociated depth and intensification of meaning with transgressions or deviations from the expected or anticipated.

Such strategic mechanisms will obviously operate at all levels of communicative action from the paradigmatic and syntactic to the semiotic and pragmatic. The deep link that this forges between communication, transgression, and the poetic is a primary factor in enabling deep, innovative communication, which illustrates the importance of exploratory and experimental cognition in the ecology of communication. Although the concept of poetry and art moving beyond limits has been recognized since the beginnings of the history of poetics and emerges regularly throughout that history, for modernism and postmodernism the very use of techniques of disjunction or discontinuity within artistic technique is initially transgressive, seeking to shock, disorient, and decontextualize.

The radical juxtaposition of elements characteristic of imagist and post-symbolist poetry, collage, montage, atonality, and decontextualization (e.g., found art) are transgressions of expectations in the here and now. Eisenstein's or Pound's explanations of montage as ideographic and vorticism's transformation of imagism through ideographic techniques are transgressive both in their 'mis/use' of Japanese or Chinese characters or of hieroglyphs and in their justification of the consistency of such techniques with the newspaper, the new urban complex, and jazz;[20] Duchamp's *Fountain* (the urinal as found art) and Schwitters's assemblages of bits and pieces (the flotsam of early twentieth-century urban debris) are transgressive both with respect to their material and in their use of radical decontextualization and radical juxtaposition.

The idea of transgression takes on a more prodigious depth when artists recycle ancient rites and aboriginal or folk art. Examples can be found in Stravinsky's *Rite of Spring*, Giacometti's exploration of the 'Oceanic' in *Invisible Object* ,[21] Bartok's use of naïve and folk music, or Klee's use of child art in such works as his illustrations for *Sinbad the Sailor*. The very core of the transgressive is revealed in the art of the 'unconscious,' the fascination with decadence or disgust, and the sado-masochistic attainment of the sublime that appear during the Weimar period in aspects of Dadaism and surrealism. This fascination quickly finds its way into the scarcely cloaked sado-masochism of the popular comics of SF (e.g., *Flash Gordon, Buck Rogers*) and the early super-heroes.

The transgressive taken across its full range of action effectuates that break which has also been described as 'a grace beyond the reach of art' – a break achieved through a 'brave disorder' that provides the requisite 'making it new' of the poetic communicative process.[22] This traditional, neo-classical use of 'grace' as transgressive is ambivalent, for it results in such writing as the erotic and scatalogical humour of Fielding, Pope, Sterne, and Swift's satire. The figures of clowns and grotesques which more recently engrossed the imagination of Picasso, then Chaplin, and later Fellini are yet another aspect of transgression of administrated society by lower and outside elements.

Proust and Joyce probed the very depths of the transgressive in sexuality, prejudice, and social hierarchy. As Pound observed, Joyce specifically explored the excremental base on which society is founded. Such involvement with transgression disassembles the official view of society (the accepted understanding of the surfaces), opening up new possible modes of seeing, speaking, hearing, and listening – the very heart of renewed or intensified communication. Baudelaire's poetic vision of transgressive wandering through the city of Paris had opened up new poetic potentialities and subsequently new possiblities for communication. The twin motifs of investigating the new urban metropolis and new modes of movement and communication clearly connect Baudelaire's writings with Proust and Joyce.

This *modus operandi* reaches a high point of intensity in Joyce's *Ulysses*, where the poet's method embraces the myth of the epic and the matter-of-fact low life of everyday Dublin; the official life of the church (Father Conmee) and the state (the vice regent of Ireland) counterpointed by the low life of the pub, bedroom, and whorehouse; a new union of the suppressed history of the past with the everyday life of the lower elements of society. Benjamin thematizes this by concluding his essay 'Some Motifs of Baudelaire' by quoting Baudelaire's dedication to his *Spleen of Paris*: 'Who among us has not dreamt, in ambitious days, of the miracle of a poetic prose? It would have to be musical without rhythm and rhyme, supple and resistant enough to adapt itself to the lyrical stirrings of the soul, the wave motions of dreaming, the shocks of consciousness. This ideal which can turn into an *idée fixe*, will grip especially those who are at home in the giant cities and the web of their numberless interconnecting relationships.'[23]

Baudelaire anticipates and Proust and Joyce build upon Bergson's insights concerning the concepts of the 'new' and *durée* in *Matière et mémoire*, which, Benjamin has argued, 'towers over' the works of Dilthey and Jung.[24] Baudelaire, Proust, and Joyce pursue an art focused on shocks, which the new cinematic art extensively develops as one of its formal principles. Benjamin and they are all fascinated with the technology of switching, inserting, and pressing characteristic of the photograph, the friction match (i.e., lucifer), the newspaper, the phone, and the mechanization of the crowd.[25] Each of these elements surfaces during various incidents in Joyce's *Ulysses*: meditations on photography and photographs, Bloom's lighting of a match, the movement of trams through the city, the production of newspapers, the dialing and ringing of telephones, and the mechanization of people's movement through a modern city (especially in the eleventh episode, 'Wandering Rocks').

Such technologies have not only brought about changes in communication, but they have also change the very foundation of communication itself through transformations within the language of gesture. To understand this statement, it is necessary to think of an integrated semiosis, a body of signs from all modes of perception which can be used separately or together, or some elements of which can be invoked by others – the way a word invokes a visual strata or a visual symbol invokes a verbal complex. Changes in the very foundation of communication can then come about by the way the material existence of machines, media, and organizations transform the body of signs, both by opening up new potentialities for generating signs and by transforming the ways the existing body of signs can be utilized. While this process cannot be divorced from the social fabric within which it occurs, neither can it be isolated from formal and technological changes that are part of that fabric. A little technological determinism is a desirable thing as long as it is not regarded as the sole or primary social force acting at a particular moment in history.

Artists are culturally sensitive to this ambivalence in the technological – that to some extent it is determining, and to a substantial extent it is to be shaped, determined. The evolution of the automobile may demand a network of roads, service points, and the like, but it hardly determines the type of road, the regulatory structure of its use or their use, the potential human hazard or protection created by the development of service points, the environmental hazard of the fuel, or the safety hazards of the automotive experience. Still the automobile does determine some changes in the overall pattern of transportation and the improved mobility of people and produce which this permits. The same ambivalence resides in the growth of the machinery of state – the bureaucracy, the army, the judiciary, the police, and politics. In the wake of the First World War, Kafka in *The Trial* and *The Castle* uses such an insight in exploring the evolution and operation of bureaucratic or judicial structure as techno-structure. In the aftermath of the Second World War, Kubrick in *Dr Strangelove* and Pynchon in *Gravity's Rainbow* trace the exfoliating effect of interaction of the seemingly all-pervasive technologies of destruction.

Poetic perceptions generated by the imaginary materials implicit in technologies, whether those that are relatively determinate or those that are uncircumscribed and relatively indeterminate, are quite complex and persist across various historical stages. At least in the modernist and postmodernist period, a recognition of this aspect of poetic perception has enhanced – across a broad spectrum of social and cultural phenomena – artists' contributions towards understanding the relations of culture and technology and their even more extensive, though little understood, contributions towards understanding communication and communication theory. First and foremost, artists have shown how their activity and the related activities of the popular arts and the rhetorical craft of the arts of persuasion contribute to shaping the material of communication itself – the universe of signs by and through which people communicate. As a corollary, they have demonstrated that all human creative activity is potentially ecologically oriented to regenerating the 'languages' of the community.

Second, artworks (implicitly and often unconsciously and unintentionally) provide a critique of the limits of communication existent at a particular place and time. Their very excess in achieving the difference or distinction by which they operate leads to a transgression and subverting of limits. Third, through the link between the mind-body and its sensory systems, these art works explore what the *Wake* calls the rhizomic 'feelful thinkamalinks' through which the complexity of communication and the formation of communities actually take place. Fourth, these art works, which are machines constructed to communicate, exhibit a predictive sensitivity to the actual changes occurring in society. The poets and artists become 'prophets' (or futurologists) showing the way processes of communication might, could, would, or should develop.

While traditionally the poet had been considered a prophet, modern society through its secularization has somewhat lost sense of this potentiality in the creative process. Nevertheless, modern artists have themselves suggested the existence of such a 'prophetic' role, as implied in modernist slogans like 'the artist is the antennae of the race.'[26] Diverse cultures throughout the world have assigned the poet the role of prophet, a theme strongly emphasized in the Hebraic and the Graeco-Roman traditions. Frequently the idea of the poet as prophet had to do with the divine and divine vision, whether in the biblical conception of the Psalms, the Roman of the *vates,* or William Blake's view of himself as poetic visionary. In medieval scholasticism, theologians such as Thomas Aquinas developed a concept of 'natural prophecy' in contradistinction to divine prophecy. Natural prophecy can be looked on as a sort of medieval futurology; the individual who reads the signs within nature intuits what will come to be.

Poets could then be described as natural prophets. Even if they are not consciously aware of their capability, the very imaginative action by which they reassemble the flows and ruptures of a particular period into an imaginary world effected a kind of predictivity by the use of a probable potentiality. While differing from Aristotle's view that 'poets should prefer probable impossibilities to improbable possibilities,'[27] the two ideas share the notion of the production of art as an assemblage of probabilities. Since the middle of the last century, the very activity undertaken in exploring the changing concepts of time, space, technology, and communication lured modernists and postmodernists into assembling probable imaginaries – virtualities that may not be realizable in the here and now but might be realizable in some potential future.

Historical examples of art as natural prophecy abound. The introduction in the Renaissance of the concept of Utopia provides a classic example. Utopianism, a term which has accrued almost half a millennium of history, arises from the title of a work that Sir Thomas More, a scholar-poet, consciously constructed as an intellectual plaything. Utilizing the words, images, and thoughts that pervaded the scholarly discourse of his colleagues, he presented his plaything using a well-recognized genre of 'ludic' rhetoric, the imaginary voyage, associated with Lucian of Samostha. In the oldest sense of the concept of *scholium* (intellectual leisure), More (the first lay chancellor of England under Henry VIII) and his friends investigated the implications of their intellectual world in a spirit of playful exploration. In that era, More was so highly regarded as a participant in such intellectual play that his close friend, Erasmus, played with More's name when entitling his most famous paradoxical encomium, *The Praise of Folly,* (i.e., the *Encomium Moriae*).[28]

The ludic spirit of transformation permeated the lives of these two individuals, who were to alter profoundly the future of European attitudes towards tolerance and the domination of church and state. More's playful exploration of the flows and ruptures of Renaissance individualism and of the evolving new modes of planning, controlling, dominating, and governing this world led him to construct an imaginary (admittedly a satiric, likely an ambivalent) world which, while a 'probable impossible,' provided a guide to much of what might become possible and implanted suggestions of what people might make possible. Within a few years after its publication, More's *Utopia* was actually used as a model by the Spanish government for colonial organization in Mexico. In the following centuries, particularly after the rise of socialism, *Utopia* became a focal point for debate as to just what aspects of a socialist program More had anticipated consciously and what his own position towards Utopia had been. *Utopia* successfully prefigured the emergence of a series of significant movements in the intellectual history of succeeding centuries.

The intellectual connection between Utopian literature and science fiction has become a familiar feature of contemporary discussions of the relation of literature and paraliterary forms. There is a futurological or natural prophetic aspect present in SF and fantasy, just as there is a close affiliation with the Lucianic genre involving the creation of imaginary worlds. The current popularity of SF writer William Gibson's stories of cyberspace (*Count Zero, Neuromancer,* and *Mona Lisa Overdrive*) involves the same rhetorical lineage, in which he extrapolates from the present to create a probable imaginary. Gibson's particular prophecies are intimately related with questions of communication and the nature of poetic communication. Their perspicacity was made clear when he was attacked in a major computing journal by a leading executive for being responsible for the rash of viruses and worms that were harassing the networks and particularly for the virus launched against the National Defence Network in 1989 by Robert Morris, a graduate student in computing at Cornell University.

The prophetic motif is broader than the Utopian tradition and its continuation in SF and speculative fiction: Pope's major comic epic poem, *The Dunciad,* prognosticates the emerging power of mass culture linked to mechanical modes of reproduction; Dickens's *Hard Times,* which analyses the everyday world of industrialization and the management of people by the very power of selection, condensation, and disjunction, prefigures the more fully developed ideology of post-post-industrial capitalism; Velázquez's painting *Las Meninas* ('The Maids of Honour,' 1656) prefigures the crisis in representation, as Foucault explains in his introductory analysis to *Les Mots et les choses* [*The Order of Things*];[29] and Leonardo da Vinci, who combined the role of artist and engineer, is so much the master of anticipating possible futures through imaginary probables that he has fascinated the modernist and postmodernist mind.[30]

This prophetic or predictive feature of the arts increased exponentially in the modernist period and continues to increase, with contemporary audiences adopting SF as a major genre. Visual artists in para-artistic modes (such as the comics) predicted the unfolding possibilities of the exploration of space; while Duchamp and Léger in constructing their artistic machines probed the implications of changing patterns of time, space, and distance. This affiliation of contemporary artistic activity with a predictive, prophetic, or futuristic aspect is aligned with modernist art's further contributions to understanding communication or communication theory. Heuristic exploration with respect to developing the regime of signs parallels the playful probing of social and technological change and their interrelationship that characterizes the cultural production of this era.

The artists and writers working in the first half of this century forecast the advent of the communication era that began after the Second World War. Avant-garde painters, musicians, architects, film-makers, and writers (who probed the potentialities of the newly emerging technologies of production, reproduction, and distribution both in their practice and in their reflections on the processes and effects of these new means of communication) intuitively foresaw the trend of increasingly mediated and multi-media communication and the ultimate merging of media through the development of computerization in the post–mass-mediated age of telematics. This process put in question the traditional status of modes of communication that were considered to be clearly distinct and separate modes of expression (e.g., visual, gestural, aural, musical, etc.). It further challenged the traditional hypostatization of speech in the idea of *logos*, and even put in question the primacy of language.

Today it is no longer possible to attribute that privileged status to Art (denominating the system of the Fine Arts) which it has traditionally held in the West since the Enlightenment. All human creative activity from the most ordinary and spontaneous productions of everyday life to the most complex works of art is poetic – a making, assembling, constructing. Nevertheless, it is still possible to recognize the intensity of the poetic motive in all those productions which permit a free, rich, dissociated play of signifiers and that facilitate our changing conceptions of what constitute individually identifiable arts. At any given moment there have always been a variety of specific individual arts that constitute a finite but indeterminable multiplicity, which is an ever-shifting, always mobile, regime of those semiotic elements that participate in making sense.

The use of phrases such as the 'art of the comics,' 'conceptual art,' 'optical art,' 'the happening,' 'the dance drama,' 'technoart,' or 'rock video' clearly illustrates what is involved and how the range of combinatory possibilities is expanding as this century draws to a conclusion. In this regard, multimedia art, the arts of virtual reality, and the poetic use of hypermedia reveal the edge of the future.[31] TV dramas, rock videos, popular movies, comic strips, crime novels, and SF have not only contributed to creating the new multimedia paraliterature,[32] they have also become prime elements in a series of ongoing critical dialogues between groups of individuals, which occurs, for example, through special interest groups, fan clubs, and conferences, but still more fruitfully through the day-by-day interchanges made possible by computer telecommunications.

Every day many hundreds of thousands of individuals make contributions on Internet, Compuserve, and other networks to bulletin boards and discussion groups for which the subject is often confined to a single interest cluster, such as *Star Trek* or *Doonesbury*, or an area such as jokes, comics, SF, cinema, and the like. These new multimedia works become part of an ongoing process of critical discussion that has involved the development of a populist form of traditional criticism of literature and the fine arts. The thirty-year success of *Star Trek* and *The Next Generation* is characteristic. Beginning with TV productions, there has been an exfoliation of video cassettes, films, animated films, novels, comic books, and a multitude of associated paraphernalia, including computer games, manuals, conventions, clubs, T-shirts, and so forth. *Star Trek* has become 'multimedia paraliterature,' exemplifying a phenomenon that in its scope, enabled by technology, is unique to the second half of the twentieth century. Today such multimedia works are characteristic of all market-place successes.

These universes constructed around 'multimedia paraliterature' have emerged along with avant-garde techno-cultural experimentation characteristic of the first three decades of this century. Joyce's major works provide the first encyclopaedic critical reflection on the possibility of such events. From the time of Baudelaire's appreciation of the importance of photography and urbanization, of Whitman's celebration of the transformative power of a new electric world, and Mallarmé's perception of the centrality of the press, there had been a gradually accumulating awareness of how social and technological change were bringing about an entire transformation of the artistic world. Eliot's writing on the music-hall and the detective novel, and Brecht's theatre designed as a place of festive entertainment utilizing techniques such as the titling associated with comic-strip balloons, exemplify some of the ways in which this new consciousness began to develop.

By the late 1920s, Wyndham Lewis could produce extensive and elaborate critiques of popular culture, the technological media, and the new sense of time preoccupying the attention of artists and popular entertainers. In *Time and Western Man* Lewis carries out a complex reflection on those changing conceptions of time, space, duration, and speed resulting from the world-view of Bergson, Einstein, and modern technology that involves a wide range of cultural productions: Chaplin, the Diaghileff ballet, and Joyce; women's fashions, advertising, and Virginia Woolf; radio broadcasting, the blossoming of a cult of youth, and Gertrude Stein.[33]

This growing fluidity of forms and genres is dramatically apparent in a world where words, images, movements, and rhythms complement and supplement one another: silent films with verbal titling (adapted to the theatre in Brecht's plays); the entitling of painting (as in Klee or Calder); the happening, integrating sound, gesture, rhythm, and vision (beginning with Dadaism). Sergei Eisenstein's reflections on film practice quickly led him to realize how interconnected all of these phenomena really were and how they were a prelude to an integrated artistic activity consonant with the urban world, the new techno-culture, and contemporary life. Yet this is not a sterile formalism; for such playing with the elements of communication immediately becomes a social activity. What begins as an exploration of technology and its implications for changing concepts of time, space, and communication quickly comes to involve cultural, social, and political questions which transform the very way people regard poetic activity in the individual arts.

Understanding communication must involve an understanding of what is happening in the arts through the interplay of poetic and dramatic action in the crafting and constructing of architectonic artefacts, one of whose fundamental *raisons d'être* is to place a central emphasis on the intrinsic satisfaction (or delight) in the use of the elements of communication simply (or at least primarily) for the sake of using those elements in and for themselves. Important contributors to recent dialogue about communication theory, such as Adorno, Barthes, McLuhan, Eco, and Williams, all shared a strong foundation in the history and critical theory of a number of individual arts, and their books have always demonstrated this. It is interesting to note also that in the institutionalization of communication study in the United States, one of the early academic pioneers of communication study as a social science, Wilbur Schramm, though his writings would hardly reveal it, had initially been an English scholar (like McLuhan and Williams) before turning to communication research.

Since Paul Ricoeur has demonstrated the importance of an expanded conception of textuality by examining the concept of 'meaningful action' as a 'text,' the interrelation of the poetry, drama, and practice of the individual arts should be recognized as fundamental to the understanding of communication. The close link which has developed in the past two decades between communication and cultural studies (which arose from earlier transdisciplinary linkages) further underlines the urgency to examine the role of the poetic in the conceptual understanding of the process of communication and of the growth of human communication which pervaded the development of modernism and the avant-garde arts.

McLuhan reiterated again and again that neither his work nor the subject of communication could be fully understood without a knowledge of the symbolist and post-symbolist poets, particularly Joyce and Mallarmé.[34] Burke used Joyce and many other modernist artists in developing his theory of the poetics of communication. The spectrum of artists whom it would be useful to study from this perspective is by no means limited to Joyce and Mallarmé or a few major figures of high modernism, nor limited to such traditional arts as literature and painting. From SF to the parabolic poetic prose of Borges, from comics to Lichtenstein, from the Beatles to Boulez, and from *Flash Gordon* and the cliff-hanging serials to Fellini and Bergman, the subject of the actual contribution of artistic practice and artistic vision to understanding communication certainly deserves extensive exploration.

5

The Book, the Press, Eisenstein, and Joyce: Changing Relations in Culture, Technology, and Communication

Joyce's multiplex method enables him to transform the dialogic nature of the novel. Inner dialogue may now appear within a character, or as the narrative voice interacting with characters, or even between characters, so that the traditional dialogic movement of styles within the novel becomes the exploration of a 'chaosmos' of 'plurabilities.'[1] These new synchronistic poems develop dialogues which include the distinctive modes of communication used by different groups of people and by mediated 'voices' of individuals. As film and other audio-visual media start to supplement (and in some ways even replace) the novel, the synchronistic poem explores the very nature of communication itself. That poetic process reconstructs language to take advantage of the differences between speaking, writing, print, and emerging post-print-related modes – 'verbivocovisual presentment[s]' (*FW*341.19) – in which multiplexity of language produces those epiphanies that illuminate and metamorphosize the trivial. Joyce, working in this comic epic form, could strongly endorse Pope's aphorism: 'What mighty contests rise from trivial things!'

This new synchronized poetry in prose intensified the novel's potential as critique; that is, this type of writing transformed and intensified the strategies which had produced novels characterized by self-criticism and criticism of the various dialogues and voices of which they were composed. This new poetic critique embraced the spectrum of communication and dramatized how the varying modes of poetry which constitute that spectrum (such as film, radio, television) also were often constituted as critique. Filmic critiques of ads, 'mass media,' fashion, bureaucratic organization, technology, or modes of production provide well known examples: for example, Kubrick's *Dr Strangelove, Clockwork Orange,* or *Full Metal Jacket.*

During the period since 1880, a number of factors have interacted to shape a potentially liberating poetic communication that pervades the expression of everyday life as well as conscious poetic production. These include: fundamental transformations in the technological modes of producing, reproducing, and distributing communication and information; the impact of electro-mechanization on the socio-economic order; a series of transformations of poetic communication (including the creation of new art forms); the creation of a new poetic (verbal) language. Examples that include advertising, film, radio, and the newspaper will provide a means of seeing the process by which modes of communication interact with poetic modes. Joyce's *Ulysses* is an obvious place to begin.

Leopold Bloom, an advertising-space salesman, who is Joyce's Quixotean or Chaplinesque 'hero,' still has, as an ordinary 'everybody,' his moments of poetic creativity; the commodified media products that he promotes are also to some extent rhetorical and often poetic productions. It is well recognized that ads frequently transmit messages quite different from the fundamental aims and beliefs of the advertisers. It is ironic that a pioneer of the modern ad agency, like David Ogilvy (of Ogilvy, Benson and Mathers), a deeply committed Puritan, through his activities in the advertising industry unknowingly contributed to generating a wide-spread hedonism that eventually contributed to significant changes in popular attitudes towards the human body and sexuality.

The mediated forms of the new urban circus or carnival, such as ads, appropriate material and formal attributes from the arts in profoundly self-revealing ways. Poetic creativity is not an absence in that urban mass-mediated world, for it utilizes those mediated products in assembling its artefacts. Furthermore, as everyday semiotic forms, these ads and other mass-mediated productions also carry potential as poetic signifiers. Ads innovatively utilize as well as transform phrases and images regularly used in everyday life (e.g., 'the pause that refreshes'). It is a common enough phenomenon for viewers of decontextualized sequential filmed presentations of a series of ads (such as, the 'World's Best Ads' of any year) to find them irresistibly funny. They are the very stuff of the urban circus; the materials which shape the humour of the modern 'market-place.'

In *Ulysses* (1922), published the same year as Eliot's *The Waste Land*, Joyce clearly demonstrates a complex awareness of how these relationships are involved in the interconnectedness of communication, poetry, and the arts. 'Aeolus,' the seventh of *Ulysses'* eighteen episodes, explores the role of the press in a contemporary metropolis.[2] Joyce describes the style for this episode as 'enthymemic,'[3] for according to his chart of the book's design, the art emphasized in 'Aeolus' is rhetoric.[4] He further suggests that the symbol for this episode is the editor (as gatekeeper – keeper of the winds). His hero, Bloom, sells advertising space for the newspaper; the young artist, Stephen Dedalus, partly supports himself by writing for the press. Joyce's vision, highly comic, partly ironic and ambivalent, reflects the ambivalence of the language and influence of the press and of the socio-political pressures on the press.

The 'Aeolus' episode opens with shots of Dublin life: the Dublin United Tramway Company; shoeblacks working in front of the General Post Office in juxtaposition with 'His Majesty's vermilion mailcars'; 'grossbooted draymen' rolling 'dullthudding' barrels; the print shop with its 'thumping presses.'[5] The rhythm of the printing press dominates, and the mechanical fragmentation of the landscape pervades Bloom's visit to the newspaper office. Through the segmentation involved in the setting of type; through the system of roads and tram tracks which shape the circulation system of Dublin; through the 'national' communication system provided by the Royal Mail; and through the division of labour, the commercial life of the city manifests its all-pervasive influence. Stressing the role of the modern newspaper in the life of the city, this section of *Ulysses* focuses as well on the ancient art of rhetoric, linking public speaking, literary communication, journalistic communication, and advertising; thus implying how the rhythms of commerce, of machines, and of technological processes shape contemporary communication.

The crafted style of 'Aeolus' uses the full panoply of classical rhetorical figures – and particularly emphasizes that condensed, probabilistic, and often incomplete syllogistic form that characterized rhetoric for Aristotle, the enthymeme. The 'enthymemic' style unfolds in the shadow of two of its post-classical definitions: first, the medieval, emphasizing its ellipsis; and secondly, that of Port-Royal, which regarded it as an imperfect syllogism on the level of language whose pleasure is marked by its concision.[6] Concision, ellipsis, and imperfect reasoning associated with journalism abound in this episode, both in its parodic headlines and its crafted rhetorical text.

Advertising is itself enthymemic: Bloom's ad for the House of Keyes (crossed keys) simultaneously suggests that Keyes's business is nationalistic and Catholic, supporting home rule (for the parliament of the Isle of Man, which has home rule, is the House of Keys) and receiving the blessings of Saint Peter and the Pope, for this is the symbol of the papacy. Paronomasia arising from the condensation of headlines becomes one type of index to Dublin's cultural complex. The solution of a riddle, posed by Lenehan, 'What opera is like a railway line?' is '*The Rose of Castile*. See the wheeze. Rows of cast steel. Gee!' This multiplex pun (which brings together the mechanization represented by printing presses and tram tracks with a romantic figure of Catholicism, Saint Rose of Castille, an Irish opera and operatic aria, and the erotic figure of Bloom's Spanish-born wife, Molly, a professional singer, who is also associated with Castille) serves as an index to the motifs of romance, pseudo-dedication, mechanism, eroticism, and communication that play behind the rhetoric and modes of action within the world of the press and the colonialized city of Dublin. Such puns also suggest ways in which the activities of the press are changing everyday perceptions of the events and experiences of contemporary life through manipulation of language.

The reduction of people and events to 'types' abounds throughout this episode of *Ulysses*. Headlines play a major role in establishing these typologies, for, as a passage from *Finnegans Wake* puts it, people are categorized (i.e., 'typed' and 'placed') through the operation of rhetoric: 'For that ... is what papyr is meed of, made of, hides and hints and misses in prints. Till ye finally (though not yet endlike) meet with the acquaintance of Mister Typus, Mistress Tope and all the little typtopies. Fillstup' (20.10–3). Topics (Latin, *topos*, place, passage in a book) and types (Latin, *typus*, print, impression, image, model) as figures, forms, images, topics, and commonplaces, the elemental bits of writing and rhetoric, in 1920 Dublin are now established through the products of typesetting. Printing sets in place the 'root language,' which resides in the types and topes of the world through a multitude of codes: sounds, images, objects, movements, and gestures.

In the *Wake* references to the production of books, newspapers, and the rise of publicity abound for 'the latterpress is eminently legligible and the paper, so he eagerly seized upon, has scarsely been buttered in works of previous publicity wholebeit in keener notcase' (356.21–3). 'ABORTISEMENT(s)' (181.33), 'newslaters' (390.1), dailies, weeklies, magazines, and other products of the printing press appear; for example, 'reading her Evening World ... News, news, all the news' (28.21), 'Fugger's Newsletter' (97.32); or 'the Frankofurto Siding, a Fastland payrodicule' (70.6). Increased mechanization and new technological organizations accompany these developments: reporters, editors, interviewers, newsboys, ad men (cf. Bloom in *Ulysses*). A new sense of urgency related to time emerges: 'Stop. Press stop. To press stop. All to press stop ...' (379.6). Further effects on the ecosystem are noted for 'All the trees in the wood they trembold, humbild, when they heard the stop-press from domday's erewold' (588.33). This motif is related back to the beginnings of language in 'woodwordings' of a different kind, for 'The war is in words and the wood is the world' (98.34).[7]

A dialectical relationship between the book and the newspaper is fundamental in Joyce's late writing, just as it is a key theme in the development of poetry, art, and popular culture throughout the early twentieth century. Poets and artists had discovered the iconic nature of the newspaper long before it was pointed out by communications theorists. The nature of the daily newspaper had been a preoccupation of modern writers and artists ranging from Pound's aphorism that 'literature is news that STAYS news'[8] – news which has no 'dateline' – to Karl Schwitters's use of it in collages, or Picasso's in *Guernica* and in still lifes. In an essay entitled 'Joyce, Mallarmé and the Press,' McLuhan demonstrated how Mallarmé and Joyce had made the important discovery that the newspaper page was really a cubist landscape.[9] The iconic nature of the newspaper layout, which McLuhan had identified as early as *The Mechanical Bride* (1952), permitted daily papers to create a universe of significance far greater than all of the words in each of the individual stories or all the photos illustrating them.

The newspaper, as a cultural phenomenon affecting all poetry and arts that shape language and communication, accomplished precisely the kind of rhetorical liberation which literary language and the visual arts required at the turn of the century. What Yeats, speaking about poetry and the arts, had called 'thinking with the body' manifests itself through symbols that interweave elements of the natural, the everyday, and the poetic. Another interweaving of such elements occurs virtually every day in the press, so that just before the twentieth century opened, Mallarmé could prophesy how advertising and the press would produce 'the foundation of the popular modern Poem, at the very least of innumerable Thousand and One Nights.'[10]

Brecht's dramatic practice, Picasso's painting, and Welles's film-making provide ways of seeing how this process evolved. Brecht was acutely aware of the significance of the press for poets and dramatists as well as society at large. The press as institution plays a role in dramas such as *St Joan of the Stockyards*, where the media through their relations with the economic system contribute to bringing about Joan's crisis. Benjamin, writing about Brecht and the contemporary role of the 'author as producer,' analyses an aspect of this relation between the newspaper and the book by observing that 'contrasts which ... used to fertilize one another have become insoluble antinomies. Thus, science and *belles lettres*, criticism and original production, culture and politics, now stand apart from one another without connection or order of any kind.' The newspaper is the 'arena' where this process happens, for the only form imposed on its content is the result of the 'reader's impatience'; 'behind it smoulders the impatience of the outsider, the excluded man who yet believes he has a right to speak in his own interest.'[11]

Editors, having learned that this impatience 'binds' the readers to the newspaper, for it demands fresh nourishment every day, develop space where readers can participate with 'questions, opinions, protests.' This gradually erodes the distinction between author and public, for 'literature gains in breadth what it loses in depth.' As an expert on his own work, the reader becomes 'one who describes, or prescribes' so that 'authority to write is no longer founded in a specialist training but in a polytechnical one and so becomes common property. In a word, the literarization of living conditions becomes a way of surmounting otherwise insoluble antinomies and the place where the word is most debased – that is to say, the newspaper – becomes the very place where a rescue operation can be mounted.'[12] This 'literarization of living conditions,' a result of authority now being grounded in polytechnical training, which makes it the common property of all, becomes a feature of other artistic practice.

In his 'literarization' of the theatre, Brecht both consciously and unconsciously utilized the techniques of newspapers and other media and took advantage of the transformation which they were bringing about in the relationship between author and audience – the ambivalences between producers and consumers. At an elementary level, his use of titles and screens in the literarization of the theatre comes from the media world. He developed his conception of brief titling devices similar to headlines from journalistic practice (and probably silent films). His theories concerning a 'theatre of entertainment,' which also is a 'theatre of instruction,' flow from the need to make the audience a co-producer, in order to produce consciousness of the structural processes implicit in contemporary society.

While Joyce makes a far more extensive use than Brecht of aspects of the press, he is acutely conscious of the major factors Benjamin outlines in his analysis of the relation of the newspaper to the author as producer. *Finnegans Wake* (written during a time of economic and social upheaval that began two decades earlier) uses the language of the everyday to achieve what Benjamin described as a 'functional transformation' – the transformation of forms and instruments of production by a progressive intelligentsia.[13]

Across the range of arts, the qualities of print journalism and the press as an institution provided one stimulus to the more penetrating criticism and satire of the socio-political world by twentieth-century artists. Joyce's shaping of a 'new language,' and the theory and praxis with which this process is associated, became essential as a stage in the development of the ways that subsequent writers such as Beckett, Borges, Burgess, Vonnegut, and Acker and, perhaps even to a greater degree, SF writers such as Aldiss, Brunner, Dick, or Lem have used media to probe satirically the contradictions of everyday life and social goals. As early as the 1930s, Karel Čapek in his science fiction novel *The War with the Newts* used journalism and the newspaper as an iconic and structural form. Pop Art more recently has reabsorbed the press into art works, picking up again that historical movement beginning with Schwitters's preoccupation with visual collage in which he made scraps of newspaper print part of a disjunctive, mosaic-like response to the fragmentary character of modern urbanization, and continuing through Picasso's use of the press as reflecting the vision of fragmentation that contributes to the anti-fascistic destructive energy of *Guernica*.

In Orson Welles's classic film *Citizen Kane*, which contributed to the work of Alfred Hitchcock in Hollywood and the New Wave in France, the press and its extension into audio-visual journalism plays a major role. Welles's exploration of the infamous journalistic and entrepreneurial career of William Randolph Hearst unfolds in a dialectical movement that plays off the cinematic newsreel against the daily press. Welles produced *Citizen Kane* shortly after Joyce had published *Finnegans Wake*. While it would be difficult to imagine two works that are more fundamentally different, they share the same fascination in probing the world of media and contemporary communication. Welles's career and his film are very relevant for understanding what the evolution of art and media have to do with the relation between poetics and communication theory.

Beginning his career in the 1930s, Welles was a genuine child of the new media world: verbally literate, traditionally trained, and yet highly sensitive both to the interplay between media and to the power of words and images. The young Welles was more than just a film director; he was a man with a peculiar sensitivity to the ways that the newer media were changing artistic practice. Before directing *Citizen Kane*, he had produced the legendary radio drama series Mercury Theatre for NBC. Mercury's best-known production was Welles's notorious radio dramatization of H.G. Wells's *War of Two Worlds: The Invasion from Mars*, considered by many to be the single most effective use of radio as a medium to achieve an impact. Extensive panic throughout the United States resulted from this broadcast of Welles's *Invasion*. (A more recent re-broadcast in Canada in the 1970s still resulted in a minor rash of inquiries throughout the Maritimes as to whether or not the invasion was real.) Broadcasting *War of Two Worlds* as a contemporary mixture of genres and media involved four different creative areas: practices of contemporary theatre, the new medium of radio (hence sound), the translation of novel into play, and SF with its growing significance as a popular art form.

When Welles turned from radio and the theatre to film-making and the production of *Citizen Kane*, he was still fascinated with the role of media in the new society. In this film, he did not abandon theatre, for the theatricality of large portions of the production contributes to the effect of mock grandiosity that is so central to its action. The plot that provides Welles's tale of a 'News-of-the-Week' film journalist researching a story on the life of Kane, a millionaire newspaper baron, entails the clash that had developed by the 1930s between the then relatively new film newsreel and picture magazines and the older daily press of which Kane had been king. This film brings together techniques not only from the stage, the press, the documentary newsreel, and the new and the old journalism, but also from radio and the graphic art of the comic strip and the front page.

André Bazin first pointed out Welles's superb use of sound as a central component in his film-making; a component which he had learned to use in adapting drama to radio during the Mercury Theatre productions.[14] Comic strips are also an evident influence, for as *The Penguin History of Comics* suggests 'his use of angles for dramatic effect, overlapping dialogue, sudden cutting from one scene to another, inset effects with one scene superimposed on another, and the opening sequence with its advancing succession of shots of an old mansion echoed the work of the comic strip artist and created a new library of film clichés.'[15] Kane's grandiose castle, Xanadu (modelled on Hearst's estate at St Simeon in Southern California), further permitted the introduction of aspects of the Gothic novel with its affiliations with silent horror films. It is significant that a film journalist, not a print journalist such as Kane himself had been, undertakes the quest for the 'truth' about Kane's life. This has the effect of placing the whole film in a quasi-documentary frame, lending a credibility and veracity to the way the camera shapes the story. Using the newspaper world as a focus, the camera exploits the technique of collage characteristic of press layout, just as reportorial film editing employs montage characteristic of film-making. Journalism as a commercial institution, a profession, and a mode of cultural production, by utilizing a semiotic style and structures specific to the press and media world, produces a cultural work that is a complex network of interrelated signs which reveal the entire media world as enmeshed in multiple contradictions between truth and prevarication, profit and disinterested reporting, dedication to business or profession and commitment of self to concern with others. The film's unfinished quest for 'truth' ultimately imbues many other objects with significance: Xanadu, the archives, an empty poison bottle, 'Rosebud.' Ultimately the prime irony – that the world of journalism (print and film) fails to realize the importance to Kane of such an apparently trivial, yet deeply significant, object as his childhood sleigh, 'Rosebud' – reveals that deep ambivalence which characterizes the journalistic quest for truth.

The telling of Kane's story is segmented and discontinuous. Technique and socio-political dimensions of traditional genres and newer modes of communication interact to generate an essentially multiplex cluster of signifiers aided and abetted by the strategy of telling Hearst's story as the fictive tale of Kane and then transforming that tale through the filter of a fictive tale-teller who is a film journalist. The particular scene where Kane discovers his wife's, Susan's, attempted suicide dramatizes Kane's domination of his world through Welles's characteristically polysemiotic use of sound techniques of radio journalism and visual strategies learned from comic strip artists. Elsewhere the camera produces effects of grandiosity and megalomania. These provide a kind of silent counterpoint to the very different use of such effects in Leni Riefenstahl's contemporaneous documentary-propagandistic film *Triumph of the Will*. In focusing on the megalomaniacal hero figure, Kane, who appeals to the modern 'everybody' as a result of the propagandistic nature of the press and film, Welles's work has its connection with Joyce's dream satire of his 'Everybody,' who in a megalomaniacal way tends to see his life as that of a mythic giant in the dimensions of the history of his country and of the world. Both of these poets explore new perceptions of the world that have influenced the way in which each person weaves and unravels stories that reveal rapidly changing life-worlds with radically transformed attitudes towards entrepreneurship.

Welles's work has had a very special impact on film history that certainly would have surprised its original audiences in the United States. *Citizen Kane* has appealed to many makers of 'art' films, such as Godard in France, who developed a cinematic form much closer to the complexities of Joyce than the deceptively transparent surface simplicities of Welles's tale of a journalist-baron. One aspect of Welles's work which appealed to Godard was his interest in documentary and in media. The *Invasion from Mars* employed the style of presentation of a documentary broadcast news report covering a major crisis. The fictional use of documentary in a complexly expanded form is also central in *Citizen Kane*. News and newsreel are modes that always had an appeal for Godard as well as the youthful Welles. In fact, Godard, discussing his film *Deux ou trois choses que je sais d'elle*, revealed that he had really wished to be a journalist: 'Actually if I have a secret ambition, it is to be put in charge of the French newsreel services. All my films have been reports on the state of the nation; they are all newsreel documents, treated in a personal manner perhaps, but in terms of contemporary actuality.'[16]

Since Godard believed that everything can be put into a film, he saw the film as discourse, as communication. Expanding on his remarks about his interest in 'news,' he emphasized the inclusiveness of film and the fascination which he had for TV, especially TV journalism: 'During the course of the film – in its discourse, discontinuous course, that is – I want to include everything, sport, politics, even groceries ... Everything can be put into a film. When people ask me why I talk or have my characters talk about Vietnam, about Jacques Anquetil, or about a woman who deceives her husband, I refer the questioner to his own newspaper. It's all there. And it's all mixed up. This is why I am so attracted by television. A televised newspaper made up of carefully prepared documentaries would be extraordinary. Even more so if one could get editors to take turns at editing these televised newspapers.'[17] This conviction that 'everything can be put into a film' appears to echo earlier conceptions of the makers of collages – whether in words, objects, or paint – who had found that the newspaper reflected modern urbanization and participated in shaping a new sensibility.

All this is implicit in Welles, for *Citizen Kane* is about the power of the newspaper and how it comes to prominence with the growing importance of the myth of the powerful megalomanical financeer – a type related to the fascist dictator and the media star, concepts which emerged from the media world of the 1920s and 1930s. In his film, Welles develops a dialectic between different modes of information and story-telling: the press, the documentary film, the newsreel, and the actual making of a film producing a narrative which encompasses his world in complex detail. While perhaps not as inclusive as Godard outlines, Welles moves in the direction of inclusiveness as the panorama of Kane's success and failure reflects the nature of his times. The tendency of the ongoing development of contemporary media has always been towards inclusiveness in time and space, from the telegraph, the telephone, the photograph, and the newspaper produced by rotary press through film and television to the newest potentialities of the marriage of computers and telecommunications or virtual reality as the means of producing a heretofore unanticipated electronic inclusiveness. Just before the beginning of the twentieth century, poets and artists had grasped the difficulties confronting the concept of 'literature' as it had been traditionally recognized. By the second decade of this century, it was quite apparent that literary language needed to be re-examined in the context of the changing world of communication. Oral or printed poetry encounters serious challenges when television and film can be so potentially inclusive and when they also can fulfil the same function as most of the major strategies of narration characteristic of nineteenth-century novels such as those of Dickens.

From his exposition of his film theories, it is clear that Eisenstein saw film as a composite art. He demonstrated that he appreciated the importance of a knowledge of Dickens or Joyce for understanding film as a mode of expression, and proposed a synchronization of older and newer modes of production and transmission. This is another corollary of gestural theory, for synaesthesia always implies the potential integration of human sense experience, either by the actual or the imaginary interrelation of different modes of expression. Prefigurations of contemporary multi-media are exemplified in liturgy, the cathedral, illuminated books, emblems, shaped poems, masques, and cantatas.

Eisenstein recognized the important activity that Joyce was carrying on within language, for in *Film Sense* when discussing 'Word and Image,' he relates the technique of the portmanteau word associated with the writings of Carroll, Freud, and Joyce to the newly emerging importance of montage in film. Portmanteau words are 'an extreme instance' of the 'tendency to bring together into unity two or more independent objects or qualities.' The 'charm' of their effect is 'built upon the sensation of a duality residing arbitrarily in a single word.' He goes on to observe that 'obviously the greatest manipulation of the portmanteau word is to be found in *Finnegans Wake*.'[18]

Joyce's and Valéry Larbaud's development of the 'inner monologue' interested Eisenstein for he considered that to be the core of the cinematic experience. Elsewhere, in *Film Form*, Eisenstein recounts how Joyce, though nearly blind, wished to see 'those parts of *Potemkin* and *October* that with the expressive means of film culture move along kindred lines.'[19] Eisenstein further cites Joyce's *Ulysses* on the need for an art of gesture,[20] and he recommends Joyce as advanced reading towards the development of 'filmic feeling,' but he criticizes him for stretching this method too far. While his argument recognizes that in *Ulysses* and the *Wake* Joyce intensified the urge of all the contemporary arts 'to strain towards ... the full embrace of the whole inner world of man, of a whole reproduction of the outer world,' Eisenstein felt this aim could not be achieved by any single one of the older arts. Therefore, he declares that 'Joyce reached a limit in reconstructing the reflection and refraction of reality in the consciousness and feelings of man.' He believed in order to achieve this Joyce paid too high a price: 'the entire dissolution of the very foundation of literary diction, the entire decomposition of literary method itself.' Writers were limited by living in a period of transition in which the cinema was emerging as the form which 'synchronized the arts': 'For only the cinema can take, as the aesthetic basis of its dramaturgy, not only the statics of the human body and the dynamics of its action and behaviour, but an infinitely broader diapason, reflecting the manifold movement and changing feelings and thoughts of man.' When any existing art tries to achieve the full embrace of the inner world of man and the whole reproduction of the outer world, 'the very base that holds the art together is inevitably broken.'[21] Eisenstein clearly regarded *Ulysses* and *Finnegans Wake* as having 'broken' the 'base' of literature, although for him there was no way for the imaginary operating through any of the arts other than film to successfully achieve integration.

While Eisenstein understood the synchronization of the arts and the specific power of film for achieving this at that time, he did not foresee a world that was moving *beyond* media, in which film culture itself could be superseded in its rage for integration by computer culture and virtual reality. Consequently, he did not realize the importance of Joyce's project in providing a new role for the poetry of language in a world where traditional conceptions of the book would wither away. For the theme of the death of the book is not a theme about an instantaneous demise, but something akin to Eliot's announcement of the 'death of the novel,' implying that afterwards what had been recognized as the role of poetic prose narrative before the appearance of *Ulysses* would not survive in the same type of form, nor would it have the same central role to play in social production.

Eisenstein also refers to Joyce while he is discussing the cinematographic principle, the haiku, and the ideogram, for Eisenstein shared with Ezra Pound the conviction that 'the principle of montage can be identified as the basic element of Japanese representational culture.'[22] Eisenstein also believed Joyce to have been the poet who develops 'in literature the depictive line of the Japanese hieroglyph.'[23] This principle is 'denotation by depiction' and, incidentally, radical juxtaposition, which does not necessarily depend upon whether or not the attribution of it to the ideogram is correct or not. Eisenstein characterized montage as 'collision ... the conflict of two pieces in opposition to each other.' Therefore, whether or not he fully grasped the significance of Joyce's project or the tendency to develop increasing inclusiveness and comprehensiveness in the evolution of contemporary communication, he clearly recognized how the importance of 'inner speech' and its relation to the new poetics of the ideogram, Joyce's major works, the visual arts, jazz, and the newly developing film culture presupposed a new understanding of communication and expression.

Communication, so conceived as a continuum within the social life-world, embraces all aspects of activity, such as the popular expression of jazz, the everyday use of certain symbols, the ways in which gesture and hieroglyph operate, and the specific processes of the various modes of poetic and practical expression and communication. This is consistent with the era in which Eisenstein developed his cinematic practice, and it clearly foresees the breakdown between levels of culture which characterized the Joyce era and which eventually contributed to the development of cultural studies. To explore, however, the way in which the limitations of Eisenstein's perceptions spawned later problematic analyses, the question of what it means to *move beyond media* arises.

While Eisenstein discerned the power of film-makers to achieve greater inclusiveness and comprehensiveness in orchestrating the full range of modes of expression available, as his discussion of Dickens and Griffith illustrates,[24] and although he recognized the importance of *Ulysses* and its grasp of cinematic effect, he still failed to understand fully what Joyce was about in his revolutionary work, *Finnegans Wake*. Verbal texts necessarily possess a special position in this process because of the peculiar problems presented to language by contemporary developments in communication and because of the historically critical function that language has performed in our making sense out of 'things.' Joyce's use of language and signs in *Ulysses* and the *Wake* demonstrates how by being aware of the influence of a changing world on the role of communication, he consciously contributed to the forging of a new language which would enable verbal poetry to engage with the realities of the changing role of communication media in the age of technology.

Some of the many other writers who re-examined the role of communication and can be cited as reflecting on as well as experimenting with communication include Baudelaire, Proust, Mallarmé, Valéry, Benjamin, Kraus, Pound, Yeats, Wyndham Lewis, and Tzara. A large number of the key proponents and practitioners of the newer arts in the first third of this century also reflect on and experiment with communication. The search for new *languages* by artists (such as Klee in painting, Schönberg in music, or Eisenstein in the cinema) clearly underlines the importance of the changing relationships taking place and how that necessitated the transformation of the community of signs by which people communicate.

In *Vision in Motion* Laszlo Moholy-Nagy, an early Hungarian constructivist who had joined the Bauhaus in 1923 and moved to the United States to establsh a new Bauhaus in 1937, describes Joyce's unique role in the contemporary movements which involved 'the orchestration of the arts.' A designer and experimentalist who had worked in a variety of media, Moholy-Nagy was deeply sensitive to the changing relationships between the arts and to their relationship with the new technologies. As a constructivist and a teacher in the Bauhaus, he was familiar with the affinity of the artist and engineer. As polyglot European, he was equally sensitive about the new character the arts of language would have to assume in the emerging techno-culture. Therefore, he readily recognized the central importance of Joyce's contributions and of the necessity for contemporary artists to try to understand them.

Launching into a discussion of Joyce's work, he warns his reader of the dangers implicit in the explanation that he is undertaking, for it can destroy 'the fresh impact of surprise' of the privileged moment of a first reading in which the 'fluidity' of feeling has an inexplicable 'plastic impact.' He denies the commonplace that puns are the lowest form of humour, singling out the inaccuracy of such an idea when applied to *Finnegans Wake*. In the *Wake* the reader is 'willing to go on with the rather complex task involved in reading the book' because Joyce's wit is 'candid':

> The gaiety implicit between the lines, between the words and within the composite words, makes one feel happy. At the same time there is a feeling that the author himself enjoys most of all the great spectacle of life in spite of his murderous knifing of human petulance. When he scourges social and individual deficiencies, he does not sound as if he were preaching in gloomy rage. His humour grows beyond the obvious in word combinations with their ambivalent or multiple meanings.

Quoting Joyce's phrase 'panaroma of all flores of speech,' he shows how it appeals to all five senses:[25] 'There is something to see: "panaroma"; but also something to smell, "flores" (flowers) and to taste "aroma" and things to touch and feel' – such as floors, a peach, and a speech. Moholy-Nagy goes on to argue that at this point the synaesthetic, the technological, and new modes of communication meet:

> Has he [Joyce] achieved here the coordination and interchange of senses which Rimbaud meant? Is his an X-ray technique of verbalization? Probably. It is the approach to the practical task of building up a completeness from interlocked units by an ingenious transparency of relationships. The method parallels the cutting of motion pictures. The editor of a film sometimes relates (pastes) units of different shots made at different places in different times into a new entity.
>
> If one presupposes that there is an underlying unity of all creative work in one period, one can find in Joyce's writings analogies to contemporary ethnological terms. In these terms Joyce's agglutinations (often constructed from German, Hungarian or other composites which is normal in these languages but strange in English) appear to be similar to the industrial process of assemblage by bolts, rivets and screws ...
>
> outohelloutof that

wavyavyeavyheavyeavyeveyevy hair
bronzelidded
softcreakfooted
whitetallhatted

Joyce's fusion of words, like

panaroma
immarginable
erigenating
celescalating
bootiful

are again equivalent to the present technology of mass production as it occurs in welding, casting, moulding, stamping.'[26]

Moholy-Nagy goes on to point out that there are some approximations to this strategy of fusion in some surrealist and abstract films, but that it has also been adopted by the language of contemporary advertising and media: 'girlesque' instead of 'burlesque'; 'brunch' for breakfast and lunch; Pittsburgh 'smog' meaning a mixture of smoke and fog.[27]

Moholy-Nagy's discussion merits extended consideration since it reveals the common understanding of those changes which had been emerging throughout the arts and shows how Joyce provided many new fundamental insights into the process. His views closely parallel those of Eisenstein, up to the point where Eisenstein criticizes Joyce's 'failure,'[28] for Moholy-Nagy stresses Joyce's success in doing something unique in, for, and to language which he stresses also performs an essential function for all the other arts since it is the special role of the verbal to provide a reflective, recollective intelligibility to the underlying unity of all cultural production that is undertaken during a particular period of time.

Both this artist-designer and the film director Eisenstein call attention to how Joyce's concern with structural and semiotic features of the literary work is considerably in advance of their time. Their observations on the *Wake* reveal how extensive the inter-animation of the arts had become and how the importance of the 'coordination and interchange of senses,' the impact of technology, and parallels between artists' methods actually was widely recognized. In film, in visual arts, in fact, across the spectrum of the arts, there emerged a feeling that human communication is integrated and each of the traditional modes has its own role to play in the integration. Moholy-Nagy goes further and associates the contemporary artistic method and Joyce's method with the joining of mechanization and electricity: a 'completeness' built up from interlocked units; a method parallel to montage in editing; the similarity to industrial assemblage; the final goal being 'an X-ray technique of verbalization.'

These strategies, though, are common to surrealist and abstract films (and, for that matter, visual art) and to advertising. Joyce goes even further, for his language embraces the technological changes which occur within the production of signs, which involves all of the media and their shifting interrelationships within the activity of 'the orchestration of the arts.' There is a direct line from this type of artistic thinking, with its implications for communication, and the current intense interest in the arts among scientific and technical communication researchers at MIT's Media Lab. This institute, which was founded by Jerome Weisner and is exploring the potentialities of computers and telecommunications for the development of new modes of communication, has directly inherited the insights of Moholy-Nagy, Gyorgy Kepes, and other modernist artists working with the new technologies. Since it was McLuhan's who first enabled many of the early researchers at the Media Lab to grasp the importance of art and poetry to their work, he remains an important figure there, where he is still sometimes spoken of as the inspiring prophet of the telematic age (a fact confirmed by *Wired* magazine's elevating him to the role of a patron saint).

Newer communication technologies have tended to become more and more inclusive of all of these potentialities, so that contemporary microprocessors are being designed to permit the simultaneous use of signs derived from all of the differing sensory capacities of the human person. The Aspen Movie Map designed in the MIT Media Lab as a response to whether 'experiential mapping' could be simulated on a computer is already an older stage of what is yet to come:

> 'Aspen' wasn't a travelogue ... It was the whole town. It let you drive through the place yourself, having a conversation with the chauffeur. There was a season knob – any street you were driving down, any building you were examining could be seen Winter-Spring-Summer-Fall. Many buildings you could go into. Some, like restaurants, you could go in and read the menu. Some had micro-documentaries – brief interviews – inside. Some had a time knob – you could see historical pictures of the building. And much more.
>
> 'Aspen' shook people. Scales fell from eyes at conferences where it was demoed about what computers could do, about what videodisk could be, about how *un-authored* a creative work could become.[29]

This new mode of communication, a living map, dramatizes the necessity for Joyce's having X-rayed language and transformed the architectonics of poetry, as well as the necessity for other artists and writers to have developed such an extensive self-consciousness of the evolving integration of the arts and of the emerging centrality of the transformations implicit in electro-mechanical technology.

6

Beyond Media

Marshall McLuhan used to be fond of talking about people's everyday unawareness of the environment in which they lived by pointing out how a fish is not aware of the water in which it is swimming. In his writings, he specifically applied this image to the information age, for the information environment could become so all-pervasive that it became invisible. Unfortunately this comforting image is far from reality, since most of us readily experience information overload in a social setting where information is not only all-pervasive, but all-obtrusive. Yet there is a way in which McLuhan's fish story still holds. For while people are negatively aware from time to time of what they perceive to be a glut of information in their life-world, on a continuing basis they often find themselves unable to retain a conscious awareness of this all-pervasive presence. Consequently, people frequently find it impossible to deal rationally or critically with this aspect of their social and cultural environment.

Since the media's contribution to the creation of this all-pervasive milieu is largely unconscious, McLuhan's writings dramatized the importance of the effect of *any* medium on how and what people communicate.[1] 'Concern with *effect* rather than *meaning* is a basic change of our electric times; for effect involves the total situation, and not a single level of information movement.'[2] Consequently, in 1964, McLuhan proclaimed that 'the medium is the message.' A little more than twenty-five years afterwards, it is now necessary to revise that famous aphorism, since today the microprocessor is *the* medium, and so *the micro is the message.*

All media that have developed since the birth of print have tended towards the goal of a more and more all-inclusive medium. The recent coining of the term *info-tainment* reflects a world where it is again possible for leisure and knowledge to coexist simultaneously in the same human act; or at least where this will be an opportunity open to all those who desire it. Therefore, since the micro is the message and that message is popularizing electronic networks, virtual reality, and cyberspace, there is every reason now to grasp what modern artists and poets have been saying for many decades: all sensory information forms one complex, far-ranging semiotic system – the human communication system!

The micro opens worlds of time and space by interlinking with telecommunications networks, so that it provides the individual who uses it with access to masses of information, including readily available access to all the resources of the entire communication spectrum: sounds, images, gestures, simulated movement, and languages; and now through computerized multimedia; computer graphics, computer animation, sound synthesization, and desktop publishing. A post–mass-mediated world is emerging in which it is relatively meaningless to speak of media, for all media are becoming *the* medium of the microprocessor. Users are placed directly in the centre of the drama of communication, in which language becomes one central, but subordinate, aspect of the continuum of communication through which we exchange thoughts, feelings, and emotions.

Modernist poetic practice developed in reciprocity with those social and technological movements that engendered this trend towards the micro as medium. The vision of early contemporary artists transcended the then current limitations of thinking about the arts or about technologies of communications in terms of media. Intermedia, multimedia, and mixed media gradually became 'buzz' words for talking about 'expanded cinema,' marriages of art and technology, and automated poetry – genres not limited by pre-existing conceptions of language and media (or, perhaps better, *mixed forms)*. The popularity of *McLuhanism* (confirmed by how McLuhan's name generated a word in many world languages, such as English, French, and Japanese) is an index to how important this interaction really is.

In *Understanding Media* McLuhan was aware that he had used the term 'media' as a cliché to establish it as an archetype to signify all processes of communication and exchange that governed the broadest interactions between people and things and between people and their bio-social life-worlds. Although McLuhan adapted his concept of media from the work of his Canadian colleague Harold Innis, Innis had used 'media' as an inclusive term to cover:

1. the material basis of what is communicated (e.g., stone, papyrus, newsprint);
2. the production and/or distribution mechanism within which this material is realized (manuscripts, books, radio programs, moving pictures);

3. the nature of that which is actually disseminated; the matter or its means of distribution (the daily newspaper, the book, a broadcast, a cable transmission, film distribution, video-cassette, papyri, stone tablet, or oral telling of tales);
4. the community of interest which generated and/or controlled the distribution of that which is carried (the scribes, the legislators, the poets, the press, the broad-casters, the advertisers, the professional writers, and the directors and producers).

In his books, Innis adhered to the gradually evolving practice within the social sciences, government, industry, and society itself which encouraged using the term to embrace all of these various senses with all of its attendant ambivalence.

McLuhan did nothing to clarify this ambivalence. He exploited it by using the term 'media' to encompass all the ways in which people in the action of transferring or exchanging information, knowledge, attitudes, and states of feeling could be described as communicating interactively – intrapersonally, with their environment, or with others individually and collectively, either through direct personal contact or remotely across time and space. In doing this, he built upon the early work of Bateson, who with Jürgen Ruesch in *Communication: The Social Matrix of Psychiatry* (1951) had outlined a cybernetic and systems-oriented, trans-disciplinary approach to the study of human communication considered as a concept inclusive of all communicative action from intrapersonal to cultural communication across time and space.[3]

McLuhan and, through his propagation of Innis's work, Innis are relevant chiefly because of the importance McLuhan's writings had in situating media as a fundamental concept in communication theory, the history of communication, and public awareness of communication technologies. Midway through the twentieth century (1948), Innis published three books which have been described as a 'cartography of communication.' The first of these, his *Empire and Communication*, mapped out a history of communication in relation to a history of the physical media used for communicating.[4] McLuhan, who initially became interested in communication, culture, and technology independently of Innis, shared Innis's concern with media and the history of communication.

Communication scholars are indirectly indebted through McLuhan to those modern critics, artists, and poets who are still developing theories about the relation of gesture and oral and written language to human communication. McLuhan's earliest interest in problems of orality and literacy, predating his developing interest in communication after 1950, emerged from his study of contemporary art and literature, Elizabethan literature, and the history of the trivium (grammar, logic, and rhetoric). He developed an early interest in orality, literacy, and gesture from two major sources: his reading of Joyce, whose interest in orality, literacy, gesture, and Jousse's gestural theory of language and communication predated Milman Parry's research; and his own study of the history of the trivium for his doctoral thesis, which predated the publication of Eric Havelock's writings on the oral world of ancient Greece.[5]

While McLuhan's prominence has declined and his contributions continue to be not overtly acknowledged by most academics, his description of how media themselves transmit messages beyond whatever they contain or carry has provided a major legacy of unexamined assumptions which he has bequeathed to all those who have subsequently examined questions about contemporary communication and technology. In particular areas, he is still regarded as an important figure; for example: groups of AI or VR researchers such as those involved in the Media Lab at MIT, where Negroponte and his colleagues still speak of McLuhan as the inspiring prophet of the telematic age; in Joshua Meyrowitz's *No Sense of Place* and subsequent studies on television;[6] or among the artists, writers, and cognitive and computer scientists associated with *Wired*. He also is a significant, but largely unacknowledged, presence who still affects the agenda of cultural studies, mass media studies, communication policy, and most communication theory, for his ideas permeated popular and intellectual discourse concerning communication during the 1960s and early 1970s, when McLuhanism became for a brief period (1965–75) a worldwide institution contributing to the establishment of new interdisciplinary studies involving communication, culture, and technology.

The very trademark of communication in the 1990s – the microprocessor as symbol – challenges some of McLuhan's ideas, even though micros are a species of a conceptual genre with which McLuhan's thought has been most closely identified: media. Implicit in both Innis's and McLuhan's writings is a message that the development of the concept of media in its contemporary sense is a specific product of the mass age. In entitling his first *essai concrète*[7] or 'mixed media book' *The Medium Is the Massage* (message + massage + mass age), McLuhan humorously contemplates his own most quoted epigram, for implicit in the tendency of communication technology to develop at a rapidly moving rate of change has been the demystification of the concept of media and the unmasking of its ambivalence.

Earlier, during a moment of fanciful McLuhanizing, it was suggested that for the present moment the micro is the message and, therefore, the *medium* is the micro. Television, as videotext, is one obvious content of this new medium. The micro as chip and processor is the metamorphosis of media. The only features of the world of speech that are not yet immediately open to development in the micro are the full re-creation of features of actual physical presence: touch, smell, taste. There is no reason to believe that such possibilities will not emerge in the future through combinations of genetic engineering with our current synthesis of computers and telecommunications (which might be designated *compunications*, in preference to telematics or informatics, since such a term would underline the union of the numerate and the literate with the full potential range of human communication that has resulted from the marriage of computers and communication devices). Already today compunications holds out the promise of vital, fully enhanced synaesthesia.

What such speculative McLuhanitic flights suggest is that McLuhan himself originally led us Beyond Media: that *Understanding Media* in retrospect might have been entitled 'Undoing Media.' This is not mere semantic game-playing. There are real problems in the term 'media' as it has been used in the twentieth century. As Williams's *Keywords* points out, seventeenth-century writers used *medium* in the sense of an intervening or intermediate agency, as in Bacon or Burton's *Anatomy of Melancholy* (1621): 'To the Sight, three things are required, the Object, the Organ and the Medium.'[8] Williams then continues to explicate and criticize contemporary usage of 'media': 'There has probably been a convergence of three senses: (i) the old general sense of an intervening or intermediate agency or substance; (ii) the conscious technical sense, as in the distinction between print and sound and vision as *media*; (iii) the specialized capitalist sense, in which a newspaper or broadcasting service – something that exists or can be planned – is seen as a *medium* for something else, such as advertising ... especially in thinking about language, this idea of a *medium* has been dispensed with; thus language is not a *medium* but a primary practice.'[9]

While Williams is not precisely correct in ruling out a definition of medium which includes language (since many theorists still include speech and writing as media), in other respects the convergence he speaks about is key to why discussions of media so easily lead to confusion. An additional complication arises from our world having now moved into an era of post–mass-mediated communication,[10] which is also characterized by the appearance of more and more inclusive media and more complex individual choices concerning access to media, so that it is meaningful to say that society is moving beyond media (that is, beyond finding the term 'media' useful for the description of all modes of communication). In fact, it could be said that communication has always been moving beyond media, as McLuhan himself suggests in *From Cliché to Archetype* (1970), where he investigates the role of cliché in generating and retrieving archetypes, which he defines as 'old clichés' that are 'retrieved awareness or consciousness.'[11] In the posthumous *Laws of Media*, the so-called laws are actually 'observations on the operation of human artefacts,' and human artefacts are 'extensions of the physical human body or mind.'[12]

Bateson, who substantially influenced McLuhan at the time he co-founded *Explorations* with Carpenter in 1953, developed an ecology of mind (or ideas) as a monistic theory of communication based on cybernetics, systems theory, and evolutionary concepts. Bateson's theories are far from a media-oriented approach to communication, although they tend towards describing an integrated system of communication for the entire biosphere. His work classifies communication into modes of communication rather than speficic media. In spite of the awareness that has developed in human sciences and in the arts that it would be preferable to speak about modes of communication rather than media, now when it is crucial to go beyond media to make sense of evolving communications technology, many researchers, policy makers, and the public still surprisingly hypostasize media when they talk about communication

Beyond media? Obviously part of the intent is to query, extend, and reinterpret the work of McLuhan and his precursor, Innis, and challenge the problematic usage of media in academic discussions about communication. Print and broadcasting in the technical sense should, therefore, be more strictly designated as material *forms* and sign systems. In developing their theories of media, both Innis and McLuhan demonstrate an awareness of the ambivalence of the term and implicitly conceive of each historically crucial medium as a moment of technological transformation or metamorphosis. This is why McLuhan can speak of an immediately preceding medium becoming the content of a succeeding one.

A medium then is identifiable as such, while it is a dominant factor in the socio-political sphere, as radio was from the sinking of the *Titanic* to the Second World War. Later, radio and film, while still continuing partly to operate independently, become, in McLuhan's sense, the content of TV. Being good Romantics, Innis and McLuhan were primarily interested in moments of transition or transformation. They both structured grand historical narratives about such moments, bracketing in the process the detailed searching out of slow, gradual change and complex interaction between social, economic, political, cultural, and material factors that must be taken into account in the future within any genuinely detailed history of media (e.g., Elizabeth Eisenstein's history of printing; Carolyn Marvin's history of the telephone in *When Old Technologies Were New*).[13]

From Innis's analysis, it is clear that he considered key moments of transition to arise at times such as the period just prior to the emergence of writing and the decline of the oral tradition in Athens, when a relative democracy emerged accompanied by an increase in cultural diversity. This archetypal model is adapted from Parry's and Havelock's writings concerning the transition from speech (or orality) to writing (or literacy) in ancient Greece.[14] Innis chooses to speak about speech and writing rather than orality and literacy, for he sees speech not merely as a medium but as a mode of being. Writing may appropriately be described as 'a technologization of the word,' or perhaps more precisely of speech, but for that very reason the conceptual opposition of orality to literacy undercuts the fact that Innis is interested in this dynamic moment as producing for a brief period more flexible and direct communication as opposed to more remote, codified, and mediated communication.

McLuhan adapts Innis's analysis, attributing to writing or literacy all of the characteristics of a Blakean vision of the original fall from grace. In McLuhan's writings, humanity 'falls' into writing, though naturally this fall is also metaphorically the discovery of the knowledge of good and evil. As an individual who had striven to model himself on the late eighteenth- and nineteenth-century 'man of letters,' McLuhan embraced the ambiguities of literacy striving to preserve the integrity of the age of print, while maintaining a theological and a Romantic commitment to orality. It is important to note that his book about the emergence of electric media is entitled *The Gutenberg Galaxy*, situating print culture and its prospects centre stage in the new electric age. In contradistinction to Derrida, McLuhan does not consistently argue that a primal 'writing' is actually the precondition of speech, though he does intuit this in his awareness of the primacy of tactility and the kinaesthetics of gesture.[15]

As a central classificatory concept in the study of communication theory, the term 'media' has often been more misleading than helpful. Whatever value there is in the work of Innis and McLuhan must reside in their ability to bring to our attention clusters of associated communication activities. For example, in Grecian times: the effect of the melding of the physicality of the oral tradition with the new authority of writing and its influence on the composition of the later dialogues of Plato; the emergence of a complex Alexandrian tradition of interpretation; enigmatic literature; libraries; encyclopaedias; the growth of gnosticism; and the subsequent political organization of Greece. A medium, then, should be treated as an interactive node, and as a mode of producing, transmitting, and/or distributing communication that has a formative power over how the everyday world evolves, but which is also modified by the priorities of that everyday world. Technics do not rigidly determine certain events; they interact with them, opening up various possibilities, amplifying programs, undermining resistance to change, and in the process being themselves transformed.

Writing is a practice – a practice for manuscript production, letter writing, and then print. With typing, an aspect of the practice of writing changes. Word processing (a major transformation of typing) is itself a practice, since it transforms as well as extends the activity of composition and it also reduces the gaps between writing, typesetting, and printing. But writing itself already is an 'ambivalent' conception, since it is both a practice and a material form and a system of signs, not just a medium. In his discussions of that important moment when writing emerges as the dominant form for intellectual intercourse in Greece, Innis, like McLuhan, often telescopes these differing implications of the term 'writing.'

While McLuhan has been sharply criticized for speaking about Innis's use of ambiguity, wordplay, and 'humour,' in actuality these attributions do quite aptly apply to an aspect of Innis's writing since the same ambivalence necessarily permeated Innis's terminology as McLuhan's: speech, writing, media, space, time, centre, and margin. Furthermore, the posthumous publication of Innis's notebooks, *The Idea File,* indicates that he used a modernist technique of composition through accretion of fragments that marks his rather discontinuous and slightly telegraphic expository style.[16] This compositional strategy is less radical, but similar, to McLuhan's. McLuhan's assemblages of fragments, with their radical use of discontinuity through juxtaposition, are permeated by the difficult shifts in terminology that this strategy permits. When McLuhan speaks of the opposite of the oral, sometimes he speaks of it as the written word (or printed word) and sometimes as writing; on occasion, writing can be construed as a pre-linguistic concept and other times as referring to the post-oral.

Using media and certain media-affiliated words as key terms can conceal the fundamental complexities inherent in the fact that human communication is constituted as a single interrelated expressive system utilizing a 'universe of interacting signs.' For it is through orchestrating these signs (which appeal to differing senses and utilize different modes of reproduction) that the process of communication discussed above occurs: a process in which people simultaneously use gestures, sounds, rhythms, images, demonstrations, speech, self-presentation, and settings in differing mixtures to shape their messages. Newer communication technologies have tended to become more and more inclusive of all of these potentialities, so that contemporary computer workstations are being designed to permit the simultaneous use of signs derived from all of the differing sensory capacities of the human person.

Technologies are creating other kinds of convergence as well. Ever since the introduction of visual, auditory, and audiovisual media, the means for production, reproduction, and transmission or distribution of knowledge and information have been converging. Tools of production, such as the computer, function also as tools of reproduction and transmission. Further, modes of communication converge, as in hypermedia. At the moment, we can only discern some of the potential for the future in fictional visions such as Gibson's *Count Zero* or *Neuromancer*, which, like McLuhan's work, interest researchers such as those at MIT's Media Lab, the University of Washington's HIT Lab, or VR researchers at the University of North Carolina. MIT's Aspen Movie Map, dating from the 1980s, is just one example of what such 'texts' are coming to be.[17]

Technologies are also opening up a limited potential for liberation. Jürgen Habermas has distinguished, on one hand, between the liberatory potential implicit within communication technologies and the production of cultural industries, and, on the other, the actual distortions projected through the way that the organization of technology (the 'technology of technologies') operates through the economic modelling of culture as a cultural industry: 'They [communication technologies] free communication processes from the provinciality of spatiotemporally restricted contexts and permit public spheres to emerge, through establishing abstract simultaneity of a virtually present network of communication contents far removed in space and time and through keeping messages available in manifold contexts. These media publics hierarchize and at the same time remove restrictions on the horizon of possible communication. The one aspect cannot be separated from the other – and therein lies their ambivalent potential.' Habermas's view is confirmed by communications research which allows for 'dimensions of reification in communicative everyday practice,' yet still finds that 'ideological messages miss their audience because the intended meaning is turned into its opposite under conditions of being received against a certain subcultural background,' and that 'even when they [the programs] take the trivial forms of popular entertainment, they may contain such critical messages as "popular culture as popular revenge."'[18]

The dialogic theory of the development of the novel explains how the intrusion of the languages of the 'people' within the official language (in this case, those of the 'cultural industry') contributes to democratization by carrying out just such critiques. Rabelais, whose function in the sixteenth century had substantial similarities with Joyce's today, provides a complex model of such a dialogical imagination. In his writings on Rabelais and in *The Dialogic Imagination* on the history of the novel, Bakhtin has shown how the development of novelistic prose came about through the interplay of different languages that correlate with the practice of differing social groups within the same society.

In Faulkner's novels, the languages of the Afro-American community and of the poor white community infiltrated and subverted the language of the aristocratic South. In Joyce's *Ulysses*, the adopted language of European immigrants (for Bloom is Hungarian), the Anglo-Irish English dialects of Ireland, and the 'official' English of the English administration interact. As Bakhtin's discussion of the heteroglot dialogic imagination of the everyday forms of communication suggests and Joyce's practice confirms, ambivalence is the very lifeblood of everyday discourse, and when this is crafted from actual encounters with those everyday forms the resulting vision will lead to effects like 'popular culture as popular revenge.'

This 'discourse' occurs not only between levels of language, but between all levels of communication – in film, television, the visual arts, and music. Throughout the sphere of communicative interaction, there is an extensive ongoing social conversation which cannot easily be controlled by the management of media. In fact, even at a generic level, the so-called media themselves become undermined by the constant invasion of materials from other genres: novel into film, comic book into animated TV, rock concert into video, radio drama into TV and book, and SF into TV. The wide-ranging dialogue of signs is paralleled by a dialogue of genres. Fellini carries on a complex dialogue with his own films and with those of other film-makers; Godard consciously adopts the style of an essayist, which not only makes complex reference to the cultural productions of a mass society or the traditions of film-making, but is itself, as he has indicated, a kind of journalism.[19]

In most of his films, Kubrick derives the action from a book that contributes to the film strategies of complication, amplification, and critique. Normally he uses the book as a foil that the film counterpoints and supplements, as in *Dr Strangelove, 2001,* or *A Clockwork Orange*. He also develops a dialogue with the extended context of the book, which involves a multifarious range of socio-political and cultural factors, and constructs an audiovisual dialogue within his film that includes a complex range of other socio-political and cultural productions (such as the Coca-Cola machine and the Army recruiting advertising and propaganda in *Dr Strangelove*).

A Clockwork Orange, which uses Burgess's novel for its basic plot, utilizes a complex range of sensory effects to explore the problem of violence, its embeddedness in human experience, the dangers of treating it solely as a problem to be medicalized and psychologized through treatment, and the very presence of violence within the treatment itself. Objects of art (e.g., Beethoven's 'Ode to Joy') and other films (e.g., Leni Riefenstahl's Nazi-sponsored *Triumph of the Will,* which will be discussed later) become intertwined with the violence, so that behavioural treatment removes the creative play of the hero's mind-body as well as his antisocial attitudes, while the violent environment which engendered him is still left in place. The language of Burgess's novel and Kubrick's film, like that of Joyce's *Wake,* which partly inspired Burgess, contributes to breaking up the distorted discourse of a world artificially protecting itself against violence through sophisticated control of minds and bodies, which nevertheless fails to rectify the fundamental forces which produce the violent behaviour.

A society existing on the provision of pseudo-security and pseudo-satisfaction of needs symbolically reveals its real bankruptcy of values in the way it maintains the public spaces and public life for a majority of its citizens – thus generating that violence which leads to violent mob behaviour among the youth of the less privileged. Kubrick's film treats the social life-world as a fragile and distorting artificial assemblage, which is constantly threatened by the frustration of the new generations which such a society produces. Youths wander erratically, traversing the surfaces of the world and periodically undertaking to break it apart. In the process, they create their language, which is a stylized rhetorical response to the even more stylized and paralysed visual, verbal, and auditory rhetoric which bombards them: garish colours, packaged sound, artificial comfort, and the creation of a pseudo-hierarchized class structure. The dramatic violence perpetrated by the gangs on suburbanized professionals, who themselves live in a similarly stylized world of the rhetoric of fashion, design, and pseudo-control, recapitulates the mechanistic life of all those involved.

Rather than using a specific book, *Full Metal Jacket* uses as a foil a whole cluster of contemporary war films ranging from *Apocalypse Now* to *Platoon. Full Metal Jacket* then becomes a complex critique of war films, military life, the totalistic technologization of life, and the forms of disorientation, madness, and estrangement they produce. The portrait of the dehumanized and dehumanizing drill sergeant, whose function is to inculcate recruits with an ideology supported by unquestioning enthusiasm, concludes with his brutal and insane slaughter by one of his own recruits whom he has victimized. Entering into and inviting complex dialogic interaction, *Full Metal Jacket* entails a strong element of black comedy operating within the satiric form of the film, which is chiefly achieved through the compositional construction of film form, especially its success in creating 'artificial' (or virtual) realities. The prime dark joke of this order is the fact that the drill sergeant is 'played' (or better, 'presented' *not* 'represented') by an actual U.S. marine drill sergeant.

Any individual work of everyday cultural production can create a complex world of its own, as well as engaging in a complex intertextual relationship with other productions within the same mode of production or different ones. *Star Trek,* conceived originally as a space opera, has since become a complex cluster of works and events which have created a dialogue with SF productions and other cultural forms. The remarkable popularity of this series of programs, produced until his death by Gene Roddenberry, is marked by the fact that it is one of those rare TV series whose initial replays on television were virtually forced onto the network by the fans. *Star Trek* now typifies a successful TV series developed with the conscious intention of reaching a potentially massive audience. It has engendered an entire industry, which provides an ongoing context within which it continues to thrive and develop.

Star Trek is exemplary in having created a cult which has spawned a series of films, a completely new sequel in the TV series *The Next Generation,* and a spin-off series from that sequel, *Deep Space Nine,* as well as fan clubs, a series of original *Star Trek* and *Next Generation* SF novels (not just books which re-present originally televised stories), and a wide variety of other *Star Trek* materials, a small selection of which includes such items as: *The Making of Star Trek,* by Gene Roddenberry and Stephen Whitfield; *The Trouble with Tribbles* (the birth, sale, and final production of one episode), by David Gerrold, the writer who provided the story and then the script for that episode; *The World of Star Trek;* a *Star Trek Concordance; The Star Trek Technical Fleet Manual* (which was actually used by the actors of the various episodes); and *The Star Trek Blueprints* (which are the general plans of the *USS Enterprise*). Now similar *Next Generation* materials are appearing: for example, *Star Trek: The Next Generation Companion;* and *Star Trek: The Next Generation Technical Manual.*

Besides all these TV, film, and print productions, there are illustrated comic books, collections of fan materials, fan clubs, and discussion groups by e-mail on Internet and other networks. It is also possible to buy *Star Trek*–inspired toys, costumes, and other paraphernalia. The papers, especially the specialty press, have kept up a fairly constant flow of material about *Star Trek* and its major participants such as William Shatner and Leonard Nimoy as well as its sequel. A phenomenon such as *Star Trek* exists not just as a television presentation, but as part of a complex, total context of words, images, actions, and ideas. The *Star Trek* complex comes to create a universe of its own. Talk about it rapidly becomes a necessary part of what it is!

Star Trek is one of those popular culture phenomena, like the Oz books in children's literature, *E.T.* in film, or Elvis Presley, the Beatles, and Madonna in music, which respond to, develop, and exploit fundamental desires by shaping a regime of signs within which that desire proliferates. It is a phenomenon of the order of *Superman, Batman, Marvel Comics, Doonesbury, Bloom County,* or *Garfield.* Yet not only these individual items, but the entire sphere of cultural productions – the arts, TV, advertising, the press, etc. – provide a regime of signs within which a continuous complex dialogue takes place. The dynamics of this dialogue generate transverse paths that permit the participant to interrelate randomly different levels of social discourse.

All these cultural phenomena form part of a complex ongoing everyday discourse by which the material evolved through the multitude of interpenetrating modes of communication and expression is disseminated throughout society as a whole. The effect is discontinuous; flows of meaning are constantly broken down and reassembled. The movement is an unpredictable zigzag which is related to a perpetual becoming. This process involves a multitude of social machines spanning most of society's major activities and institutions. Yet in this process, the gradual accretion of a regime of signs which form a multi-modal critical vocabulary intensifies self-consciousness about communication for ever-increasing sectors of society.

Finnegans Wake, with its machinic assembling of the flotsam and jetsam of an emerging international culture, embraces all contemporary and historical modes of communication, cultural production, and social machinery, including such differing modes of communication as gesture language, drum language, manuscripts, newspapers, radio, TV, films, telephones, telegraphs, and possible future combinations of them; and such differing genres as liturgy, drama, broadsides, poems, cartoons, comics, operas, and oral tales. Dada, aleatory music, and happenings provide other strategies for embracing assemblies of some of this flotsam and jetsam.

The growing recognition during the last thirty years that the borderlines between the so-called higher and lower arts are either not very definite or completely non-existent breaks down the definitions of genres, just as the evolution of communication has broken down the definition of media. This is reflected in the interest manifested in terms such as 'paraliterature' or 'hyper-aesthetic.' Baudrillard speaks of a hyper-real world lost in an ecstasy of communication where simulacra are the reality; Eco, of hyper-reality;

Arthur Kroker of the hyper-aesthetic; Marc Angenot, of paraliterature. All these terms have somewhat different implications; but all of them speak of a realm that is above or beyond literature, poetry, and the arts – or so far beyond as to undermine the original basis of the distinction between the 'fine arts and the popular arts.'

I have used the term 'paraliterature' to suggest the continuity of poetry from oral and printed literature to the complex productions of film, television, and computerized media. (In the early 1970s at a symposium in Montreal with Marc Angenot and Darko Suvin, I coined the terms 'para-aesthetic' and 'parapoetic' to more properly cover the full spectrum of cultural production, but I now use 'multimedia paraliterature,' since the term has become familiar. It appears to have been used first in France in 1970.) Paraliterature here is used in a sense of 'beyond literature.' It also embraces the contextual proliferation which is naturally part of the multimedia-paraliterature complex: productions in different modalities (e.g., comics, animated films, talking books, etc.), fanzines, hot lines, clubs, etc. For a discussion of the whole thrust of going 'beyond media,' which this really implies, see Donald Theall and Joan Theall, 'Marshall McLuhan and James Joyce: Beyond Media.' To put the problem in context, note the ambivalence of the prefix 'para-.' The *Oxford English Dictionary* contains the following entry: 'As a preposition Greek *para-* had the sense "by the side of, beside" whence "alongside of, by, past, beyond, etc." In composition it had the same senses, with such cognate adverbial ones as "to one side, amiss, faulty, irregular, distorted, wrong," also expressing subsidiary relations, alteration, perversion, stimulation.'

This introduction is followed by two sets of entries, one from natural history and anatomy, where 'para-' is used in the sense 'beside or near or standing in some subsidiary relation to,' and another from chemistry, where it is placed before the name of substances which are supposed to have been modifications of other substances, such as 'paraformaldehyde.' This is interesting, for many of the examples of the various genres that might be classified as paraliterary appear to be parallel to the literary (e.g., utopian science fiction or Le Guin's *The Dispossessed*); some may go beyond literature in their explorations, such as some of the work of Brian Aldiss or Stanislaw Lem, though most of the examples are generally seen to be subsidiary to literature or literature gone amiss, such as novels by Dean Koontz; some finally may seem almost to be outside of literature (beyond the bounds) like Heinlein's *Stranger in a Strange Land* (beyond because of the peculiar breakdown between imagination and execution that marks a work of this kind). Similar examples could be brought forth from other genres, even comic strips. *Pogo*, it is arguable, and, in a different way, *Krazy Kat* are flirting with the activity of extending the bounds of literature and certainly are strong examples of paraliterature, though naturally such conceptions when related to literature will certainly still strike many as a 'perversion' or 'distortion' of a serious kind. It is important, however, that many scholars of literature, art, and cultural theory now suddenly want to give a name to such activities, which I have here labelled multimedia paraliterature and/or para-artistic or parapoetic, in order to make them part of a continuum of cultural production along with the literary and the traditionally artistic. It is also crucial that we be aware that these and similar names which seem to be gaining popularity are susceptible of rather ambivalent interpretations, making them attractive to different people for different reasons.

Using such a term as 'paraliterature' or 'parapoetic' exemplifies what Burke describes as a verbal strategy. This particular strategy is first used for getting a production, which has not yet been legitimated, recognized as worthy of inclusion within the categories of the 'grand' theory of genre and is later used to disassemble and reassemble the boundaries between the traditional fine arts and other modes of creative expression. If 'parapoetic' is adopted as a term, it indicates an awareness that all those products classed as popular culture (popular film, TV series, advertising, print and electronic journalism, and a wide range of other modes of info-tainment) have come to assume an importance within the everyday communication processes that makes them as socially significant, if not even more so, than the traditional arts. As an index to the radical cultural changes of the twentieth century, *Finnegans Wake* betokens the way that these forms have been and are becoming more extensively intermeshed with the modes of expression and communication of contemporary artistic practice.

While in the past paraliterary or parapoetic works have usually tended to become models for, or at the least, components of later literary or artistic works, the speed with which this adaptation now occurs has contributed to breaking down the effectiveness of the socially imposed distinction between the arts and the 'para-arts.' Even though historically parapoetic forms have always played a role in creative activity (e.g., the broadsheet in Shakespeare; the carnival in Rabelais; Grub Street pamphleteering in Pope; ritual and folklore in the masques; popular story-telling in Chaucer and Boccaccio), this contemporary self-consciousness concerning the parapoetic is indicative of the radical change produced through the capabilities of the new technological modes of communication.

Umberto Eco, as one of the leaders in the development of semiotics, has actively explored a wide variety of parapoetic modes, ranging from *Marvel Comics* to detective stories, from cult movies to Disneyland, and from Hollywood castles (e.g., William Randolph Hearst's real castle in San Simeon, California, which appears as Xanadu in *Citizen Kane*) to International expositions (e.g., Expo '67).[20] Eco favours using the prefix 'hyper-' and speaking of this as the realm of hyper-reality, a usage that carries the implications of 'excess' and simulacra, for the difficulty with such verbal strategies as 'paraliterary' or 'para-aesthetic' is that they very rapidly conceal the continuum between the so-called exemplars of what is 'para-' (Stephen King novels, the *Lucy* show, *Jaws, Miami Vice, Blondie,* Earle Stanley Gardner mysteries, or Frederik Pohl space stories) and what has already become literature or video or cinematic art (such as Le Guin, Chandler, *2001, The Next Generation,* and Ernie Kovacs). Concealing this continuum creates considerable confusion when criticism speaks of genres such as science fiction, detective stories, SF films, or satiric TV, for these classifications lump together works that many might consider to be differentiated forms that should be prefixed by 'para-' and works that could genuinely be considered as 'poetry' or art (SF includes the work of Dean Koontz and Norman Corwin as much as it includes the more poetic work of Philip Dick and Stanislaw Lem). Yet both the 'para-' and the literary, poetic, or artistic clearly can be members of the same genres. The situation is still more complex since many works participate in a multiplicity of genres: the Western has been identified as a pastoral, and Arthur Clarke and *Star Trek* as archetypal and psychological (Jungian).

What is really at stake here is that the artificial distinctions, generically oriented and socially reinforced, have been demystified. 'Poetic' or 'artistic' have either become value terms distinguishing the well-made from the more poorly conceived and crafted; or they have become terms indicating a more exclusive commitment on the part of the 'maker' to the maximization of the potential of the symbolic act. Just as it has been possible to speak of going beyond media, it is also necessary to speak of going beyond such distinctions as the 'fine arts,' the 'popular arts,' and 'kitsch.' This rise of interest in the parapoetic underlines the increasing importance of viewing the production of sensuous and verbal signs as part of a whole symbol-making process which is involved in people making sense of their world.

But whether regarded as above or beyond, the dismantling of the universe of traditionally privileged delineations of the poetic, the artistic, or the literary, invoking modes that had previously been thought of as a lack or absence of the poetic – the supposedly sub-poetic world of popular culture – is a crucial corollary to a more complex understanding of communication with its assemblage of transverse networks and a full appreciation of the individual creativity involved in any communicative act. As interpreters like Eco have demonstrated, an immediate implication of this dismantling is that research into communication must necessarily involve what has been considered literature and art as well as what has been considered popular culture or mass media productions. Burke's theoretical principle, articulated in the 1930s, that the poetic, including literature and all other arts, has a vital function to serve in exploring and understanding the phenomena of communication takes on renewed significance.

Can the poetic really be part of an ecology of communication – an ecology of sense? One of the questions raised by this dismantling is whether the dissolution of the boundaries between high art, popular art, and kitsch represents a descent of society into a maelstrom of metamorphoses, a labyrinth of simulacra, from which there is no escape and no desire for escape. The recent emergence of the parapoetic has often been viewed as a symptom of a world where the simulacra of the regime of signs have become reality, so that reality itself has become a simulacrum in which people are reduced to living in a world where all is imaginary, for the imaginary is the reality. In one of his later works, Baudrillard described the current state of people in the contemporary world as being lost in an 'ecstasy of communication.' This is a world which has passed beyond the negative dialectic of Marcuse's perspective of a critical function for the arts,[21] since 'the simulacra have passed from the second order to the third, from the dialectic of alienation to the giddiness of transparency.'[22]

In *Simulations* and *The Ecstasy of Communication*, Baudrillard goes beyond Bataille's philosophy of excess in which communication necessarily implies loss of self, for he argues that the dialectic of transgression – of the negative – which Bataille elaborated has now metamorphosed: 'Today the scene and the mirror have given way to a screen and a network. There is no longer any transcendence or depth, but only the immanent surface of operations unfolding, the smooth and functional surface of communication.'[23] Baudrillard playfully adopts McLuhan's concept of the former medium becoming the content of the new one, so that the mirror and scene of drama and poetry have been absorbed by the form of the monitor and the telecommunications net. 'The medium is the message' then defines the state in which the simulacra reign supreme and all people participate in the ecstasy of communication.

Baudrillard is the obverse of McLuhan, for he accepts the vision of the McLuhanistic world and metamorphoses it into a pessimistic vision rather than an optimistic one. Still his vision is that of a world where the medium is the message, and the micro is the latest and possibly quintessential medium. Baudrillard overlooks that the actual way in which the micro functions in this role is radically different from the way the medium does. The micro is an instrument of bits – of logic and elements which become signs. The micro restores the legitimacy of the entire complex of human communication as the privileged mode instead of only language. Baudrillard appears to regard this as the epitome of the hyper-real world, which eliminates the possibility of a transcendence based on language.

Over half a century ago, Burke's critical theory stressed drama as the nucleus of a theory which would illuminate the relationship of the arts, popular life, and everyday expression within the evolution of human communication. He grounded such a theory in the social critique that the artistic process provides. Dell Hymes, as an ethnolinguist, adapted this theoretical approach to the development of socio-linguistics and an ethnology of communication.[24] At some points, Burke's discourse closely addresses the same issues as Baudrillard's more recent theories on mirrors, simulacra, the political economy of the sign, and the ecstasy of communication. The problem that Baudrillard explores as the 'ecstasy of communication,' which can be related to Bataille's theories of communication and loss of self, is examined by Burke with respect to the role of 'phatic communion' in understanding communication. To begin to explore the problems raised by the relation of phatic communion and communication and to investigate the question of the poetic as an ecology of sense, it is essential to consider the relationship of polysemy to communication and the crucial relationship between polysemy and drama as a prolegomenon to understanding human communication among individuals and within their societies.

7

The Comic, Wit, and Laughter: Dramatic Engineering of Communication

The poetic engineers of the first half of this century realized that the poetic work, whatever its mode or modes of expression, is an assemblage of bits. Klee's pedagogical notes and his magic squares clearly exemplify a self-consciousness about painting as an assemblage of bits, just as Schönberg's recrafting of music through the new twelve-tone scale does. The modernist artistic work not only reflects the relativity of time and space; it often reflects the quantum principles of uncertainty and of the wave-particle duality of discrete particles that produce light.

Joyce consciously identifies his work with quantum theory when in the first part of the *Wake* he has his prime critic, Wyndham Lewis, mockingly declare, 'Talis is a word often abused by many passims (I am working out a quantum theory about it for it is really most tantumising state of affairs) ... (149.34–6). Later this same critic charges that the author is confusing the 'tality' or 'suchness' of a thing (its substance) with the 'quality' of a thing (its role in the transitory): 'may be said to equate the *qualis* equivalent with the older socalled *talis* on *talis* one just as quantly as in the hyperchemical economantarchy the tantum ergons irruminate the quantum urge so that eggs is to whey as whay is to zeed' (167.4–8). Joyce does not idly associate his book with theories about quanta and light, for the book concludes as dawn breaks with a debate about the nature of light that Joyce in a letter suggested is 'the defense and the indictment of the book itself.[1]'

That debate between the Archdruid Balkelly (Bishop Berkeley) and Saint Patrick (a contemporary realist), which involves Newton's and Helmholtz's theories of light, is resolved by an argument that if you can only see a specific colour reflected from a body and not the rest of the spectrum which remains absorbed within it, observing other bodies or the same body under different conditions will reveal other bands of the spectrum. So in the language of the book, if you cannot grasp the whole in any single reading, multiple readings will provide opportunities within which you will observe other aspects of the text. The two debaters, the Archdruid, a sage, and Patrick, a saint, are described as governed by complementarity – '(for beingtime monkblinkers timeblinged completamentarily ...' – and by uncertainty, for they are 'murkblankered in their neutrolysis between the possible viriditude of the sager and the probable eruberuption of the saint)' (612.21–3).

This playful developing of theories of light and of verbal communication in the critic's attack and the climactic debate between saint and sage clearly situates the book as propounding a theory of intersubjective communication and language. The linguistic equivalent of the quantum effect can only be achieved through the molding of a multiple series of styles and figures of speech that take advantage of the fact that language is always 'ambiviolent,' being governed by an uncertainty principle and consequently operating much as light itself does: one moment being a flow, the next a series of particulate entities. Joyce underlines this relation of atom to the diachronic and synchronic aspects of the word when in the TV scene the 'charge of the light barricade' by the 'missledhropes' with their 'bitts bugtwug their teffs' leads to the catastrophic 'abnihilisation of the etym' (349.10–11, 353.22).

The pun is a node of semantic energy where the material realization of the pun (e.g., in print) is an entity which radiates and disseminates signification. Therefore, it is a major example of the process of the 'abnihilisation of the etym.' It breaks down the apparently unified bits of sound and sense, of phonology and orthography, to break the flow of meaning. Punning is a species of that multiplexity which is a predominant characteristic of Carroll's *Alice* books (doubleness, etc.), where there is an unresolved pendular movement between sense and apparent nonsense. Samuel Johnson suggested that Shakespeare would lose the world for a quibble. Shakespeare's fondness for his quibbles demonstrates the natural dramatic intensity implicit within puns and the way that they can become a heuristic strategy that functions by dislocating the flow of meaning and enforcing a 'dialogue' or 'debate' between conflicting meanings.

Joyce countered one critic of his puns with the rejoinder: 'Yes, some of them are trivial and some of them are quadrivial.'[2] While 'trivial' refers partly to trivia, indicating trifles or insignificant scraps of information, it also refers to 'of the *trivium*,' the medieval name for those studies which concern the basic arts of communication and language (grammar, logic, and rhetoric). The pun is a constant reminder of the complexity, multiplexity, and ambivalence of communication. It is a microcosm of communication, where transverse connections create competing lines of sense. The apparently humble pun, as typifying all the different ways of achieving effects of polysemy, is crucial to understanding the relationships between polysemy, drama, and communication, for it is essentially comic and the prime exemplum of wit. It is both the archetypal and the cliché aspects which typify wit – the generic name for various comic strategies that involve ambiguity, ambivalence, or doubleness, essentially multiplexity of meaning. In a way, the pun encapsulates within itself the system of codes, transgressions, deviations from expectations, conflicts, and dynamic resolutions which any adequately complex act of communication requires.

Although details of traditional classifications of the pun and its subcategories have differed, the sense of doubleness or multiplexity and disparity of meaning characteristic of puns and portmanteau words is always present, along with the resulting effect of fascination and allure.[3] The pun reaches across the gap between the code within which one speaks/writes and the actual act of speaking/writing itself. This is why it has a structural side (embedded in the phonological and/or orthographic) and a semantic side (manifesting the polysemic nature of the word). Freud's 'Wit and the Unconscious' uses the pun as an exemplar of *Witz* and other devices which bring to the surface of discourse the ability to communicate about something which had previously been incommunicable.[4]

Joyce brings the dark humour of the puns in *Hamlet* into conjunction with the death motifs of the *Wake* to make a statement concerning the reading of a manuscript, which is his book, every book, and all symbolic actions:

> ... the lubricitous conjugation of the last with the first: the gipsy mating of a grand stylish gravedigging with secondbest buns (an interpolation: these munchables occur only in the Bootherbrowth family of MSS., Bb — Cod IV, Pap II, Brek XI, Lun III, Dinn XVII, Sup XXX, Fullup M D C X C: the scholiast has hungrily misheard a deadman's toller as a muffinbell): the four shortened ampersands under which we can glypse at and feel for ourselves across all those rushyears the warm soft short pants of the quick-scribbler ... (*FW*121.30–122.3)

Joyce deliberately intertwines his work with that of Shakespeare through the intricate interplay of alpha (first) and omega (last), for the last page of Joyce's book, concluding 'A way a lone a last a loved a long the' (628.15–16), links back to the first, which begins 'riverrun, past Eve and Adam's, from swerve of shore to bend of bay, brings us by a commodius vicus of recirculation back to Howth Castle and Environs' (1.1–3).

Motifs of death and sex, of black humour, of reading manuscripts and masticating bits, tie together Shakespeare and Joyce, while 'grand stylish gravedigging' and 'secondbest buns' specifically echo the 'Scylla and Charybdis' episode of Joyce's *Ulysses*, which takes place in the National Library, where Stephen analyses *Hamlet* and bases his biographical interpretation of Shakespeare's works on the poet's having willed Ann Hathaway his second-best bed. Food and sex references also abound in this passage from the *Wake*: 'buns', 'munchables', 'Bootherbrowth', 'Pap', 'Brek', 'Lun', 'Dinn', 'Sup', 'Fullup', 'hungrily', and 'muffin'; 'lubricitous' introduces lewdness and the slipperiness associated with the general transgressiveness of the passage, the 'secondbest buns.' 'Dielectrick' (322.31) interplay is established between eating, reading, living, dying, writing, acting, conjugating, lewdly and chastely. In the process, 'secondbest buns' (i.e., puns as well as bums and buns) mark the role of verbal play in the 'prepossessing drauma' (115.32). Joyce uses these motifs to construct his fictional night world, with its satire on the vanities of communication: 'Vannisas Vanistatums! And for a night of thoughtsendyures and a day. As Great Shapesphere puns it. In effect, I remumble, from the yules gone by, purr lil murrerof myhind, so she used indeed' (295.2–6).

Through the study of Joyce, who performed and pre-formed symbolic acts which unexpectedly tease communication theory out of social praxis through the use of the pun and other polysemic devices, Burke developed a heuristic technique that he called 'joycing.' 'Joycing' became a major aspect of Burke's dramatistic theory of communication by providing strategies for utilizing expanded rhetorical figures in understanding social dynamics. 'To joyce' is deliberately and systematically to tease out verbal transformations by using series of puns, near puns, and verbal twists for heuristic purposes.[5] Although Burke's term has never been widely adopted, it still reveals Joyce's significant role in the contemporary revolution in the understanding of language and communication.

Joyce must be regarded as one of the central figures in developing a contemporary understanding of that poetic ecology of communication which is an ecology of sense – his 'reading' of his 'writing' of his 'reading' – a 'raiding' (482.32) of the symbolic acts of his world, 'whirled without end' (582.20). The 'decentred' universe discovered or uncovered by Derrida in the 1960s is implicit in the way Joyce and Burke teased out transformations of symbolic action to explore communication and society. As Burke explains, 'to joyce' does not 'prove anything,' does not effect closure; it is a 'heuristic' leading 'to critical hunches' or to the 'discounting' of critical hunches. 'Joycing' is achieved through the use of conscious intellectual techniques to explore the social unconscious, the Freudian unconscious, and possibly the collective unconscious. Therefore, this strategy is not limited to working with materials produced by the individual psychoanalytic unconscious through the examination of verbal slips, jokes, and dream material generated during therapeutic dialogue.

Through such 'joycing,' the *Wake* satirizes psychiatric discourse and the psychiatric 'confession' as voyeuristic, paternalistic, and libidinous: '... we grisly old Sykos who have done our unsmiling bit on 'alices, when they were yung and easily freudened, in the penumbra of the procuring room and what oracular comepression we have had to apply to them!' (115.21–4). 'Joycing' frees all words and language, signs and symbols, from apparent univocity and reveals those elusive, surreptitious, and cloacal aspects of the social world which people are not otherwise prepared to confront directly. While this opens up the possibility of an interminable discourse of signs signifying other signs, Burke, following Joyce, does not see this free play freeing artists and critics from problems of significance and value. Like Baudrillard, Burke can envision an uncontrolled ecstasy of communication and he utilizes strategies which decentre and demystify; but he speaks about them as 'debunking,' 'perspective by incongruity,' or 'stealing back and forth of symbols.' Within these strategies, he develops a rhetorical exploration of motives using 'pivotal terms' to 'track down symbols' such as 'being driven into a corner,' 'secular prayer,' 'casuistic stretching,' 'discounting,' or 'bureaucratization of the imaginative.' Unlike Baudrillard he does not see the modern world as inevitably ensnared in an ecstasy of communication, for his acceptance of the chaos of life and the multiplicity, indeterminacy, and relativity of his world still involves moral action and reconstruction.

In Burke's first major work, *Permanence and Change*, which he originally thought of entitling 'A Treatise on Communication,' there is a discussion of the difference between humour and the grotesque. Humour, which ultimately favours the status quo, 'flatters us by confirming as well as destroying.' In contrast, Burke supplies such examples of the grotesque as Socrates (in opposition to Plato), Spengler, Marx's 'formula of class consciousness,' and the 'humorous,' but far from laughable, death-bed scenes of Mann's *The Magic Mountain*. He concludes that 'humour tends to be conservative, the grotesque tends to be revolutionary.'[6] Dreams and dreamart, he suggests, which are permeated with grotesqueries that result from their logical distortion, foster transgression by countering common sense with the nonsense of dream.

Joyce is the contemporary master of the grotesque for, as Burke points out,

... blasting apart the verbal atoms of meaning, and out of the ruins making new elements synthetically, [he] has produced our most striking instances of modern linguistic gargoyles. He has accomplished the feat of dreaming most laxly while most awake. In the portmanteau words of his latest manner [this was written in 1933 while fragments of the future *Finnegans Wake* were appearing under the title *Work in Progress*], he seems to be attempting to include within the span of one man's work an etymological destiny which may generally take place in the course of many centuries, as the rigidities of education gradually yield to the natural demand that the language of practical utility and the language of 'unconscious' utility be brought closer together and their present duality be mitigated.[7]

Burke clearly perceives the motivation of Joyce's disassembling and reassembling, blasting apart to make new elements out of the ruins. Joyce's reconstructive process rises out of a destructive process, for he describes the action of the *Wake* as receiving 'dialytically separated elements of precedent decomposition for the verypetpurpose of subsequent recombination' (614.33–5). This reconstructive process is associated with cycles of falling and rising: 'Phall if you but will, rise you must: and none so soon either shall the pharce for the nunce come to a setdown secular phoenish' (4.15–17).[8] Yet this is surely a very ambivalent reconstructive process, for it implies that the phallic cycle of rising and falling leads to a 'secular' finish – to a secular resurrection (phoenix), a secular ending (finish), and a secular language (Finnish). A Joycean pattern of ricorso is central to Burkean dramatism, where, if one form of communication or social organization burns out, through the operation of the comic perspective and its grotesqueries, a new form will be produced from its wreckage.

In *Finnegans Wake* the hero's 'wake' is a comic grotesque 'celebration' which establishes new, revivified communication and socialization processes through the ritual festivities:

... all murdering Irish, amok and amak, out of their boom companions in paunchjab and dogril and pammel and gougerotty, after plenty of his fresh stout and his good balls of malt, not to forget his oels a'mona nor his beers o'ryely, sopped down by his pani's annagolorum (at Kennedy's kiln she kned her dough, back of her bake for me, buns!) socializing and communicanting in the deification of his members, for to nobble or salvage their herobit of him ... (498.19–23).

The *renewal* of communication in the passing of what has been is implicit in the process involved in 'waking' a body. But here the new communion – 'pani's annagolorum,' suggesting *Panis Angelicus*, the eucharist or communion, the bread of angels – is the emergence of socialism and communism, and yet it is also the age-old coming to terms with the dirt of the body and the world within which it exists: 'with a hogo, fluorescent of his swathings, round him, like the cummulium of scents in an italian warehouse' (498.29–30). 'Communicating' and eating are again woven together in the pun on the *panis* as bread, 'buns' (see above p. 111).

Henri Bergson, who in 1911 first introduced *wit* as an important contemporary theoretic concept for the arts, suggested that it is 'a certain *dramatic* way of thinking. Instead of treating his ideas as mere symbols, the wit sees them, he hears them and, above all, makes them converse with one another like persons. He puts them on the stage, and himself, to some extent into the bargain ... In every wit there is something of a poet – just as in every good reader there is the making of an actor.'[9] While Bergson limits wit to the purely intellectual aspect of the poet's activity – for to become a wit, the poet must resolve to be 'no longer a poet in feeling' – he achieves the important insight that wit is seeing things *sub specie theatri*, which makes *ideas converse with one another as if they were persons.*

Joyce relates the concept of *sub specie theatri* with the *Wake* in the 'Feenichts Playhouse' episode (II,1) of the dream action in which the children's play hour is presented as a cinematic drama 'wordloosed over seven seas crowdblast in cellelleneteutoslavzendlatinsoundscript' (219.28–9). This theatro-cinematic interpretation of the Earwicker children playing in the nursery consists of 'jests, jokes, jigs and jorums for the Wake lent from the properties of the late cemented Mr T.M. Finnegan R.I.C.' (221.26). This mimetic, mini-dramatic microcosm of the *Wake* concludes with the invocation:

Loud, heap miserics upon us yet entwine our arts with laughters low!
Ha he hi ho hu.
Mummum. (259.7–10)

The 'entwining [and also en-twin-ning][10] laughters' make the *Wake*'s dream a dramatic conversation of 'feelful thinkamalinks,' for Joyce moves beyond Bergson by relating the activity of wit to complexes of intellect and feeling. The cinematic absorbs the dramatic, for the yet broader principle of montage, inclusive of film and other complex forms, is central to the dream structure, which permits the fusion of characters interacting with complexes of thought and feeling to be a 'conversing': 'But, the monthage stick in the melmelode jawr, I am (twintomine) all thees thing' (223.8–9).

While 'wit' as a term derives from the realm of poetry and drama, 'montage' as a term comes from the realm of engineering: *montage* (F.) = 'the assembling and erection of mechanical equipment.' The term 'montage' was appropriated by the Berlin Dada group for their application of collage to photography and later extended into film theory by Eisenstein.[11] By now this term has been extended to include virtually any type of compilation in any art, such as music or dance, or any medium, such as advertising or the arrangement of the front page of the newspaper.[12] Montage emphasizes the conception of the work of art or communication as a mechanical assemblage – the product of a poetic or communication machine.

Eisenstein understood montage as assemblage when he spoke about its architectural or architectonic function; Godard in his journalistic film essays carries this sense of the director as engineer near to one of its limits. As an exploration in light, colour, movement, and form, Brakhage's nearly five-hour silent film *The Art of Vision* is unadulterated assemblage, which he conceived as a twentieth-century visual equivalent to Bach's *Art of the Fugue* and as a new lexicon for cinema equivalent to Schönberg's twelve-tone scale. Fellini concludes *8½* on a complex SF set, in which he brings together all the characters in a symbolic celebration of the director as engineer. The developing possibilities for integration among the arts has permitted individual productions to include more and more differing media by utilizing the technical strategies of wit: collage, montage, and juxtaposition. Today the micro as medium is a master of montage.

Benjamin, analysing Brecht's drama and dramatic theories, perceived the importance of montage for this new era: 'the ability to capture the infinite, sudden or subterranean connections of dissimilars, as the major constitutive principle of the artistic imagination in an age of technology.'[13] Benjamin understood how the forms of Brecht's 'epic theatre' arose in response to 'new technical forms of film and radio,' which favoured a discontinuous and episodic shaping of the dramatic action that paralleled the radio audience's new-found freedom of selection by turning a switch on, off, or to a different item that the phonograph and radio had made possible.[14] In what now has become one of his best-known essays, Benjamin traced the impact of the new era of 'technological reproducibility' on the work of art. In film, he argues 'the audience's identification with the actor is really an identification with the camera. Consequently, the audience takes the position of the camera; its approach is that of testing.'[15]

Montage operates throughout Brecht's works as a corollary to his doctrine of cognitive estrangement (or alienation principle) by encouraging probing and exploration; for, as Benjamin explains, Brecht realized that film has enriched our perception with particular methods of disjunction – for example,

Freudian verbal slips, dreams, or *Witz* (jokes and humour). Here the comic principle is associated with 'negative dialectic' and with art as critique, bringing to fruition a potential that is predominant in neo-classical satire – for example, in Pope's wordplay, which is enhanced by the structure of his closed heroic couplets:

> Know then thyself, presume not God to scan
> The proper study of mankind is man.

Such encapsulations of a logical square produce forms of negation; what Joyce later describes as sense 'involted' in the 'zeroic couplet.'

In the closing decades of this century, Baudrillard has associated *Witz* (and the principle of montage) in 'our contemporary world of hyper-reality' as being the 'fatal strategy' for language (communication) in which the historical workings of the negative are replaced by the workings of reduplication: 'In the *Witz*, language makes itself more imbecile than it really is; it escapes its own dialectic and concatenation of meaning only to hurl itself into a process of delirious contiguity, into instantaneousness, into pure contiguity, into pure "objectality." The evil demon of language resides in its capacity to become object, where one expects a subject and meaning. The *Witz* is the predestination of language to become nonsense from the instant it is caught in its own devices. In this there is passion, *a passion of the object*, which could very well make us rediscover an aesthetic force of the world, beyond peripeteia and subjective passions.'[16] This particular contemporary interpretation of wit describes a principal part of the substructure of our society of simulation, where the products of art and media have become the only reality: for reality itself has become a product of cultural industry.

These dynamic processes of wit are actually machinic[17] processes that play across the signifying surface of all modes of communication, not just verbal language. Pope, for example, found wit in his grotto and his gardens; while Joyce or Borges discover wit across the entire regime of signs, regardless of any particular medium or mode of expression. Baudrillard's suggestion that the play of wit could 'make us rediscover an aesthetic force of the world' describes what has always taken place in the activity of wit, which is now occurring even more intensely within such genres as advertising, journalism, TV soaps, and comics, within which there is a constant unintended, inadvertent questioning, challenging, and undermining of the very homogenizing agenda of mass media.

Although Baudrillard challenges Barthes's critique of sales promotion in *Mythologies*, when we examine Barthes's essay 'The New Citroen' (as a typical example), his 'poetic' unmaskings actually use the principle of montage (or wit) to reveal the hidden assumptions, elusiveness, and perverseness of the social unconscious. In 'The New Citroen,' Barthes leads up to a conclusion with the encounter between the driver and the car. 'One is obviously turning from an alchemy of speed to a relish in driving.'[18] Exhibited for promotion to the public, the DS19 is 'explored with an intense, amorous studiousness.' This is that moment which brings about new approaches to car production that have resulted in the BMW, the Lexus, the Porsche, and other driver-oriented and driver-caressing vehicles. Relish in driving rather than pure speed results in a tactile relationship with the object: 'the moment when visual wonder is about to receive the reasoned assault of touch (for touch is the most demystifying of all senses, unlike sight, which is the most magical). The bodywork, the lines of union are touched, the upholstery palpated, the seats tried, the doors caressed, the cushions fondled; before the wheel one pretends to drive with one's whole body. The object here is totally prostituted, appropriated: originating from the heaven of *Metropolis*, the Goddess is in a quarter of an hour mediatized, actualizing through this exorcism the very essence of petit-bourgeois advancement.'[19] Barthes's essay on the Citroen involves a conception of the car which is simultaneously spiritual and material, erotic and technological.

The DS is a Gothic cathedral of modernity, a Goddess, a gift of heaven, yet it is a physical object marked by relationship ('junction') rather than substance, a magical lightness and an 'exaltation' of glass, and ultimately 'the very essence of petit-bourgeois advancement.' But 'the *Déesse* is *first and foremost*, a new *Nautillus*' – an object from another universe. This does not derive from a narratology, but a presentation; a *showing* not a *saying*.[20] Here driver and car unite in a new way that Eco relates to Italian actresses', and McLuhan to Brigitte Bardot's, driving barefoot to feel at one with the car, to humanize the drive through a sense of feeling in touch.[21] Driver, car, the industry of 'Metropolis,' and the spirit of modernity interact in a moment of drama. This permits semioclasm, simultaneously endorsing in part, while decisively exposing, this new mythology. Barthes's essay is an exercise in *esprit* deliberately constructing a dialogue with the object, which reveals and questions the social function of the object and the processes which it represents. It is a mini-drama of communication through the senses; an extended multiplexity in which the DS19 involves visual-verbal wit.

The startling effect of demonstrating the poetic drama of the front page of a newspaper, a comic book, or an advertisement in McLuhan's *The Mechanical Bride* (1952) is a semioclastic revelation just as Barthes's treatment of the DS19 is. In writings permeated by pun, paradox, proverb, and aphorism, Barthes, McLuhan, and later Eco reveal the essential importance of ambivalent polysemy to drama. The complex doubling and redoubling in communication, which involves the poetic work, the symbol, the sign, and the metaphor is symbolized in the seductiveness of verbal play, play with sense. Wit is not merely a Freudian strategy for fooling the censorial functions or revealing the psychiatric unconscious, since Rabelais and Joyce clearly demonstrate how it is the essential mark of the liberating function of the dialogic imagination. The principle of montage has persisted beyond modernism (if, indeed, living 'in modernity's wake,'[22] we really are postmodern), for montage pervades the twentieth-century spectrum of the arts: literature, the visual arts, film, music, dance, architecture, and computer art. Montage naturally situates artistic activity in a comic perspective, which does not limit it since tragedy is itself embraced within the dark laughter of the comic vision. Laughter is the intellectualizing and distancing factor in contemporary poetic. Laughter involves an intimate relationship between wit (or montage) and the dramatic, and this reveals why it is embedded in the inherently dramatic nature of the pun itself. Bataille's writings have explored and expounded this deep ambivalence of laughter within which passes a 'current of intense communication.' Symbolic actions (words, books, monuments, laughter) are 'paths of contagion' by which the 'passage of warmth or light from one person to another' (which signifies 'to live') occurs.[23] The principle that releases the comic response, a 'slight error – a slipping – [which] spills out joy in the realm of laughter' is fundamental to Bataille's theory of communication:

> *When I expressed the principle of the* slipping *– like a law presiding at* communication *– I believed myself to have reached the depth ...*
>
> *I imagine today not being mistaken. I gave account at last of the* comedy *– which* tragedy *is – and vice versa. I affirmed at the same time that existence is* communication *– that all representation of life, of being, and generally of 'anything,' is to be reconsidered from this point of view.*
>
> *The crimes – and as a result the puzzles – which I recounted were clearly defined. They were laughter and sacrifice ...*[24]

The children's cinematic drama that takes place in the 'Feenichts Playhouse' (i.e., both the playhouse of the night of the fairies and the Phoenix Playhouse), a title which refers to the error of the fortunate fall, a slipping. This drama entitled the 'Mime of Nick, Mick and the Maggies,' which concludes with an invocation affirming 'the comedy which tragedy is' ('Loud, heap miseries upon us yet entwine our arts with laughters low!'

[*FW*259.7–8]), is presented for the 'Mummum' (ALP, their mother), who is 'The annamation of evabusies, the livlianess of her laughings, such as a plurity of belles' (*FW*568.4–5) even though her 'laughings' are 'laughtears' (15.9).

The problem presented by popular media is their tendency to transform 'laughtears' into entertainment or 'info-tainment' by institutionalizing the doubling and neutering it.[25] Strategies of decontextualization are a necessary move to counteract the neutering produced by the 'info-tainment' industries; but info-tainment again reabsorbs the decontextualization. Regardless, there are always gaps, breaks, which permit the exploration and exposing of info-tainment. McLuhan's aphorism concerning the 'pun' as breakthrough by breakdown pinpoints how confronting the neutered comedy of info-tainment with new disjunctions and differences can produce a renewed laughter. When artistic and poetic activity are so engaged, they produce an ecological effect as a spin-off, for the prime poetic directive is to operate within these breaks or gaps and use them to open up a liberatory making sense of our life-world. In developing the strategy used in *Mythologies*, which he calls *semioclasm*, Barthes discovers the relation between the ecology of sense and the poetic implosion.

Today the exponentially assimilative character of the cultural industries seems to make this process increasingly problematic. A prime example is that aspect of TV broadcasting that Williams in *Television: Technology and Cultural Form* described as the 'flow' of programming.[26] In the daily TV news, for example, there often are sharp discontinuities which occur between advertising, program announcements, and station presentation and the specific, often tragic, content of the news itself. Examples of how flows produce such effects include the dark comedy generated by news concerning South African apartheid preceded by a sex scandal involving an evangelical leader and followed by a shampoo ad; the black humour of placing an Esso ad between items on the greenhouse effect and the environmental pollution from an oil spill; or the barely hidden satire of inserting cries for a war against drugs between an Ibuprofen ad hawking the pharmacological road to happiness and the announcement of major job lay-offs in a local factory. If the flow is broken by splitting up and recompounding it, the audience will potentially be released from the blinkered context in which it passively views the program and its surrounding messages. A world suddenly appears where black humour, tragic comedy, dark laughter, and demonic satire emerge as the radically disparate moments of the surface of communication events that are now transversely related.

McLuhan widely disseminated Mallarmé's and Joyce's discoveries about the potential comic energy contained in the shape of the daily newspaper: the layout, the arrangement, the headlines, the placement of stories. McLuhan and Barthes demonstrate how decontexualization of communication objects and events (such as advertising, news photographs, publicity events, mass performances, sports events, political promotion, the physiognomy of an actress, a caricature, cartoon, or comic) would reveal their inherent contradictions through bringing to the surface the implicit comic processes resulting from the principles by which they were constructed: discontinuity, randomness, attention to the flow of the surface of a story, the propagandistic intent, the commercially oriented concern of the layout. The poetic principle of the arts as the 'god of all machineries' (*FW*253.33) could then magnify such decontextualization through recontextualization ('mortisection,' splitting up followed by 'vivisuture,' recompounding or reassembling), providing a potential path of liberation from the unidimensionality of the media's neutering of the effect of the previous 'mortisection' and 'vivisuture.' Still, the original potential for such unmasking is within the rhetorical structure of the pseudo-poetic activity of the media themselves.

Habermas, as noted in the preceding chapter, has pointed out the ambivalent nature of the mass media, for they are 'generalized forms of communication,' 'a specialization of linguistic processes of consensus formation that remains dependent on recourse to the resources of the lifeworld background.'[27] The phenomenon that he identifies in which the 'centralizing tendency' of these 'generalized forms of communication' is offset by 'a counterweight of emancipatory potential built into communication structures themselves' is particularly enhanced by the 'artistic,' dramatic, or rhetorical processes encouraged by communication. Their very modes of presentation invite a mode of transverse communication as much as they encourage a continuous submission to the flow of the message. The 'contradictions' that constantly arise from advertising, where the obvious effects intended often carry along with them unanticipated effects, are frequently contrary to the type of persuasion which the ad is directed towards achieving. The contradictions of the 'mechanical bride' period of Western advertising (1930s to the 1950s) contributed to sexual emancipation, feminist critique, the distrust of the myths of mechanization (only to be supplemented by the myth of electrification), and the questioning of the limits of rugged individualism.

McLuhan's early sensitivity to this process in *The Mechanical Bride* did not emerge *ex nihilo*; it resulted from his awareness of the attention which writers, poets, and artists had been giving to the exploration of the growing importance of communication and the increasing commodification of society, with its accompanying increase in advertising and promotion. Decades of artistic analysis preceded the appearance of hermeneutic and semiotic analyses of advertising and also preceded the more social science – oriented empiric and quantified analyses. Calder's playfulness with Medaglia d'Oro coffee tins, Dada's exposure of the preoccupation with publicity in bourgeois society (e.g., Richter's films), or Joyce's analyses of mass culture and technology precede by years McLuhan's interpretive analyses, Barthes's semiological demystification, or Eco's semiotic critiques.

The argument is not that such art is sufficient as a critique, but that it opens up language and communication to enable the possibility of a deeper critique to occur. The poetic activity is a necessary, but not sufficient, condition for relatively undistorted, liberated communication. People naturally take from advertising a meaningful way of semantically packaging their emotions and dreams, which is a shadowy mimicry of intense poetic creativity. Yet as McLuhan's and Barthes's work with advertising showed, there is still poetic potential within the ads themselves; an emancipatory potential that is deeply distorted and concealed within the advertising activity. The release of this process only occurs to the extent that people are able to go beyond the limits of advertising and 'read' it critically in the broader social context.

The dramatic dialogue that comes about from reading beyond (or outside) of the media's limited intent is for most people the first stage in the development of a more radical questioning. Such dialogue with media is enhanced by popular satiric modes. *Mad* magazine sustained a satiric contemplation of Madison Avenue, which popularized Dada and surrealistic critique. Lenny Bruce's satire, which questioned institutions, conventions, media manipulation, and the prejudices of everyday life, provides an intensely effective example of such probing. Cinematic sequences, such as Anita Ekberg materializing out of her erotic image on a billboard advertising milk in *The Temptation of Dr Antonio* (Fellini's contribution to *Boccaccio '70*), counterpoint purity and naughtiness, revealing the assumptions implicit in such commercial promotion. Denys Arcand's *The Decline of the American Empire,* while situated in Quebec, provides an extended questioning of a media culture which has nearly totally engulfed an entire continent.

These activities move beyond info-tainment by providing the means to question that concept. They emancipate by emancipating entertainment from amusement. In examples such as Kubrick's *A Clockwork Orange* or Fellini's *La Dolce Vita,* poetic crafting provides works which are themselves major critiques of the cultural industry. It can be objected (and legitimately so) that as much as they might suggest a solution to the problem, they are still part of it; nevertheless, it is within the very gap created by such a situation that the emancipatory potential arises. Laughter (and dark laughter) must exist in a world of ambivalence and be part of a dialogue. To prevent the dialogue from coming about because it is not purely rational is to truncate the production of the very energy needed to engender extensive questioning of such cultural activity. Openness is essential to undistorted communication. Censorship of any kind can only run counter to evolving further in the direction of the 'ideal communication situation.'

Above and beyond the communication event itself is the 'talk' about the communication event which it necessarily engenders. 'Talk' is enclosed in quotes since it is meant to include all forms of communication in which dialogue about communication takes place. The nature of all cultural productions involves precisely this type of dialogic conversation. The major media success of *Star Trek* is an example of a production which contributes to the comforting effect of info-tainment, and yet also engenders potentially strong questioning. Here is a media event which generates conferences, fan clubs, magazine discussions, books about the event, interactive on-line electronic conferences by computer network, etc. While the original *Star Trek* may itself have initially promoted the mentality of the 'new frontier,' the 'wagon train to the stars,' hierarchical military power structures, and the doctrine of 'manifest destiny,' it contradictorily encased this in suggestions of freedom, brotherhood (though only secondarily sisterhood), and ecological awareness which led to the complex questioning that arose from the subsequent 'talk.' That 'talk' involves satiric and comic critique and the bringing forth of the implicit comic disorientation hidden within these communication events. Its most recent metamorphosis, *The Next Generation*, confirms this by its adaptability to changing social attitudes in which there is a greater value placed upon cooperation through dialogue, a lesser value placed on conflict and violence, and a greater one on peaceful coexistence and multiculturalism. Yet the fundamental thrusts of exploration, glory in technology and organization, and the wisdom of hierarchy still persist in this atmosphere of freedom, social equality, human sensitivity, and ecological concern. There is a poetic but also rhetorical manipulativeness which permits its growth and metamorphoses, yet confines and limits its emancipatory potential. Its poetic qualities, however, undermine significantly its specific ideology, partly because they create a doubleness of vision.

Poetic and rhetorical interventions often play an important role in the development of modes of expression for exploring changing problems and attitudes, as exemplified in *Dr Strangelove*, for its comic vision ultimately made a significant contribution to the escalation of critical awareness concerning the nuclear threat and to the critique of the military complex and thus remotely to the protests against the war in Vietnam. The core of such comic development of modes of expression can be found in wordplay. The metaplastic function of puns and portmanteau words is like a mini-drama condensed to a moment of time. They remind us of the proximity of the oral and the written, speech and vision, in the process of communication.

As a nexus where oral and written meet, the verbal pun and portmanteau underline the proximity of sign, gesture, and language, since the gap that is created in the phonetic continuity of the flow of speech calls attention to the nature of the word as a sign and since the tension between the oral and written focuses on the word as if it were an object, converting the word into a sort of gesture which makes it the crux of the tensions between orality, literacy, and gesture. Ong's seminal studies of literacy and orality can be traced to his early attempt to understand the nature of pun and wit, for one of his earliest articles is on wit in medieval Latin hymnody.[28] The pun and portmanteau go beyond the clash of modes of expression, for they also break up meaning by breaking apart sense. Here they can intervene in the social world, for they break apart the expected flows of life and force a questioning and searching of the resulting fragments. Rather than just opening up a language for the individual unconscious, they have the more important effect of opening up that which is unconscious in the social life-world.

Puns and portmanteaus that operate within non-verbal modes of expression function in a similar way and exist at a nexus where the ambivalence of modes surfaces. Picasso's playing with mirrors and the fragmentation of the human body is a case in point, for it depends on a multiplicity of ways of seeing what is presumably the same, while simultaneously undercutting the perspectival frame of traditional painting. Puns which work within mixed modes of expression (sound, vision, movement, and word in an audiovisual medium) provide some of the most intense breakdowns. Many years ago, Arthur Koestler selected the pun as symbolic of the entire movement of human creativity. If you can see the world in a grain of sand, you can see the drama of the poetic in a pun.

Drama insists on the juxtaposition of multiple actions. This juxtaposition necessarily underlies the way we read a story, see a play, watch a film, or listen to a poem. The primary meaning of jest (or gest) is that of a legend or a tale, from which it derives its later meaning of a joke. It shares a common root with gesture, both being related to performance. What drama provides to poetics is a model from which to derive an interpretive language which not only includes a rhetoric but ways of speaking about action, passion, time, space, gesture, movement, sign, and symbol. Polysemic devices, particularly pun and portmanteau, address the immediate material basis of communication, while drama addresses that ritual aspect of communication which is spoken about by using terms such as 'participation' and 'communion.' But since drama also involves communication as transmission and interaction, for interaction occurs both between characters within the frame of the drama itself and between the actors and the audience during an actual performance, the pun and portmanteau create mini-dramas in which words and groups of words are the actors who address one another and also in which the reading practices necessitated by the complex wit bring about an interaction between the interacting words and the reader (audience).

In the contemporary world, the pun and portmanteau have increased in complexity, comprehensiveness, and quantity. The arena of the comic, the grotesque, and the carnivalesque has shifted and expanded through the artistic use of the wide variety of newly enhanced technological modes of communication that culminate in various multi-media modes of computer art, (e.g., VR), where carnivalesque jokes and language abound, even though in many quarters this is causing extensive negative reaction. Both within the operation of the official modes of communication and through alternative communication, a nomadic instinct increasingly expresses itself, moving in zigzag fashion across the lines of energy (power, force) of the official world. This performs a fundamentally ecological function in communication, which, when most effective, can only operate initially by being officially unpopular because it is threatening to the status quo. The modality through which this happens is dramatic: that conversation of ideas which Bergson found in wild, machinic, Rabelaisian-like laughter. But it is rooted simultaneously in the material and social foundations of communication, for verbal polysemy is 'a soundsense sympol' (*FW*612.29); while the complex multiplexity of overlapping modes of expression is 'communicanting' (498.21) through 'thc cummulium of scents' (498.30).

8

A Dramatic Theory of Communication

Joyce, who began writing *Finnegans Wake* in 1922, explored the shift from gesture and oral speech to writing and print and then the return to a new technologically mediated gesture, speech, and writing shortly before Milman Parry propounded his theories (published in 1928) concerning Homer's poetry as the corporate production of bards schooled in oral recitation. The *Wake* was completed well before Goody, Havelock, Innis, McLuhan, or Ong thought about such questions or their relevance to contemporary problems of communication. Imagine Joyce in the 1920s asking the question: what is the role of the book in a culture that has discovered photography, phonography, radio, film, television, telegraph, cable, and telephone and that has developed newspapers, magazines, advertising, Hollywood, and sales promotion? What people have read, they will now see transformed into film and television; everyday life will appear in greater detail and a more up-to-date fashion in the press, on radio, and in television than in books, speeches, or lectures. A new Renaissance of oral reading of poetry will emerge from the phonograph's ability to reproduce sound; a phenomenon reinforced by radio and by the sound film.

One historical factor which necessitates the exploration of all these questions is that in the act of the writing or reading of any particular book, writing and speech always confront one another. Pursuing an inquiry about Joyce and the techno-culture of the twentieth century immediately opens up the question of the role of language itself in the world of communication as well as of the role of writing in creating the concept of textuality and, therefore, of extended textuality; that is, the viewing of any meaningful action as textual.

In an important article, Paul Ricoeur provides theoretical foundations which indicate how any meaningful action can be considered as a text.[1] This way of setting up the problem suggests that the text provides a fundamental paradigm applicable to all communicative or interactive behaviour, and meaningful action is just one of many phenomena which it helps us understand. This is what Barthes does when he writes about the mythology of the Citroen, a wrestling match, or the Eiffel Tower. In the early 1930s, while small sections of *Work in Progress* (the working title of *Finnegans Wake*) were being published from time to time, Burke, inspired by Joyce's 'revolution of the word,' had already anticipated Ricoeur when he began developing a somewhat different approach to meaningful action, which he christened *dramatism*. Once drama is adopted as a model for communication, it opens up the possibility for using a 'dramatic vocabulary' as a strategy for speaking about communication. To speak about the symbolic or communicative act as dramatic, Burke devised his *pentad*[2] of dramatic terms: act, agent, agency, scene, and purpose. All communicative acts, he argued, could be described by a combination of any two terms from this set, since a specific pair dominated the description of each particular act. But, by adopting such a poetic-dramatic analysis, he further introduced an entire interpretive lexicon of related terms: narrative, motive, character, role, myth, theme, spectacle, and the like. The resulting theory of communication, art, and literature as symbolic action interlinks the phenomena described by the five terms of his *pentad* with the phenomena described by all these other terms.

Burke integrates all these terms within his theory – he does not use them as mere synonyms or individual metaphors. To examine the radical nature of communication, he supplements these historically derived terms with his own terminology, which is designed to describe a variety of actions and communicative strategies through such phrases as 'perspective by incongruity,' 'discounting,' 'attitude of attitudes,' and a number of others. His dramatistic method is developed as a social critique which is closely related to the pervasive importance of the concepts of grammar, dialectic, and rhetoric in social interaction. This theory also treats meaningful action as a text, though in so doing its emphasis is on the primacy of the dramatic rather than on narrativity.

What is important about Burke's theory is not the *pentad* or the specific details of his methodology, but the identification of the roles of the language of poetics (aesthetics, artistic theory), the poetic product (film, happening, novel, visual assemblage, dance, etc.), and poetic technique in the understanding of communication and its relationship to social ecology. His insights preceded Barthes's, Eco's, or McLuhan's practice in employing the poetic essay to probe the multiplexities of a communication object or event, or in utilizing the poetic to enhance and intensify dialogue with everyday objects and events. While only Barthes's work parallels that of Burke in adopting a socio-politically conscious critique, all of these poetic essayists contributed to developing an understanding of the importance of poetic-dramatic action for communication theory, a contribution that has been continued by Baudrillard and some practitioners of cultural studies, and then has been further extended in the work of Deleuze and Guattari.

What Burke talks about as drama in his theory of symbolic action cannot be reduced to what has been discussed in the social sciences as dramaturgical action; for example, Goffman's theories of encounter and the presentation of the everyday self.[3] The dramaturgical, which is an application of dramatic structure to a model of social action, is only a limited aspect of dramatic action as developed in poetic theory. This is why the later Burke speaks instead of symbolic action as a consummatory activity. For dramatic action to provide a critique of symbolic action, various levels or types of action included within dramatic action must be identified: action with respect to aims or purposes (teleological); action with respect to norms (normative); meaningful interaction (communicative action, if in defining communication we apply the term to a process in which verbal interaction is primary); and dramaturgical action.

Dramatic action as the mode of experimentation with and exploration of human communication involves non-verbal forms, such as gestures, visual and auditory elements, and kinaesthetic rhythm. To allow for the 'application' of dramatic action in non-poetic modes of symbolic action, Burke calls his system 'dramatistic' rather than 'dramatic'; the dramatistic being derived from the dramatic and from the logological (from 'Logology,' as used by Burke in his works) core of dramatic action. He encountered difficulty when he developed dramatism as an essentially static, classificatory theory since, as his earliest writings suggest, his fundamental commitment to a philosophy of action should have involved his theory with processes of becoming.[4]

Burke describes the poetic motive as 'treating the act of symbol-using as an "unmotivated motive"' – the finding of an 'intrinsic satisfaction in the use of symbols simply for the sake of symbol-using.'[5] Poetic productions generate a participatory process that entails a becoming: becoming woman, becoming dog, becoming pine tree, becoming dawn, or, as Chaplin explores through gesture and mimicry in *Modern Times*, becoming machine.[6] In *Permanence and Change*, one of his earliest books, which preserves the spirit of its original title ('Treatise on Communication'),[7] Burke examined the proximity of the process of becoming with the rage to communicate, an inquiry that entails his pointing out that literature and the other arts are 'equipment for living.'[8] While a literary or artistic production constitutes an act (a poetic or dramatic action), that act is also a means (an instrument, an agency) for potentially improving the quality of life.'

Poetic activity, while being 'considered prior to all purpose,' is also an ecological process that enhances society's communicative capability. Whereas the symbolic act is created for its own intrinsic delight, paradoxically the participant discovers ways of understanding the universe of motivation and how motives are communicated: '... if we were trained, for generation after generation, from our first emergence out of infancy, and in ways ranging from the simplest to the most complex, depending upon our stage of development, to collaborate in spying upon ourselves with pious yet sportive fearfulness, and thus helping to free one another of the false ambitions that symbolism so readily encourages, we might yet contrive to keep from wholly ruining this handsome planet and its plenitude.'[9] The ultimate goal of poetic metaphor 'through its great stress on the communicative' is to produce 'a society in which the participant aspect of action attained its maximum expression ... [that] would emphasize certain important *civic* qualities' which are necessary to make our urban world a society which grants maximum expression to the participant aspect of action.[10]

The poetic work provides a way of intensifying, enhancing, and questioning symbolic action. In doing this, it utilizes the very elements within which symbolic action itself occurs, but by freeing them through expressive play it permits the participant (the consumer as co-producer) to follow the multitude of traces that emanate from the symbolic materials. The product of this operation can be as simple as a minimalist work of optical and spatial art, such as Flavin's light sculptures created from fluorescent tubes or incandescent bulbs; or it can be as complex as Kubrick's 'rewriting' of Burgess's novel in *A Clockwork Orange*. Flavin's artwork involving fluorescent lights and space appears to reverberate ironically against McLuhan's dictum that the electric light is the only medium which is its own message.[11]

Flavin's *green crossing green*, with its propensity for disorienting vision immediately after the viewer leaves the environment (the daylight, for example, will turn to rose immediately after one views such a work),[12] is a silent poem concerning the awareness of our perceptions, which also environmentally sensitizes us to problems of imbalances in our daily, everyday activities. Flavin rejects the rhetoric of light, which may consist of anything from a red light at an intersection to an elaborate neon display advertising Seagram's. He unconsciously criticizes the implications of such rhetoric by transforming it into purer light that speaks of light itself and its relations to space and environment, producing a work which creates a self-reflexive awareness about the environment in which one lives and has one's being.

Works like Flavin's highlight the sensuous, erotic implications of communication and expression. The consciousness of Eros generated by them critically explores such everyday phenomena as electric illumination that have normally concealed and still continue to conceal basic implications of their social function, which are now made manifest through such poetic transformation. It is not a question as to whether Flavin actually intends to achieve such effects, but rather that he does so precisely because he probes the everyday world that surrounds us. Such transformations of the everyday world should open up new possibilities for understanding and reshaping the social environment. Even such a limited engagement with our sensory system as Flavin's minimalist environments brings about a criticism that liberates objects from habitual, automatistic perception.

The poetic activity, as an area relatively free from the persuasive concern of strategic rhetoric, allows a direct engagement with symbolic action in a playful, exploratory, heuristically oriented way. This does not mean that the entire work is free from such persuasive concerns, *but* that, to the extent to which the poetic activity is in play, the poetic with its enigmatic revelation surmounts the persuasive and strategic concerns. It invites discussion, assessment, and understanding rather than closing them off – even in such an extreme case as the Nazi-sponsored propaganda film of the 1930s *The Triumph of the Will*, whose director undertook a commission that she knew to be essentially propagandistic. While the conscious intent of Leni Riefenstahl's film provided support to the Nazi regime, which was pursuing policies of catastrophic evil and barbarity, the very poetry of *The Triumph of the Will* reveals some of the contradictions within its political subject and subverts the strategic message to which its director was committed as a propagandist.

Riefenstahl's film provides various insights into the meaning of the 1934 Nuremberg rally of the Nazi party that have subsequently assisted in understanding how Hitler's program of the 'nationalization of the masses' through art and ritual seduced a large segment of the German public by conscious control and distortion of communication. While art can be distorted, or even may be deliberately designed, for the purpose of instrumental control of society, nevertheless, because of its necessary affiliation with the poetic motive, the artistic work insists on saying more and inviting more to be said than such deliberate distortion intends. While the intended propagandistic, ideological, or strategic message will still be effective in the short run, upon reflective consideration its poetic aspect will encourage interpretive unmaskings.

Fuzzy references to or allusive echoes of *The Triumph of the Will* have subsequently appeared in other films with vastly differing intentions: Kramer's *Judgement at Nuremberg*, Kubrick's *A Clockwork Orange*, and Makavejſv's *WR: Mysteries of the Organism*. Perhaps there is a still more fuzzy allusion to the eros of Riefenstahl's camera in Kubrick's photographing of U.S. Marine recruits on parade and in their barracks in his *Full Metal Jacket*? Rejection of the intentions and objectives of *The Triumph of the Will* is an important part of the world community's self-understanding of Nazi rhetoric and ritual that both contributes to and is deepened by understanding the rhetorical and ritualistic ploys of *Mein Kampf*. Benjamin implicitly refers to this particular moment of Nazi manipulation of aesthetics in the conclusion to his discussion on the power of the new arts of 'technological reproducibility,' just as Sigfried Kracauer, Theodor Adorno's close friend and one-time mentor, stressed its importance in his theory of film.[13] In 1941 Burke, in a lengthy analysis of *Mein Kampf*, which in 1990 he still considered to be one of his most successful interpretive essays, demonstrated the peculiar value of rhetorical analysis in exposing the motives of Hitler's program.

Dramatic or poetic communication today is an assemblage of assemblages manufactured by self-reflexive poetic engineers, for it is an 'unmotivated motive' governed by rhetorical and poetic construction. Barthes speaks of rhetoric as a machine, while explaining his decision to opt for Aristotle's view of it as a *technè rhétorikè*. Considering rhetoric to be a creative ordering, he sees its way of distributing its different parts as 'a great liana descending from stage to stage, sometimes splitting a generic element, sometimes collecting scattered parts.'[14] The image of the liana suggests a rhizome-like rather than an arboreal structure, thus avoiding the rigidity and hierarchization which had led to the death of rhetoric in the later eighteenth century. This liana or network is a '*montage*,' which he compares to Diderot's machine for making stockings: 'It can be seen as a single unique reasoning whose conclusion is the fabrication of the object ...' Textiles are put in, stockings come out: 'In the rhetorical machine, what one puts in at the beginning, barely emerging from a native aphasia, are the raw materials of reasoning, facts, a "subject"; what comes out at the end is a complete, structured discourse, fully armed for persuasion.'[15] Rhetoric and poetic are arts of assemblage. Historically, poetic's archetypal (original) assemblage is drama. A poetic perspective is *the* perspective of 'Man as Communicant,' which can consequently claim to be the 'foremost principle,' since all people are members of a symbol-using species.[16]

Such a perspective is unlikely to 'set the tone' for 'implementing' communicative behaviour, but it enjoys a critical or '*corrective function*.' It is antipathetic to pyramidal authority, the bureaucratic and the hierarchical, for it works horizontally within, between, and across specific symbolic acts. Barthes, contemplating the 'mythology' of the Eiffel Tower, traverses its larger context, form, surface, location, and history to examine it as 'friendly,' as a presence 'to the entire world' which is a universal symbol of Paris, yet which 'touches the most general human-image repertoire: its simple, primary shape confers upon it the vocation of an infinite cipher,' and this makes us imagine it as symbol: 'of modernity, communication, of science, or of the nineteenth century, rocket, stem, derrick, phallus, lightning rod or insect, confronting the great itineraries of our dream, it is the inevitable sign.'[17]

The Eiffel Tower becomes a mythic machine across whose surface, within whose space, and across whose relations with its setting, a network of significance is generated. It becomes a communication about communication. As 'an object when we look at it' while on a visit, it is transformed into a 'lookout.' The Eiffel Tower provides the visitor with provisions of 'a technical order' and constitutes a 'familiar little world.' Only when the tower and its context is placed against art objects, engineering feats, communication designs, religious symbols, historical texts, and the common talk of France, Paris, tourism and the world does it assume the complex pardoxicality of its communicative action. The Eiffel Tower is a dynamic ongoing mini-drama persistently present in the city and simultaneously residual in the world's imagination. Barthes's poetic prose unfolds the tower's intricate complications and implications, rhetorically exploring the relations of art, culture, and everyday life which are intertwined in the architectonic structure itself, thus producing a kind of 'artifactual' poetry.

On the second page of one of the texts recognized as most characterstically Irish, *Finnegans Wake*, the Eiffel Tower ironically presides over the action as Tim Finnegan dreams of constructing a new global society or of his having an erection: '... he seesaw by neatlight of the liquor wheretwin 'twas born ... a waalworth of a skyerscape of most eyeful hoyth entowerly, erigenating from next to nothing and celescalating the himals and all hierarchitectitiptitoploftical ...' (4.33–5.1–2). The unexpectedness within the action during this scene arises from the zigzagging exploration of the tower that inscribes a design of differing and diverse points and moments to reassemble the tower in a new imaginary machinic assemblage. Joyce implies that the tower projects itself as a poetic, constructive energy: the 'hierarchitectitiptitoploftical' (the poetic and the architectural linked in the architectonic motif).

In Burke's theory of poetics and communication, the poetic is an intensely specialized form of undistorted, though enigmatic, communication, with a constructive, machinic (but not mechanistic) principle. Poetic machines are constructed by random horizontal movements across the signifying surface by which communication events are produced, as Lewis Carroll's 'non-sense' demonstrates. All people must find some intrinsic satisfaction in making and using symbols just for the pleasure of doing so, much in the same way that a cat finds innate satisfaction in playing at hunting through which it indulges in the pleasure of developing its natural proclivities.[18] The same process is in operation when people explore possible semiotic uses of objects and symbols from their everyday life-world in playful ways – jokes, verbal games, visual or verbal slogans, and trivial pursuits – although it would not normally be recognized by the participants that such activity was potentially poetic. Across the spectrum from children's wordplay to nonsense, human beings explore ways of expanding their communicative capabilities and potentialities. In the days of the camera, the video-camera, sound synchronizers, graphic user interfaces (GUIs), hypermedia, and virtual reality (VR), the possibilities for such exploration may have increased but the same poetic pleasure is involved.

The concept of the architectonic involves the notion of building (architecture and design) and of engineering. It is the basis of the poetic, which ought not to be conceived of as purely formalistic, for it is an intensely specialized form of communication which is intrinsically connected with the dramatic, the rhetorical, and the architectural because all the functions of the symbolic act implicate one another. The architectonic, in stressing the nature of the poetic as an assemblage, reveals that what is often embraced in speaking of art as imitation is imitation only in the very specialized sense Joyce has in mind when, in interpreting Aristotle's conception of mimesis, he comments on a passage from the *Physics*:[19] '*e tekhne mimeitai ten physin* – The phrase is falsely rendered as "Art is an imitation of Nature." Aristotle does not here define art; he says only, "Art imitates nature" and means that the artistic process is like the natural process.'[20]

The artist assembles as the *bios* assembles. The assemblage the artist produces examines the entire community in action through disassembling and reassembling the signs by which the community communicates and generating from them a renewed body ('the spectacle of redemption'). This is neither a doctrine of reflection nor reproduction; it is a statement concerning dynamic production and an imaginary partitioning of that production to display the entire community in action – that process which Joyce called 'vivisection.' In playing with the regime of signs to produce architectonic constructions where all symbolic functions implicate one another, the enigmatic communication which is generated entails the social world, although often unconsciously, just as much as it includes the formal, structural aspects of the poetic.

In *Aesthetic Theory* Adorno is quite specific about the enigmatic quality of art: 'All art works are riddles; indeed, art as a whole is a riddle. Another way of putting it is to say that art expresses something while at the same time hiding it.'[21] Art's nature as enigmatic would seem to pose a problem for those thinking of art as having to do with communication, for a corollary of this doctrine about art as riddle would appear to be that art is non-communicative: 'The manner in which art communicates with the outside world is in fact also a lack of communication, because art seeks, blissfully or unhappily, to seclude itself from the world. This non-communication points to the fractured nature of art.'[22] This fracturing arises from the ambivalence of communication and the paradoxical relationship that arises from art's being grounded in both its supposed purposelessness and indifference and the impossibility of its productions' not having some implications for the society within which it is produced. This fractured nature of art is actually the plight of communication itself, for there always is an enigmatic element in communication resulting from its significance always being interpreted uniquely by each individual (and her/his 'hermenuetic compulsion'), even if this is less prominent in everyday social communication than in poetic action.

Another aspect of the engimatic nature of the poetic is quite central to its communicative power. Information theory, since it concerns the transmission of electric signals or the behaviour of self-governing devices (e.g., a thermostat), addresses itself to purely physical situations quite different from the poetic use of language. The theory of codes which information theory discusses is a monoplanar theory, while poetic theory as part of a theory of morphogenesis is not.[23] Nevertheless, this mathematical theory involves some quite suggestive concepts for thinking about the poetic, since it examines the interplay of predictability and unexpectedness within a theory of codes.

Roman Jakobson's writings in the 1950s adapted the concept of unexpectedness from information theory to describe the type of deviation from expectancy or transgression that is the foundation of the language of poetry, of rhetorical figures.[24] The more surprising, unexpected, or deviant the encoding of a signal or a sign, the greater the amount of information it produces – an insight intuitively grasped in the importance of the concept of shock among the early twentieth-century avant-garde. Leonard Meyers's writings on music[25] and E.H. Gombrich's on the visual arts[26] developed similar analyses of the relevance information (communication) theory had for understanding their respective arts.

The crux of the tension between enigma and transparent communication in the arts certainly emerges from the operation of the unexpected. There are practical limits to the communicative potential of the unexpected, however, for while within some apparently finite set of limits, the greater the complexity any communication presents, the more informative or illuminating it is likely to be, the most extreme deviation within the encoding would fail to inform, since intelligibility would be completely lost in the absence of any probable or anticipated structure against which its differences could become meaningful. Besides, the greater the difficulty any communication presents, the greater the likelihood that the size of the group to which it communicates will be reduced.

In relation to the poetic, the unexpected, in spite of presenting problems for communication, also has the potentiality to increase the complexity, depth, and density of communication. The modes of expression in the arts are closely linked to the everyday world, since this phenomenon that is so essential to poetic innovation and consequently to the way in which the productions emerging from new artistic direction 'speak' out at their inception is a necessary characteristic of all human communication. It is also central to the 're-creative' way that historical contemplation continually discovers new relevance in the past contexts of all social objects, particularly of cultural productions, so that there is an 'unexpected' element in the renewed way in which a work of the past 'speaks' to the present.

The figural, the formal deviation or transgression, which characterizes figurative language, such as pun or metaphor, depends on such surprise or unexpectedness. This is not exclusively a question of form, for the figural arises from unexpected symbolic play with material from the life-world as well as with formal linguistic structures. The figural in all modes of communication is a complex construction that, while including material and formal elements, is also shaped by the technological factors of the mode or modes of communication which are involved. (The early use of montage or of devices such as dissolves in film and the use of printed format at the onset of printing to produce shaped poems or orthographic figures exemplify this.) All these modes of unexpectedness break the continuous surface of the expected or anticipated; they become a negation of, challenge to, or intensification of what is anticipated. Such effects characterize a dramatic intervention in an ongoing statement within a dialogue.

Taking drama as a theoretical foundation when speaking of the constructed (and fictional) text is preferable to the contemporary stratagem of privileging narrativity. First of all, the dramatic model is actually closer to the interactive structure of everyday life than the narrative, which is an abstraction from drama and action; secondly, drama is also closer to the dialogic mode in which the interaction between the range of modes of expression must take place in the everyday world. Narrative is not essentially dialogic, which is why in developing a dialogic theory of the novel, Bakhtin of necessity posits the selection and development of certain particular narrative strategies oriented to the dramatic as the means for achieving the dialogic. Storytelling need not be interactive; ritual or drama always is. Furthermore, the historical roots of poetics in Europe are in dramatic theory rather than epic, while ethnologists such as Bateson have also recognized the fundamental role of drama.

Some theorists have argued that the dramatic form is highly ideological, involving itself in the spectacle of presentation and encompassing the audience within the assumptions of the action itself, a situation which can only be demystified by examining the drama's narrative action. This interpretive act distances one sufficiently to permit a rational analysis of the motivations. Such a position assumes a purity of academic discourse arising from a distancing which situates it within rational critical dialogue. Yet this raises the question whether or not in a more remote, but nevertheless quite relevant, way, such discourse itself is not a drama, an acting out at another remove from that script which is the text. The text finally only continues to live in the ways in which it continues to be talked about, and the act of talking about it brings into play the interests and biases of those participating in the conversation.

A dramatically oriented, multi-generic (multi-modal or multi-disciplinary) theory of communication underlines the way in which all communicative action participates in the same complexity. Person-to-person communication is based on all of the combined repertoire of rhetorical interchange: gesture, setting, vocal tone, rhythm, and movement in addition to verbal language. But since it also exists in a world permeated by discussion, negotiation, gossip, rumour, and interpretation of motives, it only takes on its full significance within this context. Bateson's theory of an ecology of mind complements Burke and others in stressing the important relationships between drama and communication.

Bateson's analysis shows that our understanding of communication can only come about by our playing and experimenting with communication and then being able to communicate about the implications of that play and experimentation. In the communicative process, the poetic provides an intensive strategy for experimenting with communication and assisting in its development. This is why from 1880 to 1960 the arts tended to become preoccupied with the effects of photography, phonography, and then film and

TV and have subsequently become preoccupied with the computer and telecommunications. Film (and to a lesser extent TV) dominated the first half of this century, just as the information matrices (e.g., Internet), virtual reality, and other immersive technologies that constitute cyberspace are dominating the second half.

Bateson, as an anthropologist, related these cybernetic conceptions of communication to his understanding of aboriginal art and to the concepts of play, poetry, drama and humour. Partly sparked by Norbert Wiener's *Cybernetics: Control and Communication in the Animal and the Machine* (1948), in 1950 Bateson first tried to bring together social theory, psychiatric theory, systems theory, and communication theory in a then seminal study, *Communication: The Social Matrix of Psychiatry*. After laying this groundwork, he developed a theory of the epistemology of communication, beginning with a consideration of play, fantasy, schizophrenia, and distorted communication. In studying schizophrenia, Bateson became interested in various communication situations which involve both emotional significance and the necessity of discriminating between orders of message. Such situations involve the play principle, humour, ritual, art, poetry, fiction, and fantasy in general.[27] Stressing that humour (wit) is a 'method of exploring implicit themes in thought or in a relationship,' wit – the montage principle – and its association with play assume a central importance for Bateson's communication theory. Humour, as an example of the 'play principle,' depends on 'a condensation of Logical Types or communication modes.' The 'explosive moment' in humour, which creates this condensation, occurs when 'the labelling of the mode undergoes a dissolution and resynthesis'[28] – a destruction and reassembling.

Bateson sees poetry as exemplifying the communicative power of metaphor, since like poetry, all forms of wit (such as drama, humour or jokes, ritual or narrative) involve doublings of levels. In his presentation of his 'Theory of Play and Fantasy,' drama is the privileged member of the set of poetic activities associated with humour. Dramatic action is most 'interesting in this respect, with both performers and spectators responding to messages about both the actual and the theatrical reality.'[29] That it exists as doubleness doubled is not markedly different from all poetic forms of communication, but the poet's response to interaction with his consumers – who are also co-producers within his creation – is not as immediate or directly visible as that of the actors and spectators in the theatrical presentation of a drama. But while the double structure evident in all poetic activity produces the relationship of communication, meta-communication and 'meta-meta-communication,' the peculiar relationship within dramatic presentation is one reason why instinctively the terms 'play' and 'playing' have been associated with drama.

A dramatic action encompasses a fictive action which involves the following mimetic and imaginary aspects:

1. the representation of actors (which Burke called agents) and their motives;
2. the movement of thought both within the action and between the actors, as well as in the interaction between the drama itself and the audience;
3. the flow and ebb of speech and its rhetorical and poetic shaping;
4. the visual and gestural language of spectacle;
5. and sound, rhythm (including music), and kinaesthesia.

Drama, as a comprehensive mixture of media, provided for many twentieth-century artists, like Eisenstein, the pre-filmic example of film art; an art which is an orchestration of many arts. This set of interrelated concepts is crucial to an understanding of the difference between distorted or pathological communication and ordinary undistorted communication.

In an essay entitled 'Style, Grace and Information in Primitive Art,' Bateson expounds a view of art as an 'exercise in communicating about the species of unconsciousness ... a sort of play behaviour whose function is among other things, to practice and make more perfect communication of this kind.'[30] Bateson differentiates his concept of unconsciousness from that of Freud, since he holds that many important areas of social knowledge and the accompanying performance and competence in social action function largely within the unconscious. Art and dream are essential as aids to consciousness, for he observes: 'What unaided consciousness (unaided by art, dreams and the like) can never appreciate is the *systemic* nature of mind.'[31]

Art, then, has a positive function of maintaining wisdom, correcting a too purposive view of life, and making the view more systemic. This establishes what Bateson called a plateau in contradistinction to the purposiveness of climax. The most profound forms of communication, which are necessarily transverse and, therefore, rhizome-like, are plateau experiences, characterized by their sustained intensity. The movement of twentieth-century art towards primitive models is a deliberate recognition of the importance of such plateaus to the structure of the open work that characterizes modernism. Ambivalence pervades modern poetic practice, and while such ambivalence is also found in works of art from earlier times, contemporary art does not exhibit the conscious purposive direction of earlier works.

Shakespeare and the classical drama move beyond purposive climax to establish plateaus of intensity: *Lear*, for example, ends in an ambivalent vision of folly, wisdom, and evil. Pope's major satires, such as *The Dunciad,* maintain a persistent complex and unresolved questioning which transcends apparent climaxes. Through these strategies, both poets intensify their challenging and questioning of their respective eras and the prevailing social values. The pervasive mode of contemporary poetic practice highlights this critical element and downplays or eliminates the climactically oriented structures of preceding periods in order to design semiotic machines – a potentiality of wit that had been recognized, but not embraced enthusiastically, by earlier poets such as George Herbert (1633): 'Wit's an unruly engine, wildly striking / Sometimes a friend, sometimes the engineer' *(The Temple).*

By what means does art achieve this plateau, make its view more systemic, construct a semiotic machine, and stress its role as critique? In answering this question, Bateson identifies how the work of artists carries out the important activity of providing for more adequate communicative action, for their productions strive to counter the monstrousness of separating intellect from emotion, the external mind from the internal mind, and the mind from the body: 'Pascal asserted that "The heart has its *reasons* of which the reason knows nothing" ... the reasonings of the heart (or of the hypothalamus) are accompanied by sensations of joy or grief. These computations are concerned with matters which are vital to mammals ... matters of *relationship* ... love, hate, respect, dependency, spectatorship, performance, dominance, and so on. These are central to the life of any mammal and I see no objection to calling these computations "thought," though certainly the units of relational computations are different from the units which we use to compute about isolable things.'[32] Artists and poets construct the bridges between these two types of thought. Art is involved with 'the relation *between* the levels of mental process.' Bateson argues that those who suggest art is the expression of the psychoanalytic unconscious miss the point, for 'artistic skill is the combining of many levels of mind – unconscious, conscious and external – to make a statement of their combination. It is not a matter of expressing a single level [the unconscious].'[33]

Art, which has the function of building such bridges between different levels of mind 'to make a statement of their combination,' should enhance communicative effectiveness and potentiality, while promoting the integration of thought and feeling in the systemic nature of the mind: the 'reasons of the heart' or the 'tear' as a thing of intellectual joy. There is a interval in activities such as joking, playing, and creating poetry which permits experimentation with communicative potentiality and involves a process similar to the way in which the computer as a communication machine 'computes' experience. The concepts of doubling and redoubling are equally essential to Bateson's theory, since the ambivalence produced through the interplay of levels is essential to depth and complexity of communication and to the understanding of the nature of a communication. His well-known analysis of the double bind explores the confusions which occur when those communicating do not recognize a message of the type 'This is play!' – a meta-message reinterpreting a certain mode of behaviour; for example, two cats involved in a mock battle each have to recognize those signs that constitute the message 'I am just playing not really fighting.'[34]

From the perspective of communication, ecology, and evolution, Bateson's discussion of drama and other artistic forms of the poetic complements Burke's. While both reinforce the perspective of contemporary artists (that the dramatic-poetic activity is heuristic, which enables all the arts to contribute to the evolution of communication), Bateson places the discussion in a wider anthropological and epistemological setting and raises issues not broached directly by Burke. His theory is uncompromisingly monistic; thus involved with becoming rather than being, with a systemic theory of mind, and with the same broad theory of communication from which Burke's work arose. Burke's theories were, in fact, used by anthropologists and sociologists examining native drama.

Bateson, however, also articulated the important conception of a 'plateau of intensity,' which has passed beyond the possibility of being resolved by a climax. This conception, developed by Deleuze and Guattari in their study of capitalism and schizophrenia,[35] is crucial to understanding the evolution of communication that accepts the systemic nature of mind and realizes that communicative understanding can only be reached through the integrating of levels of mind. Planes of consistence or plateaus of intensity are where the heuristic of communication, which is a nomadic, exploratory feeling out, takes place. Poetic works consciously assemble plateaus of intensity (as Bateson noted among the Balinese). But they also do so in traditional art, such as Shakespearean drama, for here there is no question of real climax in the dénouement; as in *Lear,* life goes on, but the same anew.

The motif of the 'seim anew' (*FW*215.23) is characteristic of Joyce's poetic vision or Klee's design. Unresolved tension, quintessential ambivalence, play on the surfaces of *Finnegans Wake,* where Joyce ends where he begins to begin again:

> [Last lines:] Till thousendsthee. Lps. The keys to. Given! A way a lone a last a loved a long the
> [First lines:] riverrun, past Eve and Adam's, from swerve of shore to bend of bay, brings us by a commodius vicus of recirculation back to Howth Castle and Environs.

The climax dissolves as it does in Molly's soliloquy in *Ulysses*, for these are poetic worlds: 'continuums of intensities, combinations of fluxes.'[36] Klee, who regarded the concept of the infinite as cosmic earthly tension, realized 'space itself is a temporal concept,' that 'all becoming is based on movement,' and that the 'grid' of the magic squares was a game-board for generating dynamic approximations to the infinite. Just as Joyce shared a view of the new cosmology which was a 'chaosmos,' Klee, who delights in the assembled, such as his 'magic squares,' and in the machinic counterpointed against the narrative (e.g., *Battle Scene from the Comic Fantastic Opera 'The Seafarer'* (1923) [*Kampfszene aus der komisch-phantastischen Oper 'Der Seefahrer'*])[37] produced insights into the communicative potential of the 'new vision' of poetics that transcends postmodernist critiques of the 'grid' in art. From his black stick marching men on a red background to his changing treatment of leaves, he produced a strong monistic sense of becoming and unresolved tensions which create very visible 'plateaus of intensities' or 'emissions of particles.' The poetic and its archetype, the dramatic, constitute the beginning of an understanding of the enigmatic nature of everyday communication: communication by which people make contact; leading to very partial, yet pragmatically useful, understanding.

9

Communication and Comedy: Negativity, Satire, and Secular Communion

Joyce designed *Finnegans Wake,* primarily by playing with orthography, so that readers both have to see the text with their eyes and hear it with their ears in order to comprehend the workings of the language with its complex variety of puns and other verbal play. Joyce clearly indicates the intricate interrelationship between the poetic exploration of communication and the production of comic effects. His technique also provides a means for utilizing the differences between oral language and print for developing poetic counterpoint and for creating completely new 'words' to deal with the complexities of a modern world of innumerable new communication technologies.

The original discovery of phonetic writing had itself been a 'poetic' activity which brought into play the counterpoint between the two different modes of language – writing and speech – a counterpoint intensified by the discovery of print, which through its tendency to standardize orthography can inhibit the poetic exploitation of this counterpoint. A sleeping figure, Yawn, one of the dream metamorphoses of one of HCE's sons in the *Wake,* speaks of the poets' invention of writing and provides his audience, four inquisitors – who are simultaneously 'annalists' (historians), psychoanalysts, and the four Evangelists – with a summary of the contrapuntal process of encoding and decoding required in reading a book, which is itself characteristically mechanical:

The prouts who will invent a writing there ultimately is the poeta, still more learned, who discovered the raiding there originally. That's the point of eschatology our book of kills reaches for now in soandso many counterpoint words. What can't be coded can be decorded if an ear aye sieze what no eye ere grieved for. Now, the doctrine obtains, we have occasioning cause causing effects and affects occasionally recausing altereffects. Or I will let me take it upon myself to suggest to twist the penman's tale posterwise. The gist is the gist of Shaum but the hand is the hand of Sameas. Shan - Shim - Schung. (482.31–483.4)

In this passage, which is simultaneously a comic embodiment of the communication processes associated with voice, script, and print, the complex *modus operandi* of the poet's 'raiding' is achieved through processes of coding and decoding by eye and ear, and of transformation from oral to written and from written to oral. The poet, as a Hermetic thief, an 'outlex' (169.3), who discovered the 'raiding' (reading) originally, invents a 'writing.' Seeing and hearing are intricately involved in this 'raiding' of a night-book, so that the reader, too, becomes a 'raider' of the original 'raiding' through the machinery of writing. The subsequent book is compared to an artefact of visual design (a book 'in soandso many counterpoint words'), but it is 'raided' only by the machinery of decoding for 'What can't be coded can be decorded if an ear aye sieze what no eye ere grieved for.' This requires seeing it as an extension of gesture: '... I will ... take it upon myself to suggest to twist the penman's tale posterwise. The gist is the gist of Shaum but the hand is the hand of Sameas.' It is precisely because the mechanics of the 'Nichtian glossery' is 'nat language in any sinse of the world' (83.10–12) that 'the speechform is a mere sorrogate' (149.29), since night language 'communicakes with the original sinse' (239.1) by going to the 'root' language of 'the sound sense sympol in a weedwayedwold of the firethere the sun in his halo cast. Onmen' (612.29).

Finnegans Wake as a symbol of the crisis facing the primacy of literacy and the book in our century anticipates the problematic of Derridean grammatology and the subsequent contemporary elevation of the importance of writing. This occurs partly because the *Wake* becomes a symbol for the still more fundamental process implicit in poetic activity – communication. To focus first on the more immediate grammatological processes, the *Wake*'s wordplay is intrinsically related to conceptions of orality and literacy, to the interplay between the printed book and the oral language. Puns are involved in the 'decording' of 'what can't be coded,' since they depend on the counterpoint of the visual and the oral that involves complex notions of coding, decoding, unravelling (i.e., 'de-cording'), and musical sounds (de-*chord*ing) – the chord as a symbol of musical sound.

Still another type of wordplay is at work in 'if an ear aye sieze what no eye ere grieved for,' which depends for its effect on the chain: 'ear-ere-aye-eye.' Here the verbal wit is much more overtly dependent on the interplay between close visual attention to each of the written words and close auditory attention to their realization in speech. Writing when he did,

Joyce developed the 'root' language of *Finnegans Wake* with its counterpoint and 'decording' not because he had to force readers to read his book as a printed text, but because he had to make them become aware that this book also had to be spoken and *pronounced*, at least silently, *preferably aloud.* This process of coding, decoding, reading, listening, and sensorily participating underlines the way in which a language that is 'punny' is itself a symbol for the drama of communication.

Drama provides a paradigm for the study of communication; the archetypal form of drama is comedy, so that the *Wake* announces, 'Outragedy of poetscalds! Acomedy of letters!' (425.24), for Joyce concluded the Phoenix playhouse section (the children's mime) with 'Loud, heap miseries upon us yet entwine our arts with laughters low!' (259.7–8). Burke considered the comic perspective rooted in the affinity of language for 'joycing' as one fundamental aspect of a theory of communication. Barthes, Bakhtin, Eco, Wyndham Lewis, and McLuhan all exploit 'comic' techniques for writing about communication phenomena. Comedy and satire entail what Burke called gargoyle elements, grotesque caricatures exemplifying 'typical instances of planned incongruity' – just that type of planned incongruity that characterizes Barthes's *Mythologies* or McLuhan's *The Mechanical Bride,* both of which use the artwork as a means and a technique for interpreting communication events and products.

'Perspective by incongruity' is certainly one mark of the modern avant-garde for 'an incongruous assortment of incongruities' had become a dominant feature of modern art.[1] Before structuralism or postmodernism, Burke's concept of analogy, which he related to his conception of planned incongruity, stressed difference and a negative dialectic, employing the difference to intensify the process of emerging meaning. This clearly differentiates his concept from traditional conceptions of analogy grounded on similarity. The negative and negativity occupy a distinctive role in Burke's dramatistic theory of human language and provide a means for treating the social realm as itself having an unconscious element which must be brought into relation with other levels of mind through strategies such as 'joycing.'[2] He saw such strategies as a way of using language for going beyond language to the realm of human communication where different modes of expression and communication, such as gesture, movement, sound, and image, all interact.

Joyce tells the readers of the *Wake* that he has developed a 'Nichtian glossery,' a night language, which is 'nat language,' a nonsense language and a language of the negative as well as a non-language. Joyce's language, which has affinities with Carroll's nonsense – even though Joyce denies having read

Carroll or Rabelais before starting to write the *Wake*[3] – is a more complex and comprehensive nonsense language. Furthermore, his is also a dramatic language that most effectively integrates the interplay of negation, opposition, conflict, and the imaginary with the sensory and the significant. Comedy, with its bias for the negative, the incongruous, and the rage for chaos, is the dramatic modality that most readily acts as a mode of critique.

Comedy is *the* mode of critique because it arrests desire by allowing people to take intellectual possession of the work through the operation of 'the schizophrenic laughter ... the schizophrenic line of breakthrough, and the process of deterritorialization with its machinic indices,' as Chaplin's schizoanalytic laughter exemplifies.[4] Comedy promotes possession by dramatizing the machinery of our social life. This is the point of McLuhan's insight that the pun is breakdown as breakthrough. Deleuze explains why this process of breakdown is so important for understanding communication from the standpoint of the community. Discussing 'Which comes first, the chicken or the egg – but also the father and mother, or the child?' he concludes that the adult is 'never an afterward of the child, but in the family both relate to determinations of the social field.' He states that the point of view of the community 'is *disjunctive* or takes account of the disjunctions in the cycle': 'The genetic revolution occurred when it was discovered that ... there is no transmission of flows, but a communication of a code or an axiomatic, of a combinative apparatus (*combinatoire*) informing flows. Such is also the case for the social field: its coding or its axiomatic first determine within it a communication of unconsciousness. This phenomenon of communication, which Freud touched on only marginally in his remarks on occultism constitutes in fact the norm ... It appears that in the common social field the first thing the son has to repress is *the unconscious of the father and the mother*. The failure of that repression is the basis of neuroses. But this communication of unconsciousness does not by any means take the family as its principle; it takes as its principle the commonality of the social field insofar as it is the object of the investment of desire.'[5]

Bateson also perceived the significance of the unconscious in relation to understanding communication within the social field, for he claimed that Freud had turned the problem of communication with the unconscious upside down. He suggests we now recognize that the unconscious is continually active, necessary, and all-embracing, while consciousness is mysterious. Artists communicate messages about this interface between conscious and unconscious, messages that also indicate 'what order or species of unconsciousness (or consciousness) [to] attach to [them].'[6] Since Joyce speaks of comedy as arresting desire, as creating a feeling of possession of the object, and thereby generating joy, he implicitly recognizes that the dramatic or poetic machine is essentially comic and that the audience enjoys the sense of possession of a good. The audience possesses the machinic structure, which itself is the source of desire, for desire is in the assemblage.

The dramatic, generating an immediate sense of relationship with the poetic machine, develops a code that creates the gaps which release the full force of the unconscious as it exists in the social field, so that even in the mass media – produced parodies, there is a partial critique of everyday life. Joyce observed 'that art is dramatic whereby the artist sets forth the image in immediate relation to others.' Drama is not mediated; nor, is it in the strictest sense a medium. Epic, as the basis for narrativity, is a mediated form, for 'that art is epical whereby the artist sets forth the image in mediate relation to himself and to others.'[7] Joyce later modified his view when he disassembled the epic in *Ulysses* and developed a theory of the author as producer and the audience as co-producer. The immediacy of the drama is the foundation of the poetic; the comic is an essentially dramatic form, for narrative and lyric forms are derivatives of the dramatic, not vice versa, the very notion of an action being central to all poetic form. Taking 'folk criticism' as an example which deserves tribute just as 'folk art' does, Burke shows how a comic orientation operates in bringing to the surface the comic nature of popular culture. Consequently, the comic condition is the fundamental condition of drama, for it is what immediately roots the dramatic in the social. Joyce declared that 'comedy is the perfect manner of art' and that 'even tragic art may be said to participate in the nature of comic art so far as the possession of work of tragic art ... excites in us feelings of joy.'[8]

The sense of reintegration with the social world so frequently associated with the role of comic drama is neither integration, submission, nor irresponsibility, but the production of a machinery of envelopment and development which explicates (explains) by producing partial objects (fragmentation), effects of resonance, and forced movements.[9] The enveloping and developing proceed by way of disassembling and reassembling, or 'precedent decomposition' for 'the very petpurpose of subsequent recombination' (*FW*614.34–5).

In *Dr Strangelove, or How I Learned to Stop Worrying and Love the Bomb,* Kubrick presents the drama of the nuclear disintegration of world order as a comic recording of such partial objects as the stylized cockpit of a B-52; a surrealistically lighted and disorientingly photographed war-room; a Coke machine decontextualized by its standing untouched amidst the rubble of a room destroyed by an infantry attack; a Bell Telephone booth that *also* remains intact and demands coins from RAF captain Mandrake, who is desperately trying to follow orders by calling the president; the sexual relation of people and technology revealed in the relationship of the flight crew with their aircraft; and, finally, the sexual relation of political and military leaders with their war machines, which is reproduced in the play on sexual excitation mimicking technology as General Turgeson tells his secretary-mistress to start her countdown for copulation and orgasm, while he visits the war-room.

The lines of force which constitute the movement of the film run counter to one another, but move inexorably to an ambivalent Armageddon, generating a complex of forced movements that lead to the final counterpointing of mineshaft sex and death in Strangelove's closing reflections on the necessity, for those who survive the fallout by living in the mineshafts, of preventing a mineshaft population gap between East and West by energetically copulating to perpetuate humanity.[10] The fragments of social communication are transversely reoriented in *Dr Strangelove,* enveloping, developing, and explicating, while maintaining an irresolvable plateau of consistency. A corollary to positing a role for drama in social theory is to posit the primacy of the role of the comic in social theory.

Bataille's writings relate drama and comedy to communication and posit the importance of a concept of community: 'The human reality which yoga determines in them [the sanyasin of India] is no less that of a community; communication is a phenomenon which is in no way added on to Dasein, but constitutes it.'[11] While Bataille, who stresses the supression of subject and object in the action of communication, is in sharp contrast with Joyce's relative optimism, he nevertheless ties bacchanalia and the comic to depth of communication: '*From one end to the other of this human life which is our lot, the consciousness of the ... profound lack of all true stability, liberates the enchantment of laughter. As this life suddenly passed from an empty and sad solidity to the happy contagion of warmth and of light, to the free tumult which the waters and the air communicate to one another: flashes and the rebounding of laughter follow the first opening, the permeability of a dawning smile. If a group of people laugh at an absent-minded gesture, or at a sentence revealing absurdity, there passes within them a current of intense communication.*'[12] Isolated individuals emerge into a community within which they become 'like the waves of the sea,' for any partition between them disappears as long as the laughter lasts.

Nietzsche's laughter had affirmed a community of experience. Bataille asserts that '*it is from a feeling of community binding me to Nietzsche that the desire to communicate arises in me, not from an isolated originality.*'[13] Just as community requires a suppression of self – in fact, of the subject-object relationship – drama has a particular relevance to the subject-object relationship in social interaction, since in the process of stressing the reciprocity of actors and observers, it also underscores the way in which the social system forms the subject; yet the subject contributes to the formation of the system. Implicit in the very foundation of drama is the ironic remove of consumers from the primary action and the urge of the consumers and producers to overcome that distancing through a mode of dramatic communion.

Some of Bataille's major themes (the centrality of transgression, laughter, and sacrifice to communication; communication as an ecstatic experience; the vision of the sacrifice as a comedy; the accompanying insight that 'the path of communication is in anguish') reappear in Burke's secularization of concepts such as 'scapegoat,' 'original sin,' 'secular mysticism,' and 'comic corrective.' Burke's primary mode of understanding, 'perspective by incongruity' (wit as symbolic action), is situated in the 'thinking of the body' and its revelations through the lower (sensual) activities: defecation, urination, and copulation. A dramatic theory of communication essentially makes all modes of expression and communication aspects of a communion achieved through a common regime of signs. This emerging convergence of genres, characterizing modernity and postmodernity, parallels the movement beyond media and the dissolution of traditional views of art in the emergence of the parapoetic.

A similar emphasis on this centrality of communion and the comic condition in drama marks the early introduction of Burke's dramatistic analysis of society into social theory through the writings of H.D. Duncan.[14] The comic has a privileged role, for as Burke asserts, 'the proper study of mankind is man's tendency to misjudge reality as inspirited by the troublous genius of symbolism.' Comedy as condition, rapport, feeling, or natural characteristic provides a perspective which has frequently been associated with criticism and rectification. This 'comic corrective,' Burke says, is the 'attitude of attitudes' (an 'attitude' being the naming of a process from a meditative, moralizing, or hortatory point of view): '... saturating the lot is the attitude of attitudes which we call the "comic frame," the methodic view of human antics as a comedy, albeit as a comedy ever on the verge of the most disastrous tragedy.'[15] Most of the artists mentioned earlier (e.g., Joyce, Proust, Brecht, Chaplin, Fellini, Kubrick, Bataille, Klee, Picasso, and Schönberg) share this sense of the intermingling of the comic and the tragic affirmed by Nietzsche. Joyce's exposition of how the tragic is a component of the comic was readily grasped in traditional practice as illustrated by both Shakespearean tragedies such as *King Lear* and by tragicomedies or romantic comedies such as *Measure for Measure*.

The 'comic frame' as a method of study ('of making man the student of himself') depends on a translation of attitude.[16] This can be accomplished in two ways: using tropes to change the formula by which the attitude is expressed; or merely 'changing our attitude towards the formula.' Both are exemplified in those strategies of decontextualization which divorce an object or event permeated with persuasive, manipulative rhetoric (e.g., ads, mass-produced objects, or popular cultural events) as in Barthes's *Mythologies* or McLuhan's writings: 'We "discount" it [i.e., the expressive formula] for comic purposes, subtly translating it, as Marx translated Hegel, "taking over" a mystificatory methodology for clarificatory ends.'[17]

Such discounting strategies are also extensively utlilized in the writings of Erasmus, Swift, Machiavelli, Voltaire, and Veblen. Bakhtin, in his analysis of Rabelais's *Gargantua*, argued that the Renaissance is the historic moment when it finally became possible to construct a model of historical change within the domain of laughter, although this phenomenon did not become a matter of self-conscious reflection until the latter part of the nineteenth century. Bakhtin and Burke are both aware that subsequent to Marx's work an ongoing recognition of this model begins, for Marx identified the last phase of universal historic form as its comedy (perhaps in some way reminiscent of the apocalyptic vision of the New Testament): 'History acts fundamentally and goes through many phases when it carries obsolete forms of life into the grave. The last phase of the universal historic form is its comedy ... Why such a march of history? This is necessary in order that mankind could say a gay farewell to its past.'[18] But both Burke and Bakhtin are further aware that only contemporary poetry links dramatic transformation or metamorphosis with a fully self-conscious awareness of the comic foundations of social theory. Today, as Baudrillard's critique of hyper-reality satirically unmasks the pretensions of postmodernism, the dramatic and the comic corrective are predominant.

The repertoire of 'folk criticism,' which Burke notes and McLuhan later uses in *Understanding Media* and *From Cliché to Archetype*, is not invoked 'to cultivate such terms "aesthetically," for their purely "picturesque" value. We are considering them as collective philosophy of motivation, arising to name the relationships, or social situations, which people have found so pivotal and so constantly recurring as to need names for them.'[19] Burke illustrates his point from the working vocabulary of everyday relations, a method that is now thoroughly familiar. His critiques are permeated by such phrases as 'ganging up on' or 'putting on the spot,' and if they had been written in the 1990s, would include such phrases as 'rationalizing our resources' or 'being a team player.' Usages like this result from a 'metaphorical migration' of terms.

The 'comic frame,' as a 'methodology,' makes such terms more efficient 'by encouraging still further migrations.' Consequently, Burke can take phrases like 'Heads I win, tails you lose' or 'Being driven into a corner' and 'extend their orthodox range by a perspective of totality.' Such a phrase as 'Being driven into a corner,' then, becomes an 'amplifying device' with theological applications to the notion of heresy and subsequent excommunication; it can subsequently refer to the rhetorical tactics used by the authoritarian mind against dissent. Through the comic corrective of successive metamorphoses, what is primarily metaphorical, but has become cliché, is transformed into another metaphor by a process of further transformation which renews the phrase's expressive possibilities.

This device is not too different from Picasso's turning bicycle handlebars into an icon in which the bars allude to the horns of one of his many images of minotaurs. Comic frames also often bring about migrations of a more tragic or profoundly serious kind, such as Picasso's use of newspapers and the glaring electric light-bulb in his *Guernica,* which blends the modality of the comic strip with a horrific tragic visual presentation of an historic event. Comedy and paradox, like play, have important roles to assume in the poetic motive's providing depth and flexibility to communication. Burke suggests that in living according to his or her nature, a person 'works best as a perpetual student, smilingly morbid, tragicomically warning himself about the powers and limitations of the symbol-systems he necessarily lives by and thinks by.'[20]

Although all other 'attitudes' limit or restrict an exhausting of sense, the comic frame encompasses perspectives such as the tragic, the idyllic, the plaintive, and the satiric in order to 'perfect' as far as possible the assembling of a regime of signs: 'The comic frame of acceptance but carries to completion the translative act. It considers human life as a project in "composition," where the poet works with the material social relationships.' Burke traces the path from the multiplicity of significance of the 'major tropes' to the 'comic frame' as the necessary methodology for making further sense through further 'composition[s], 'translation[s] or revision[s],' which provide the 'maximum opportunity for the resources of *criticism*.[21]

Comedy's major role in social analysis is its ability to 'bridge' the abstract, heroic, intellectual side of people with their natural, physical, and animal side. Awareness of the need to employ ambivalence as an 'essentially comic notion' prevents the excesses of a 'methodology' of debunking, which through its unmitigated thoroughness could result in a totalistic devaluation of humanity and nature – a devaluation which has already occurred in some areas. This is what Burke conceives as a new transformed 'humanism,' for 'we have advocated, under the name of "comedy," a procedure that might just as well have been advocated under the name of "humanism."'[22] It is more properly a radical modernism which comically decentres humans from their traditional position as the prime figures of earthly existence.

This radical modernism permits the development of a social ecology which enables people '*to be observers of themselves, while acting,*' and to reach for the ultimate of '*maximum consciousness.*'[23] Understanding the problem of ecology involves recognizing the ambivalence of freedom and bondage implicit in any collective realization of community. Burke realized that the notion of *ambivalence* employed as a *comic* notion is of key significance to the understanding of communication and of a cluster of terms related to communication: 'communicant,' 'communion,' 'community,' and 'communism.'[24] The comic frame, in contributing to a well-balanced ecology, not only enables people '*to be observers of themselves, while acting*' and thus to achieve '*maximum consciousness,*' but also shows us how 'an act can "dialectically" contain both transcendental and material ingredients, both imagination and bureaucratic embodiment, both "service" and "spoils."' The comic frame 'also makes us sensitive to the point at which one of these ingredients becomes hypertrophied, with the corresponding atrophy of the other.'[25] Comedy 'meditates upon' that 'process of processes' which Burke called the 'bureaucratization of the imaginative.'[26] The material embodiment of the pure vision of imagination involves a fundamental tension in the social system.

For the contemporary arts, the comic becomes an 'attitude of attitudes.' Brecht sums up the modern attitude when he declares: 'A theatre that can't be laughed in is a theatre to be laughed at. Humourless people are ridiculous.' Modern self-reflexiveness has elevated the importance of comedy, which also underlies our post-Nietzschean preoccupation with Burke's calling people inventors of the negative – the 'nichtian' language of negation. Today Burke's use of the 'comic corrective' to provide a means for critically evaluating the processes of communication must be directly associated with a growing sense that all forms of cultural activity, including the arts, are essential aspects of ecology. Prophesying as early as 1937 that people would come to pay far more attention to 'one little fellow named Ecology' (i.e., the total economy of this planet), Burke identified the comic-dramatic theory of communication that he proposed in *Attitudes Toward History* as a fundamentally ecological approach. In so doing, he realized that in the future major problems would result from forms of exploitation that would cause extremely extensive disruption to planetary balance,[27] and that 'a cult of comedy,' with its sense of incongruity and the negative, would be crucial to any redress of this balance.[28] The relation of this ecological theme to communication continues in Bateson's *Steps to an Ecology of Mind.*

What I have called the 'ecology of sense' is a necessary corollary to Bateson's theory of the 'ecology of mind,' which designates the role that the poetic process, both in everyday culture and in the arts, plays in making sense of the world by permitting the intertwining of different levels of mind. Recognition of the importance of the ecology of mind and of sense decentres the role that people occupy in relation to nature, but it does not dehumanize them by eliminating their specific potential capability as people, who are complexes of sense, feeling, and thought (the characteristics of the human animal), for empathizing with the environment and with one another.

The comic mode emphasizes the dialectic and dialogic elements of expressive communication. As the expressive mode which is most inclusive and least tolerant of generic specialization, it involves an interplay of the significant and counter-significant, of sense and nonsense, across the spectrum of communicative experience. It is equally at home playing with the transcendent (language and ideas) and with the immanent (the sensory and sensual aspects of the human animal). That is the point of speaking of an *ecology of sense,* since the very term sets up an ambivalent middle ground where the transcendent and immanent are both present in nature and the body. This makes comedy the monitor of communication, since it monitors both the relation of levels and the interaction of bodies. Comedy occurs when subject and object dissolve into participants in communication and potentially in communion.

The emergence of comedy as central to the agenda of the arts in this century – whether under the guise of humour, black humour, satire, parody, or the absurd – is closely linked to the concept of the poet as engineer. Wyndham Lewis, who shared Joyce's view of the author as engineer, articulated one of the strongest defences of satire, laughter, and the comic. 'The root of the Comic is to be sought in the sensations resulting from the observations of a *thing* behaving like a person,' Lewis declares in 'The Meaning of the Wild Body.'[29] He recognizes that this means all people are comic, since they are all 'things' or physical bodies behaving as 'persons.' Laughter arises from people relieving their emotions after contemplating themselves as mechanical puppets. Some of the attributes of laughter that Lewis catalogues in 'Inferior Religions' and which recapitulate the themes of this chapter include [Lewis's numbers]:

1. Laughter is the Wild Body's song of triumph.

2. Laughter is the climax in the tragedy of seeing, hearing, and smelling self-consciously.
3. Laughter is the bark of delight of a gregarious animal at the proximity of its kind.
6. Laughter is the emotion of tragic delight.
9. Laughter is the sudden handshake of mystic violence and the anarchist.
11. Laughter is the one obvious commotion that is not complex, or in expression dynamic.[30]

Lewis relates laughter here primarily to assemblages of desiring machines and to the recognition of those assemblages. Bergson had noted the mechanical patterns on which all comic effect depends. Deleuze associated this with the way that contemporary artists, such as Proust or Kafka, structure their works. Generations accustomed to the cinema and to the composition of the television image find this a natural mode for thinking about the arts in a world where mechanization has taken command and where its effects have been exponentially multiplied through electricity. But it ought to be just as natural and just as correct in such a world to identify communication itself as an electrified machine, for all animal communication, including human communication, is intrinsically tied up with electrically controlled neuromuscular systems.

To invoke the association of comedy with the machine-like should be an immediate reminder of the association of contemporary concepts of the machine and its involvement with ideology (such as how it relates to the contemporary arts' function in the construction of desiring and communicating machines) and with technologies of power. When Mumford turned away from his relatively optimistic analysis of the new age of electricity that had characterized his earlier writings, such as *Technics and Civilization*, to explore *The Pentagon of Power*, he began to speak of the mega-machine and the technologies of power – that same power which Valéry feared when he wrote: 'Our civilization is taking on, or tending to take on, the structure and properties of a machine, as I indicated just now. This machine will not tolerate less than world-wide rule; it will not allow a single human being to survive outside its control, uninvolved in its functioning. Furthermore, it cannot put up with ill-defined lives within its sphere of operation.'[31] That fear was magnified by the fact that 'the most redoubtable machines, perhaps, are not those that revolve or run, to transport or transform matter or energy. There are other kinds, not built of copper and steel but of narrowly specialized individuals ...' These technocratic administrative machines were the core of what Valéry feared in 1932 and what Mumford came to fear in the 1950s.

McLuhan rejected that fear in the mid-1960s, expousing a technological apocalypse. Still the problem of power remains; a problem usually confronted in one of three ways: first, by conservative intellectuals such as Valéry or Wyndham Lewis, who predict that the Bergsonian celebration of mechanism and flux can only lead to disaster (this position, which he later abandoned, seemed to attract McLuhan when he wrote *The Mechanical Bride*); second, by those who embrace technology as ultimately leading to a new world of liberation and uncritically accept the power of technologies and the technologies of power; third, by comprehending the perennial presence and the essential ambivalence of the machine and allowing for its Protean capability of undoing that which it organizes – of collaborating in establishing the world as a 'chaosmos.' One of the subsets of this third position, the one most central to further evolution, is marked by the tolerance and capability of anarchistically accepting the cosmos as chaos, the propelling force of the systolic and diastolic, deconstructive and reconstructive, movement of the poetic.

Film, because of its proximity to the mechanical, reflects this ambivalence in a most forceful and authoritative way. Chaplin's satiric vision (which Wyndham Lewis, naturally, criticized for its mechanistic Bergsonianism) turned the mechanical against the industrial, using the potentials of his filmic communicating machine to subvert the industrial and the bureaucratic. His sense of the machinery of the body provided a special system of signs from which to assemble his communicating machines. Deleuze perceives in Chaplin 'the understanding of the nature of schizophrenic laughter' and cites an article by Michel Cournot on *Modern Times*: 'If laughter is a reaction that takes certain circuits, it can be said that Charlie Chaplin, as the film's sequences unfold, progressively *displaces* the reactions, causes them to recede, level by level, until the moment when the spectator is no longer master of his own circuits, and tends to spontaneously take either a shorter path, which is not passable, which is barred, or else a path that is very explicitly posted as leading nowhere. After having suppressed the spectator as such, Chaplin perverts the laughter, which comes to be like so many *short-circuits of a disconnected piece of machinery*.'[32]

Fascination with the machine and power pervades contemporary cinema. Kubrick's *Dr Strangelove* and *Full Metal Jacket* have to do with the satiric thrust of schizophrenic laughter generated by his very sensitivity for the machine which he himself is making. Fellini incorporates images of machines and of the body itself as a machine in his rich realizations of the diversity and sensuousness of the human person in films such as *8 1/2*, *Amacord*, or *Fred and Ginger*. Dušan Makavéjev, a Rabelaisian Godard, is fascinated with machines, real and imaginary, ranging from the Orgone box of *W.R.: The Mysteries of the Organism*, through the machines for the slaughtering and preparing of food in *Montenegro*, to the Rube Goldberg nightmare vision of a psychiatric institution as torture chamber in *Manifesto*.

This interplay of machines and people is a recurrent theme in the cinema, for it is an art intrinsically preoccupied with communication and with the machine. Herein lies the fascination and greatness of film animation as an art form and its intimate relation with the popular arts of the comics and advertising of the twentieth century. The micro as medium and message, an inclusive machine, advances the range and scope of animation, image production, and projection. If the medium is the message, it is the medium not the message that becomes transparent, which is one reason why approaches to film, artwork, drama, or dance as text became attractive to theorists. Because the dramatic is primarily poetic, approaches to popular culture, advertising, fashion, and the media as text all emerged simultaneously. Qualities of the dramatic may be recreated in other forms of expression by minimizing the mediated effect. This does not mean minimizing the optimal qualities of the particular expression (such as sound or light or montage in film), but utilizing the expressive signs in such a way as to place the work in immediate relation to the audience; in other words, to recognize the consumers as producers, thus absorbing the machinery of the medium and the message in the communicating machine which is produced.

Wyndham Lewis's ambivalence towards the machine is characteristically modern, for while he could condemn Bergson, Joyce, and Chaplin, he still believed in people as comic machines and in utilizing that insight for the satiric vivisection of society. His position that all great modern art is satire associates the critical, the comic, and the social. It is not necessary to fully embrace the schizoid aspect of his views to grasp schizoanalytically his fundamental insight. Kubrick's *Dr Strangelove*, as mentioned earlier,[33] provides a typical example of how the poetic work assists in providing a regime of signs with which to communicate about contemporary reality, criticizes the inadequacies of communication taking place in that reality, and provides a comic-satiric critique of society.

But *Strangelove* is clearly an assemblage which does not moralize and which may itself become an object of critique for another assemblage. It is a 'voice' in a dialogue, which because of its comedic ability to wander across the surfaces of key socio-political problems is naturally dialogic. In true Burkean style, new pivotal terms in language, sound, and image are probed; for example: the U.S. military's advertising slogan 'Peace is our profession'; the super-national mystique of the Coke machine; the dialogue of power concerning containment in the Cold War; technology as a controlling medium in the object of the B-52 and its technology of control through the top secret flight plans; the ambivalent beauty of destruction visualized in the photography of the mushroom cloud. *Dr Strangelove* is particularly illuminating for understanding the ecology of sense, since it is both a popular artwork and it is complexly involved with the tension between the person and the machine. Like Joyce, Kubrick sees people, society, and his films as machinic. Technology is probed throughout the film as it traces the critical breakdown of the ability to control the 'technoverse' and as it reveals the character of its overseers – the generals, the politicians, and Dr Strangelove. This episodic, disjunctive film, through its machinic construction, amplifies satiric effects through a deliberate structuring that simultaneously distances the viewer from, and involves her or him in, the excesses of Kubrick's vision.

All poetic assemblage involves such breaks and disjunctions, but modern poetry produces machines which make the transverse connections between sharply separated moments the primary, frequently the only, mode of communication. The beginning of the erotic countdown which General Turgeson advises his secretary to commence before he leaves their hotel room for the war-room can be fleetingly related in some 'readings' of the film to General Ripper's discussion of bodily fluids with Mandrake, to the B-52 pilot's love affair with his plane and later with the bomb which he rides to destruction, to Dr Strangelove's meditations on descent into the mineshafts to survive the fallout, accompanied by obligatory polygamy to repopulate America and to the closing moments of Vera Lynn's sentimental song juxtaposed against the cinematography of mushroom clouds following an atomic explosion.

What is most significant is the variety of potential wandering paths which this poetic machine generates, different for different readers, intensifying ambivalence, yet inviting an infinite intensification of the exploratory behaviour which is characteristic of all art. The very use of technological machinery and technological organization dramatizes the gaps inherent in people's attempt to control their biosphere. The very realism of the management of a military aircraft itself becomes a component of and contributor to the satiric dance of sounds, images, words, gestures, and movements by which the machinic nature of the poetic assemblage is generated. Kubrick delicately balances the centrality of the human body and the machinic nature of the world; the body becomes a sensuous and sensual machine poised against, and yet also implicit in, the destructive machines that it has produced.

10

Tactility and the Intersensory: Body, Dance, and Communication

The immediate sensual presence of the human body distinguishes dance and drama from poetry, literature, photography, sculpture, film, and television. In the theatre and allied spectacles (such as operas, ballets, modern dance, liturgy, evangelical meetings, circuses, rock concerts, and variety shows) there is an ongoing interaction between audience and actor in the shaping and modifying of the original text. Sensory feedback flowing in both directions modifies the physical, emotional, and intellectual responses of those involved; here is a dialogue between fleshly, sensitive bodies. Similar processes also occur in the legislature or the courtroom; sites together with the theatre that originally formed the imagination and intellect of ancient rhetoricians and rhetorical theorists. In all these actions (judicial, legislative, dramatic) and their settings, the audience participates in an interactive spectacle in which the performance of those engaged in the action (actors, dancers, lawyers, clients, witnesses, legislators, etc.) can be affected by the role of the unspeaking (though not necessarily silent) observers.

Ancient rhetorical theory provides evidence that the classical world was aware of the multi-media component in human communication. This perspective on classical rhetorical theory helps us to elucidate why Aristotle's *Poetics* presents a powerful example of how a multi-media model of communication was essential to our earliest understanding of the nature of the poetic. Aristotle's theatre blended together music, spectacle, movement, dance, gesture, mime, and the arts of language. His model for the poetic is drama, not epic or lyric, because the drama was more inclusive and more immediate. While his initial insight into the mixture of media in poetic communication is of major importance for the history of poetics, he differs from modernity in his insistence on tragedy as the highest art form and his privileging of reading and writing in spite of his respect for theatrical drama.

In the present century, the importance of 'the dance' as a persistent motif in the poetics of modernity manifests a critical awareness of the phenomenon of communication through a mixture of media, just as does the desire of many modern writers to create from language alone constructions approximating as closely as possible the effects of dance; that is, a poetry of gesture and movement often associated with a gestural theory of the evolution of language, like bp Nichol's in his *Martyrology*. It has been noted earlier in this discussion that Bateson describes Isadora Duncan's dance as a way of communicating messages from the unconscious. Bateson recognized that it is important in the construction of any contemporary theory of communication to understand the relevance of this interplay of consciousness and unconsciousness within dance and its significance for poetry and the other arts. Duncan's action appropriates the meaning of the dance, which when it first occurs is a message that can only be danced, since it is the only way of saying what is to be expressed – that is, by showing, by making manifest.[1]

Contemporary artistic fascination with the image of the dance further highlights the centrality of drama to the act of expression, the crucial aspect of human communication. In a powerful, beautifully crafted Socratic dialogue, 'L'Ame et la danse,' Paul Valéry wrote of dance and the soul: 'By the gods, the bright dancers! ... How lively and precious an introduction of the most perfect thoughts! ... Their hands speak and their feet seem to write.'[2] The body writes itself. In its movement, the body becomes its thought, the blazing image reflecting the unity of its exterior and interior reality. Valéry's Socrates envisions this as a struggle of body to be its soul:

> This *One* wishes to play at being *All*. It wishes to play at the universality of the soul! It wishes to atone for its identity by the number of its acts! Being a thing, it bursts into events! – It is transported! – And just as thought, when stirred, touches all substances, vibrates between time-beat and instant, o'erlaps all differences; and just as in our minds hypotheses take shape and possibles line up and are counted – so this body exercises itself in all its parts, joins in with itself, assumes shape upon shape, and goes out of itself incessantly! ... At last we have it here in that state comparable to flame, in the midst of the most active exchanges ... We can no longer speak of 'movement' nor distinguish any longer its acts from its limbs ...[3]

The dance is not abstract, for it is a medley of body, sound, music, movement, setting, vision; it is its own form of speech and of writing, for, as Valéry declares, hands speak and feet write, and Yeats could speak of the poetic, rooted in the dance, as a 'thinking with the body.'

Yeats, writing some of the best-remembered lines of modern poetry about dance in 'Among School Children,' stressed the unity of dancer and dance, of the creator of the form and the form itself, of benign generation through production and the product:

> Labour is blossoming or dancing where
> The body is not bruised to pleasure soul,
> Nor beauty born out of its own despair,
> Nor blear-eyed wisdom out of midnight oil.
> O chestnut-tree, great-rooted blossomer,
> Are you the leaf, the blossom, or the bole?
> O body swayed to music, O brightening glance,
> How can we know the dancer from the dance?[4]

If the dance and dancer are integrated as the blossom and the roots, the dancer is communicating a message which cannot be communicated in any other way than she or he does, not even in words (except by the use of such transgressions of communication in which the words become poetry and approximate, but only approximate, the meaning of a dance).

The dance exemplifies how 'art becomes ... an exercise in communicating about the species of unconsciousness,' which involve a wide spectrum of knowledge that is possessed but not consciously known. Bateson's unconscious is not strictly a traditional psychoanalytic concept of the 'unconscious,' for he felt that too much early Freudian theory was upside down (see p. 58). Arguing that Freud is too committed to an Enlightenment conception of reason, Bateson stresses that Pascal spoke of the heart as having precise algorithms – a position he also claims is present in Claude Lévi-Strauss's anthropological thought. Consciousness and unconsciousness are a set of relations between levels of the mind, and consciousness only arises within a regime of mental signs that has a pressing claim of priority upon attention. Metaphor and iconic communication are the discourse of the primary processes. Duncan's dance is a precise algorithm of the heart, communicating that which cannot be communicated in any other way.

Logopoeia – 'the dance of the intellect among meanings' – is the term Ezra Pound used for the poet's act of playing with the purely linguistic and semantic aspects of verbal poetry.[5] Joyce's radical and extensive use of *logopoeia* in *Ulysses* and the *Wake* is unique, and the form of the *Wake* is said to be that of a four-part dance, for 'the party begs the glory of a wake while the scheme is like your rumba round me garden' (309.6–7). Burke says, 'The symbolic act is the *dancing of an attitude*.'[6] In this 'attitudinizing' of the poem, the body is involved. Poetry's potential value as socially corrective action lies in the dialogue which art elicits through tropes and semiotic play: verbal, visual, auditory, gestural, as well as that synaesthesia involved in the synthetic architectonics of the multi-modal arts themselves. Such dialogue is both a liberating and a playful activity. Dance, like mime, plays with the movements and gestures of the body, creating an artwork formed from the figures produced through bodily gesture, movement, and rhythm (usually combined with sound or music), elements which provide the foundation of our capability to create figurative language. Freud's preoccupation with the figures and gestures of dream language, of verbal slips and of jokes, recognizes them as verbal gestures involved in communication with the unconscious.

Consequently, Bateson used dance as a way of exemplifying communication with the unconscious, because he was sensitive to the fundamental ambivalence of Freud's conception of the unconscious, a problem corroborated by the dialogue in which those transgressive figures of speech participate. While at the turn of the century many thinkers considered the conscious mind to be normal and the unconscious mysterious, today with the re-enchantment of the world we think of consciousness as mysterious 'and of the computational methods of the unconscious, e.g. primary process, as continually active, necessary, and all-embracing.'[7] The dance prefigures the mysteries of consciousness; wordplay can easily be conceived as a dance of the mind, reflecting the same mysteries of consciousness, for wordplay leads the mind back to the sense of the word and thus back to a sense of the world. In Joyce's grounding of language as gesture, word emerges from gesture, the language that is rooted (i.e., Joyce's 'root language' [*FW*424.17]) in the human person; dance unites gesture with the kinaesthetic mobility of the body to permit it to inscribe its own figures. In his final artistic work, based on his most mature theoretical understanding, Joyce identified drama and dance as fundamental for understanding all poetic creation and all communication. The association of this work with rumba or dance becomes coterminous with the dream action itself: 'Me drames, O'Loughlins, has come through! Now let the centuple celves ... by the coincidance of their contraries reamalgamerge in that indentity of undiscernibles' (*FW*49.32). His dreams (or perhaps drams of whisky), producing dramas, have come through (attained intelligibility) and come true (attained veracity – *veritas* is found *in vino, in riso,* or *in somni*!). The dreaming or drinking enable the 'centuple celves' to 'reamalgamerge,' a reassembling of multiple selves into a persona, which occurs by a 'coincidance' (coincidence + dance) of contraries forming an 'indentity of undiscernibles': a new ambiguous and ambivalent message only fully realized in the world of dream, drunkenness, or drama.

A 'coincidance' is the natural movement within a world which is a 'chaosmos,' yet just as in contemporary chaos theory, it is also the constructive power by which the contraries are 'reamalgamerged':

And as I was jogging along in a dream as dozing as I was dawdling, arrah, methought broadtone was heard and the creepers and the gliders and flivvers of the earth breath and the dancetongues of the woodfires and the hummers in their ground all vociferated echoating: Shaun! Shaun! Post the post! with a high voice and O, the higher on high the deeper and low, I heard him so! (404.3–9)

If the *Wake* involves a dance within the labyrinth of words, even more precisely a dance within the labyrinth of signs, it is from the conflict between, within, and among words and signs that the drama of communication arises. 'The war is in words and the wood is the world. Maply me, willowy we, hickory he and yew yourselves' (98.34–5). The wood here evokes the memory of the Irish letters as constituting a tree alphabet with elm (= [Gaelic] *ailm*) standing for the letter *a*.

The conflict of signs and words (wood = trees) reflects the world drama itself. The metaphor of the forest as the world parallels that of the garden as the medley of signs (the 'flowers') which transform the world into intelligible design. Ben Jonson, who in the seventeenth century entitled his 'common book' on criticism *Timber, or Discoveries* and one of his books of poems *Underwoodes*, exemplifies the ongoing familiarity of authors throughout historical and prehistorical time with such symbols. Speaking of woods and flowers in this manner is also ecological, since it suggests that people are co-partners with nature in the process of cultivating the world, making sense of creation.

This is a tradition within which the opposition of people and nature does not exist, since people, especially in their poetic role, are a part of nature. Shakespeare vividly expresses this idea in *The Winter's Tale* when Polixenes (then disguised) explains to Perdita that human creativity itself is a natural power:

Yet Nature is made better by no mean
But nature make that mean: so over that art,
Which you say adds to nature, is an art
That nature makes. You see, sweet maid, we marry
A gentler scion to the wildest stock,
And make conceive a bark of baser kind
By bud of nobler race. This is an art

> Which does mend nature – change it rather – but
> The art itself is nature. (*The Winter's Tale*, 4.4.89–97)

To think in terms of cultivating gardens, then, is equivalent to thinking in terms of protecting forests today, for in each of these ecological processes, human art is cooperating and changing nature. To transfer such thought from cultivation to culture, from gardening to acting, speaking, and writing, is to recognize the natural physicality of gesture, orality, and literacy. The action of *The Winter's Tale* moves quite naturally from the discussion of gardening to the performance of a dance. Since some messages can only be 'danced' and others can only be 'played,' in his 'ecology' of communication Bateson tries to understand how and why people select different modal forms from within the repertoire of signs.

Synaesthetic effects, nonsense, and semiotic play are the means by which poetry generates meaning, for expression itself is an artistic activity associated with those psychological and social processes employed in constructing reality by which people make sense of the world and communicate within it. The very term used in speaking about this phenomenon (making *sense*), whether in English, French, or German, reflects this ambivalence. The communality of the senses required in the process of understanding and communicating (in fact, the traditional concept of common sense as a mediator in the processes between sensory input and mental operations) refers to this situation. Communication so conceived takes place in a milieu of discontinuous fragments, which may be part of a single system (such as a natural language) or interacting components of different systems contributing to the creation of a more complex system (such as that of multimedia communication). Fragmentation is an essential aspect of all communication, since it is involved in the very activity of framing a message, whether verbal, visual, auditory, or a combination of media.

The twentieth century has experienced a heightened awareness of discontinuity and fragmentation as well as increased self-consciousness about the role that they play in enabling people to communicate. This has been associated with a recognition of the growing fragmentation of social lifeworlds (urbanization), of the shrinking of the globe (globalization), and of the rapidity of social change, as well as an increasing awareness of the centrality of discontinuity and fragmentation in the construction of our biological world and in the evolution of mind. The arts have played a complementary role in enabling these perceptions to become part of our understanding of how we communicate. Chaplin, Fellini, Makavéjev, and the surrealists are typical of contemporary artists who exploit awareness of this fragmentation of society and the life-world which has been accelerated through ever-increasing electrification and mechanization, through changing conceptions of space and time, and through radically new modes of social and political organization. Artists like these exemplify how the production of the erotic is fundamentally related to discontinuity and fragmentation, since the very power of eroticism derives from the sensory impact achieved through the transgressing of the flows, continuities, and orderliness of day-by-day existence.

A carnivalesque spirit releases disorder, tempts chaos, and deifies transgression. As such it activates that fragmenting machine of wild laughter of which Wyndham Lewis spoke so eloquently in 1917. Over a decade later, Lewis deliberately turned this 'wild laughter' against the world of mechanization both in his creative writings such as *Childermass* and in his critical writings such as *Men without Art* and *Time and Western Man*. In *Time and Western Man* Lewis argues that Joyce, Gertrude Stein, Russian ballet, Chaplin, and popular novels like *Gentlemen Prefer Blondes* all reflect the new Bergsonian time philosophy that celebrates the rapidly expanding mechanization which characterized everyday life in the 1920s. Yet the paradox is that Lewis himself has to use the very same strategies of *mechanical* laughter (which are naturally machine-like and correspond to Bergson's comic theory) to expose the dangers inherent in the Bergsonian world-view.

Lewis, as enemy or critic, sees his role to be that of exposing the mechanical movements of the world, which are presumably manifesting themselves in the shortening of skirts, the glorification of youth, the inanities of *Gentlemen Prefer Blondes*, the worship of time-motion study, and the efficiency of the typewriter. Lewis particularly singled out Joyce for attack, since he saw him as a prime exemplar of the new Bergsonian world of machinic process, as the poet who favoured a glorification of the flow of time at the expense of respecting the stability of space. Nonetheless, Joyce's *Wake* actually is a laughing-machine of wild satire unleashed against the technologization of the 'taylorised world' (356.10), a phrase he uses to allude to Frederick Winslow Taylor, the grandfather of modern scientific management, the assembly line, and time-motion study, whose name he overlays on that of the late eighteenth-century neo-Platonist and mathematician Thomas Taylor.

Finnegans Wake, characteristically of modernist poetry and art, weaves together multiple allusions to war, the destructive transformation of the natural world by technology, and the transmutation of speech and writing in a super-mechanized world as a way of highlighting the significance of this fragmentation of the life-world and the resulting effects of grotesquerie – clearly another aspect of the 'abnihilisation of the etym' (353.22). Media as mediators and interfaces between people and machines or machines and machines epitomize the fundamental social fragmentation and the way that the instrumentality of a regime of signs is also a machine. Even the movement of the body can become a grotesque assemblage of mechanical movements, as the comic and animated films of the period underline. The grotesque, in fact, is a major aspect of the force Bataille described as emanating from anatomical reflection on parts of the body such as the artists of the 1920s and 1930s had incorporated in their productions, utilizing the erotic potential of fragmentation, the breaking of flows, the creating of gaps. Bataille's pornographic work of art, *Histoire de l'oeil,* illustrates the intimate relation between the fragmentation of the mechanical bride or bridegroom and pornographic effect. He later theorized about the erotic in various essays in *Documents* and in a monograph, *L'Erotisme,* in which he drew attention to the sensory effects of fragmentation of parts of the body – eye, mouth, the big toe, the severed ear of Vincent van Gogh:

> The big toe is the most *human* part of the human body, in the sense that no other element of this body is as differentiated from the corresponding element of the anthropoid ape ... man moves on the earth without clinging to branches, having himself become a tree, in other words raising himself straight up in the air like a tree and all the more beautiful for the correctness of his erection. In addition, the function of the human foot consists in giving a firm foundation to the erection of which man is so proud ...
>
> But whatever the role played in the erection of his foot, man, who has a light head, in other words, a head raised to the heavens and heavenly things, sees it as spit, on the pretext that he has this foot in the mud.
>
> ... Human life entails, in fact, the rage of seeing oneself as a back and forth movement from refuse to the ideal, and from the ideal to refuse – a rage that is easily directed against an organ as *base* as the foot.[8]

The involvement of the toe with human erectness and with contact with dirt and excrement underlies that polymorphous seductiveness associated with foot fetishism. Bataille speaks of its 'base seductiveness,' which explains the 'burlesque value' that unfortunately accrues to 'the pleasures condemned by pure and superficial men.'[9] The erotic power results from the tension arising from the discontinuities – the back and forth movement from base to ideal – that pervade the human desiring machine. The grotesqueness of the big toe weds 'wild laughter' to a perverse eroticism. Joyce draws attention to some of these ambiguities of his era when he describes Anna Livia, the heroine in his dream work, as walking in her 'nudiboots' (136.10). This is the stuff from which the icons of the 'mechanical bride' in the 1940s and 1950s were constructed, and it is specifically associated with the movements of human desire; desire which shapes the rhetoric of that eros involved in all communication. These become the figures of advertising and propaganda as readily as they form the figures of the visual, dramatic, or verbal arts or of the intimate communication of desire.

Figures are fragments of discourse; the result of the comings and goings of the artist's mind moving through the community of signs. There is a co-naturality between rhetorical figures as the 'body's gesture caught in action' and Bataille's bodily fragments. Figures exploit the gaps in the flow of signs creating shocks – disorientations – that seduce the audience. Poetic tradition speaks of the figures as abuses or violations of speech, often in language bordering on the idea of the sinful, such as 'trespasses' or 'transgressions.' Puttenham's *Arte of English Poesie* (1589) is exemplary, for he speaks of these 'instruments of ornament' as being 'also in a sorte abuses or rather trespasses in speach.' He continues, 'All our figures be but transgressions of our dayly speach,' which work to 'beautify' poetry if they be 'fitting'; that is, if they produce a suitable proportion between 'the sence and the sensable' as nature herself does.[10] The erotic force of his terminology is also reflected in a number of Puttenham's examples, such as his discussion of *synecdoche* (or the 'figure of quick conceite') with which he concludes his exposition of the 'sensable figures' (e.g., metaphor, irony, metonymy, allegory, periphrasis, etc.):

> it encombers the minde with a certaine imagination of what it may be that is meant, and not expressed: as he that said to a fair young gentlewoman, who was in her chamber making her selfe unready. Mistresse, will ye geve me leaue to vnlace your peticote, meaning (perchance) the other thing that might follow from such unlacing. In the olde time, whosoeuer was allowed to vndoe his Ladies girdle might lie with her all night; wherefore, the taking of a womans maydenhead away, was said to vndoo her girdle. *Virgineam dissoluit zonam*, saith the poet conceiving out of a thing precedent, a thing subsequent.[11]

Hollywood, under the Hayes' Office, came to be a master of visual synecdoche: the device by which what was to happen next off-screen was reflected in gesture, action, and setting. A typical example can be found in *It Happened One Night* (1939), starring Claudette Colbert and Clark Gable. (Ironically, *Playboy* continued the tradition into a presumably more liberated era by air-brushing photographs.) The detached legs of the advertisements of the era of the 'mechanical bride' had their own teasing synecdochic relation with the coital. The relation of transgression to division or fragmentation becomes central to all the figurative processes which are so essential for everyday communication.

Transgression, which produces erotic messages, laughter, or meaning justifies the underlying relationship between communication and anarchy. Figures of communication (for all sign systems have their figurative transgressions) are associated with processes of desire. McLuhan's stressing the tactility of a TV generation reflected in a way his own past history as an historian of rhetoric and scholar of Elizabethan drama. The discourse of figures touch the body of the audience as part of the communicating machine. McLuhan's positive reception by artists and intellectuals, as well as by advertisers and communicators, is inextricably tied up with his analysis of tactility and movement. Figures weave networks of interaction which themselves illustrate the processes of communication about which they talk.

To explore the relationship of tactility, eroticism, mechanization, and communication, in which McLuhan's work reflects the insight of contemporary arts, let us trace images of the foot and the toe, since we have already examined Bataille's penetrating analysis of these fragments of the body. Such fragmentation is not only an important theme of McLuhan's first book, *The Mechanical Bride,* but the particular images of foot and toe do appear in a number of his works.[12] McLuhan's early interest in the fundamental ambivalence of tactility within the organizational rationality of the mechanical world led to his writing about advertising and popular culture in *The Mechanical Bride.* It is now fully understood that the foot shod and unshod can serve as part of an image-complex suggestive of this ambivalence as it appears in productions of the advertising industry. Together with images of chests, hair, breasts, legs, and hands, the foot is also related to the commodification of the human person, particularly women, as well as with fetishism. While used in practice, as McLuhan's work illustrated, the significance of the ambivalent motif of the bare foot had by no means been as widely and overtly recognized, or, at least acknowledged, before the 1950s.

One knows that the image of the shod and unshod for McLuhan is associated with an earlier religious poet he greatly respected, Gerard Manley Hopkins. Hopkins developed what McLuhan believed to be an intrinsic opposition between tactility and the organizational rationality of the mechanical world; in 'God's Grandeur,' in an historic image of the shod, Hopkins criticizes the loss of spirituality in the contemporary world:

Generations have trod, have trod, have trod;
  And all is seared with trade; bleared, smeared with toil;
  And wears man's smudge and shares man's smell: the soil
Is bare now, nor can foot feel, being shod. (ll. 5–8)[13]

Here the bare foot as an openness to tactile stimuli and uninhibited movement is juxtaposed against the mechanistic deterioration of the ecosystem viewed as a gift of divine grace. Hopkins utilizes the complex ambiguities of the imagery of being shod and going barefoot, since the sensuous potentialities of such images were considerable. The bare foot puts one in communication with the earth.

In the late Victorian world in which the wearing of strong, heavy shoes became a necessity of a mechanized workplace, the shod foot had also become equated with civilization and the conversion of the savage. Paradoxically, the barefoot also had long-standing visual associations with humility (as developed in ecclesiastical art), while in other traditional associations footwear had represented freedom and domination, since slaves in Greece had to go barefoot. While the evolution of the workboot in industrial society generally reversed some of the social values associated with shoes, the fashion industry could still continue to produce discriminatory styles of footwear. The social protests of the 1960s, sensitive to such significance, simultaneously adopted both the workboot and the bare foot as signs of dissent to the status quo.

Hopkins's poem involving the image of the foot begins with a reference to the new electric world previously celebrated by Walt Whitman:

The world is charged with the grandeur of God.
  It will flame out, like shining from shook foil;
  It gathers to a greatness, like the ooze of oil
Crushed. Why do men then now not reck his rod? (ll. 1–4)

The image of static electricity is meant to generate the energy which fragments and permeates the world in which Hopkins lived, so that a poem he entitled 'That Nature Is a Heraclitean Fire and of the Comfort of the Resurrection' [Poem 72] abounds in mechanical images of energy:

in pool and rut peel parches
Squandering ooze to squeezed | dough, crust, dust; stanches, starches
Squadroned masks and manmarks | treadmire toil there
Footfretted in it. Million-fueled | nature's bonfire burns on.

But quench her bonniest dearest | to her, her clearest-selvèd spark
Man, how his fast firedint | his mark on mind, is gone! (ll. 6–11)

This same tension between tactility and the mechanization of society is central to McLuhan's *The Mechanical Bride,* for the then world of popular culture is conceived of as a world of look, but not touch, and of a world that is out of touch with its own sense of sensuous integrity. The body is viewed as an assemblage of parts; the viewer is bombarded by assemblages of images in and out of conflict. Advertisements using a detached leg dressed in stockings and high heels, comparing women to cars (Body by Fisher!), or seeing impact in the juxtaposition of a fist and face (a Young and Rubicam ad promoting their own advertising agency) illustrated the world of mechanization reflecting itself in the world of advertising.

This still was a world of tactility, since titillation and tickling the emotions through the eyes is itself associated with arousing sensory sensations. But the taboo against touch made it also essentially a world of double-bind. While, primarily, all of this activity occurred in the context of an ideology of technological rationalization and economic acquisitiveness geared to preserving the dominant social order, it also had to play with the surfaces of the world of sense and of the senses co-opting them to promote control through communication. Yet by playing with sense and with the senses in this manner, the ad men, publicists, and producers of popular culture were also playing with the breakdown of accepted rationalities and misleadingly seducing the unsuspecting members of the supposed mass audience into pseudo-promises of the pre-Edenic liberation of unrealizable Utopias.

Duncan's barefoot dancing is another more secular association – contemporary with Hopkins's writings – of openness and sensuosity implicit in the development of modern dance. Her filmy gowns and bare feet, which were then considered in many quarters as scandalous, became an important symbol of liberation as well as an important part of the kinaesthetic freedom of modern dance. Duncan's moving image celebrates liberation and criticizes the image of the 'mechanical bride'; the dominated yet dominating woman of the advertising myths which McLuhan explores. The reaction contemporaneous with Duncan's first presenting her new dances strongly underlines the analysis that Bataille presents concerning shoes and 'modesty of the foot,' since her bare feet became the primary sign of the message of bodily liberation and tactile projection which permeated her dancing: an intense mode of communication.

When apparent changes in lifestyle (triggered by the avant-garde and youth) appeared to emerge as dominant, McLuhan revised his understanding of mechanization, divorcing it from being a natural product of the new urban and mass media world (which he had argued in *The Mechanical Bride*). Now media seemed to him to be producing a very paradoxical effect; not that feared from a totalitarian mechanization fostered by the Futurists, but an apparent liberation of people from the effects of the mechanical by opening up a new world of apparently total sensory exposure. While radio, comics, ads, and newspapers had all seemed to be relevant to mechanization taking command, now they were also elements of a new world, where television, conversation, mod fashions, and dance became even more important factors in this total sensory involvement.

In *Understanding Media* one of the images McLuhan had focused on as indicating the new tactility was Brigitte Bardot, whose freedom from bra and shoes had become a trademark of liberation. Bardot driving barefoot became an image of the new sports car driver's desire to be in touch with the vibrations of the road. In the *Medium Is the Massage* the momentary aberration of a cellist who performed nude, encased only in transparent plastic, projected an image of the total sensual massage. Nevertheless, the foot remained a prime symbol, since the centre-piece of *The Medium Is the Massage* (perhaps deliberately suggestive of Bataille's writings on parts of the body in his periodical, *Documents*) is a close-up of the face of a somewhat uncomfortable-looking male (could it be W.C. Fields?) sniffing the big toe of a bare foot.[14] All of the ambiguities about modernity which pervade McLuhan's satiric work are present in this key image of his *Massage*. The pervasive ambivalence of the seductiveness with which Bataille analyses 'The Big Toe' reflects an ambivalence in McLuhan which he never directly confronted, since in his own puritan support of censorship and opposition to abortion, one aspect of his sensibility was that of one of Bataille's 'pure and superficial men.' Yet the centrality of dirt to the impact of this centre-piece – visual, tactile, olfactory, and imaginary – is inescapable.

Even though McLuhan has had substantial impact on our thought about communication, these aspects are virtually never a matter of comment or criticism. Yet such erotic imagery is not only a pervasive part of McLuhan's books and was an important factor in his popularity, but it also is an intrinsic theme in the artistic worlds that influenced not only McLuhan's thought but that of many European theorists who grappled with problems of communication. The important consideration, apart from the complex associations with freedom and domination involved in this play of the erotic and the tactile, is the identification of tactility with the interplay between the surface of the world's body and the surface of the human body. This is the moment of sense experience for it brings the surface of the earth in contact with the person and simultaneously breaks that surface and its interface with the body up into discrete and different bits of sensory information. This encounter recapitulates what happens in moments of intense communication, for they also involve this experience of the surfaces of existence and the breaking down which precedes the breakthrough. As much as they differ in so many aspects, Deleuze and McLuhan appear to explore the same communicative interplay within the labyrinths of our life-world. Tactility, therefore, is the essential symbol for the intersensory operation of the body's processing of sensory material. Tactility as a powerful metaphor for the interplay of the senses is associated, like bodily movement, with the machine-like operation of the central nervous system (CNS). Although frequently tactility may appear to be a mere synonym for sensuality, it is an appropriate term for the machine-like nature of this sensory interplay, since it links the intercommunication of the sensory systems with the digital organization by which they codify information. The CNS is a powerful combination of electrical and mechanical conceptions that far outstrips the capability of the computer. The image of technologies as extensions of the senses (or really of the CNS) is tied up, on one hand, with the operation of tactility and, on the other, with our conception of the human body and of the extended social body within which humans exist. A gestural theory of communication, communication as 'the dancing of an attitude,' squarely grounds the process in the body and the body's primary avenue of communication with the earth and its world – tactility and the intersensory processing of the CNS. Literacy, when widely disseminated, ultimately transforms the uttering or outering of the voice back into the body, as a dance which inscribes by depositing its traces in time and space.

11

Electro-Mechanization and the Global City: Poetic Engineering and the Open Text

After writing *Ulysses*, Joyce provided some friends with a detailed chart outlining its complex structure.[1] Each episode of his book not only relates its action with a specific scene (temporally restricted to a specific hour of the day and spatially confined to a particular region or regions of the city of Dublin) but also interrelates it with a specific episode of Homer's *Odyssey*, a specific symbol, a specific style, a specific art, a specific colour, and a specific organ of the body. Dublin, the city (*civitas*) where the entire action of *Ulysses* transpires, takes shape as a *community* through the superimposition of organs, symbols, arts, and the movement of people.

Just as in the everyday life of any city, the great organs (institutions) produce that city's distinct shape and social existence, Joyce's epic of the everyday urban waking world is centred about the intrinsic connection between the embodied individuals who inhabit the city, their daily life, and the drama of their symbolic interaction. In *Ulysses* the different modalities of each communication technology inscribe themselves upon each person's body and on the corporate body which is the city of Dublin; in the *Wake*, the continuous mental and neuromuscular activity of one who sleeps and dreams receives and processes the imaginary (and unconscious) inscription of the daytime life-world. The imaginary nomadic wanderings of people through a city in the daytime or imaginarily through the interior landscape of dream at night shape and inscribe, structure and give form to, the production of a sense of place.

Joyce's charts of *Ulysses* are concerned with the complexities involved in taking diagonal cuts of the terrain of Dublin as a living *community* and retracing the new communication flows within the *community* that are produced by the movement of its inhabitants within the city. The movement of people, sensory experience, and information that produces Dublin's geoscape also creates gaps, generating a disjunctive, labyrinthine movement across earth, air, and river, which further varies the play of light and colour. This movement inscribes a mapping of networks on the surface of the city, for the social body (individual or corporate) is uninscribed (like Artaud's body-without-organs) without the operation of the poetic-dramatic machine or other semiotic machines associated with social praxis (economic, political, etc.).

In the nocturnal world of the *Wake*, the interplay of bloodstream (ALP as river) and nerves (marked by HCE's stuttering) produces the dreamscape of an archetypal city, which is still just a rendition of the clichés shaping any modern European city. This, then, is the very stuff of communications (the action within which the social communications of everyday life are always embedded), re-establishing movement between the gaps created in the normal or predictable flows of human life. Joyce envisages the living, moving bodies of his Dubliners as transforming the body politic of the city through its citizens' secular consciousness of the city as a machine, which provides for them an ability to participate in intensive communication (a secular communion – a sort of secularized *Corpus Christi*)[2] and permits them to remain individuals within the contemporary 'community of redemption,' a community of redemption in which secularized social communion occurs through the momentary feeling of joy at being in possession of a 'sense' of one another. The symbiosis between the person and the *city* as the site of communication defines the action of *Ulysses*, within which Joyce's dialogic epic maps the territory in, through, and by which people communicate.

The city has provided a dominant symbol for modernist literature and other arts: Eliot's *The Waste Land* (London); Baudelaire's Paris, as explicated by Benjamin; Benjamin's own odyssey of European cities; Kraus's Vienna; Garcia Lorca's New York; Picasso's *Guernica;* Eisenstein's *Potemkin* (Moscow); Lang's *Metropolis;* Britten's London; and later, Fellini's Rome. The city, as in Le Corbusier's theory and practice, became the vision of the new schools of architecture, design, and urban planning: the Bauhaus and ILTAM. The growth of the city interacts with the growth of communication and transportation, encouraging the development of the 'Great Metropolitan Dailies' of *Ulysses*' 'Aeolus' episode and Welles's *Citizen Kane;* and the development of radio and the camera eye of Dos Passos's *U.S.A.*, Joyce's *Wake*, and Lewis's *Childermass* and *The Apes of God*.

Raymond Williams, who has studied the transformations of the city and its relation to the countryside in literature and art,[3] observes that the new relationships of industrial workers in city homes, with the consequent increased privatization and self-sufficiency, required regular funding, supply, and information from the outside: 'This relationship created both the need and the form of a new kind of "communication": news from "outside," from otherwise inaccessible sources. Already in the drama of the 1880's and 1890's (Ibsen, Chekhov) this structure had appeared.'[4] Broadcasting emerged as a means of meeting the 'contradictory pressures' of this phase of *mobile privatization* in industrial capitalism.[5] Williams's remarks identify some ways in which the arts explored changing modes of communication, because they also explored changing perceptions of the lifeworld resulting from politically, economically, and technologically induced social change.

It is not only in those artworks which specifically encompass the city that the interaction between communication and community takes place, but in other artworks as well. The city and our everyday environment provide the elements from which contemporary artists and poets produce their works. Throughout this century, frequently because of the new differing mixes of ethnic origins, sensitivity to the urban experience through the conversion of forms considered exotic (e.g., Gershwin's *American in Paris*, Schönberg's Vienna, jazz) typified most modern music. Architecture and the layout of the city occupy a prominent place in Eisenstein's discussion of film elements, just as the city is the primary source of the vivisected bits and pieces that make up Joyce's poetic worlds, for cities are sites where multitudes of people first utilize a wide variety of multi-faceted modes of expression of everyday life:

> We have only to glance at a group of cubist paintings to convince ourselves that what takes place in these paintings has already been heard in jazz music.
>
> This relationship is just as evident in the architectural landscape – classic architecture bearing the same relation to the classicists in music composition as the modern urban landscape bears to jazz.
>
> Indeed, Roman squares and villas, Versailles' park and terraces could be 'prototypes' for the structure of classical music.
>
> The modern urban scene, especially that of a large city at night is clearly the plastic equivalent of jazz.[6]

Eisenstein provides a detailed description of such a night-time cityscape, ranging from the 'nocturnal sea of electric advertising' to the 'headlights on speeding cars.'[7] These are the elements which combine syntactically to form the hieroglyphs composing the message projected by the landscape and which recombine to recreate the different elements of cubist painting or jazz music that create a complementary vision. The 'litter' of the cityscape itself creates letters which reveal the new sensibility shaped by the signs of the everyday world. Such principles of Eisensteinian grammar shape the content of the filmic imagination just as much as its style of composition and editing. Film semiology is born in the awareness of fragmentation that marks the nature of the modern landscape.

The 'vivisective' method, of which Joyce speaks, provides a means for recontextualizing the world of commercial objects, of mediated forms of human communication, and of mechanized life to explore them within their living mode. The diagonal and transverse cuts across the Joycean city use decontextualization and recontextualization as a technique for bringing attention to the 'ambiviolent' (*FW*518.2) language (ambivalence and violence) implicit in these images and processes by placing them within a deliberately designed imaginary reconstruction of everyday life. A detailed look at the structure of one of the four books of *Finnegans Wake* will demonstrate how central to the entire work are technology, machines, and electricity. Joyce uses Vico to explore the role of the poetic in human development and communication in Book II. The four chapters of Book II make manifest the centrality of the poetic principle in human affairs and the perpetual process of destruction and reconstruction by which people shape and reshape their life-world through communication.

The chapters superficially seem to move from the dramatic to the expository then to the narrative and finally to reminiscence, but looking more closely at this pattern reveals how complexly Joyce exploits the poetic activity of art that is part of every body's existence. The first chapter, 'The Mime of Nick, Mick and the Maggies,' begins this history, using children's play as an originary 'model' of mime and drama. In this opening of Book II, chapter 1, the children in their nursery are playing the game of angels and devils. The game is an exemplary 'model' of mime and drama, appropriately dubbed by the dreamer as 'The Mime of Nick, Mick and the Maggies,' a mime staged in the 'Feenichts Playhouse' (219.2) and reproduced in film form.

This production encompasses the 'gossipaceousness' of a tabloid for it is '... wordloosed over seven seas crowdblast in cellelleneteutoslavzendlatinsoundscript. In four tubbloids' (219.16–18). This medley of multimedia, involving suggestions of film, newspapers (i.e., acts introduced by Brechtian headlines – tubbloids), puppetry, ballet, liturgy ('masses for the good folk'), dance, music, and spectacle, concludes like a contemporary masque 'to be wound up for an after-enactment by a Magnificent Transformation Scene showing the Radium Wedding of Neid and Moorning and the Dawn of Peace, Pure, Perfect and Perpetual, Waking the Weary of the World' (222.16–19). As this Viconian multi-mini-drama moves towards its comic conclusion, 'For the producer (Mr John Baptister Vickar) caused a deep abuliousness to descend' (255.26–7), it is described as a medley of comic method: 'your wildeshaweshowe moves swiftly sterneward!' (256.13–14).

As the first chapter of Book II ends there is 'upploud!' and laughter mixed with prayer and invocation – 'Loud heap miseries upon us yet entwine our arts with laughters low!' (259.7–8) – that lead to the next Viconian stage of development, which unfolds in 'Triv and Quad' (chapter 2). Here childhood gives way to adolescence, as the forms of communication and expression shift from drama and play to those of the schoolroom – disputation, the diary, the epistle, and the management of symbolic systems (mathematics, geography, science, etc.). As Joyce indicated in a letter to Frank Budgen, the entire chapter is 'a reproduction of a school boy's (and a schoolgirl's) old classbook complete with marginalia by the twins who change sides at half-time, footnotes by the girl (who doesn't), a Euclid diagram, funny drawings, etc. It was like that in Ur of Chaldees too, I dare say.'[8] The disputation, the epistle, and the commonplace book were forms studied within the medieval and Renaissance liberal arts of grammar, logic, and rhetoric that Jesuit pedagogues used to teach the arts of communication, expression, inquiry, and memory to develop the understanding of sign, symbol and gesture: 'Where flash becomes word and silents selfloud' (267.16–17).

As adolescence yields to maturity, the action shifts from the schoolroom in the second chapter to HCE and his customers in the pub below in the third. Here Joyce explores the development of the public and social arts of entertainment and conversation. The model is story-telling, the telling of a tale. Over one-quarter of the words in the *Wake* that directly relate to 'tale,' and the same proportion that relate to 'story,' occur in this chapter. Communication mediated by people (e.g., story-telling, singing, conversing, gossip) and by technologies (TV, radio, film) present motifs of people as builders, broadcasters, recorders, and transmitters, presenting issues that range from the peer pressures of the 'cummanity' to politics and beliefs.

In the fourth and final chapter, 'Mamalujo,' four old men mull over and recount (retale, retail) parodically the tale of Tristan and Isolde, illustrating how old age preserves the past for the future through a history that transmits corporate memory chiefly through an anecdotal medley of nostalgia, remembered rumour, and gossip – the very stuff that creates myths and legends. This parodic blend of sentimental poetry and near senile indulgence in malicious gossip characterizes the evangelist and the historian as annalists, makers of Barthesian 'mythologies,' for every night 'the four old oldsters ... all puddled and mythified' look 'to see was the Transton Postscript come,' for from reading the paper (393.30–6) (i.e., *Boston Evening*

Transcript, cf. 111.9 and 617.23),[9] they can produce their 'gastspiels' and 'dreams of yore,' these spinners of 'oldpoetryck' (393.10), who 'collect all and bits of brown, the rathure's evelopment in spirits of time in all fathom of space ...' (394.9–10).

Book II of the *Wake* explores how a society makes itself by developing competence in poetics and communication, thus demonstrating the poetic as rooted in play, in dream, and in drama, from which other forms of the imaginary derive. New or recent technologies of production, reproduction, and dissemination occupy a prominent role throughout this book, for they are the foundation for the new communicative semiology of the closing century of the second millennium. The third chapter of this book, which explores adulthood, clearly indicates the centrality of the techno-scientific in Joyce's vision. The pub provides a milieu replete with allusions to language, dance, speech, and nonsense, but also to photography, radio, film, television, and other technologies.

HCE as hero, like Lewis's Bailiff in *Childermass*, or Horace Zagreus in *The Apes of God*, is imaged as a broadcaster. But Joyce goes still further, literally presenting HCE as an electronic man (a telecommunications machine), because, like Giedion, Joyce discerns the continuity from mechanical to electrical and electronic devices. At the beginning of this bar-room scene, the Host, HCE, is said to be the 'birth of an otion' (echoing the title of Griffith's film *The Birth of a Nation*):

> ... their tolvtubular high fidelity daildialler, as modern as tomorrow afternoon and in appearance up to the minute ... equipped with supershielded umbrella antennas for distance getting and connected by the magnetic links of a Bellini-Tosti coupling system with a vitaltone speaker, capable of capturing skybuddies, harbour craft emittences, key clickings, vaticum cleaners, due to woman formed mobile or man made static and bawling the whowle hamshack and wobble down in an eliminium sounds pound so as to serve him up a melegoturny marygoraumd, eclectrically filtered for allirish earths and ohmes. This harmonic condenser enginium (the Mole) they caused to be worked from a magazine battery ... which was tuned up by twintriodic singulvalvulous pipelines (lackslipping along as if their liffing deepunded on it) with a howdrocephalous enlargement, a gain control of circumcentric megacyles. ... (309.14–310.7)

The human body is imaginarily rendered as a magnetic high fidelity device of tubes and dials hooked to antennas, sending as well as receiving, with a capability for 'emittences' and 'key clickings,' all of which is accomplished by electrically filtered ohms, harmonic condensers, engines, and batteries.

This passage has been analysed both as suggesting a radio transmitter-receiver (e.g., 'hamshack') and as an otological description of the ear ('otion'). Obviously, while both of these are involved and as John Bishop has shown the ear is primary and prominent,[10] the motif of transmission and reception is still central to Book II, particularly the pub scene (as well as the entire *Wake*). This places the head containing the brain, the 'howdrocephalous enlargement' ('hydrocephalous,' partly as water on the head and partly because electricity can be mapped as a hydraulic system) – the nervous system – at the core of this 'harmonic condenser enginium,' which is H.C. Earwicker.

Through such imaginary vivisection of the electric city as the body of an electric man, the *Wake* clearly demonstrates a continuity between the perception of mechanization taking command and the rise of the electric world, since the principle of discontinuity and fragmentation implicit in the former is expanded exponentially in the latter. Throughout the *Wake*, the design of the language deliberately mirrors the phenomenon of electrification. This insight of Eisenstein, Joyce, and many other twentieth-century artists was discursively developed by Giedion, who, as an historian of architecture, demonstrated in his *Space, Time and Architecture* an intense interest in the changing structures of time and space in the contemporary cityscape. The implications of this for communication study are of prime importance, for Joyce associates the shape of the contemporary city with the emergence of electricity and its impact on communication and transportation.

Multiple new mixed modalities of modern communication and cultural production emerge from the coalescence of mechanization and electrification accompanied by an increase in flexibility in generating and manipulating communicative signs. As Eco's semiotic writings about the contemporary period suggest, major artworks now become detailed encyclopaedic guides to the newly forming rhizomic networks that ensue from the transformations brought about by such social and technological developments.[11] The electro-mechanical urban world, when transformed into the stuff of dreams and fiction with which it is necessarily concerned (owing to the encyclopaedic nature of signs), possesses simultaneously the ability to suggest an intense sense of place and to leave the participating audience with no genuine sense of place, as key modernist and postmodernist artists have demonstrated.[12] Today the regime of communicative signs is established by the interaction of the urban world, electro-mechanical technology, and communication.

In the same chapter of the *Wake* (II,3) in which the hero is presented as an electric cyborg, the history of language as an evolving communication system is examined through Grimm's Law (which describes the consistent vowel shifts that occur in the evolution of Indo-European languages) and the problems of the Gaelic movement, which wishes to enforce a rebirth of Irish that plays counter to the course of history: 'And smotthermock Gramm's laws! But we're a drippindhrue gayleague all at ones. In the buginning is the woid, in the muddle is the sound-dance and thereinofter you're in the unbewised again, vund vulsyvolsy. You talker dunsker's brogue men we our souls speech obstruct hostery. Silence in thought! Spreach! Wear anartful of outer nocense!' (378.28–33). In the midst of and in the confusion of language in use, the wordplay of the sound-dance is a bridge between word and void, for 'in the muddle is the sound-dance.'

This bridge between speech and silence, sense and non-sense, places the unconscious in communication with the conscious; so quite aptly we are 'in the unbewised' again, for 'unbewised' links together German words for the unconscious and the unproved.[13] Communication evolves from the structure of these differing and conflicting conditions and the oppositions which consequently arise: of order and chaos, word and void, middle and muddle, conscious and unconscious, proved and unproved, since these contraries emanate from the fragments, divisions, and differences that proliferate on the ground of the earth's body. The inner speech of modern man 'obstructs hostery' because, as the pun suggests, it is 'abstract history,' while 'hostery' (hospitality, history)[14] is a type of secular communion through which the physicality of sense makes communication possible – which arises from knowing sense not by being 'artful' but through nonsense and 'anartful of outer nocense!' (no sense + know sense + nonsense + guilt [Lat. *nocentia*], a heart full of guilt and an art full of nonsense + not artful nonsense).

Just as people at earlier stages in history became one with the ways their societies developed and utilized the regime of signs (through writing, signing, signalling, singing, dancing, and drawing), people today are becoming one with their electronic networks. Those networks form extensions of every body's nervous system, or, better still, they merge with everyone's body in a symbiotic relation with the CNS. In either case, media and people become a continuum – similar to what McLuhan outlined in saying that technologies are extensions of the nervous system. Joyce's reading of Vico in the *Wake* also develops this very same theme – that technologies become extensions of a person's CNS (nerves and brain). If this is true, then the CNS, like the various technologies themselves, is a machine. A divorce between 'the whole person' and the nervous system is just as impossible as a divorce between 'the whole person' and the social field.

When communication technologies inundate the social field, people can eventually be dominated by these technologies; unless, they treat the occurrence of this symbiosis disjunctively. This requires conceiving of the act of human creativity as engineering, enabling people to invent and control expressive poetic machines. Any person in the act of such invention becomes a poetic and communicating machine producing another expressive or communicating machine. This, apparently, is part of what McLuhan believed when he spoke of the privileged ingenuity of the pun as a breakthrough through breakdown – a process which also breaks up continua, creates gaps, and opens up new possibilities. Without such a disjunctive process continuously taking place, it can genuinely be said that human communication would 'obstruct hostery' by 'abstracting history.'

The crafting of the dream language of the *Wake* involves a variety of motifs: communication, communion, and sensory experience. Poetic communication is usually associated with an act of communion and that act is usually associated with eating (e.g., the 'host') and/or other forms of sensory consummation. It permits a coalescence of ideas and states of feeling usually characteristic of those processes by which different levels of consciousness communicate about their relationships through dreams, jokes, the verbal slips of everyday life, other kinds of play behaviour, or artworks. Here, with respect to communication itself, the language of the *Wake* weaves together the dependency of communication on the interaction of the body with the gaps and transgressions resulting from engagement with the earth – its mud, dirt, and dung. It relates communication to our bodily activities of sensation and consummation and sees our body as being involved in a kind of secular communion with the life force.

During a dream presentation of the wake of the hero in *Finnegans Wake*, the odours of the corpse become a 'cummulium of scents' (498.29) – a communion of scents (punning on the communion of saints and a communion of sense), while the partying of the mourners in order to console themselves becomes a 'socializing and communicanting in the deification of his members' (498.20–1). Communication as grounded in the most fundamental interactions of human flesh and sense (scents) with the world is presented in *A Portrait of the Artist as a Young Man* (Joyce's first novel) by Baby Tuckoo's (the poet as infant) sniffing, tasting, and touching his surrounding world. Such communion depends on the fragmentation of our world, like the mourner's salvaging their 'herobit' of Finnegan at his wake. Both of these are acts which 'communicake with the original sinse,' underlining the dependency of communication on organs such as the mouth, embedding it in a world of transgression and trespass – of original sin – and going back to the original sense, the rootedness of communication in needs to eat, to survive, to reproduce, and so to sense what makes our world. This rootedness of communication in eating, surviving, reproducing, and sensing our world is ultimately grounded in community.

The concept of a *global village* was a satiric romantic transformation of the idea of a *global city* because the latter phrase, while more accurate, does not carry the overtones of comfortable primitivism.[15] The fragmentized, cosmopolitan conglomerates of psychological nomads who are part of the world of *Ulysses, The Waste Land,* or Proust's Paris already reveal a reaction to the multifarious multitude of privatized people who live in late industrial society. It is not accidental in such a community (like Dublin, which is an overgrown small town now composed of Dubliners and immigrants) that Leopold Bloom (an Austro-Hungarian Jew who is married to Molly, the Gibraltan daughter of an Anglo-Irish officer and a Spanish Jewess) strives to communicate significantly with Stephen Dedalus, a native Dubliner who is on his way to becoming a future exile to Paris. Such a city, as a communication system, works not only by transforming human social interaction, but also by transubstantiating people through the extension and subsequent transformation of their CNS, which involves an outering of people through interaction and an innering of society through the subsequent transformation of the people. The poetic reproduction of this process is an act of assemblage: 'These fragments I have shored against my ruin!'

If it can be said of Malcolm Lowry by Malcolm Lowry and then applied by Gilles Deleuze to Proust that the artist is a maker of machines, how much more penetrating is such an insight in interpreting Joyce's view of *Finnegans Wake* as an 'engine.' In April 1927, Joyce wrote to Harriet Shaw Weaver, his benefactress: 'I am glad you liked my punctuality as an engine driver. I have taken this up because I am really one of the greatest engineers, if not the greatest, in the world besides being a musicmaker, philosophist and heaps of other things. All the engines I know are wrong. Simplicity. I am making an engine with only one wheel. No spokes of course. The wheel is a perfect square. You see what I am driving at, don't you? I am awfully solemn about it, mind you, so you must not think it is a silly story about the mouse and the grapes. No, it's a wheel, I tell the world. *And* it's all *square.*'[16] Since the poet of the *Wake* and his hero, HCE, that 'eclectrically filtered Harmonic Condenser Enginium,' are both communicating machines and builders, assembling communicating machines, then ALP, the hero's wife, can see her husband, HCE (Here Comes Everybody), as her 'enginedear,' naturally concluding: 'But there's a great poet in you, too' (619.31).

Joyce, as one of the 'greatest engineers,' sees the communication event as poem and product, its receivers (or consumers) as poets and producers, and his particular imaginary dream, like Freud, as a productive work. His 'book of the depth' (the *Wake* as a contemporary *Book of the Dead*) links Egyptology and hieroglyphs to cosmology, alchemy, and Freudian dream, a complex or cluster of concepts associated with the regime of signs. As Deleuze says of Proust, of himself, and of other students of the arts and communication: 'We are not physicians or metaphysicians; we must be Egyptologists. For there are no mechanical laws between things, nor voluntary communications between minds. Everything is implicated, everything is complicated, everything is sign, meaning, essence. Everything exists in those obscure zones which we penetrate as into crypts in order to decipher hieroglyphs and secret languages. The Egyptologist, in all things, is the man who undergoes an initiation, an apprentice.'[17] The Egyptian theme unites the individual experiencing the erotic through the rites of resurrection with the Egyptologist as interpreter and discoverer of the true language, those hieroglyphs, with which Joyce deals so extensively.

The question which this raises is whether or not the cryptic or the hieroglyphic is the opposite of communication. Clearly, for Proust, Lowry, Deleuze, and Joyce, there is no opposition between the crypsis of a secret language and the process of communication. Sign, meaning, and essence in both are implicated and complicated, for Joyce's own description of his problems in composing the *Wake* brings together the themes of complications and complexity with making, engineering, and interpreting.[18] Its mode, like that of the hieroglyphs, is a breaking up of flows, a shaping of fragments. As a poet, Joyce designs a machine that will eventually create an audience for his work from the same type of people that he says assisted in its creation.

Joyce's preoccupation with letters as hieroglyphs and with the book as a designed construct (like the famous Irish illuminated manuscript of the gospels, the *Book of Kells*) manifests itself in an interest in writing systems, codes, signs, gestures, icons, etc. Runes become a kind of point of coalescence for each of these forms, for they are an alphabet, a magic language, signs, and a language of gestures. The runic theme is introduced at the very beginning of the *Wake* and is frequently associated with the art of the comic book: 'Arrah, sure, we all love little Anny Ruiny' (7.25) (i.e., *Annie Rooney*, the U.S. comic strip launched in 1929 to compete with *Little Orphan Annie*, which had been published first in 1924). In another incident, two prehistoric types, Mutt and Jute, meet – an allusion to a meeting of Mutt and Jeff – and Mutt tells Jute: 'This ourth of years is not save brickdust and being humus the same roturns. He who runes may rede it on all fours' (18.4–6).

What is to be read then is this 'claybook': '... if you are abcedminded, to this claybook, what curios of signs (please stoop), in this allaphbed! Can you rede (since We and Thou had it out already) its world? It is the same told of all' (18.17–20). The runes are rules, and rules can produce the texts of the comic-book world as readily as the open text of the *Wake* – again the association of runes and comics, rules, and games: '... but I learned all the runes of the gamest game ever from my old nourse Asa. A most adventuring trot is her and she vicking well knowed them all heartswise and fourwords. How Olive d'Oyly and Winnie Carr, bejupers, the reized the dressing of salandmon and how a peeper coster and a salt sailor med a mustied poet atwaimen. It most have been Mad Mullans planted him' (279n1.19–24). Olive Oyl (girlfriend of Popeye the Sailorman) and Moon Mullins were comic strip characters of international fame in the 1920s and 1930s. Joyce considers the art of the comics closer to a primitive visual alphabet, suggesting a relation with the relatively primitive characteristics of runic script and the even earlier Irish ogham.

Runes and comic strips; letters, illuminations, and Klee's magic squares; codes, photography, and the Alice books; gestures, nursery-room play, and cinematic dramas clearly indicate that Joyce is using language and the book to play with the entire universe of codes and to allow that universe to play through the book. Colours, heraldry, tree alphabets, and animated cartoons suggest the range of codes which are co-present in this work. They constitute part of a radically secularized realization of a new modern universalism, echoing and criticizing the vision of medieval universalism and an Enlightenment encyclopaedism. The point, though, is that this is not some specialized vision of Joyce's. He is just acutely aware of the then rapidly developing modern encyclopaedism, which has become the all-pervasive fact of the cyberspatial teleglobal communication of the 1990s. In this anticipatory prognosis, his practice exhibits a theoretical sophistication which in 1939 was far in advance of his colleagues and which, even today, remains in advance of ours.

Joyce's work creates an awareness of what it means to say that the arts are an experimental ground for the opening up of communication. In his play with the bits and pieces of speech, writing, and sign, he anticipates many of the agendas of structuralism, postmodernism, cultural studies, and communication. He even augurs the work of Bataille, Barthes, Eco, and McLuhan. But most important, his work opens up new possibilities for post-structuralist, semiotic interaction. Barthes generalizes such an insight about modernist arts in discussing how the original impetus of the structuralist movement as it united with semiology in France came as much from artists as from academics and intellectuals: 'We can in fact presume that there exist certain writers, painters, and musicians, in whose eyes a certain exercise of structure (and no longer merely only its thought) represents a distinctive experience, and that both analysts and creators must be placed under the common sign of what we might call *structural man*, defined not by his ideas or his languages, but by his imagination – in other words, by the way in which he mentally experiences structure.'[19] Noting that the 'structuralist activity' has two moments (dissection and articulation), he cites the moment of dissection using the examples of 'a *square* by Mondrian, a *series* by Posseur, a versicle of Butor's *Mobile*, the "mytheme" in Lévi-Strauss.'[20] The moment of articulation demonstrates that 'non-figurative works are to the highest degree works of art,' since they are characterized by a serendipitous 'regularity of assemblages.'[21]

The repeated play in the *Wake* with the close similarity in sound and spelling between 'letter' and 'litter' purposefully generates a complex interplay of allusions intricately implicated in structuralist and semiotic discourse: an epistle (the letter as correspondence), an alphabetic sign (the letter as a unit of writing or print), a carrier (the litter as something in which to carry things - perhaps letters), and a dung or garbage heap (a litter as mess). A letter (an epistle) written in letters becomes one of the central dream images of the *Wake*, where a key symbol in the dream is a letter written from Boston, Massachusetts, and pecked up from a dung heap by a curious hen. All this is grounded in Joyce's central concern with how letters, as those minimal elements from which books or letters are composed, inscribe the imaginary: a concern that squarely situates the *Wake* and *Ulysses* as exemplars of that contemporary semiotic consciousness of bits and pieces, of those minimal elements which make artistic machines work.

This same interest in *the elements* becomes a dominant theme among the contemporary arts in the early decades of this century. The Bauhaus, for example, represents a typical expression of such an interest in the elements of the visual arts, of design, and of architecture. Walter Gropius, the founding director, speaking of the Bauhaus program pointed out: 'The basis of its training was a preliminary course introducing the pupil to the experience of proportion and scale, rhythm, light, shade and color, and allowing him at the same time to pass through every stage of primitive experience with materials and tools of all kinds, in order to enable him to find a place where, within limits of his natural gifts, he could obtain a secure footing.'[22] As Gropius points out, such an approach involves a concept of a 'language of vision,' which meant that 'intensive studies' were required 'to rediscover the grammar of design in order to furnish the student with a knowledge of optical facts.'[23]

Others, too, were interested in such grammars, which are grammars of the 'letters' (i.e., the -etic and -emic units) utilized by the particular modes of expression and of the means by which these diverse modes deliver their 'letters'; that is, the processes of communication through which the works are expressed. Gropius, who pointed out that study of the elements, although essential, does not constitute 'a recipe for works of art,' explained that this is best understood by analogies to music. Schönberg's observations on his method confirm this:

> The introduction of my method of composing with twelve tones does not facilitate composing: on the contrary, it makes it more difficult. Modernistically-minded beginners often think they should try it before having acquired the necessary technical equipment. This is a great mistake. The restrictions imposed on a composer by the obligation to use only one set in a composition are so severe that they can only be overcome by an imagination which has survived a tremendous number of adventures. Nothing is given by this method; but much is taken away. The possibilities of evolving the formal elements of music, melodies, themes, phrases, motives, figures, and chords out of a basic set are unlimited. One has to follow the basic set; but nevertheless one composes as freely as before.[24]

Artists developed this interest in the 'basic set' – the elements – during the early part of this century just as a parallel interest was developing among linguists and anthropologists in structuralism and semiology as a result of the publication of de Saussure's lectures on semiology and linguistics.

Since collage involves a similar emphasis on minimal elements as one way of coping with contemporary experience, Eisenstein explains that the juxtaposition of images (like the elements of a hieroglyph) provides 'a means for the laconic imprinting of an abstract concept,' and when transposed into creative form (such as literature) it produces 'an identical laconism of pointed imagery': 'Applied to this collision of an austere combination of symbols this method results in a dry definition of abstract concepts. The same method, expanded into the luxury of a group of already formed verbal combinations, swells into a splendour of *imagist* effect. The concept is a bare formula; its adornment (an expansion by additional material) transforms the formula into an image – a finished form.'[25] It is interesting that this technique, based on an extension of playing with 'letters' (i.e., hieroglyphs or, as Eisenstein illustrates, the Chinese ideogram), is related in Eisenstein's mind with generating a syntax or grammar of film, an activity which he sees as paralleling similar activities taking place in the other arts as well as elsewhere in the study of society (e.g., anthropology). Commercial objects or light itself can equally well serve as minimal elements for the artist.

Warhol's adaptations of the image of the Campbell's Soup can to create a work of pop art is a classic example of the transformation of an object through decontextualization by using it as a semiotic element.

Minimalist, conceptual, and kinetic art movements in the 1960s and 1970s continued the work of earlier artists such as Mondrian in investigating the elements of the newly emerging technologies and the fundamental elements for experiencing visual art. Nam June Paik's *Video-Synthesizer*, produced for the opening of WGBH's station in Boston (1970), is described by the artist as 'moving wallpaper.' Here a multitude of visual, audiovisual, and optical elements are utilized precisely as minimal ingredients of an ongoing audiovisual experience aimed at everyone. Paik anticipated the interests of the Media Lab and similar projects at MIT.

Paik's work also anticipates the infinite power of the new technologies to generate new media and new experiences, to democratize the arts, and to transform the potentialities of communication. Paik's *Synthesizer* is clearly moving in the direction of breaking down distinctions between consumers and producers, encouraging a kind of do-it-yourself creativity. But elemental exploration marked in differing ways such works as Roy Lichtenstein's *Modular Painting with Four Panels, no. 2*, Donald Judd's *Untitled* (1968) assemblage of stainless steel and plexiglass, Tingueley's machines, Vaserely's op art, or Andy Warhol's *Electric Chair*.

The intrinsic connection of this type of sensibility to the everyday through popular and mass culture can be found in Claes Oldenburg's notebooks, which abound in surprising combinations of minimal images, such as imagining a hypodermic needle as a skyscraper, or an old-style circular ink eraser mounted over a brush as an ear. Throughout the movement of the 1960s and 1970s, disassembling, reassembling, and metamorphosing paved the way for a massive re-examination of the processes of communication. From Flavin's lighting or Mondrian's geometry of the grid to Paik's experimentation anticipating the metamorphic micro, there is a natural extension of the Bauhaus's concern with elements. Such works unconsciously criticize the implications of commercial rhetoric by transforming it into purer, elementary forms that speak of the process of composition itself and its relation to space and environment. Such works, therefore, create a self-reflexive awareness about the environment in which people live.

A parallel conception, using bits of sound and sense, is implicit in Joyce's 'allforabit.' A key passage about the Trivium and Quadrivium (the traditional basis of studies in the liberal arts) utilizes all the various senses of the word 'letter.' This schoolroom scene of the dream shows the twin brothers and their sister, Izzy, learning their reading, writing and arithmetic. The action is presented in a manuscript format – as a copybook. At one point, next to the marginalia inscribed in the right-hand margin, 'INCIPIT INTERMISSIO' (278.R) (a jotting which indicates a brief pause in the actual lesson), the following passage appears in the main text, illustrating and discussing the use of letters and their combination in the *Wake*:

All the world's in want and is writing a letters. A letters from a person to a place about a thing. And all the world's on wish to be carrying a letters. A letters to a king about a treasure from a cat. When men want to write a letters. Ten men, ton men, pen men, pun men, wont to rise a ladder. And den men, dun men, fen men, fun men, hen men, hun men wend to raze a leader. Is then any lettersday from many peoples, Daganasanavitch? Empire, your outermost. A posy cord. Plece. (278.13–24)

The parallel construction of the surface structures in the above text calls attention to the nature of language as a carrier – as structure making meaning manifest. For example:

When men want to write a letters
men wont to rise a ladder
men wend to raze a leader.

'Bits' of difference are employed to call attention to the paralleling of the processes of *writing*, *constructing* (i.e., 'rise a ladder'), and *creating government* (i.e., 'raze a leader'). A change in only one element (want-wont; write-rise) gives way to a change in one or two elements (rise-raze; wont-wend). This change is paralleled by the repetitions of 'men' with different modifiers from 'When men' to 'ten men ... pun men' to 'den men ... hun men.' But the entire set of structures is an extreme example of a basic syntactic patterning set forth in the second sentence: 'A letters from a person to a place about a thing.' (Cf. 'A noun is a name of a person, place, or thing.') The letter is a reflection of the book as the universal book encompassing the history of the world, for from the writing in letters comes the creation of rulers: 'wend to raze a leader.' The history of letters is the Viconian history of empire – empire and communication.

Such types of minute verbal play with the elements of expression and communication are central to the act of writing that Eco calls an 'open work.' The combinations of redundancy and entropy created by Joyce's minute wordplay, producing rhyme, meter, pun, homoioteleuton, and paronomasia, merely illustrate how this potentiality can be activated at the most elementary levels of the act of writing with letters or of speaking; the level at which children play games with language in exploring their own possible range of communication. These devices invite, in fact, insist on, openness in reading, the poeticality of the text. As combinations of these elements or elementary clusters become more and more complex, there emerges through them the 'curios of signs ... in this allaphbed' (18.17–18), Joyce's 'claybook' (18.17) and dreambook for the 'abcedminded' (18.17). This is the root of a technique using minute detailed alterations of form that allow a reader to 'rede ... its world' (18.18–19), for like human life, books present worlds for 'patternminds,' though in reading them the ideal 'patternmind' reads projectively.

Joyce's 'claybook' (= the key + Klee + clay), which refers not only to the *Wake* but to Klee's works and the *Book of Kells,* is composed from a labyrinthine elaboration of verbal design involving the interaction of different levels of designated signs (the visual, auditory, tactile images, etc., the conceptual, the ideological, the imaginary, which are signified) with different levels of designating signs (the letters themselves, the words, the verbal figures, the sounds and sound combinations) – the signifying. The reference to 'claybook' implies that neither speech nor print is privileged, for it indicates that this is a book of the earth. This is a carefully crafted book (like a piece of pottery) and assembled as if a type of brickwork; poetically crafted to parallel the manner in which some of Klee's work looks back at the illuminated books of the pre-Gutenberg world (e.g., *Book of Kells,* a medieval Irish illuminated manuscript).

Joyce's complex peregrinations through the regime of signs, dramatized by his obvious fascination with verbal play, are reinforced in the way he also utilized connections that exist between iconography, design, and text. His comparison of the *Wake* with the *Book of Kells* is not aberrant, since Henri Foçillon has observed how one of the unique qualities of the *Book of Kells* involves an elaborate use of labyrinthine patterns of embellishment associated with stylized codings of traditional mythic and religious figures and signs in the illuminations.[26] Klee's equally elaborate use of signs and figures generated through labyrinthine designs and his particular technique of 'magic squares' produce a proximity to the same type of stylization.

Escher exemplifies another form of labyrinthine patterning that Douglas Hofstadter has associated with the work of Lewis Carroll, Kurt Gödel, and J.S. Bach.[27] Escher, like Klee, also exhibits parallels with the highly formalized medieval genre represented by the *Book of Kells.* The *Wake,* playing a variation on the treatment of the text of the New Testament in the *Book of Kells,* is stylistically embellished in a design *not of but by* the letters of the text, so that the visual labyrinth of the illuminators becomes a verbal one whose words encompass visual design as well. This implies a further complication which results from the co-presence of aspects of the signifying and the signified, both in the signs in the book and in the signs that the signs in the book evoke.

Foçillon comments on Celtic illumination and Gothic art in *La Vie des formes*, where he notes that the *Book of Kells* shares the labyrinthine quality of Gothic art: 'What I may call the "system of the series" – a system composed of discontinuous elements sharply outlined, strongly rhythmical, and defining a stable and symmetrical space that protects them against unforeseen accidents of metamorphosis – eventually becomes "the system of the Labyrinth," which by means of mobile synthesis stretches itself out into a realm of glittering movement and colour.' The Celtic gospels provide an ideal example of this 'system of the labyrinth, for the ornament which is constantly overlayering itself and melting into itself, even though it is fixed fast within the compartments of letters and panels, appears to be shifting among different panels at different speeds.'[28] The 'counterpoint' that is described here is paralleled in Joyce's use of the 'counterpoint words' that take part in the intrasensory transformations in *Ulysses* and *Finnegans Wake* as well as the 'counterpoint' signs in Fellini's films, Klee's drawings, Escher's works, early animated film, and comic books.

Joyce, who gives the name Dedalus (after Dædalus, the maker of the original labyrinth) to his young artist, speaks in the *Wake* of the poet Shem's 'lovom of labaryntos' (187.21). There were a variety of serpentine-like ancient dances that are labyrinthine dances, one of which was the *troia* or troy-game, which Joyce mentions: 'The essence of the labyrinth is movement. The building has no meaning by itself. It only takes on a meaning when people walk through it ... The movement can exist without the building and actually does in places where nothing is known about a labyrinth.'[29] Foçillon also stresses movement, commenting on the eye movement involved in looking at the *Book of Kells*: 'As the eye moves across the labyrinth in confusion misled by a linear caprice that is perpetually sliding away to a secret objective of its own, a new dimension suddenly emerges which is a dimension neither of motion nor of depth, but which still gives us the illusion of being so.'[30]

Many major contemporary works incorporate the design of the labyrinth, utilizing its relationship to the labyrinth of cognition and to the labyrinthine structure of the ear: Picasso's *Guernica* with its Minotaur, Eliot's *Waste Land*, Proust's *Á la recherche du temps perdu*, many of Borges's stories, Stravinsky's *Rite of Spring*, and Fellini's *Satyricon*. In composing *Ulysses*, Joyce selected the labyrinth to describe the technic of that episode which maps the movement of various Dubliners, including his major characters, throughout the city; an episode which is also associated with the science and art of mechanics.

Contemporary interest in the Gothic sensibility, complementing the labyrinthine, is partially reflected in the disposition towards the grotesque exemplified in Picasso or Appel, Fellini or Kubrick, science fiction or comic strip. In addition to the way this echoes Bakhtin's insights, the Gothic also is a fragmented mode of expression and communication. The medieval art historian Emile Mâle observed that the Gothic is a script, a calculus, and a code.[31] All three terms might be applied to the *Wake*, for they are actually present in Joyce's discussions of the work itself. Mâle suggests that the most successful way in which to approach the gothic sensibility is in terms of Vincent Beauvais's *Speculum Magis* and to treat it as mirrors of nature, instruction, morals, and history. The conceptions of code, script, calculus, and mirror are part of a complex of relationships which also include the encyclopaedia, the labyrinth, reflexivity, drama, and communication. The image of the labyrinth fits well with the 'openness' of contemporary artistic communication. In his later works, Joyce demonstrated that his bias as an artist was also encyclopaedic; a bias characteristic of medieval authors, Vico, and many Menippean satirists (e.g., Rabelais, Swift, Pope, Carlyle, and Wyndham Lewis). Eco goes further, identifying the labyrinth with the principle of an encyclopaedia, although he limits this conception primarily to that form of labyrinth which could be described as a 'net' (or rhizome).[32]

Patterns of expectancy and surprise which occur in such spaces are characteristic of most contemporary artworks, their presence depending on processes of coding. Inspired by information theory and early Bloomfieldian structuralism, Meyer discussing music and Gombrich commenting on the visual arts spoke of the importance of the reading of a code based on a calculus which had been realized in a script which provides the ground for encountering a work of art. While information theory has created a peculiarly contemporary awareness concerning the role of code in communication, speech, and linguistics, the conception of code and decipherment had already occupied an important role in the literary mind for a substantial time.

The basis for some of Edgar Allan Poe's aesthetic theories, for example, rises out of his interest in codes and cryptograms. Carroll's Jabberwocky should bring to mind how Poe in 'The Philosophy of Composition' discusses the composition of his own poems. Poe's creating the poem by retracing the labyrinth of cognition parallels Carroll's logical play.[33] Poe's theories are applied in the writings of Jules Verne and of some *symbolistes*, who viewed language and the world of symbols as codes and cryptograms. Baudelaire's doctrine of *correspondances* and Mallarmé's that the poem should be a riddle (a labyrinth sealed at both ends) substantially extended these potentialities of language, as Mallarmé demonstrates in *Un Coup de dés* and in his application of his knowledge of English linguistics to his poetry.[34]

Eco has noted that the strong sense of code implies 'the whole of the encyclopedic competence as the storage of that which is already known and already organized by a culture. It is the encyclopedia, and therefore the Rule, but as Labyrinth. A Rule which controls but which at the same time allows, gives the possibility of inventing beyond itself, by finding new paths, new combinations within the network ... A code is not only a rule which *closes* but also a rule which *opens*. It not only says "you must" but says also "you may" or "it would be possible to do that." If it is a matrix, it is a matrix allowing for infinite occurrences, some of them still unpredictable, the source of a game.'[35] Klee's *Pedagogical Sketchbook* and his notebooks provide a powerful example of how preoccupation with code, calculus, and script is a predominant concern for many contemporary artists. There are many other examples: the development of dance notations (e.g., labanotation); preoccupation with musical structure in Schönberg; Eisenstein's film grammar; Brecht's quest for 'literarization' in the drama; Dadaist and surrealist experimentation. The contemporary emergence of multi-media arose from the realization of the combinatorial possibilities of the codes within new technologies of production and reproduction.

Eco has observed that the artists of Joyce's era create open texts. Open texts differ sharply from the process of communicating through closed texts usually carried out in the everyday world in the interest of manipulation or persuasion. Such open texts use the 'poetic' as a way of inviting the audience to participate actively – 'to commune.' In developing such 'open' texts, contemporary artists manifest an intense self-consciousness of semiotic structure, which expresses itself partly in the minimalist concern with elements and construction and partly in the conceptualist concern with the integration of all of the arts and with the relation of art to context and environment. Approaching communication from such a poetic perspective seems to create a paradox. The more open the artistic text becomes, the more complex the artistic 'message' becomes. To achieve greater depth and intensity of communication, the more difficult the process of communication becomes. So those who have come to equate the effectiveness of communication with its transparency and with ease in understanding the message, in all likelihood will oppose art and communication on the grounds that art, directed to an elite, limited audience, is increasingly obscure and esoteric. In so doing, they fail to grasp the ecological processes by which cultural productions abet the process of achieving relatively undistorted communication.

12

Memory: The Crux of Communication

The early modernist movement in the first half of the century clearly dramatized the conception of the artist as obscurantist. In 1948 the conflict which occurred in the United States concerning Ezra Pound's being awarded a Library of Congress prize after having 'betrayed' his country zeroed in on the esotericism and obscurantism of that twentieth-century poetry then being written by the established modernist poets writing in English who were praised and promoted by the New Criticism. Eliot, Pound, Faulkner, the Southern poets (e.g., Ransom, Tate, Randall Jarrell), and Joyce all exemplified this type of complexity and density. The popular media pointed out that obscurity was a characteristic of all the contemporary arts, whether in the visual art of Picasso, Duchamp, or the abstract expressionists, the music of Berg, Weber, or Schönberg, or the drama of Artaud, Jarry, or Unamuno. Their defenders retorted with the argument that artists faced by an explosion of mass and popular culture distributed through the mass media had abandoned 'easy' communication that did not communicate with any meaningful depth, in favour of difficult, even obscure or esoteric, communication, which strove to communicate in a more challenging and complex way. This debate decisively raised the problem of whether more complex and difficult modes of expression were ultimately the only means for communicating with meaningful depth.

Although this historical moment is now generally forgotten, because of the development of an attitude among many cultural theorists that in a populist society it would be desirable to eliminate any privileged communication, this issue was not really new. In the seventeenth century, by contrast, Bacon in *The Advancement of Learning* could praise the value of 'Poesy Parabolical' because in 'ancient times' people had wanted 'both variety of examples and subtility of conceits ... to express any point of reason which was more sharp or subtile.' Even in his own time, the Elizabethan age, the 'parabolical' in which 'the secrets and mysteries of religion, policy or philosophy are involved in fables or parables' in order to conceal and obscure was approved.[1] Earlier still, Dante could construct his *Commedia* using a complex allegorical structure.

Modernism challenged populist assumptions about a readily comprehensible and easily democratized form of artistic communication; Benjamin, Joyce, and others attributed a new relevance to complex allegory. While the allegorical tradition had frequently involved a deep and mysterious inwardness within the mystical or poetic text, from the perspective of the twentieth century populist this reflected an elitist cultural orientation. Nevertheless, this populist reaction should really be placed in perspective, for the history of artistic expression again and again records the charges of confusion, difficulty, complexity, or obscurantism being brought against the contemporary mode of expression, even though it is frequently necessary to develop the new mode in order to attack and replace the preceding mode that is unable to adapt to new circumstances.

While 'making it new' in order to regenerate the poetic language was sometimes considered by poets to be a move towards simplification or clarity and at other times towards complexity, the newness of the mode of expression seemed to render the product equally 'difficult' to critic and reader. Examples of such transitions in the history of English poetry include that from Metaphysical poetry to neo-Augustan poetry around 1650; or that from the later eighteenth century to Romantic poetry around 1800. These shifts are marked by periods of socio-economic and techno-scientific change with which the artistic changes correlate. Consequently, the manifestos which mark the beginnings of English modernism (such as Pound's 'Imagist Manifesto' or 'Retrospect' and Lewis's 'Manifestos' in *Blast I*) primarily announce another fundamental transition. In this respect, it should be noted that Eugene Jolas called his surrealist journal, in which Joyce's *Work in Progress* first appeared, *transition*.

Pound's slogan – 'make it new' – does not differentiate the modern, for such a phrase really designates an ongoing process of change in the semiotic regime of the poetic. But he does differentiate an important aspect of the modern when he amplifies it by pointing out the crucial importance of radical juxtaposition, which he illustrates through his analysis of the Chinese written character. Pound further specifies that differentiation in noting that the poem is an assemblage of fragments taken from different places and different times. In *The ABC of Reading* he demonstrates the value of shock – the poem is 'news that makes news' – and the principle of playing the new poetic language off against the base line of the prosaic, for the poetic is language charged with meaning – rhythmically, visually, and polysemically. Poetic communication necessarily must have a base line or foundation against which it can consciously create surprise and disorder to achieve that reordering through and by which communication occurs. In the twentieth century, this necessarily meant a move towards the complex and the parabolical.

In the process of poetic communication there is a *dismembering* of the base line which is also a *remembering*. In the process of remembering there is an exploration of a network which supports the mind in remembering. Marvin Minsky speaks of this network as 'societies of memories' formed from K-lines.[2] Complicated by a multiplicity of kinds of memory involving different processes and frequent rearrangement of memories, the action of complex remembering should be conceived of as transverse, employing rhizome-like networks rather than tree-like ones (suggested by the K-line conception), which are limited to creating a hierarchy of levels. While long-term memory (as Minsky explains it) is arborescent, Deleuze has suggested that short-term memory is rhizomorphous: 'Short-term memory is in no way subject to the law of contiguity or immediacy to its object; it can act at a distance, come or return a long time after, but always under conditions of discontinuity, rupture and multiplicity.'[3] The arborescent memory is Majoritarian; the rhizome-like memory is actually an anti-memory, for 'becoming is anti-memory.' Eco recognizes this in his development of the opposition between the dictionary, which is arborescent, and the encyclopaedia, which is labyrinthine.

Memory is the crux of communication, for only through the processing of a body of recognized experience converted into signs can the process of interchange occur in which each person loses herself or himself in the action of communicating. Remembering is associated with pattern; but not with the rigidity of pattern characteristic of structuralism. It is a wandering, transverse movement which in interaction with the making of assemblages forms a rhizomic labyrinth. In contemporary terms, it is not dissimilar from random searching of the net-like structure of a hypertext or hypermedia. Klee is aware of such complexity in visual memory when he articulates a philosophy of line without punctuality ('*A system is termed punctual* when its lines are taken as coordinates ... or as localizable connections')[5] in which 'the line does not go from one point to another, but runs *between points* in a different direction that renders them indiscernible. The line has become the diagonal, which has broken free from the horizontal and the vertical ...'[6] and the eye, as it reads the design, wanders while retaining where it has been, like Theseus tracing his course through Daedalus's labyrinth. Robert Henry, dealing with the problem of temporal continuity in the arts as it regards the theory of kinetic painting, observes that 'the existence of a chronological sequence in a work of art in the sculptural, architectural, literary, terpsichorean, cinematographic, or kinetic-sculptural media compels the artist to consider the problem of temporal continuity ... Memory performs an active role in one's perception of a performance of this nature. Imagery, gesture, plot, rhythm and melody subserve the function of establishing relatively stable points and sequences that form a substructure of experiences available to memory and psychological ordering.'[7] This is not restricted to kinetic or optical art for, at least two decades earlier, Gyorgy Kepes (discussing how modernism is trying to move 'toward a dynamic iconography') observed that 'visual experience is more than the experience of pure sensory qualities. Visual sensations are interwoven with memory overlays.'[8]

Discussions of orality and literacy, which have stressed the centrality of oral memory and its beginnings in Plato's reservations about writing in the *Phaedrus*,[9] have dominated many areas of contemporary communication theory. New stress on the role of memory in oral cultures and on the importance of orality as opposed to the logic of writing has emerged from the work of McLuhan, Ong, and Goody. Alternatively, among postmodernist literary, artistic, and philosophical critics, the primacy of orality has been challenged by grammatology, on one hand, and theories about mutli-modal post-mediated communication, on the other.[10] Discussion of memory necessarily cuts across all these divisions; for it functions within the verbal, auditory, visual, rhythmical, kinaesthetic, and gestural. While visual memory is distinct from oral memory, both may also be interwoven within the same experience, which may also involve kinaesthetic and gestural memory. Jousse, whose work Joyce used (and who also predates these debates), had stressed gesture,[11] so that Joyce could say of the core of memory as well as of communication, 'In the beginning was the gest' (*FW*468.5), thus implicitly explaining why oral memory in rhetoric and the theatre was accompanied by an art of memory intricately related to the visual and the sensory.

Frances Yates, who explored the history of the art of memory and its relation to the emerging importance of the hermetic tradition in the Renaissance, provides an elaborate description of the importance of visual memory, whose role in oral cultures is the preservation of tribal knowledge within crafted artefacts. In the classical period, an elaborate memory system was worked out that persisted throughout the Middle Ages and the early Renaissance. This memory system associated topics (*topos*, place) with actual physical locations, selected from within specific buildings or along roadways, or from works of art, architecture, and visual design, and with the specific real or imaginary images which were situated in the chosen physical locations.

Quintilian's commentary on the art of memory (developed by the poet Simonides) explains how this works: 'Places are chosen, and marked with the utmost possible variety, as a spacious house divided into a number of rooms. Everything of note there is diligently imprinted on the mind, in order that thought may be able to run through all parts without let or hindrance.'[12] Quintilian explains how real or imaginary images identified with specific notions to be interrelated within an act of memory are placed in different rooms, nooks, crannies, or artefacts within a house, so that by retracing this path 'however numerous are the particulars, which it is required to remember, all are linked one to another as in a chorus.'[13] What is at stake here is the retracing of an inscribed network – the Thesean thread through a labyrinthine movement.

This provides an interesting bridge between visual sensation and oral recall. An art of memory based on the visualization of images is not the same as the visibility of writing trying to provide a mnemonic substitute through recording. Although in the classical period Memory was regarded as the fifth part of rhetoric, it seldom figured centrally in the tradition of written handbooks. Nevertheless, the 'art of memory' had its own history, which developed in relation to theatre, oratory, and the evolution of an occult practice, culminating in the work of Bruno and Renaissance alchemy.[14] This 'art' had a central impact on the design of the Elizabethan theatre and on the history of the rise of science in the sixteenth and seventeenth centuries.

As it evolved in practice, the art of memory is not just associational, but labyrinthine. The intricacy of the pattern has been encountered earlier in Joyce's interweaving of eye-ear and bodily gesture within 'if an ear aye sieze what no eye ere grieved for ... The gist is the gist of Shaum but the hand is the hand of Sameas' (*FW*482.35–483.4; see above, pp. 142–3). Joyce brought the matter to bear within the characterization of his 'electric everybody.' Joyce's HCE is Earwicker (an earwig, an insect which legendarily was supposed to invade the labyrinth of the ear; note also German, *Irrweg* = maze!). Earwicker is described early in the *Wake* as 'Earwicker, that patternmind, that paradigmatic ear, receptoretentive as his of Dionysius' (70.35–6). HCE demonstrates his 'receptoretentivity' by setting out a long list of over one hundred abusive names he has been called, ranging from '*Firstnighter, Informer ...*' to '*Guilteypig's Bastard, Fast in the Barrel, Boose in the Bed, Mister Fatmate, In Custody of the Polis, Boawwll's Alocutionist, Deposed*' (71–2).

This 'patternmind' with his paradigmatic ear and his receptoretentive memory has many of the characteristics of 'structural man,'[15] although Joyce's investigation of meaning and his social critique move beyond a narrow structuralism closer to post-structuralism. Remember that Earwicker as pattern and paradigm predates by two decades the emergence of structuralism and even predates Leonard Bloomfield's seminal work in the United States on structuralism. Joyce's structuralist empathy would seem to have been derived (if derived at all) from de Saussure's original semiological enterprise; although it should be obvious that he could easily have discovered this perception of pattern and paradigm in the Stoic traditions of semiology or in its medieval equivalent or even in Ogden's outline of C.S. Peirce's semiotics.[16] Pattern and paradigm as they relate to poetry and dream are part of the labyrinthine world; but so, too, as Eco has pointed out, is any complex or evolving communication. While the myth of the avant-garde appeared to suggest that modernism displaced or overthrew memory, at least in the sense that memory was directed towards history and the past, the very nature of its strategy of shock demanded a remembering of the past against which it was rebelling and of the complex networks which it dismembered and remembered to achieve its intended communication.

But memory of signs of the immediate past gathered across space is also the only way of grasping diversity distributed through space, serving a function similar to Pound's poetic 'Great Bass.'[17] Essentially, time and space will interpenetrate and be composed of diversities in time as well, for our mode of constructing such a 'basis' is naturally a mixture of the historical past, the more immediate present, the proximate, and the remote. By gradual stages, film, TV, and now 'compunications'[18] and virtual reality are shaping the contemporary foundation just as the *new* periodical press of the late seventeenth and early eighteenth centuries supplemented the inculcated traditions of humanism. Contemporary modernist and postmodernist writing, and visual, auditory, and kinaesthetic arts, popular and avant-garde, construct their assemblages on this foundation shaped by the new technologies. Joyce's work anticipated and embraced these factors, for his is the earliest and most comprehensive realization that *the practice of writing* is the only approach to writing as practice and, more centrally, that the *practice of communication* is the only approach to communication as practice.

The involvement of memory with the central nervous system, conceived as a common sensorium, is more fully developed by Joyce than any other modern poet in any of the art forms. The fundamental texts, which comprise his ideas about memory, run throughout the whole of *Finnegans Wake,* so that what follows is an abstract of Joyce's insight into the problem of memory. The universe of Joyce's 'Everybody,' as 'patternmind ... [and] ... receptoretentive,' is inextricably involved with memory; intellectual retention follows sensory reception, for 'after sound, light and heat, memory, will and understanding' (266.19). His account of the memory process, which speaks of 'memories framed from walls,' echoes that classical account by Simonides about wandering through 'places,' which Yates so brilliantly recreates in her discussion of Memory Theatres.[19]

Although Joyce plays with the 'arts of memory' and the basics of nineteenth- and early twentieth-century physics, on one hand, and nineteenth- and early twentieth-century philosophy and psychology, on the other, he is still establishing a connection between the receptive function of the nervous system and the centrality of memory to all mental activity. At one point in the *Wake*, exploratory thinking is called '*Meminerva*' (61.1): 'A halt for hearsake. A scene at sight. Or dreamoneire. Which they shall memorise' (279.36–280.2). In a reversal of McLuhan's analysis of auditory space as holistic and visual space as analytical, Joyce's remembered assemblages are composed for 'the ear that annalykeses' (analyses) as well as the eye that grasps the totality that 'sumns' (fr. *summa*). The memory process works by 'seeming' to mirror the world. It is described as 'In effect, I remumble, from the yules gone by, purr lil murrerof myhind' (295.5–6). Drama, story-telling, and wordplay – 'as great Shapesphere puns it' – are the inevitable necessities for the mind to reconstruct (not reproduce) that world in the memory, which is engrammed through genetic inheritance, prenatal life, and infanthood.

Within this dream, as in waking life, what the ear hears and the scene at sight are dismembered and remembered, which is noted in remarks such as 'It scenes like a landescape from Wildu Picturescu or some seem on some dimb Arras, dumb as Mum's mutyness' (53.1–2);[20] or 'Television kills telephony in brothers' broil. Our eyes demand their turn. Let them be seen!' (52.18–19). These remarks about 'landescape' and TV frame the paragraph, for the audiovisual recording of a story in a dream machine parallels the broadcasting of it through TV or film (cf. the Hollywood Dream Factory!). Since the world of the imaginary is the daytime world filtered through the fictions of the night-time world, memory is discussed in terms of the mechanics of the telescope by playing on the phrase 'When I'm dreaming back like that I begins to see we're only all telescopes.[21] Or the comeallyoum saunds' (295.10–12).

'Comeallyoum saunds' is a complex, polysemic compound consisting of the following items: come-all-ye sounds; a song, 'Come all ye Roman Catholics, who never went to Mass'; excremental (i.e., from L. *cumulus*) sands; and 'communion of saints' (cf. also 'cummulium of scents' [see p. 115]). 'Telescopes' and 'dreaming back' supplement the eye references by bringing the ear into conjunction with eye in the memory process. Sounds, sight, words, and gestures interplay in assembling the *Wake* from the fundament – 'comeallyoum saunds.' While the combination of the two sentences includes people seeing, hearing, and sensorily experiencing, the entire text is then remembered through a secular communion, since communion is a violent 'doing in commemoration' through eating, drinking, and speaking, a communication that ends in a tentative, momentary community.

Shortly before Anna Livia's closing monologue in *Finnegans Wake*, there is a remarkable passage that links the processes of memory with a semiotic account of the textual writing and rewriting performed by the imagination and intellect. Eating, digesting, consuming, producing, and communication are among the processes that form part of the web that Joyce weaves in order to demonstrate how the poetic engineering generated by the imagination and memory in the mind works. This account of the crucial relationship between memory and communication opens with the dreamer meditating on the subject of memory as he begins to awake. The *Wake* as dream and as a communication about dreaming is a becoming; for the dreamer who wakes is transformed from the dreamer who went to sleep – that dreamer has died and been reborn.

The very way in which the dream as a communication is inscribed on the reader's (producer's and consumer's) body is produced by the zigzag lines of movement of the gestures and the words as remembered after their inscription on the body – 'It will remember itself from every sides' (614.20). Whether drama, story, or dream, the *Wake* is an assemblage created by nomadic wanderings – 'liberty of perusiveness' (614.23–4) – through the labyrinth of sensation and cognition. This freedom produced through transversality, or 'liberty of perusiveness,' generates communications about the global city – 'the world' – which are also becomings, a creative evolution: the flows, the river – communication as life itself. The *Wake* is the archetype of all cultural productions in any mode or combination of modes of expression and of all meaningful action considered as text.

Throughout the *Wake* there are many references to a letter written by Anna, the dreamer's wife, different versions of which are repeatedly quoted. When it appears in the dream action, this letter is usually treated, along with the *Wake* itself, as a symbol of the book as written text. Both the *Wake* and the letter, which is a book in miniature, can be described as electrochemical engines designed on a helical pattern of evolution following Vico's theory of history, so that this culminative passage begins: 'Our wholemole millwheeling vicociclometer, a tetradomational gazebocroticon' (614.27–8).

Like all books (or texts or cultural productions), Joyce's is dominated by four dimensions (tetra-) and as a book is a beacon, that is, a pivotal combination of gaze (observation), sight, form, expression, critical judgment, and memory (gaze + book + wrote + rote + icon + gazebo + *kritikos* – able to discern, critical). The book is a printed object (a '-boc-') which is composed of visual, secondary sensory, and mnemonic aspects (for '-rot-' is a pun on 'rote' as well as 'write' and 'rite'). This way of describing a book also plays with the concept of enlightenment, for 'gazebo-' refers to a particular kind of garden-house with a turret-light, perhaps in this context symbolically illuminating the 'garden' of 'flores of speech' in the book.

This printed text, 'the gazebocroticon,' is 'autokinatonetically preprovided with a clappercoupling smeltingworks exprogressive process' (614.30-1); for rhythm and sound become crucial to its 'sound sense' (109.15). The process functions 'autokinatonetically' (auto + kinetic + tone + autokinetical [that is, possessed of spontaneous activity or perpetual motion]), since the book is a self-perpetuating unfolding of a dialectical tension through gestural movement and sound. Books consist of 'homely codes' (614.32) that function in a self-perpetuating realization of tension through sound. This permits fragmentation and then reassembly, since the book in process (*Work in Progress*, the pre-publication working title of the *Wake*) 'receives through a portal vein dialytically separated elements of precedent decomposition for the verypetpurpose of subsequent recombination' (614.34–6). The process of reading and re/writing, like the process of digestion in the liver (i.e., the hepatic portal vein), is conceived as a recombining of the 'dialytical' and dialectical separation, which can be a mechano-chemical separation of smaller and larger molecules or colloids and crystalloids, an organic dialysis, or an intellectual division.

The book as 'gazebocroticon,' then, works through a dialectic of decomposition and recombination (dismembering and remembering) which, since at least the eighteenth century, has been overtly recognized by theorists as a central theme of poetics and aesthetics, especially in discussions of the poetic act at work. That work, which is a 'recombination' of the elements that have been separated dialectically in the 'precedent decomposition' (614.34), is virtually identified with the fragmented body of existence represented by the deceased everyman hero, HCE-Finn. In *Biographia Literaria*, Coleridge stresses this doctrine of poetry as the reconciliation of opposite and discordant qualities when he describes the Secondary Imagination (or the imaginary of each individual person), which 'dissolves, diffuses, dissipates, in order to recreate; or where this process is rendered impossible, yet still at all events it struggles to idealize and unify. It is essentially vital.'[22]

This dialectic process in such a creative act instinctively moves along a semiotic path, probing the significance of elements in the life-world of the 'producer-consumers,' the audience. These elements which are initially 'decomposed' by the work are recombined in new figures, which is the 'very-petpurpose' (614.35) of such activity, since in the process they are also made new – the theme of the 'seim anew' (215.23) which Joyce develops from the Viconian cycles.[23] The 'seim anew' is produced through a metamorphic or tranformational process. It is the ability to generate this process of 'amply-heaving metamorphoseous' (190.31) which is specifically attributed to Shem, the son-poet figure of the dream.

This activity of the memory and imagination provides a way of encompassing the 'heroticisms, catastrophes and eccentricities' (614.35–6) – the heroic, erotic, catastrophic, and unique motifs of historical moments – which are 'transmitted by the ancient legacy of the past' (614.36), the flows arising from the unfolding of history. This transmission through the poetic work is only realized through the semiotic devices of grammar, rhetoric, written language, and poetic presentation, for it must be shaped 'type by tope, letter from litter, word at ward, with sendence of sundance' (615.1–2). This shaping is a reflection of the way in which the 'ancient legacy of the past' itself transmits history. Joyce, like Vico, recognizes the central relationship of the poetic to the historic – in the indissoluble connection between aesthetics and history.

The 'sendence' (sentence, transcendence, and dense), a message projected by the 'sundance,' is generated 'type by tope,' rhetorically and mnemonically through types and places (*topoi*) in a tope-like manner of intoxication (tope = drinking); 'letter from litter,' re-creating and carrying through letters, print messages about the world (i.e., 'litter' = world as garbage heap); 'word at ward,' that is, verbally but by a watchful and defensive use of language. 'Sendence of sundance,' the movement of the natural and the human, the light of the sun and the dance to the sun, the Tantric dance of Shiva, relates the poetic communication to dance and illumination. This is the process of the poetic incorporating the signs of nature and transforming them into the signs of art, which then transform our sense of our relation with nature and history.

The book as archetype of the communication product is essentially an assemblage of multiplicities, quite different from a synthesizing or totalizing moment, for it occurs by the crossing of pluralistic branches of differing motifs, through a process of transmission involving flows, particularly the flowing of blood, water, and speech, and breaks the discontinuous charges of electrical energy, telegraphy, punctuation, and 'the end speaking nots for yestures' (267.9). Recombination, anastomosis, assimilation ('anastomosically assimilated' [615.5]), and 'preteridentification' function so the 'wholemole millwheeling vicociclometer ... may be there for you.' This 'anastomosical' assimilation which indicates a process of intercommunication through interconnection between past and present counterpointing the particular and already identified ('paraidiotic preteridentification'), involves a method of dialectical doubt, which brings out the intrinsic contradiction within the poetic fiction. It is a 'hophazard' (615.7) process, a process of chance and of leaps in knowledge, and it is the understanding of the same process that goes on in everybody's mind: 'the sameold gamebold adomic structure ... highly charged with electrons' (615.6–7). This is how the codes, signs, and symbols operate.

This 'ideal game' of 'the sameold gamebold' Everybody, which can only be created in thought or art and only thought about as 'non-sense,' has captured the contemporary imagination. Game as conceived in the *Wake* cuts to the very heart of contemporary concern about communications, for it rises out of the problem of language as it arises in the games of Lewis Carroll or in Wittgenstein's description of our perpetual language-games, which are themselves the activity of philosophy. Game-playing has entered extensively into discussions of very diverse aspects of communication theory: human encounters, intrapersonal theory, and even mass communication. Bateson's student, Paul Watzlawick, used games and works of art to explore the 'pragmatics of communication.'[24]

Reading, viewed projectively as Joyce does, naturally engages reader and writer in a game in which the writer's attempt to construct his world involves him in a series of moves which the truly projective reader plays in order to achieve her own orientation to and understanding of the work. Klee's 'Magic Squares,' especially when considered in the context of Joyce's *Wake*, should be considered as setting out a game board in which the elements of the painting and their juxtaposition to the stylized verbal titles form counters in a game between artist and viewer. In any case, semiosis as an aesthetic factor and semiosis as the base of communicative encounter become intelligible for many modernists through peoples' endless fascination with game-playing, especially board games such as chess, Japanese Go, and children's games, which are an essential part of their social, intellectual, and emotional development.

Game and play, though somewhat distinct, are at various points interrelated. The game-playing of the artist is meant to be a more open game than the games with enclosed boundaries, such as chess, even though these latter may be quite complex. Open games lead to a liberating possibility, just as enclosed games are the kind of authoritative regime from which Alice in the Carroll books is constantly trying to escape. Chess is parodied in the *Alice* books, as is the formal structure of croquet. Open games and play have direct relationships to the mimetic and learning instincts of the body as well as to the development of imagination and memory. Just as Bateson weaves humour, play, games, and art into his ecological theory of mind as ways of going beyond the schizophrenic, so Joyce relates these to the projects of art and human communications as they are interrelated within the ecology of sense.

All arts of writing, speaking, and electronic production involve game-like aspects. Those processes of print communication that move between the present and the past, vibrate between the arts of living, the sensuality of the body, and our history. They are an archetype of the processes of all communication and of the production and active consumption of arts, whether practical ones like cooking or fictive ones like an epic poem or panoramic film. The arts counterpoint a sense of movement against aspects of arrest and contemplation, implying the way that the ideal communication game involves the interplay of arrested mosaic and flowing musicality in order to create the 'anastomosically assimilated' effect. Taking into account the 'gamebold' aspect of the human person is one way to alert people to the type of critique which must be performed by an extensive 'reading' of other texts and sign systems and of the text written on us by the natural history of our world, which is itself human history.

Joyce's mock newspaper or television presentations become means of illuminating not only the formal limitations implicit in the content, but also the social history involved. That bar-room scene in which there is a televised presentation of a fight between Butt and Taff reflects the action of the Crimean War and becomes a critique of the process of nationalist and imperialist war activities as well as of the exploitative activities of conflicting empires. Yet Joyce roots this in the competitive aspect of the human person within the oedipal family and then society as reflective of the larger outside structure. The making overt of the shape and nature of the media as participators in such promotion of the competitive instinct, therefore, becomes one of the goals of this word-game; but that can only be made clear through this particular word-game, which dislocates the object from its usually concealed presence in the ambience surrounding the media world.

While other theorists ultimately may provide insight into game and play that leads to a greater depth of understanding, Bateson's writings provide a direct illustration of the central importance of comedy, wit, game-playing, and the poetic to the development of contemporary theories of communication. In studying schizophrenia, Bateson became interested 'in various sorts of communication which involve both emotional significance and the necessity of discriminating between orders of message. Such situations include play, humour, ritual, poetry and fiction.'[25] In a 'Theory of Play and Fantasy,' he added fantasy to this list.[26] Drama, which is central to this set of interests (it entails play, ritual, poetry, and fiction), is particularly interesting, since both performers and audience respond to messages about the reality of their immediate presence and of the theatrical environment. As early as his writing *Communication: The Social Matrix of Psychiatry* with Jürgen Ruesch, Bateson appeared to use Joyce's *Ulysses* as a model for the networks of communication that he had uncovered in the typical daily schedule of an average person on an average day.

In 'Form, Substance and Difference,' Bateson outlines this cybernetic epistemology:

> The individual mind is immanent ... not only in the body ... but in pathways and messages outside the body; and there is a larger Mind of which the individual mind is only a sub-system. This larger Mind ... is perhaps what some people mean by 'God,' but it is still immanent in the total interconnected social system and planetary ecology.
>
> Freudian psychology expanded the concept of mind inwards to include the whole communication system within the body – the automatic, the habitual, and the vast range of unconscious process. What I am saying expands mind outwards. And both of these changes reduce the scope of the conscious self. A certain humility becomes appropriate, tempered by the dignity of my being part of something much bigger.[27]

This 'new approach to the problem of mind' stresses the importance of patterned relationships which arise from differences that make a difference. For Bateson, meaning would appear to be analog in function.[28] (In speaking about the ecology of sense, the verbal play on *sense* is used to suggest this analog aspect of meaning, thus distinguishing *sense* from *signification,* which operates at the digital level.)

Making sense is, therefore, an analogic function that is dependent on the recording of differences that make a difference - the process that presents a map rather than the territory. Memory is essential to the recognition of pattern, and Tony Wilden has suggested that in Bateson 'memory seems to rely upon the set or networks of analog patterns retained by the "grooving" of the pathways in and between the organism or the system, and recall could be described as a sort of "plucking" at these patterns. (Bateson, personal communication).'[29] This difference that makes a difference is reminiscent of Derrida's concept of *différance*, the formation of form; or perhaps, as Wilden better puts it, the information of form.

Bateson, who starts by considering communication, cybernetics, and the problems of mass communication, reaches his 'Theory of Play and Fantasy' by way of speculations on art in primary societies which he had studied, such as that of Bali. In an essay on 'Style, Grace and Information in Primitive Art,' he used concepts from cybernetic theory to arrive at a view of art as an 'exercise in communicating about species of unconsciousness ... a sort of play behaviour whose function is among other things, to practice and make more perfect communication of this kind.'[30] To account for this particular ecological function of art, Bateson discriminated between a purposive view of life and a systemic view (associating, as Wilden observes, the purposive with digital modes of communication and the systemic with analog modes of communication, in a manner somewhat similar to Jakobson's distinction of metonymy and metaphor).

While life has to be a balance between regarding the total mind as an integrated network and allowing for purposive action, Bateson notes that art plays an important systemic role for 'what unaided consciousness (unaided by art, dreams and the like) can never appreciate is the *systemic* nature of mind.'[31] Art, then, has a positive function of maintaining wisdom, correcting a too purposive view of life, and making the view more systemic. But by what means does it achieve this activity? Bateson began by exploring the problem of the double bind and logical types in humour, fantasy, and play, from which he developed a thesis that had obvious associations with his cybernetic theory of communications.

His development of this theory led to his stressing 'the necessity of the paradoxes of abstraction.' People ought not 'to obey the Theory of Logical Types in their communications' for these paradoxes of abstraction 'must make their appearance in all communications more complex than that of mood signals ... [for] without these paradoxes the evolution of communication would be at an end. Life would then be an endless interchange of stylized messages, a game of rigid rules, unrelieved by change and humor.'[32] This theory recognizes that the evolution of communication arises through open games as differentiated from the closed structures of chess that Carroll destroys by translating the chessboard into imaginary beings pursuing 'hophazard' actions. Deleuze explains the phenomenon of the open game when he contrasts the state-like movements of chess along the grid of the board to the nomadic movements of the game of Go. Chess is striated, while Go is nomadic; chess, the *polis* and Go, the *nomos*.[33] Joyce's strategy of 'paradoxmutose' creates the gaps that permit transverse movement. Klee's squares, because of his interest in the supremacy of the line – the line of flight – do not create grids, but jagged maps inscribed to deterritorialize an established territory of sight.

Bateson claims that art, especially in its dramatic modes, has a privileged place to play in the evolution of mind. The title of Bateson's essay, 'Style, Grace and Information in Primitive Art' indicates that he considers serendipity to be 'the quality of art,' for 'Art is part of man's quest for grace.' Grace then fundamentally becomes a problem of integration: 'what is to be integrated is the diverse parts of the mind.' Therefore, 'the central question is: In what form is information about psychic integration contained or coded in the work of art?'[34] In selecting the term 'grace,' Bateson introduces a word into his aesthetic discussions which had been present in discussions about art from the Middle Ages to the Enlightenment. Pope, a poet fascinated with the playing of games, made a classical statement involving art and 'grace' in his *Essay on Criticism*:

> Great wits sometimes may gloriously offend,
> And rise to faults true critics dare not mend;
> From vulgar bounds with brave disorder part,
> And snatch a grace beyond the reach of art.[35]

Poetry may reach beyond art in the sense of the knowledge of a craft, for it responds to the rage for chaos. Since Bateson stressed the importance of grace in contradistinction to style or information, it is consistent that he was intrigued with precisely those aspects of the artistic process which have to do with paradox and surprise – qualities such as humour and play. Paradox and surprise in Bateson's mind are also associated with the negative entropy of communication theory; the 'transgression' (or deviation) which increases the quality of communication by increasing the quantity of information. This way of using such concepts as grace and information becomes itself a witty playing with the paradigm of cybernetic thinking; a metamorphic transformation of a systematic cosmos into a nomadic 'chaosmos' of hypertextuality.

As the 'gamebold' play along the surface of the signifiers, wandering among them in a labyrinthine, rhizomic dance, the multiple memories, corresponding to Harold Gardner's multiple intelligences, include the Linguistic, the Musical, the Logical-mathematical, the Spatial, the Bodily-kinaesthetic, and Personal forms of intelligence (intra- and inter-).[36] These active memories exist both within and outside of the person, for they are founded in the 'heroticisms, catastrophes and eccentricities' transmitted. Their reassemblage occurs as inner and outer integrate within the activity of the mind-body, the 'livivorous, feelful thinkamalinks' (*FW*613.19). Memory, then, relying as it does on the 'grooving' of the rhizomic, labyrinthine wandering, has its roots outside as well as inside, since mind must embrace both outer and inner. Memory and imagination function as play and game. Bateson's theories of the ecology of mind, which imply that the ecology of sense in which memory mediates between mind, body, and world, constitute a theory of communication based on the recognition that the fundamental activity of communication is directed towards social evolution.

13

History of the Poetic: A Major Aspect of the History of Communication

The suppressed iconography of Picasso's art refers to the history of art even in the process of breaking with that history. The women in mirrors, the transfigured, multi-planar still lifes, the collages permeated with classical allusions, the fascination with the mythology of the Western world, all indicate an involvement with history and an awareness of the historical involvement of his work. But this is a new sense of history; subsequently delineated in Foucault's critique of history. The same tension between the historical and the break with history is characteristic of Schönberg's development of the twelve-tone scale or Le Corbusier's revaluation of the cathedral. It resurfaces in a new way in postmodernity with its mixtures of differing layers of historical and cultural allusion.

The artists who produced works between the beginning of the First World War and the end of the Second World War are the first to have become thoroughly self-conscious about the complex involvement of their artistic practice with changing concepts of the urban community and the rapidly developing technologies of communication. Their contributions were key to an increased understanding of how radical the ensuing transformations would be and of how transformed conceptions of communication and transportation would shrink the effective size of the world, creating a global metropolis. Modernism is distinctive in its virtually comprehensive self-consciousness about the relationship of art, technology, and the process of communication. Modernists imaginarily anticipated the development of telecommunications machines like the computer (e.g., Kafka in *Amerika*, or Valéry in *Remarks on Intelligence* or *Politics of Mind*) – hardly surprising, considering that the computer's lineage goes back to Leibniz, Babbage, and the nineteenth century. Furthermore, they imaginarily anticipated the transformation of what then appeared to be a variety of different media into a common technology – an intuition of cyberspace – where the visual, auditory, verbal, mobile, rhythmic, kinetic, and gestural could be readily blended, obviating the differences as technological forms between TV, radio, film, phonography, and the like, thus underlining their role as specific social formations of a particular moment. The universe of signs would then be dealt with technically as one set of expressive possibilities, just as previously the imaginary had dealt with them conceptually.

Mallarmé's 'revolution in language' marks the beginning of the self-consciousness about this process in literature. He reassesses the book, the printed page, the relationship of foreign languages to a writer's native language, the aleatory factor in artistic production, the exceeding of limits, the synaesthetic, and the interrelationship of modes or expression. This results in his revaluation and rejection of literature and the accompanying realization that the poetic provides a bond between all cultural production, a position epitomized in his famous interchange with the painter Degas when he exclaims that poems are made of *words*, not *ideas*. English writers came to know these motifs through the writings of their major modernist writers: Yeats, Pound, Eliot, Joyce, and Wyndham Lewis. In spite of extended debates concerning these artists' presumed indifference towards communication, their discursive prose writings clearly indicate a persistent interest in effect, technique, audience, social function, and communication.

Pound's interest in communication is evident in his use of images from the new media world and its techniques (the press, radio, montage, datelines, layout), his sensitivity to problems of communication intensified by the new technologies of his world (multilingualism, modes of writing; e.g., ideograms), and in his acute awareness of the importance of flows of information (economic and cultural theory). Eliot's quest for community and his concern for poetry as purifying the language of the tribe (directly inherited from Mallarmé) involve questions of communication that are specifically related to language and communication in the *Coriolan* poems and the *Four Quartets*.[1] While his position ultimately may have developed as a radical conservatism (not dissimilar from McLuhan's), his earlier vision of the communicative problems of the modern metropolis (*The Waste Land*) parallels the modernist preoccupation in Europe with the metropolises that were the sites of the new communication revolution, as exemplified in Benjamin's writings – Paris, Berlin, Rome, Moscow, and Vienna. Ozenfant's *Foundations of Modern Art*, a seminal work on modernism and the visual arts, clearly identifies the new artistic movements and their utilization of new media (such as photography, film, recorded sound, mobiles, and optical displays) with a new consciousness of communication, partly associated with defining how the new art differed from what had come before. Klee, Kandinsky, Gropius, and others involved in the Bauhaus explicitly raised problems of communication, which also became an intrinsic aspect of discussions of architectural theory and history for Le Corbusier and Giedion. Klee's interest in exploring the crossing of the boundaries of the arts is exemplified in the synaesthetic motif of his *Table of Colour (in Grey Major)* (1930), where he arranges his magic squares in spatial form like sounds, the effect of which has been described as being 'like the notes of Webern, each has its values and sounds clearly, although it is conditioned by adjacent sounds or colour.'[2]

In works such as *Twittering Machine* (1922), Klee 'renders visible' the machinic roots of auditory communication, associates this phenomenon with his unpeopled cosmos, and randomizes (or labyrinthinizes rhizomically) the inscription through the carnivalesque, comic use of the comic-strip quality of the assemblage of elements.[3] The machine is the key to the assemblage. Klee can range from the primitive simplicity of his 1939 work of men marching across Europe as a sombre meditation on the ascent of Hitler to his witty, abstract elaborations of aquaria and circuses. For him all of this constitutes an elaborate playing with the 'life of forms' in art and a fundamental re-examination of the communicative potential of how the entire visual realm 'renders' visible, which is quite similar to Joyce's exploration of the impact of the evolving worlds of photography and film on writing.

Mallarmé said that the Book needed a people. Kafka said literature is the affair of the people. Klee said that the people is essential *yet lacking*.[4] Like Klee, Joyce struggles to rediscover and recreate the people whom he had addressed, for his consumers must be his producers, since communication and communion are consummatory acts. In that struggle, Joyce as 'alshemist' transmutes the book, for the same reasons that Klee transmutes the visual image. His recognition of the people as co-producers of the work of art and his acceptance of the significance of all cultural production – like Klee and his abstract expressionist and Bauhaus colleagues experimenting with visual form – leads him to explore the encounter between history and the rapidly developing techno-culture.

Stephen Kern, who reviews the beginning of the era of Joyce and Klee in his study *The Culture of Time and Space*, explores the interrelationship of art and the technosphere from 1880 to 1918, and examines changes in communication as well as space, time, and culture, just as Innis, Williams, and Carey do. If time and space were central concerns of the cultural developments from 1880 through 1918 to 1940 and beyond, it is obvious that the modes of production, distribution, and reproduction of communication were intricately involved as well. If new electronic communication altered the conception of space, artists simultaneously explored the new altered perceptions in poetry, mobiles, montage, and the exercise of the imaginary.

Eliot's use of anaesthesia and X-ray in 'The Love Song of J. Alfred Prufrock' is a simple, well-known example of how technologies affected the entire sense of interior as well as exterior space. Léger's and Picasso's cubist visions reintegrated people with a space that was rapidly transforming under the impact of time (and the impact of film movement on time and space), while the Futurists explored the metamorphoses of distance with changing concepts of speed. Such efforts had their technological as well as semiotic impact, for cubism contributed during the First World War to the development of camouflage of military operations, as Kern demonstrates,[5] just as the experiments of the abstract expressionists brought about the exploration of the semiotics and technical effects of visual communication by the Bauhaus and its successors in design and visual communication. The road to the Media Lab, virtual reality, and cyberspace began with artistic experimentation in the second half of the nineteenth century.

While modernist artists' overt awareness of how the entire spectrum of communication is radically changed by social and technological transformations may appear 'new,' that artists have always been interested in modes of communication and their relation to the semiotic universe is far from 'new.' The history of artistic theory and practice has always played an important role within the history and evolution of the theory and practice of communication, beginning, as Giedion demonstrates, with the birth of art and architecture – a history that is coterminous with the history of civilization. Cave paintings are the forerunners of writing stories, painting, sculpture and even cartoons and comics: the root of that persistent classical commonplace of painting and sculpture as silent poems, and poems as speaking pictures, the forerunner of recorded gestures and the interplay of light and rhythm.

Vico, exploring the role of ancient cultures and primary mythology in the development of civilization in *Scienza Nuova*, reveals an awareness of these aspects of the history of communication and their relation to the poetic. Joyce, a friend and associate of Giedion and a lifelong student of Vico, selected Vico's work as the 'ground bass' for his own exploration of the evolution of communication into the electric age, for Vico provided a method of understanding the process of communication or language coming-to-be that established a continuity between gestures, rhythms, visual signs, and the emergence of language. Vico's classification of those three languages which mark the progress to human speech is as follows: first, a divine mental language of liturgy; next, heroic blazonings; finally, articulate speech.

Liturgical and heraldic materials abound in *Finnegans Wake* side by side with telegraphy, radiophony, and television. The morphogenetic approach to semiosis pursued by Vico establishes a pattern for the continuum of communication, which Joyce dramatically brings up to the last century of the millennium by dramatizing the very language transformed and reproduced by urbanization, communication, and internationalization. John Bishop has shown how Joyce adopted from Vico the strategy of playing on webs of meanings generated from an aboriginal root in Indo-European languages. In *The New Science,* Vico himself uses 'an assemblage of words originating in the same aboriginal root **gen-* ("to come to be").'[6] Joyce deconstructs and reconstructs English in the new world of international communication, using webs of words emanating from common Indo-European roots.[7] Such relationships form rhizomic networks that permeate the surface of texts, revealing the complex and multiplex density of history/communication.

Vico went further and showed that polysemy is a to-be-expected feature of this ongoing becoming-communication through the exercise of the poetic faculty. As Bishop puts it: 'In Vico's etymological vision, Joyce found that every normal particle of language was inherently a quadruple pun of sorts. Beneath its current denotation, every word concealed two meanings revelatory of existence in history, one reflecting internal evolution of social forms and the other reflecting wider international forces whose play modified those forms ... all words finally concealed the aliterate thinking of the body.'[8] The book as 'vicociclometer' emanating from bits of code and digested like bits of food is a transformation of the Viconian conception of communication in an electro-mechanical era. Vico opened up the path by which to see the history of communication through a dialectic of socio-semiology and morphogenesis, the transformation of forms counterpointing the transformation of society. He viewed his method as a poetic wisdom that, as a corollary, introduced the history of poetics and the arts as a necessary complement to the genesis of communication and society.

Marx refers to Vico in *Capital* when speaking about a need for a history of technology: 'And would not such a history be easier to compile, since, as Vico says, human history differs from natural history, in this, that we have made the former, but not the latter?'[9] Gramsci expanded on Marx's insight into Vico's dialectic, suggesting that Vico's 'ruses of nature' demonstrated 'how a social impulse, tending towards one end, brings about its opposite.'[10] While there are profound differences between Marx's historical materialism and Vico, the Viconian way certainly opens up a path for examining people making technology and technologies making people. What Vico does for communication studies is to open up the history of poetics as centrally relevant to the history of communication and to establish the history of poetics itself as socio-political history.

Within the Western world, the recorded history of poetry's or art's contribution to communication theory begins at least by the time that classical poets speak about 'silent poems' and 'speaking pictures.' Poems playing with orthography, calligraphy, and spatial arrangement of written signs are present in the Greek repertoire, where poets newly exposed to literacy explore some of the potentials of the written form. This same fascination emerges again in the Renaissance with the emergence of print, as attested by the practice of a poet like George Herbert, whose poems include some in the shapes of birds or altars, and by the earlier theories of Puttenham, who discusses in detail the visual layout and the visual shape of poems in his *Arte of English Poesie*.[11]

Quarrels about the effect of print on poetry which arose in the sixteenth century, such as the one between Spenser and Harvey, were actually discussions about the conflicting communication potential of a new technology. Spenser, arguing against Harvey's wish for a standardized orthography, raises the question of the density of communication which can be achieved by playing with the simultaneous impact of eye and ear, while Harvey stresses the vast advantage of providing a more transparent medium of communication.[12] Such debates, while directed towards poetic practice, were not divorced, however, from social and political positions, since Spenser's courtly commitment certainly did not have the same intense interest in the immediate and widespread dissemination of the word that the new Puritan cultures did.

The history of the poetic as it cuts across all of the arts parallels the history of the transformation of communication as well as of that continuous becoming which marks the evolution of the poetic. Therefore, Bateson's treatment of grace (see above p. 205), which rewrites texts from the early eighteenth century, is not quixotic, since it marks the awareness that the poetic affects this process of evolution. A critique of the final sections of McLuhan's *The Gutenberg Galaxy* on Pope's *The Dunciad* will permit reconsideration of a key example of a text that exhibits this historical relationship between the poetic and transformations in communication. McLuhan argues that *The Dunciad* predicts how the evolution of print technology in the eighteenth century will result in delirium.[13]

In the first half of the eighteenth century, the idea of the writer as a professional emerges, periodical literature and newsletters appear, commercialized publishing begins to replace patronage, a new and improved printing technology comes of age, and attitudes towards the advancement and dissemination of knowledge are transformed. These changes cannot be separated from social and political changes that occur during the same period: for example, the beginnings of industrialization or the rise of the mercantile class. Pope, as one of the landed Catholic gentry, is politically a conservative, yet a radical conservative who is naturally critical of the Protestant majority and the British government. Demonstrating in Viconian terms that 'a social impulse tending towards one end, brings about its opposite,' Pope, like Pascal and Racine in France, adopts a 'quietistic' scepticism, using all the *finesse* of a Pascalian play with the *esprit de géometrie*.[14] He develops his own specific poetic device for negativity by optimizing the satiric potential and complexity of the heroic couplet – an achievement which Joyce recognizes when he speaks of how 'samething ... may be involted into the zeroic couplet' (*FW*284.9–10). The British writer Charles Williams confirmed this when he analysed the negating movement of the Popean couplet as an anticipation of the negative moment of the Hegelian dialectic.[15] Through the use of such poetic devices, Pope and Pascal criticized the Enlightenment from the marginality of their respective social roles. Completed at the pinnacle of his career, *The Dunciad* shows how Pope adapts such techniques to investigate problems of communication.

Pope and a group of his closest literary friends (Jonathan Swift, Dr Arbuthnot, Thomas Parnell, John Gay) formed the Scriblerus Club, dedicated to ridicule 'all false tastes in learning.' The members discussed and began drafting papers and parts of books which would be corporate works. In the tradition of Menippean satire, the anti-hero of many of these projects was to be one Martinus Scriblerus, a learned gull and pedant, who was an editor (i.e., textual scholar, philosophist, speculator, and man of letters). Pope's major comic epic poem on poetry, learning, and communication technology, *The Dunciad* (and, for that matter, Swift's *Gulliver's Travels* as well) had its roots in the Scriblerian satiric program.[16] The composition of the final variorum version in four books took fifteen years from its first inception, because Pope carefully engineered the context from which it would emerge.

To attract attention to his project and build up a body of criticism from those he wished to attack in *The Dunciad*, Pope first published a comically conceived, rhetorically oriented poetic treatise written by Martinus Scriblerus, the *Peri Bathous*, or *Art of Sinking in Poetry*. This satire attacks those new writers who were trying to cultivate the expanded audience made available through technological changes in print, increased literacy, and developing commercialism by indulging in enthusiastic, uncritical, extremist use of Longinus's *On the Sublime* and by promoting misleading populariza-tion of criticism and learning.[17] Throughout this satiric manual, poetry is reduced to a rigid kind of mechanics, so that Scriblerus provides directions for making epic poems just as one provides recipes for cooking partridge.

Scriblerus sets out, as critics have previously done, to lay 'down many mechanical rules for compositions of this sort,' but he undertakes to do so in a way in which 'epic poems may be made *without a Genius*, nay without Learning or much Reading.'[18] He associates this entire project with the economic and technological characteristics of the age: 'To which end our Art ought to be put on the same foot with other Arts of this age. The vast improvement of modern manufacture ariseth from their being divided into several branches, and parcelled out to several trades: for instance, in Clock-making one artist makes the balance, another the spring, another the crown-wheels, a fourth the case, and the principal workman puts all together: To this economy we owe the perfection of our modern watches, and doubtless we also might that of our modern Poetry and Rhetoric, were the several parts branched out in the like manner.'[19] Rhetorical *topoi* thus come to be like watch parts or slugs of type – a topic quite literally becomes type – in this brave new world of print. *The Art of Sinking* provides a remarkable example of Pope's consciousness of the new modes of communication that were opening up in his era.

Having provided a point of attack to draw the missives of the writers, printers, and publishers who were his satiric targets, proceeding step by step, he first published *The Dunciad* (1728), a poem in three books (episodes) to stimulate still further attack. This was followed by *The Dunciad Variorum* (1729), an edition of the three-book poetic text(complete with commentary, critical apparatus, extensive notes, appendices, tables, indices, etc.) under the editorship of Martinus Scriblerus, incorporating many of the earlier critical attacks and further castigating those who had been the original targets. The 1729 *Variorum* clearly launches a profound examination of the movement of communication towards romantic diffuseness and populism marked by a full consciousness of the interaction of the technology with the forms of producing communication and the impact of the changing economic forms on the beginnings of a culture industry.

During the years following the 1729 *Variorum*, Pope and Swift's *The Memoirs of Martinus Scriblerus* appeared; Pope collected all the attacks on the three-book *Variorum* and on the *Memoirs*. Then, in 1741, he published the *The New Dunciad*, a poem in four books. This was followed by *The Dunciad, in Four Books* (1743), a new variorum edition in which the hero figure has changed from the pedantic Tibbald of the three-book *Dunciad* to the writer, publicist, playwright, and laureate, Colly Cibber. In *The Dunciad* project, stretching from 1728 until 1743, Pope demonstrated a thorough awareness of the role that the book played in the eighteenth century as a material form of communication which provided authors and publishers with new potentialities made possible by improved technology and the beginnings of mass production.

Concern with the mechanics of the book is an important aspect of *The Dunciad*, for as Scriblerus observes in a note, the poet was moved to write this poem because 'he lived in those days when (after providence had permitted the Invention of Printing as a scourge for the Sins of the learned) Paper also became cheap, and printers so numerous, that a deluge of authors cover'd the land.'[20] He opines that mass publishing has opened the way to free and easy publication made possible by the unlimited 'Liberty of the Press.' This theme is clearly stated in the opening of the 1728 *Dunciad*: 'Books and the Man I sing, the first who brings / The Smithfield Muses to the Ear of Kings' (A:1.1–2).[21] Smithfield, as the site of Bartholemew Fair, is associated with mass entertainment characteristic of any fair, which was now being imported into the theatres. The increase in scholarly editions and the multiplication of critical books are also satirized, along with Richard Bentley, ('the eminent') professor and textual editor, for in *The Dunciad* Bentley is Dulness's servant:

Thy mighty Scholiast, whose unweary'd pains
Made Horace dull, and humbled Milton's strains.
Turn what they will to Verse, their toil is vain,
Critics like me shall make it Prose again. (B:4.211–14)

This Scholiast, described as 'the critic Eye, that microscope of Wit' (B:4.233), uses the power of print to produce information overload:

For thee I dim these eyes, and stuff this head,
With all such reading as was never read:
For thee explain a thing till all men doubt it,
And write about it, Goddess, and about it. (B:4.249–52)

Dulness obfuscates sense, memory, and intellect:

Here to her Chosen all her work she shews;
Prose swell'd to verse, verse loit'ring into prose:
How random thoughts now meaning chance to find,
Now leave all memory of sense behind (A:4.273–6)

She continues to show her followers the value of 'frittering' poetic texts into notes and how 'index-learning turns no student pale, / Yet holds the eel of science by the tail' (B:1.278–80).

The entire 1743 *Dunciad, in Four Books,* which extends the range of the satire to a critique of the advancement and dissemination of knowledge, is a prophecy about a world moving into the dark night of a Romanticism geared to simplification, massification, and industrialization. The poem moves from the day world into the darkness of chaos and old Night. *Finnegans Wake,* published two hundred years later, is *The Dunciad*'s alter ego; moving from the night world of Romanticism to an acceptance of a new day world of para-modernism, where the evolution of the electro-mechanical technology and attendant industrial capitalism will eventually free the book and the journal from many of the specific tasks which would interfere with its appropriate utilization. While McLuhan suggests that for Pope print leads to delirium (that is, Dulness, for all distinction is lost in the process), Pope's insight is much stronger and more profound.

Pope's real delirium is a vision of a world where a multitude of contradictions, brought about by the co-presence of quantities of printed material, will lead to a helically accelerating movement towards negativity and nothingness. Contemporaries of Pope, such as Swift in *The Battle of the Books,* shared this position, and as the minority opinion they were prepared to use the aesthetics of transgression and the carnivalesque world as a means of exposé. Such strategies used to attack the alleged mechanization of the art of thinking (in keeping with the mechanization of physics and mechanics) rise out of their opposition to the inappropriate mimicry of technology, which was being reinforced by the development of a professional and industrial approach to publishing.

Pope's style tries to achieve a balance of orality and print, since he affirms the co-presence of orality with writing in the printed text. Devices of print often highlight the oral realization (e.g., italicization, capitalization, punctuation, syllabification). The mechanized word will become increasingly divorced from the physical realization of orality; for such effects as standardization of the language are a necessary corollary to the mechanization of the word, since it is assumed that to achieve maximum effectiveness, print itself must become transparent. Addison, in the *Spectator* papers, and later Samuel Johnson, in his *Preface to Shakespeare,* condemned Shakespeare's puns or verbal quibbles. Both represent a critical extreme which wishes to suppress those aspects of rhetoric that pose potential conflicts between oral and printed modes.

The *Dunciad Variorum* achieves its climax in a vision of an 'uncreating word,' which by negating creation opens up an abyss. Although this is only one of the potentialities of print, it is an inescapable potentiality in a world where knowledge as well as its communication and dissemination become mechanized. In this conclusion, communion is Pope's means of defining the symbolic action of adequate communication; but what interferes with that communion is the way in which the mechanical nature of the cultural industry encourages a cumulative scepticism (characteristic of Pope's own sceptical nature). McLuhan viewed this as print unleashing the new collective unconscious; a theme he found to be developed fully in *The Dunciad, in Four Books*. The headline introducing this section of *The Gutenberg Galaxy* announces:

The last book of *The Dunciad* proclaims the metamorphic power of mechanically applied knowledge as a stupendous parody of the Eucharist.

And he continues in the text: 'The entire fourth book of *The Dunciad* has to do with the theme of *The Gutenberg Galaxy*, the translation or reduction of diverse modes into a single mode of homogenized things.'[22] The irony, though, is that Pope is prophesying the eventual emergence of modernism. It is not the technology in itself, but the evolution of the technology in the specific social, political, and economic context which is Pope's concern.

It is interesting to remember that the same William Warburton whom Derrida rediscovers and Paul Heyer speaks about in his study of communication/history is Pope's friend and editor.[23] In fact, Warburton's *The Divine Legation of Moses* is of intrinsic importance to the structuring of *The Dunciad* for it provides the insight for Pope's 'ground bass,' the Eleusinian mysteries. Historians of communication will discover a close relation between theories about communication and the concerns of students of language, poets, and artists; a relation which will only temporarily have been bracketed in some areas of communication studies in the past century or so. While communication studies have always embraced the history of rhetoric, there is now a need for communication studies to explore the interdependent link existing between communication theory and practice within all of the arts and the impact of the poetic on the history of communication.

In the Elizabethan age, Shakespeare's use of bawdy tavern humour, popular song, broadsides, and the like constantly challenges the high, courtly rhetoric of the ruling factions, thus providing an expanded capability for the communicative faculties. The so-called low life of Shakespearean drama is an intrinsic factor in the poet's exploration of new modes of communication. The transgressive puns in Hamlet's conversations with Ophelia and Polonius provide an excessive intensity which criticizes the everyday world of court and of commons. In *The Tempest* Shakespeare confronts the clandestine, convoluted politics of the official world with the hermetic, esoteric force of the subversive 'underworld' or occult world, fusing a magical past with a subversive present through the art of Prospero.

Shakespearean dream and memory cut through the hierarchical order, since they are the possessions of fools, jesters, and clowns that are operative for the commons as well as the court. In *A Midsummer Night's Dream* as Bottom wakes up after dreaming, an interchange occurs between the lovers Demetrius and Hermia:

> *Dem*: These things seem small and undistinguishable,
> Like far-off mountains turned into clouds.
> *Her*: Methinks I see these things with parted eye,
> When everything seems double.
> ...
> Are you sure that we're awake? It seems to me
> That yet we sleep, we dream. (4.1.192–5, 199–200)

About which Demetrius finally concludes:

> Why, then we are awake. Let's follow him;
> And by the way let us recount our dreams. (204–5)

Recounted dreams or remembered time – life reconsidered – for 'We are such stuff / As dreams are made on, and our little life / Is rounded with a sleep' (*The Tempest*, 4.1.156–8).

Again, Bottom exclaims:

> I have had a most rare vision. I have had a dream, past the wit of man to say what dream it was. Man is but an ass, if he go about to expound this dream ... I will get Peter Quince to write a ballad of this dream. It shall be called Bottom's Dream, because it hath no bottom, and I will sing it in the latter end of our play. (*A Midsummer Night's Dream*, 4.1.209–22)

Remembrance, dream, and imagination permeate the social field, so that the dream of the weaver, Bottom, is *the dream*, yet in its doubleness, is it a dream or a waking dream? Poetry, not interpretation, can recount this dream for:

> The poet's eye, in a fine frenzy rolling,
> Doth glance from heaven to earth, from earth to heaven;

And as imagination bodies forth
The forms of things unknown, the poet's pen
Turns them to shapes and gives to airy nothing
A local habitation and a name. (Ibid., 5.1.12–17)

As 'imagination bodies forth / The forms of things unknown,' it becomes the ecology of sense, creating a new space from the remembered dreams, just as 'the art that nature makes' is said to have done in Polixenes and Perdita's discussion of the garden and language of flowers.

Such a vision springs from *A Midsummer Night's Dream* through the action of the play and playing of the people: Peter Quince, Bottom, and their entourage. Proust appropriately echoes Shakespeare when he entitled his *Recherches* ('The Remembrance of Things Past').[24] The Shakespearean dream is a perspective on the cartography of communication in the Elizabethan Renaissance. While that perspective is not the same as that of the contemporary world, the analysis of communication still indicates the transverse and transgressive functioning of the poetic. Classical and medieval artists experimented with the modes of communication, transforming and extending them in the process. The emergence of Western drama from the liturgy of the early Christian church is just such a specific case in point. Furthermore, it is important to note the conjunctions which arose between print and visual materials, or between print and printed music. In the former case, there is the practice of emblem poetry (introduced in 1531 in Alciati's *Emblemata*, the woodcut first appearing in Europe around 1400), which explores the possible relations of the visual print in the printed text; or the role of the semiotically oriented engraving in the emerging interest in the preservation of information and the transmission of ideas, such as the iconographic engravings used in treatises throughout the Renaissance (material the scholarly understanding of which Panofsky pioneered in his explorations of iconography). Vico's frontispiece in the *New Science*, which is a mnemonic device figuring forth the 'idea of the work,' represents one such application of a long and complex tradition, transforming the technique of memory into a visual *aide-mémoire* and guide to reading. Yates has explored the evolution of this iconographic mode in relation to discussions of theories of memory and memory theatres in the Renaissance in her *Art of Memory* and other writings, in which she demonstrates that this mode was preserved within the hermetic tradition of the Renaissance in opposition to its diminished importance within the development of the Enlightenment concepts of science and method. This use of iconography implies radical changes in communication as well as mnemonics, for such polysemic iconography preserves aspects of the dialogic, pre-print tradition within print, stressing an interplay between surface and depth. Vico's exegesis of his icon takes twenty-three pages in the Bergin translation! That interplay of the dialogic and print is further underlined by the aphoristic style of presentation of the 'new science.'

In painting, the new technological orientations had a profound effect. Gombrich has related the understanding of the development of perspective to a conception of painting as a form of communication.[25] He argues that perspective represents a major change in the system by which paintings are interpreted through a rhythm of schema and correction. In *Through the Vanishing Point* McLuhan examines the significance of the newly emerging vanishing point in painting and discovers that it is an index of how a commitment towards a new way of seeing and other new technological modes (i.e., printing, print-making) generates new ways of communicating. He goes on to show further connections of the relationship of this newly conceived device of perspective to new modes of governing, new social organizations, new religious beliefs, and new modes of discovery.

While there is always some experimentation taking place among artists, which is one of the reasons for closely associating art with the history of how humans think about communication, nevertheless, classical, medieval, Renaissance, and early Romantic discussions of poetry and art did not self-consciously reflect on how the artistic process itself can affect or transform everyday communication, nor how the symbol-making power can function apart from political and religious belief or specific tradition. While Dante, Shakespeare, Racine, or Pope do not overtly recognize it, their poetic practice implies certain theories and practices of communication.

Dante, for example, experiments with the limits of a complex symbolic tradition in which writing is dialogically reinforced by the art of oral memory. Yates points out the role of the 'Inferno' as a 'memory theatre' and the whole of the *Commedia* as a system of mnemonics oriented to the purgation of the past (Hell) through envisioning the hope of the future (Heaven).[26] It has been demonstrated how in *The Dunciad* Pope provides an early critique of the ambiguities of mass communication. Rabelais experimentally transforms the language of reflective discourse through the confrontation of scholastic, ecclesiastic, and legalistic expression with the carnivalesque grotesque modes of everyday life in the late medieval world. He plays with many of the potentialities of the new print medium; potentialities which included the possibility for the revolutionary emergence of the individual.

According to Mikhail Bakhtin, in Rabelais's *Gargantua* 'the carnival-grotesque form exercises the ... function; to consecrate inventive freedom, to permit the combination of a variety of different elements and their rapprochement, to liberate from the prevailing point of view of the world, from conventions and established truths, from clichés, from all that is humdrum and universally accepted.'[27] He describes Rabelais's use of all the resources of verbal and logical play, of the encyclopaedic nature of the realm of the signifier, and the jokes, jests, and malapropisms of the market-place. This example is even more explicit than some of the others in demonstrating that an implicit concern for how communication works in a particular society is centrally involved in the poetic process.

No one before Joyce sets out to explore communication technologies with the same exhaustiveness and comprehensiveness. No one, until our century, attempted to design a work which would exploit fully the interplay between different modalities of writing, print, and speech. While, subsequent to the introduction of print, many rhetoricians recognized the importance of 'orthographical' figures and figures based on punctuation, capitalization, and the like, they usually regarded them merely as aids to highlighting features of the oral language. Joyce, however, designed *Finnegans Wake* primarily by using orthography in such a way that the reader has to both see it with his eye and hear it with his ear to fully comprehend the workings of the language and the range of the puns. This also provides a means for utilizing the differences between oral language and print to develop a poetic counterpoint and 'language' for generating completely new forms by which to explore the complexities of this contemporary world where the variegated multiplicity of communication technologies has demonstrated the interdependence of media of expression.[28]

14

High Decibel Dialogue of the Electronic Fairground: Mediating Communication by Talking about It

Books and telecommunications gadgets, the organs imposed on bodies, or the geography imposed on spaces, or meanings imposed across pluralities of signs and gestures are all part of the world of 'Annah the Allmaziful, the Everliving, the Bringer of Plurabilities' (*FW*104.1–2). Probabilities are plural only by being recompounded in the mechano-electro-chemical structure of 'Finnius the Old One' (615.7), the Awakener of you, 'the Cockalooraloora-loomenos' (615.8). Finnius is the boundary, the limit – the limit of the oneness of nature itself. A body or the body of a book or the screen on which images are projected are surfaces, topographies, across which a multitude of 'plurabilities' play. Upon each such body are inscribed assemblages, abstract machines – 'The mar of murmury mermers to the mind's ear' (254.18) – which create the inscriptions, the wandering lines, that make communication possible.

The presence of modes of mediated communication pervades the *Wake*. First, there are the verbally based forms: the tale, the story, rumours, and gossip. At the conclusion of Book I of the *Wake*, two washerwomen washing laundry in the river tell stories and gossip about the relation of the innkeeper and his wife:

> O
> tell me all about
> Anna Livia! I want to hear all
> about Anna Livia. Well, you know Anna Livia? Yes, of course, we all know Anna Livia. Tell me all. Tell me now. You'll die when you hear. (196.1–6)

But tales are told by a wide variety of means; bells, for example: 'Spell me the chimes. They are tales all tolled' (275.24). In one case, they ring about

Anna: '*Telltale me all of annaryllies* ... (ringrang, the chimes of sex appealing as conchitas with sentas stray, rung!)' (268.2–4). Tales are also told by drums, stamping feet, telegraph, telephoto, and wireless. The telling of the tale of the *Titanic* by wireless is even retold.[1] The electric world is buzzing with telling everyone about everything – whether through talk, verbally mediated communication, or electrically and mechanically mediated communication.

There is an interminable ongoingness of communication. Besides theoretical reflection on communication, each and every person is always involved in communicating about communication; not only with regard to that metalinguistic activity which governs particular communicative acts, but as an infinite regress of communicative acts about communicative acts. Put more simply, the arts live and thrive in and through 'talk about' the arts; but this is a specialized case of communication itself, which lives and thrives in 'talk about' communication, for people constantly communicate about communication. In the *Wake* there would be no endless talk about Anna if the original story, when it had first been told, actually was *the* story.

Since a story is always an assemblage involving selection of events, another selection can speak about it in another way. It is possible to talk about how the story has been told and to discuss the means by which the story has been communicated. When in HCE's pub a 'verbivocovisual presentement' of a horse race – 'the worldrenownced Caerholme Event' (341.20) – is telecast: 'Hippohopparray helioscope flashed winsor places' (341.23–4); the story is then recounted, commented on, and evaluated by those watching it, so that the 'presentement' itself becomes part of the subject of their interaction. Talk and reflexive communication, both critical and social, are an intrinsic part of the arts and what the arts are about. The arts are a concentrated model of the process of communication, for they are a realm in which one can experiment with expression and communication.

This historical association between art and interpretation should also strongly suggest that there is a close relation between art and conversation (or human discourse); for the act of interpretation is an extension of conversation, a kind of talk. In this process, it is impossible to distinguish between high art, popular art, and those products of the mass media which many try to distinguish from either high or popular art, since all such activities, which Benjamin described as the 'post-auratic' arts, exhibit traits of being enmeshed in an ongoing conversation by means of radio broadcasts, reviews, journalistic coverage in media, books, academic criticism, research reports, and so forth. In spite of all disclaimers, there is a close relation between art, literature, popular discourse, and academic discourse. Much of the talk about non-verbal or mixed modes of art arises in written forms which are themselves a kind of literature, such as the writing of Pauline Kael on film or the writing in *Rolling Stone* on rock music. It appears to be necessary that in order to participate, to share, to commune with art and popular culture, people have to communicate or talk about it.

This is hardly new; for painting, the most silent of the arts, has always existed in a world of communication: the talk of collectors, gallery owners, museum viewers, critics, and academic students of the art of painting. Medieval cathedrals have thrived by producing centuries of talk. In *Mont St Michel and Chartres* Henry Adams very perceptively compared the cathedral to a world's fair, for it was for its community a *summa* or contemporary encyclopaedia. As a complex multi-generic assemblage of the arts – drama (i.e., the liturgy), music, painting, sculpture, architecture, and poetic prose – it became a space to move through, to interact with, and to talk about that permeated the lives of the community within which it existed. And it also entered into a conversation with the works which it contained and encompassed.

Many contemporary art forms are self-reflexive with respect to this 'conversational' interaction: Godard's cinema, Lichtenstein's pop art, Brecht's theatre. All art is of necessity not only a *kind* of discourse, but a *part* of discourse – an ongoing communicative interaction and conversation. For this reason, in spite of some of our modern heresies, talk and other communication about cultural productions does not corrupt those art forms, since it arises naturally from within the form (as Eisenstein realized with respect to film in the controversy over silent versus sound films). Even a critic of sound film, such as the dean of underground film-making in the United States, Stan Brakhage, ultimately became enmeshed in talk defending the purity and independence of film. Brakhage's own masterly silent film, *The Art of Vision* – nearly five hours in length – is a colour exploration of the orchestration of visual perception in motion. Brakhage places his film activity in the context of his own poetic talk about his work, through such writings as his 'Metaphors of Vision' in *Film Culture*, as well as by his practice of entitling films: for example, 'The Art of Vision' or 'Songs' or 'Window Water Baby Moving' (the title verbally playing on the use of camera movement in the film).

Talk about communication, communication about communication, is an all-pervasive feature of our communication universe. It underlines the way that the entire process of communication is an outering, an uttering, which basically exists in externality. Just as earlier people became at one with the ways their universe of signs developed through writing, signing, signalling, singing, dancing, and drawing, moderns are becoming at one with their electronic networks. Those networks become extensions of the nervous system, as they merge in a symbiotic relation with that nervous system. In both the pre-modern and modern instances, the means and modes of communication and people form a continuum.

This is what McLuhan tried to describe when he said that technology is an extension of the nervous system. Since this is so, the nervous system, like the structure of the various technologies, is a machine. Divorce between the whole person and the nervous system is impossible, just as divorce between the whole person and the social field is impossible. When communication technology inundates the social field, the people become one with these technologies, unless they are able to treat the assumed symbiosis disjunctively. This requires people to act as engineers, potentially capable of constructing and controlling machines, since everyone, to the extent they exercise their creativity, does so by constructing a poetic and communicating machine.

This is evidently what McLuhan appears to have been trying to say when he pointed out that with 'the arrival of the new electric technology, man extended, or set outside himself a live model of the central nervous system itself.'[2] This is inevitable, for 'art as a means of developing immunity to society's new extensions or techniques is itself also an extension of human awareness in contrived and conventional patterns.'[3] In *Ulysses* Joyce has shown how the city is an extension of man's physical body. The rise of the phenomenon of the interminability of communication clearly confirms the way people as communicating machines continually communicate about communication and communications.

All of these communications and meta-communications inscribe themselves upon the body of the recipient; for the body, without the poetic-dramatic machine or other semiotic machines associated with social praxis (economic, political, etc.), is unstructured. Like a body-without-organs, the body receives through communication the wandering inscriptions of its environment. The city of *Ulysses* emerges as a *socius* from the imposition of organs and symbols, just as in everyday life the great organs of each of our own cities produce its social existence. Joyce's chart, which he presumably used in producing *Ulysses*, is concerned with the complexities of the shaping of the *socius* and naturally how the new flows of communication within the *socius* are produced by the gaps created through the disjunction of the flows of earth and river which produce the geoscape of Dublin.

In the *Wake* the interplay of bloodstream (ALP as river) and nerves (marked by HCE's stuttering) is the very foundation of communications; the action within which the social communications of everyday civic life are embedded – re-establishing movement between the gaps created in the normal or predictable flows of human life. Joyce envisages the city of the people, an imaginary global city, as a secularized Corpus Christi transformed through the secular consciousness of the city as machine, thus providing people with an ability to participate without absorption; to remain individuals within the community of redemption, a community of redemption in which a secularized social communion occurs through the sense of joy at being in possession of the logic of sense.

The productions of communication institutions, even the least commendable of them (e.g., advertising or propaganda), all have the characteristic of creating the potential for such gaps, even when their explicit intention is to reinforce the expected or anticipated flows of daily life. The more self-conscious communication becomes, the more likely it is that these gaps will generate paradox and contradiction, develop signs of negation and of the schizoid, and lead to a comic analysis of society. Talk about advertising permits a distancing from it, since it decontextualizes the ads; but poetic or artistic contemplation of advertising achieves the same end, only more powerfully, by simultaneously preserving and exposing the qualities within the ad which gave it its original power. Communication about such art provides a more complex 'vivisective' text from which to continue that critical discourse, opening up an ecological approach to communication.

McLuhan's *The Mechanical Bride* (and a less well known work, *The Astonished Muse*, by a colleague of David Riesman, Reuel Denney) first concentrated on how a dialogue between the arts and popular culture, and the treatment of popular culture as if it were art, would utilize this communication about communication as a critical strategy. Both McLuhan and Denney focused on advertising, the comics, the popular press, Hollywood, radio, and the beginnings of television. Ragtime, cubism, and symbolism illuminated the format and layout of the daily press; Dali, surrealism, and Disney confronted the movie mags; Li'l Abner, William Faulkner, and *Finnegans Wake* provided a complex illustrating Al Capp's artistic success; D.H. Lawrence, Budd Schulberg, Edmund Wilson and Charlie Chaplin demystified the myth of the mechanical bride. With *Pogo* in the 1960s, comics reached a stage where they became a mode for questioning the intellectual establishment (e.g., Kelly's strips on the 'new criticism'). *Pogo* became a critique of political communication in the broadest sense (the politics of culture as well as government), to be followed by the more intensely satiric *Doonesbury* and *Bloom County*.

In 1967 John Berger's BBC TV series *Ways of Seeing* made a considerable impact. In that series as well as the resulting book, Berger quite consciously extends McLuhan's strategy to a more direct critique through the juxtaposition of semiotic elements, works of art, advertising and publicity images, cultural objects, and commerical objects (categories which naturally overlap). Here communication's ideological dialogue is revealed; yet by implication that ideological dialogue is also revealed to be a necessary aspect of the evolution of communication. When Duchamp tampered with the image of the *Mona Lisa,* just as much as when he displayed a urinal as his *Fountain,* he opened the way for a more reflexively conscious awareness of the continuity between artistic activity and everyday culture. The semiotic, ideological, and critical approaches to advertising – still more importantly, the very fact of taking advertising itself as a cultural object seriously – owe a substantial debt to the cultural dialogue generated by the arts.

Ulysses' hero, an advertising salesman, is fascinated by exempla of his profession: a handbill picked up in a butcher shop advertising a project in Israel; an advertisement for an evangelist meeting that he eventually throws away in the river; five sandwich men carrying signs around Dublin, which viewed together spell out 'HELYS.' He mulls over the manipulative publicity of the clergy, slogans for canned goods (Plumtree's potted meat), promotional photography, outright pornography, and finally his own contribution to the art of innuendo, an ad for the House of Keyes, which consists of crossed keys – a symbol that suggests home rule (since these are the symbol of the Isle of Man), but also the power of Rome (since the crossed keys are the symbol of the Papacy). All of this relates to that aspect of Bloom as nomadic wanderer in a bourgeois city.[4]

Joycean strategies succeed in making a formidable satiric critique of the world of advertising and mass communications. When the formulae of the ad-world sales pitch are transformed through the dream displacements of the language of the *Wake,* they provide new indices into the nature of Joyce's society: '[Johns is a different butcher's. Next place you are up town pay him a visit. Or better still, come tobuy. You will enjoy cattlemen's spring meat. Johns is now quite divorced from baking. Fattens, kills, flays, hangs, draws, quarters and pieces. Feel his lambs! Ex! Feel how sheap! Exex! His liver too is great value, a spatiality! Exexex! COMMUNICATED]' (172.5–10). Set off from the text by framing brackets, this is an audiovisual ad for a butcher shop, which primarily transforms an ordinary visual sales presentation, with its accompanying oral pitch, into a disclosure – in this case, of the slaughter that it conceals.

Simultaneously, this parodic advertisement is also a take-off on the British author and painter Wyndham Lewis, which further suggests that he has slaughtered the *élan vitale* through his obsessive critique of temporality in works such as *Time and Western Man*. In this publicist-style attack on the contemporary fascination with the 'time mind' complex within popular and high culture (and the accompanying reductionism of distinction between them during the 1920s), Lewis had identified Joyce as the central spokesperson for those embracing the Bergsonian philosophy of time[5] and its implicit undermining of our sense of space (and place) in favour of the new modernist vision of space-time. (Lewis's critique later inspired McLuhan in his early study of popular communication and popular culture that led to writing *The Mechanical Bride.)*

The strategy of Joyce's parodic ad involves a dislocation or estrangement from an expected context combined with the conscious shaping of a creatively distorted language: for example, 'next place' (next time, with reference to Lewis's space bias), 'tobuy' (today), 'sheap' (cheap and sheep or lamb), and 'spatiality' (speciality). The innuendo of slaughter simultaneously provides a powerful symbol for the hypocrisy of commercialism and mechanization of processes. Giedion's *Mechanization Takes Command*, which is another of the fundamental inspirations for *The Mechanical Bride*, devotes an entire chapter to the slaughterhouse, which Brecht also uses as the location of the action of *St Joan of the Stockyards*. Consequently, slaughter becomes an especially powerful sign for unmasking the ideological, commercial, and technological implications behind advertising, particularly in the period between the two world wars.

The association of the ad with communication and excommunication introduces an ambivalent analysis of the way such messages operate. The interplay between the 'exexex' ('Ex! Feel how sheap! Exex! His liver too is great value, a spatiality! Exexex! COMMUNICATED'), reminiscent of Aristophanes' comedy *The Frogs*, with its satire on commercialistic pseudo-communication, and the booming 'COMMUNICATED' calls attention to the undermining of genuine social communication through such manipulated social communication. To excommunicate designates a cutting off from communion; a removal from the realm of common society.

The recipient of such notice of excommunication becomes an outsider (Lewis, under his adopted guises as Tyro and Enemy), a deviant, and the ultimate object of the slaughter described in the mock ad. The separation of the terms designates that communication has been achieved – 'COMMUNICATED' – at one level that imparts information concerning the slaughter; at another level, the same communication that imparts the information through the advertisement has brought others into communion with the action involved in the slaughter. Turning back to earlier discussions in which communication has been linked to speaking and eating, this reference to communion and slaughter is deeply rooted in the rich anthropological associations of communication and sacrifice. As an example of what is later designated as an 'abortisement' (181.33), this item powerfully satirizes the way advertising co-opts the regime of signs.

Dada and surrealism, both of which inspired Joyce, are generally recognized as sharing some similarities with 'Pop Art,' for their practitioners, frequently through the distortions achieved by displacing the focus of advertising language and images, created new potentials for communication and a new communicative understanding of the original commercial sources.[6] Long before the 1960s there was a clear awareness of the 'announcements' inherent in commercial images in such examples as Picasso's *Plate with Wafers* (1914) and in the evolution of Schwitters's productions (from the early collages using fragments of everyday images to his later use of comic-book figures in work such as *For Kate 1947*) – artworks that preceded those of Oldenburg, Lichtenstein, and other Pop artists. In the United States, Pop started with a positive celebration of the raw energy and commercialism of postwar America.

That celebration, through the effect of shifting context, very quickly came to have a 'negating' relationship with the original images. Warhol's Campbell's Soup cans became the archetypal figure of this movement, setting up the most complex type of dialectic between the work of art and society. As beer cans, Brillo boxes, coke bottles, hamburgers, and frankfurters became the staple images of a whole art movement, a new intensive scrutiny of the manipulation of images arose from the close scrutiny of those images that absorbed the symbolic attention of North Americans and Western Europeans. Images of commercial packaging and advertising were set forth in their ambivalence; no longer condemned as banal and beneath notice. During this period, the same patterns and images came to be used by film-makers such as Makavéjev and Godard. In *Pierrot le fou*, for example, Godard structures the action of a scene at a cocktail party by using advertisements as structural joints in people's conversations, showing how they condition the participants' lives.

A Pepsi-Cola TV ad in the late 1970s, which almost seemed to be a parody of the Oedipal triangle, dramatized a family visit to the grandparents' ranch. This ad was roughly structured into three segments: the first segment shows the family arriving by car at the ranch; the second, the family riding on powerful horses, with close-ups of the youngest son on a black stallion, accompanied by the music 'Come on, come on, come on'; the third shows the family and friends at an old-style barbecue while the camera, paying considerable attention to a variety of food-processing and cooking machines, emphasizes the eroticism that accompanies the anticipated consumption and actual eating of the food. The sequence concludes as the mother rides off with the youngest son on the horse with her and pulls a large black stovepipe-style hat down over his head.

The symbolism is a highly charged, almost blatant, sketch of the Oedipal situation. It is hardly the kind of situation in which the interpreter 'reads into' the advertisement, for the ad is almost comic in its invitations to engage the viewer in superficially Freudianized analysis, including the phallic Pepsi-Cola bottle. This is an ad which clearly manifests what Joyce calls the 'eatupus complex' (128.36), a revelation of the psychoanalytic politics which Oedipalize and oversimplify in order to dominate.[7] The particular Pepsi ad analysed here tells a story involving a psycho-social dimension and employing traditional historical and mythological symbols. The narrative is dramatized, cinematically shaped, and accompanied by sound and music.

Superficially, then, this ad is a film in miniature. It can be analysed semiologically or interpretatively or both; it has cultural, intellectual, and historical dimensions involving the familial, the psychiatric, and popular American mythology. It is engaged in a process of making sense both by interpreting part of the world and its relations with Pepsi-Cola and also by being itself interpretable as part of a world in which Pepsi-Cola has a significant place in the social and economic structure as well as the cultural and ideological superstructure. Common sense suggests that the action, which produces this ad, is contrived and manipulated in the narrow interests of selling a specific product, so that it is not a contribution to some ecological process by which people posit themselves in relation to their life-world. Yet the structure, the signs, the dramatic and mythical elements, the ingredients of fantasy and dream, and especially the arousal of desire are all present here just as they are in other types of cultural production.

A more complex example than the Pepsi-Cola ad will illustrate how advertising co-opts socio-political and cultural values. Extended ad sequences consisting of a series of episodes are sometimes used on individually sponsored specials (e.g., by ATT, IBM, Dupont). One particular example, from the same period as the Pepsi ad, which has complex roots in film and literature, was used during a made-for-TV presentation of a new version of the classic Hollywood film *The Man in the Iron Mask*. The program, an expensive period costume extravaganza of eighteenth-century France, including location filming at Versailles and starring Richard Chamberlain, provided a pseudo-cultural vehicle with considerable nostalgic interest for the older portion of the viewing audience and for others hooked on Hollywood film history who would remember the original 1939 version.

The sponsors of this TV event were the Bell 'family.' The Bell advertising breaks consisted of an interrelated group of ads which together constituted episodes in an extended ad, one episode being presented at each program break. This extended sequence is a single unified 'story,' the parts being connected by a voice-over narration delivered by the well-known SF writer and futurist Arthur Clarke, who had only recently finished his collaboration with Stanley Kubrick on *2001* and who had also provided commentary for the CBS presentation of the first landing of an astronaut on the moon – the *Moon Odyssey*. Science fiction furnished a bridge uniting technology and culture. The use of Clarke as an on-camera narrator connected the ad with film, literature, science, prophecy, and the historic event of the first moon landing.

Through such an ad sequence, Bell's agency could play on virtually every theme, motif, key, and subject area, relating the corporate institution of ATT to the heart of the social and cultural fabric of a new internationalism. Clarke's presentation included: historical and nostalgic glances at the growth and development of Bell services through their operators; comic presentations of computers as new anthropomorphic members of an office management team; an impressive presentation of Bell's super-technology, with the use of the moving images of thousands of cars flowing along a metropolitan thruway system at night, which became a mobile artistic metaphor of the flow of messages through the Bell system and thus of the beauty of the power of modern telecommunications technology.

The climactic episode in this sequence of ads, a futuristic cultural *pièce de résistance*, opens with Clarke (whose name also conjures up that of Sir Kenneth Clark lecturing on PBS TV about art history and culture) in a sensuously erotic cultural setting, amid the massive architecture and sculpture of ancient Ceylon. Narrating about the wonders of the past in this ancient environment, Clarke subtly shifts from the distant past to the distant unpredictable future, associating new possibilities of intergalactic communication with our ability to explore the ancient culture hypertextually – an encounter with the mystery of a totally unimaginable 'other,' whose possible existence evokes the fear and fascination aroused by our preoccupation with UFO's. ATT's technology can provide us with images from the historical past for the study and enjoyment of the immediate present through transmitted image and computerization, just as its technology will also aid in opening up future prospects of intergalactic communications and transportation. This grand finale comes complete with visions of the Stargate from Kubrick's

2001 and all the accompanying innuendos of 'Beyond Jupiter' and its mysticism imported via Arthur Clarke himself.

The allusions to Kubrick's *2001* raise complex questions about technology and its future, which ironically the Bell ad sequence attempts to suppress. This attempt at suppression is achieved by the introduction of more 'stock' virtues of the everyday world: the comforting myth of the familiar, intimate home town suggested by family and children, by pseudo-erotic camaraderie in office byplay, and through the pseudo-liberating technology provided by ATT. To the extent that the suppression is successful, the ad has levelled the polysemy that characterizes Kubrick's film. On the other hand, Kubrick's *2001* provides a commentary on the inadequacies of such an ad and on the inadequacies of cultural programs like the one which exploits Kenneth Clark to promote its own specialized vision of officially defined culture.

The films of Makavéjev and Fellini provide examples of cinema that contribute talk about and means for talking about communicative actions such as the ads that we have just examined. The poetic process in their works begins a critique that leads to a destruction of the facile and superficial manipulation of meaning such as that which occurs in the Oedipal Pepsi or the pan-cultural Bell ads. In Makavéjev's deeply subversive film *Sweet Movie* (1974), the fetishization of women's bodies is neatly presented as an example of the 'sweetness' of advertising rhetoric – one of many manipulative uses of rhetorical sweetness that this film examines in detail. But critiques of the ad world are by no means limited to such individual intensive treatments as *Sweet Movie,* for one can readily recall other examples, such as the scene from Fellini's *The Temptation of Dr Antonio* in *Boccaccio 70,* where Anita Ekberg voluptuiously emerges out of her own image on a billboard advertising milk. Fellini's billboard or Makavéjev's play with milk and sugar in *Sweet Movie* helps make sense of ads, such as the Pepsi-Cola ad above, in a manner quite different from the way that the creator of the ad intended. The films magnify one's feeling that the images and actions in these ads are quite familiar, having been borrowed after being used many times before. Conventions become dead conventions. Whatever play may be present is the play of repetition rather than the playfulness of discovery.

Makavéjev, owing to the controversial nature of *Sweet Movie* and *W.R.: Mysteries of the Organism,* is not as well known as his abilities as a film-maker would justify. Since he uses a Rabelaisian-like comic and satiric perspective in his work and since he links some of his work directly to communication and popular culture, he is of central importance in understanding relationships between art and communication. The most genuinely penetrating examples of the ecological function of the poetic frequently invite the most stringent censorship, direct or indirect. Joyce's *Ulysses* is the classical literary example. The reason Makavéjev's work, which is quite central to the contemporary ecological functioning of the arts, is not better known is that *Sweet Movie* met with direct and indirect censorship, from both Marxist and capitalist societies and even from his star actress, Carol Laure, and his assistant director, Gilles Carle. The shocking transgressions of this film are too stark and striking in the way they reveal the paradoxical and ambiguous sources of the sweetness of propaganda and PR. The Rabelaisian and Aristophanic carnivalesque unfolding of the social unconscious can be deeply disturbing and frightening.

W.R.: Mysteries of the Organism, Makavéjev's film that immediately preceded *Sweet Movie*, won unanimous approval from the jury for the World Council of Churches award for the best film of 1971. *W.R.* is a cinematic essay on the life and teachings of Wilhelm Reich which, like *Sweet Movie*, is simultaneously a study of communication, of film theory, and of the nature of film practice. Makavéjev weaves documentary material, historical film footage, ingredients of television advertising, Hollywood film, Eisensteinian montage, underground, porn, and pure poetry into a complex mosaic of sounds, actions, and filmic ideas. Blending documentary reality and fictional narrative and dealing directly (often shockingly) with erotic material, he develops a multi-sensory and multi-sense (i.e., polysemous) mode of exposition that is not only essential to the making of his film, but which is affiliated with many of the strategies implicit in the dialectically conceived film essays of Godard.

Makavéjev, who in the 1960s consciously challenged anyone who would dissociate art film from being a discourse about what matters in the world around us, noted that '... concerning the political film by Eisenstein and Godard – I was conscious of it. But I wanted to do it with soul. To do it with feeling, to do it with humor, and to do it so you can feel that you can *touch* it. Not to have it as just images.'[8] Makavéjev's own image of his productions as a network of connections is very close to the etymological sense of text as a web. His filmic texts, the product of his essay technique, like Brechtian theatre, insist on an intellectual response from his producers-consumers through the use of cognitive estrangement within a context that simultaneously engages the audience as sensual and emotional beings.

Sweet Movie expands *W.R.*'s interest in the psycho-sexual and the erotic to link the ecology of sense and human sensuality to a concept of social therapy for, as Makavéjev tells us, *Sweet Movie* 'will be a pulsating film essay on HUMAN SENSUALITY. The idea of SENSUALITY as the basic criterion of human relationships commits the *actors and camera* to a "sexe à trois," to *a research laboratory of micro-relationships*, compels them to carefully *look at, smell, touch, lick, taste, listen, carry* and support each other. The idea of SENSUALITY commits the attitude of the actors toward *speech* as a SENSUAL ELEMENT: men feed one another with their speech; by aggressive speech a forced listener is "sucked" by the speaker.'[9] *Sweet Movie*'s ecological and therapeutic aspects are involved with the manner in which the film pursues the understanding of 'sweetness.' This is achieved by Makavéjev's conscious development of the semiotic multiplexity in this open text.

Commenting further on *Sweet Movie*, he speaks in considerable detail about 'film structure':

> In an open, non-authoritarian structure of film, basic material is made up of non-verbal elements, ingredients and contents. The verbal elements, definitions, clichés, are that part of the material which helps the construction of the basic illusion, namely that the story is important. The non-verbal material which hovers and flutters around the main story titillatingly tells us that the story itself is not important but that there is actually 'something else.' Having found out from the very first frames that somewhere beside the main story there is something else, something elusive and quintessential, the spectators join in the game and at various points discover 'hidden messages,' those that we have 'planted' in the film, uncovering things that we have never even dreamed about, and adding on various connotations and meanings based on their own personal experiences.'[10]

Arising out of the collision, the dialectical interaction of verbal and non-verbal elements actually tells the viewer that there is something else, something elusive, ambivalent, and quintessential.

This film technique has been called dialectical montage, a description with which Makavéjev concurs; for, while criticizing the Russian revolutionary films, he argues that 'they never thought about the montage and distance. Because when you pull together something from here and something from there in the same manner, then you have people recalling; you have not only a kind of one plus one equals two, but you have also two plus two equals five. If you take very distant things that have something in common, so people can be shocked at it and say, "Impossible!" ...'[11] Makavéjev's dialectical montage triggers a network of connections; connections in the verbal text, in the music, in the images, in the cutting. In doing this, he believes that he is making a new kind of comic dialectic film that uses many of the major strategies of Eisenstein and Godard. Polysemic multiplexity rather than simple juxtaposition is the textual principle of Makavéjev's films;

for there is a complex relationship between dialectical films, fiction, musical form, and the essay, as Godard suggested when speaking of *Deuxoutrois choses que je sais d'elle*: 'Actually, when I come to think about it, a film like this is a little as if I wanted to write a sociological essay in the form of a novel, and in order to do this had only musical notes at my disposition.'[12] Sound, image, verbal design, and motion pervaded by a comic sense of incongruity interact to produce Makavéjev's complex film.

Dream is also a central influence on his film-making, for one of his primary effects is to create overlapping shapes which bring his audience 'close to this feeling, these hypnogogic images that you have when you dream and you wake up.' This technique involves major connections between the beginning, middle, and end, 'like a network of ideas,' using 'shifting gestalts' so that in different viewings the audience may see different connections. He is clearly aware of the relation of these double images of dreaming and waking with the work of surrealists such as Breton, Magritte, and Dali, who shared an interest in the psychological effect of dreaming and hypnogogic imagery. The creation of such 'borderline experience with this double image is actually your emotional content put into some shape that is really something else.'[13]

In *Sweet Movie* (1974), Makavéjev probes the complex interplay of the sweetness of rhetoric, the erotic seductiveness of sweetness in sugar and candy, the sweetness of sex and polymorphous perversity, and the implicit threat in the manipulation of sweetness that can sometimes result in death. The film plays this quality of sweetness off against simulations and manipulations of sweetness in the world of advertising, propaganda, and persuasion. The heroine of *Sweet Movie* ultimately drowns in a vat of chocolate while making a TV ad. In a parallel plot, two young children and a sailor are slaughtered by Anna Planeta, the enthusiastic, prosletyzing socialist, who is captain of the *Karl Marx*, a riverboat carrying sugar and other sweets.

Carefully managed mass-publicity media events, one of the manipulative activities of the controllers of advanced capitalism, are refocused through satire by the use of hyperbole. An early scene in Montreal features a milk bottle, perched on the top of a dairy to advertise the purity of milk, which becomes an ambivalent symbol of pseudo-purity – a theme that first arises in the opening scene of the film, a TV beauty contest for the most desirable virgin to be Miss World 1984. This event is sponsored by Mr Kapital's mother, Martha, chair of the Chastity Belt Foundation (played by Jane Mallet), who preaches voluntary self-restraint – 'YOUR OWN BODY KILLS THE ANIMAL!' – and features an on-camera examination of the contestants by the eminent gynecologist Dr Mittlefinger, who, when he encounters

Mademoiselle Canada with her glittering sex radiating light, exclaims: 'A Rosebud!' She wins the prize – the power-hungry, frozen-phallused Mr Kapital (played by John Vernon), who offers her Niagara Falls. This hyperbolic device dramatizes the fetishistic use of the female body as a commodity, always implicit in such events.

Makavéjev then uses the natural landscape transformed by tourist promotion (in this case, Niagara Falls) to exhibit the sweetness of commercial exploitation. The Falls are revealed as the artificially exploitative nature show that they have become. When Mr Kapital takes Miss World above Niagara Falls in his airplane, he expresses his desire to possess them as he does her and to convert them into the world's greatest *son et lumière* (a wish filmically reinforced by a jolting cut from the billionaire on his wedding night urinating through his silver-clad penis, back to a shot of Niagara Falls). After a failed wedding night followed by a failed murder attempt on Miss World by Kapital's mother, she is taken by an Afro-Canadian bodyguard up into his apartment in the large model of a milk bottle above the dairy in downtown Montreal, where the purity and sweetness of the milk is counterpointed with the black comedy arising from the racial tensions between the two of them.

Paralleling the odyssey of Miss World, who travels from Niagara to Montreal and then France and Germany, there appears the complementary figure of Captain Anna Planeta in Eastern Europe with her folksy boatload of sweets, representing the earthy sweetness of Eastern Bloc dogmas. The critique of capitalism now extends to the false seductiveness of the official Communist party messages of the Eastern Bloc; posters of Stalin, Eastern European propaganda material, and pix of movie stars decorate the quasi-Romantic seductive sentimentality of the interior of the boat captained by this mentally unstable, ritualistic serial killer Anna Planeta – the craft on which she hawks sugar, chocolate, sweets, sex, popularized Marxism, and ultimately *death*. Throughout the film there are a multitude of other allusions to sweetness and its proximity with deception or death, ranging from incidents on the use of advertising sentimentality to the intricate interplay with milk, chocolate, and sugar. The filming by a British production crew of the Mexican singer El Macho (played by Sami Frey) on the Eiffel Tower with Miss World comically exposes how commercial persuasion utilizes popular national or ethnic music for an effect of false sentimentality.

From this interplay of sweetness and death, Makavéjev weaves a labyrinthine network of signs, which interrelate transversally throughout the texture of the film. When Anna Planeta seduces and then murders a young sailor in a vat of sugar, the murder had been symbolically anticipated in an earlier scene in which we see the sailor being bathed by Anna in her bathtub. Both scenes will also later be echoed in the climax of Miss World's odyssey when she drowns in a vat of chocolate during the filming of a TV advertisement. All these death motifs are also linked with documentary film footage that shows the exhumation of corpses of Polish soldiers who had been massacred by Soviet troops in Katyn Forest. One of the 'moral' ambiguities of war and persuasive propaganda is represented by the words of Sir Owen O'Malley concerning this Katyn massacre, written in a letter to Anthony Eden on 11 February 1944: 'Let us think of these things always and speak of them never.'[14] Ultimately, the film's web weaves paths that trace all of these deaths back to the machinations of Miss World's billionaire husband, the milk and sugar king whose fortune has resulted from the commercial 'sweetness' of marketing products, and to his Soviet counterparts.

One of the apparently least sweet scenes in this film is a shocking Rabelaisian-type orgy at the Milky Way Commune, a psycho-therapeutic community organized by the German film-maker/psychoanalyst Otto Muehl. Even though many of the specific practices of this particular radical commune will revolt the average audience, this orgy scene, featuring a highly anal 'shitfest' (Makavéjev's own term) banquet, celebrated to the accompaniment of Beethoven's 'Ode to Joy,' hints at some implicit, though ambivalent, modes of salvation within the exploitative society through the openness of genuine and uninhibited, but perhaps covertly totalitarian, human communalism. Sweetness becomes a sign through whose redefinition a whole radical rethinking of society should take place; a rethinking which challenges the 'sweet talk' of advertising, propaganda, false rhetorics, and the empty formulae of most politics. The modern grotesque is permeated by the interior, the depths, the unconscious, which are part of the discourse of the twentieth century. That is why *Sweet Movie* involved filming the Milky Way Commune, a post-Reichian phenomenon that still can be related to the erotic philosophy of *WR*.

Defending these commune scenes (which have frequently disgusted, even repulsed, rather than amused, film-goers since the film's first showing at Cannes), Makavéjev makes three telling points: (1) the non-participatory nature of the documentary camera in handling this material; (2) the use of the camera as an agent and a constituent of behaviour, which therefore becomes a deliberate stimulant and brings a sexual offering to the audience – an offering relating to the broad and diffuse perspectives of polymorphously perverse sexual stimuli which pervade the rest of *Sweet Movie* and *WR* as well; (3) that the total effect is to reveal a veiled and distanced 'pit of existential despair.'

This 'voyeur-lens,' as Makavéjev calls this effect, becomes a means of communicating the bitterness within the sweetness of the confusion of Eros and Thanatos within the audience's world and the way in which this excludes them from understanding the deep processes of socialization through which the Milky Way Commune members are seeking salvation and an awareness of self. While there will be an ongoing debate as to whether Makavéjev's shocking scenes in the commune, where the camera is a participant observer, work or not, their affinities with Bataille's understanding of the erotic and the intensity of communication accomplished by his transgressive camera are indisputable and particularly relevant to the development of communication about the contradictions within desire.

The scenes with the Milky Way Commune also present a carnivalesque world where, in a quasi-Rabelaisian contemplation, the camera presents individuals who are ritualistically acting out inner conflicts which they experience. The insertion of this event into a fictional story, and the insertion of the tragicomic heroine of that story into the documentary, construct a filmic machine for probing the extent of the contradictions of the 'sweet.' Makavéjev speaks of adopting an 'amorality principle,' a starting from zero or minus, the beginning of a negative dialectic with the more apparent sweetness of other parts of the film:

> All that starts as an expression of horror, awe, despair,
> nothingness, etc. (and that is where we shall arrive at)
> all that each person hides and will not admit even to
> himself, when looked at through the eye of the camera
> will become *beautiful,* shall reveal its *freaky charm.*
> its *truthfulness* and ATTRACTION. Thus, the horror shall
> be transformed into poetry, humour and charm.
>
> Do not worry, it's going to be funny. It's going to be
> dreadfully funny.[15]

The anal, orgiastic, gorging activities of the feasts and dances, the 'shitfest' and the breast feeding, all have a highly functional place in this anti-Oedipal, post-Freudian, Rabelaisian-style vision. It is the purging of the de Sades, the Hitlers, the Stalins by descent and degradation, instruments of the grotesque which must always invoke the lower elements of bodily life. In the context of the twentieth century, this differs radically from that of the sixteenth, which is precisely Makavéjev's power as a post-Marxist and an historian.

Makavéjev's film-making is directly related to the Freudian problem of eros and civilization. Seeing the erotic principle as a prime civilizing and liberating principle in human society, he consciously identifies the artistic avant-garde as revolutionary. Makavéjev's camera and microphone deliberately explore 'polymorphous perversity,' illustrating in the process an affinity between the discovery and development of film and more liberated communication and the emergence or re-emergence to the consciousness of the 'polymorphously perverse' aspects of people's nature. The contradiction and pervading irony of *Sweet Movie* is the confused relationship between Eros and Thanatos that has emerged in the contemporary world; a world where 'sweetness' conceals only as through a veil the essential aggressiveness which results in the sugary death of Luv (the *Potemkin* sailor), the children, and Miss World. In his earlier film, *WR*, his heroine, Milena (who is decapitated by her lover, Vladimir Ilyich, a Russian super-star figure skater), is comically resurrected at the conclusion when her decapitated head starts speaking in the autopsy room – an allusion to an earlier autopsy scene in his film *The Switchboard Operator* (1967). Both of *Sweet Movie*'s odysseys – Anna's and Miss World's – characteristically lead to death and destruction; but they also result in a resurrection which preserves the comic quality of the whole. Anna Planeta, as a ritual murderess, seduces children and other innocents and buries their corpses in the sugar she carries on her boat. At the conclusion of *Sweet Movie*, these children (the Innocents) murdered by Anna Planeta on her boat (the *Karl Marx*) are resurrected, rising from the body bags in which they had been laid out by the police along the shore of the river, unlike the vicitms in a true story of a mass murder of twenty-seven children that was discovered in Houston, Texas, in August 1973, to which the filmic situation alludes. So these resurrections are counterpointed against deaths without resurrection. In *WR*, Reich's death in prison is a real death, and in *Sweet Movie* neither the sailor nor Miss World undergoes a resurrection at the end. Makavéjev deliberately moves transversally across the border between pathos and comedy, between light and dark satire, a movement that is closely associated with his constructing a contemporary filmic equivalent of Rabelaisian satire relevant to the twentieth century.

Makavéjev uses myths ancient and modern as part of the equipment of a social and cultural criticism in encounter with the here and now *and* with the immediate history of the present-day world, not to establish the archetypal structure of a mythicizing film. Eros and Thanatos are not mere abstractions borrowed from Freud, but forces like those of Bataille that permeate his films. The contents of an egg sensuously passed back and forth between people's hands in the opening moments of *WR* may be suggestive of folk cult or Orphic mysteries yet still be the focus of a highly sensual tactile experience. Film's kino-audiovisual capacities permit Makavéjev to develop a poetic for making sense by means which are simultaneously sensory, sensual, and intellectual; producing both a form of revolutionary ecological therapy (social as well as psychological) and a dialogue of liberation.

Speaking of Makavéjev's particular sociological filmic essays, I have on occasion referred to Makavéjev and his 3 *M*'s: Marcuse, Marx, and McLuhan. His cinematic psycho-sociological discourse shows a keen awareness of McLuhanism and the concept of a media revolution, as well as manifesting a deeper understanding of advertising and propaganda and what is concealed behind the apparent sweetness of its persuasion: 'persuade' and 'sweet' share the same Indo-European root, *-*swad* (sweet). While Makavéjev had satirized Coca Cola and Maybelline ads (among others) in *WR*, an obvious Godardian touch, *Sweet Movie* presents a world of sell, show, and advertisement, moving towards a conclusion with the complex ambivalent denouement of Miss World's death by drowning in chocolate. As that fatal ad scene begins, the producer instructs her: 'I want, when people buy chocolate in the future, and eat it – at least this particular brand – I want them to feel as if they were eating you.'[16]

In this sequence, as Miss World drowns in the vat of chocolate, the cameraman (who continues to roll his camera) remarks that 'chocolate selling will never be the same.' Makavéjev is fully aware of the mock communion aspects involved and wants also to show the ambivalence which makes the techniques of 'sweetness' work: 'Every move [he says] even drinking a coke or moving a camera, has some little particle of the general joy of life, some kind of play, excitement of Doing Something that has Never been Done Before.'[17] Eating and speaking, taste and persuasion, are motifs fundamental to communication. In *Sweet Movie* this goes further, for the drowning in chocolate is transversally related to the eating of feces in the earlier orgy scene involving Miss World, which takes place at the Milky Way Commune, where she has sought refuge from Mr Kapital.

Art, whether it occurs as part of everyday life or as the dedicated activity of individuals or groups of individuals, can be crucial in establishing the marks and traces which unmask distortions and inadequacies of communication conceived in the interests of hegemonic power. While ads and other products of cultural industries will to some extent provide their own unmasking (an unmasking that can be intensified through decontextualization, as Barthes and McLuhan have demonstrated), it is only the sensitive semiotic range made available through the arts and the festive energies of the people that exposes the critical problem implicit in contemporary mass communication: the mock or pseudo-communion. While the sensitivity of poetics certainly is not a substitute for those queries advanced by historical studies, critical theory, or a hermeneutics, such queries ought not to proceed in complete innocence of comic contemplation, for their practice will be considerably enriched by a thorough understanding of the theory and practice implicit in comedy, carnival, and poetry.

15

The Ambivalence of the Poetic as Critique: Science Fiction and Fellini Films

In the postmodern era, it has become well recognized that art frequently serves as an instrument for the dominating powers in society. The myth of the neutrality of art has been thoroughly undermined. Yet the poetic motive persists as a mode of critique manifesting an ambivalence, a duplicity, which makes it the instrument of a negativity, the grounds for establishing the realm of art as Nothing: the abyss, the absence, the gap. Art has always already been committed to particular interests, though its commitment has been differentiated from that of rhetoric. All the historical examples that have been cited throughout this discussion are paradoxical and problematic in relation to the progressive historical movement of the specific times and places in which they were constructed. Without dismissing the strong self-awareness of modern artists that their works – characteristic of post-Nietzschean, modernist, and postmodern poetics – are to a large part distinctive because of their intense *ambivalence*, it is essential in order to understand the relationship between art, other forms of cultural production, and communication to recognize that ambivalence permeates all intense poetic activity throughout history.

If the poetic has an ecological function with respect to human communication, the presence of the ambivalent in the poetic work can hardly have emerged only in the twentieth century. While Pope's critique of mass culture is from some perspectives progressive, it was constructed within an essentially conservative political position, in defence of the interests of the post-recusant rural property-owning Catholic gentry. The progressive critique of the beginnings of mass culture and technology and of the accompanying stultification or numbing of the senses arises because of the perspective from which Pope explores the material of *The Dunciad* (i.e., by extending his range of vision to encompass a critique of the effect of massification and mechanization on the development and dissemination of knowledge) and the means by which he deals with it – a carnivalesque, comic-satiric treatment of the parody of communication, human community, and communion.

His building an imaginary world designed around the ancient mysteries and initiation ceremonies conjures up the abstractions of gnostic thought as a means of undoing the bodily sensitivity of communication based on the human sensorium, which he then in part retrieves through his transgression of the decencies of a Puritan commercialized social consensus. The ambivalence of *The Dunciad*'s concluding couplets opens up a vision of the abyss, quite in keeping both with his 'zeroic couplet' and a prophetic anticipation of modern and postmodern visions of Nothing:

> In vain, in vain – the all-composing Hour,
> Resistless falls: The Muse obeys the Pow'r.
> She comes! she comes! the sable Throne behold
> Of *Night* Primeval, and of *Chaos* old!
> Before her, *Fancy's* gilded clouds decay,
> And all its varying Rain-bows die away.
> ...
> Thus at her felt approach, and secret might,
> *Art* after *Art* goes out, and all is Night.
> ...
> Lo! Thy dread Empire, C H A O S! is restor'd;
> Light dies before thy uncreating word:
> Thy hand, great Anarch! lets the curtain fall;
> And Universal Darkness buries All.
>
> (*The Dunciad*, B:4.627–56)

The *Dunciad*, being an ambivalent text, differs from modernist texts in Pope's having a residual commitment to some interests situated within what he takes to be truth and in his not having a full self-reflexive awareness of the extent of his poetic ambivalence. Earlier poets, however, certainly were aware that their poetic works immediately passed beyond the limited intentionality of their interests as the creator of the work. Consequently, a work could become a form of natural prophecy, for it exceeded the conscious, immediate limitations of the poet's specific position in time and place. The poetic emphasis on the complexity of assemblage, with its corresponding intensity (for the poetic work embraces a complexity of the surface and a density of the depth of the work), generates new ways of seeing, sensing, and understanding. Since the poetic work invites discussion, judgment, and understanding rather than closure, it permits exploration and evaluation; it even may have a value when the artist is a conscious propagandistic agent.

In turning to one of the most crucial examples of a form of poetic cultural production that is most intimately linked with the evolving of the new techno-culture, science fiction (SF), it is important to recognize that its difference from past poetic forms is not grounded exclusively in its awareness of technology, its poetic motives, its ambivalent construction, or its critique of knowledge. Neither is it unique in opening up communicative discourse about new social and cultural realities. Its peculiar difference must lie in its self-consciousness concerning its ecological function with respect to a rapidly expanding, changing, and accelerating techno-scientific culture. Darko Suvin, one of the pioneers of the historical and theoretical problems presented by science fiction, has established its poetic motive and stressed the particular role that a distancing and differentiating similar to Brecht's cognitive estrangement plays in its poetic construction.[1]

Science fiction, a highly ambivalent genre which has come of age in the twentieth century, is peculiarly important for understanding key issues in the contemporary ecological role of art and communication and in tracing the activity of communication/history in twentieth-century cultural production. SF as one of the new parapoetic forms has had an increasingly important role to play with respect to the ecology of sense. Artists, AI researchers, social theorists, and computer designers, for example, have organized conferences to explore the implication of William Gibson's discovery of cyberspace. That SF writing, film, TV, SF art, and comics have emerged in the twentieth century as significant new genres is intrinsically involved with the ecological function of the poetic.

In the 1870s at the time of the very beginnings of modernism, Jules Verne's writings gave birth to modern SF. Verne's concern with technology, communication, and changing time-space relations marks the involvement of SF in exploring and developing ways of perceiving these new phenomena. Kern identifies Verne as one of the early diagnosticians of the culture of time and space, citing such works as *Around the World in Eighty Days* (1873), which envisioned the effects of changing perceptions of distance and speed.[2] He also notes how Verne anticipatorily predicted 'telephonic journalism' and an electronic computer – a 'Piano Electro-Reckoner.'[3]

In his *Metamorphoses of Science Fiction* Suvin relates Verne's project specifically to communication when he entitles his discussion of Verne 'Communication in Quantified Space: Verne's *roman scientifique*': '*Quantified time translated into quantified space* constitutes the book of Nature, which is decoded and claimed for knowledge by the act of motion through it that permits the reading of its hidden information.'[4] Changing perceptions of time and space are blended with older Utopian and visionary motifs, such as fabulous islands, trips to the moon, and life under the sea. These are the very same themes and motifs that are central to Innis's and Kern's histories and Wyndham Lewis's critique of the time mind.

In 1886, when Verne wrote about airships and air travel, he established a SF that adopts an optimistic orientation towards technological change. Beginning a few years later, the more generally recognized father of modern SF, H.G. Wells, explored the dark, destructive side of the processes of technological change that were transforming the Victorian world. What links Verne and Wells, though, is a projective imagination – the future imaginary – which opens up whole new ways of seeing and feeling through metamorphoses of the historical genres – Utopias, dreams, imaginary voyages – and by forging from a contemporary scientific perspective poetic constructions entailing radically changed artistic perception because of changing perceptions of time, space, relationship, and expression itself that result from technological change. Wells's *The Time Machine*, which seems to imaginarily typify the contemporary mind, is characteristic of the future imaginary. It is significant that Joyce imagined Wells would admire his work; but Wells did not, although later science fiction writers would.

Gibson's exploration of *cyberspace* shows how acutely self-conscious practitioners in this genre have now become of its ecological role, since his work delineates an important new aspect of the developing techno-culture: 'Cyberspace. A consensual hallucination experienced daily by billions of legitimate operators, in every nation, by children being taught mathematical concepts ... A graphic representation of data abstracted from the banks of every computer in the human system. Unthinkable complexity. Lines of light ranged in the nonspace of the mind, clusters and constellations of data. Like city lights receding ...'[5] This 'drastic simplification of the human sensorium, at least in terms of presentation,'[6] has 'no particular relationship with the deck's physical whereabouts.'[7] Cyberspace becomes an all-pervasive way of perceiving, so that it can be imaginarily experienced, as set forth in *Mona Lisa Overdrive*: 'Her father [Angela's], long ago in Arizona, had cautioned against her jacking in. You don't need it, he'd said. And she hadn't, because she'd dreamed cyberspace, as though the neon gridlines of the matrix waited for her behind her eyelids.'

Although this suggests the possibility of imaginarily experiencing cyberspace in dreamscape, this passage continues by looking at Angela's encounter with the history and theory of cyberspace: *'There's no, there.* They taught that to children explaining cyberspace. She remembered a smiling tutor's lecture in the arcology's executive crèche, images shifting on a screen: pilots in enormous helmets and clumsy looking gloves, the neuroelectronically primitive "virtual world" technology linking them more effectively with their planes, pairs of miniature video-terminals pumping them a computer-generated flood of combat data, the vibrotactile feedback gloves providing a touch-world of studs and triggers ... As technology evolved, the helmets shrunk, the video-terminals atrophied.'[8] McLuhan's 'acoustic space' with its essentially tactile orientation is an imaginary anticipation of cyberspace that aims for the ultimate in total intermedia surround. Gibson undertakes a major transformation of the genre to open up new modes for comprehending the effects of virtual reality, telecommunications, and infomatics – cyberspace.

Mike McGreevy, who developed the 'Head-Mounted Display System' at the NASA Ames Research Center, produced a relatively early real-world example of immersion in 'virtual reality' in which a 3D head Rig and a Data-Glove allow a 'virtual' experience of a 'virtual simulation' of a real room permitting the operator to reach around, pick up things, reach right through them, or to use gestures for commands. As Stewart Brand describes it: 'If you made a fist and pointed your index finger you FLEW toward wherever you were pointing. Point up, for example, and ascend through the virtual ceiling. If you look down while doing that, you see the room is getting smaller and smaller below you in the distance. Then you could swoop back down into it, soar around, fly through the floor, etc. I lost my body almost instantly, except as a command device (ultimate mouse), and thoroughly enjoyed life as an angel. Oh wings of desire.'[9] In Gibson's cyberspatial world, such immersive technologies with much more powerful interface devices than HMDs and gloves capable of manipulating nearly unimaginable amounts of data are globally interlinked through an ultimate Internet that allows for the interactive sharing of information provided by a nearly infinite number of databases.

To achieve his imaginary vision of a fully developed cyberspace and the possible dystopia that it would bring about, Gibson produces a poetic vision extrapolated from the everyday world of science, occupational specialization and division of labour, and the proliferation of subcultures. Gibson has himself stated that his language is poetic, a poetry utilizing 'a lot of phrases that seem exotic to everyone but the people who *use* them.'[10] The world he envisions is a world in which the micro as terminal – the cyberdeck – is the medium and the person 'jacked' into it becomes one with that medium. In *Mona Lisa* there is a description of Angela experiencing cyberspace:

She touched the power stud and the bedroom vanished behind a colourless wall of sensory static. Her head filled with a torrent of white sound.

Her fingers found a random second stud and she was catapulted through the static wall, into cluttered vastness, the notional void of cyberspace, the bright grid of the matrix ranged around her like an infinite cage.[11]

Here art and science seem to merge; addiction is a function of an angel-like existence as powerful as a drug in a 'hi-tech low life'[12] world where those who work the matrix necessarily become servants of the wealthy and powerful.

This is the newest frontier, replete with its cowboys, drifters, mercenaries, and legends, all revealing the essential ambiguity of the nomadic, chaotic qualities of such uninscribed bodies: 'People jacked in so they could hustle. Put the trode on and they were out there, all data in the world stacked up like one big neon city, so you could cruise around and have a kind of grip on it, visually anyway, because if you didn't, it was too complicated, trying to find your way to the particular piece of data you needed. Iconics, Gentry called that.'[13] This is a technocratic world where intuition remains the appropriate Ariadne's thread to the rhizomic labyrinth of data. Gibson's vision provides a regime of signs and structures for exploring some of the possible future directions of such an evolving world.

Stanislaw Lem's writings provide a straightforward, yet complex, example of the operation of the poetic in SF to critique and renew language, thought, and artistic perception. Three of Lem's major SF novels, *His Master's Voice, Fiasco,* and *Eden,* centre around projects directed towards accomplishing communication with extraterrestrial cultures. Consequently, their narratives involve considerable speculation concerning the problems of human communication and the questions which would arise if intergalactic contact really could occur. *His Master's Voice,* which takes place on earth, tells the story of what happens when the government has to establish a high security bureaucratic agency to deal with the reception and translation of a suspected extraterrestrial communication, a parody of the goals of genuine research resulting in frustration and personal tragedy. *Fiasco* and *Eden,* imagined in a far future when intergalactic travel has become a reality, explore the dangers of intergalactic contact between intelligent, yet alien, species; again concluding in frustration and the tragic destruction of an entire world.

These works, like other of Lem's science fiction, represent the maturation of this genre as part of mainstream contemporary literature, a coming-of-age in which the exploration of aspects of communication are primary themes. Communication and technology are two of the major concerns of Lem's writing, which normally tends to be satiric. He has explored the computerized society of the future in a collection of comic cosmic 'fairy tales,' *The Cyberiad,* and other collections of tales of cybernauts and cybernetic projectors, and he has satirized the contemporary scientific conference in *The Futurological Congress.* Trurl and Klaupucius, his cosmic constructors in *The Cyberiad,* worthy modern successors of the mad projectors of Swift's Laputa, are capable of using their powers to create an electronic bard or even the galactic equivalent of a Tower of Babel.

The Futurological Congress, not an extrapolation about a possible future but an examination of the unchecked development of elements of the immediate present, plays with ambiguities between being awake and dreaming to satirize the pretensions of academics and other researchers and the problems of communication they experience while living in the everyday world. While imagining a 'psychemized' society of the future in which all communication is mediated through drugs and the medium of communication itself reflects the metamorphic nature of drugs, Lem plays subtly with ambiguities between the dreaming and waking worlds. The dream of Ijon Tichy, his academic futurologist anti-hero, is presented so ambiguously that one is not really sure what is part of the waking action of the story or what is a dream, until the conclusion, when Tichy finally awakes in a sewer.

The waking world in which Tichy works at his profession is in its own way as much of a nightmare as the nightmarish 'psychemized' society about which he dreams. Lem creates a new language for his psychemized dream world. To live in this psychemized society, a completely new world as far as Tichy is concerned, he must learn anew those elements of the language through which this culture communicates:

Some other unfamiliar expressions I've come across: threever, pingle, hemale, to widge off, palacize, cobnoddling, synthy. The newspapers advertise such products as tishets, vanilliums, nurches, autofrotts (manual). The title of a column in the city edition of the *Herald*: 'I Was a Demimother.' Something about an eggman who was yoked on the way to the eggplant. The big Webster isn't too helpful: *Demimother* – like demigran, demijohn. One of two women jointly bringing a child into the world. See 'Polyanna, Polyandrew.' '*Eggman* – from the mailman (*Archaic*). A euplanner who delivers licensed human gametes (fe-male) to the home.' I don't pretend to understand that. This crazy dictionary also gives synonyms which are equally incomprehensible. '*Threever* – trimorph.' '*Palacize, bepalacize, empalacize* – to castellate, as on a quiz show.' '*Paladyne* – a chivalric assuagement.' 'Vanillium – extract emphorium, portable.' The worst are words which look the same but have acquired entirely different meanings. '*Expectorant* – a conception aid.' '*Pederast* –

artificial foot faddist.' '*Compensation* – mind fusion.' '*Simulant* – something that doesn't exist but pretends to. Not to be confused with *simulator*, a robot simulacrum.' '*Revivalist* – a corpse, such as a murder victim, brought back to life. See also *exhumant, disintermagent, jack-in-the-grave.*'[14]

This is merely a sample of the proliferation of new linguistic combinations which Lem uses to construct an alternative world for Tichy's dream-state. The particular examples above show how he plays subtly with the normal sense of everyday words and syllables, utilizing his understanding of their morphology and of the way a language's lexicon categorizes knowledge about a culture. Besides, he is also building a language within a language which, like the term 'psychem,' will reveal the basic contradictions of such a chemically controlled human society. He actually constructs only an extreme extrapolation from the contemporary situation at the time when he was writing the *Congress*. Such a 'pharmacocracy' has achieved Bentham's dream, while absorbing earlier forms of government such as democracy. This whole play with language actually leads to the revelation of the important role of 'linguistic futurology' in this imaginary 'pharmacocracy.'

The significance of 'linguistic futurology' in this psychemized world is explained to Tichy by a professor whom he had known in his everyday world. In Tichy's dream of the 'pharmacocracy,' this professor is a futurologian, a profession which differs from that of a futurologist, for futurologians only concern themselves with theory. Tichy's friend now deals with 'projective etymology,' which he describes as 'divination through linguistic derivation. Morphological forecasting.' This is how it works: '"Linguistic futurology investigates the future through the transformation possibilities of the language," Trottelreiner explained ... "A man can only control what he comprehends, and comprehend only what he is able to put into words. The inexpressible therefore is unknowable. By examining future stages in the evolution of language we come to learn what discoveries, changes and social revolutions the language will be capable, some day, of reflecting."'[15]

The premises here, of course, through extrapolating from some linguistic item, can lead to any type of absurdity. Yet the linguistic manipulations of the futurologians are in some way a perfect parody of the play of the poet, especially those poets, like Joyce, whose work is based on a direct play with language or other elements of semiotic communication; or the play of nonsense poets such as Lewis Carroll. Tichy selects various words, so that this enthusiastic futurologian can illustrate how they are treated by 'projective etymology' in 'morphological forecasting.' Tichy's selection concludes with the word 'trash,' from which the professor produces the following sequence:

'trash, trashcan, ashcan, trashman. Trashmass, trashmic, catatrashmic. Trashmass, trashmosh. On a large enough scale, trashmos. And, of course, macrotrashm! Tichy, you come up with the best words! Really, just think of it, macrotrashm!'[16]

This new word entrances the professor, since he discovers in it a whole new 'psychozoic' theory: 'From the word itself. Macrotrashm indicates or rather suggests, this image: in the course of many eons the Universe filled up with trash, the wastes of various civilizations. The wastes got in the way, of course, hampering astronomers and cosmonauts, and so enormous incinerators were built, all at extremely high temperatures, observe, to burn the trash ...'[17] And so forth, until the universe becomes nothing but one big trash disposal unit. To the futurologian, it does not matter whether the thing can actually come to be or not, only that it is possible to imagine hypothetically that it might.

Lem has created a satiric machine for exploring distorted communication. His play with the sense of language (with communication) creates deliberate gaps to force the exploration of what bridging those gaps will reveal about our culture and its future. Lem is a Menippean satirist interested in learned, yet outrageous and often excrementitious, satire just as are Rabelais, Swift, Sterne, Pope, Lewis, and Joyce. His poetic construct, *The Futurological Congress,* is a communicating machine in which the discovery of gaps, as in Lewis Carroll's *Alice* books, uses the surface of his world to reveal complexities and labyrinths. The crux of this play with gaps in *The Futurological Congress* is the complex critique of political, journalistic, PR, and academic manipulations of the language that people speak.

This language contributes as much towards creating the psychemized world (the 'futurologians') as the technology does in creating the world in which there is a need for psyco-chemical terminology. The accompanying breakdown of reality into a fictive world of communication eliminates the barrier or border between life-world and dream world. Lem's constructing this virtual state – his destruction of everyday reality, his critique of the very grounds of communication – permits an evaluation and renewal of contemporary expression. This transformation of language and speech further reveals new possible developments of vision, sound, rhythm, and gesture, just as his psycho-chemical wordplay has itself been inspired by the artistic exploration of that psycho-chemical 'drug' world that dominated the late 1960s and early 1970s.

In other works, such as *His Master's Voice, Microworlds, A Perfect Vacuum, One Human Minute,* and *Imaginary Magnitude,* Lem extends the strategy of probing communication to develop satiric take-offs on the implications of science and technology, political communication, book reviewing, and the writing of academic criticism and complex artistic treatises. Artists like France's Fred Forrest, who experiments with communication art that his practice defines as the art of telecommunication, are exploring other aspects of this techno-cultural semiotic 'chaosmos,' producing works that are critiques of advertising, commercialization and the rigidification of narrow techno-scientific vision. Lichtenstein's artistic play with comic strips and underground 'Comix' explores psycho-chemical experiences which contribute to the same type of process. Communication renews itself in the process; the limits of sense are transformed and redefined. *Forbidden Planet* and Kubrick's *2001* demonstrate how the SF film opened up new communication potentials, extrapolations of cinema's involvement in extending the communicative potential and the regime of signs.

A now classic film, Fellini's *8½*, perhaps closest of any film work to that of Joyce, probes the ecological factor of communication within the act of film-making itself. Joyce's interest in film is underlined by his familiarity with Eisenstein's epic films, Chaplin's comedy, Griffith's work (particularly *Birth of a Nation*), surrealist and Dadaist film-making, Hollywood spectaculars, and German expressionism. His film references include, among many others, complex allusions to Chaplin in *Ulysses*; and to Griffith, Eisenstein, Chaplin, animated films, and Shirley Temple in *Finnegans Wake*. Moreover, he actually turned a portion of the *Wake* into a film script, depicting both the mythical possibilities and the semiological ambivalence of the film form. Although Fellini denies knowing Joyce's work, he stresses that one comes to know major contemporary figures through looking at the culture that you share with them.[18]

Fellini regarded his function as film-maker to be that of an anti-journalist. He critically presents the figure of the journalist in the protagonist of *La Dolce Vita* and later sharply satirizes film journalists in the press conference of *8½*. While he develops his theory of comedy out of everyday life, in contradistinction to those who see the director as related to the journalist, he does this by learning the 'essence of comedy from comic strips and the circus.'[19] *Flash Gordon* and *Bringing Up Father* represent the comic strip fare that became central to Fellini's developing sense of comedy. He could join this comic sense derived from such strips to the perennial figure of the clown.

In particular, the 'clown-like gift for mimicry' of the actress Giulietta Masina (his wife) contributed substantially to his linking of comic strip and circus. Masina's remarkable powers as a comic actress contribute substantially to her characterizations of Gelsomina (*La Strada*), Cabiria (*Nights of Cabiria*) and Juliet (the feminine heroine of *Juliet of the Spirits*, the colour companion film to *8½*). Fellini, who made a short film entitled *The Clowns*, has frequently made comments about this perennial figure of the grotesque and the comic: 'The clown is the incarnation of a fantastic creature who expresses the irrational aspect of man; he stands for the instincts, for whatever is rebellious in each one of us and whatever stands up to the established order of things. He is a caricature of man's childish and animal aspects, the mocker and the mocked. The clown is a mirror in which man sees himself in a grotesque, deformed, ridiculous image.'[20] The proximity of Fellini's observations to Bakhtin's theories and Joyce's practice of the carnivalesque exhibits his clear sense of the critique implicit in his own work.

That Joyce and Fellini share a similar view of the fundamental power of comedy is summed up in Fellini's conviction that there is 'nothing sadder than laughter; nothing more beautiful, more magnificent, more uplifting and enriching than the terror of deep despair.'[21] It is ridiculous to try to clarify the difference between tragedian and comedian he argues, for tragic poets had to keep an ironic distance from terrible suffering, and therefore '... it is absurd to want to classify great creative men, to differentiate between comedians and philosophers, actors and authors, clowns and poets, painters and film-makers.' For Fellini, there are no essentially humorous themes: 'Humour, just like the dramatic, the tragic, the visionary, is the collocation of reality in a particular climate. Humour is a type of view, of rapport, of feeling one has about things, and is, above all, a natural characteristic which one has or doesn't have.'[22] Humour, especially in the forms of the grotesque and of the circus, always borders on the madhouse, as exemplified in many scenes from Fellini films: for example, the harem scene of *8½*; sections of *Juliet of the Spirits*, especially Suzy's party; and many episodes in *Satyricon*, particularly Trimalchio's feast.

This world of folly and madness counterpoints the world of sacred frenzy. Historians of dance have pointed out the association of the clown, the sacred frenzy, and the dance: 'As an antidote – a backward spring of the pendulum – the sacred frenzy gives birth to a roistering troop of clowns. Beside the divinely inspired dancer walks the jester – a child of the dance. (Is not the German *Narr*, jester, cognate with the Sanskrit, *nrtu*, dancer?) ... He caricatures the other participants, frightens the spectators, teases the young girls, and dips into the mysteries of life and death.'[23] In comic drama, the action usually concluded traditionally with a dance or with a masque that contained a dance as a central element. So Fellini's *8½* ends with a labyrinthine, comic dance reminiscent of the circus, and *Finnegans Wake* ends with the undulating, labyrinthine movement of Anna Livia, as the River Liffey, back to the sea, performing her own *Saltarello*: 'Saltarella come to her' (627.3).

Dance is one of the more pervasive, resolving images in Fellini's film; late in his career he finally made a film celebrating the contemporary power of popular dance films – *Fred and Ginger*. Fellini's practice confirms the theoretical orientation that views poetry as a 'grace' achieved in the process of producing a message about the interface between the conscious and the unconscious.[24] Joyce and Fellini share the theoretic awareness implicit in their practical activity that contemporary art is complexly reflective in nature, since it is engaged at a practical level in the ongoing dialogue about the nature of expressive discourse. This causes the intricately complex 'mirroring' structure of *8½* that Christian Metz describes in his discussion of the film: '... if *8½* differs from other films that are doubled in on themselves, it is not only because this "doubling in" is more systematic or more central, but also and above all because it functions differently. For *8½*, one should be careful to realize, is a film that is *doubly doubled* – and, when one speaks of it as having a mirror construction, it is really a double mirror construction one should be talking about. It is not only a film about the cinema, it is a film about a film that is presumably itself about the cinema; it is not only a film about a director, but a film about a director who is reflecting himself onto his film.'[25]

While Fellini's approach to his film text is comparable with Joyce's practice, superficially *8½* does not resemble *Finnegans Wake*, since it is not exclusively about the world of dream or the metamorphosis of language, nor does it resemble *Ulysses*, since it is not about the everyday life of an ordinary man. Instead, its protagonist is Guido, a film-maker, confronted with the problems of making a film about his film-making. Guido's tale, though he is middle-aged, echoes that of Stephen Dedalus in *A Portrait of the Artist as a Young Man*, but it also adds to that topics about maturity, making and dreaming, 'writing' and 'reading,' that echo the concern of *Ulysses* and *Finnegans Wake* with communication.

When the dreamer in the *Wake* dreams about the children and imagines them to be creating their own psychodrama by presenting a play that is presenting or re-presenting the father's dream or the mother's dream about the father, motifs of play, projection, dream, poetry, and drama are interlaced with terms that are clearly cinematic: 'With futurist onehorse balletbattle pictures and the Pageant of Past History worked up with animal variations amid everglaning mangrovemazes and beorbtracktors by Messrs Thud and Blunder. Shadows by the film folk, masses by the good people. Promptings by Elanio Vitale. Longshots, upcloses, outblacks and stagetolets by Hexenschuss, Coachmaher, Incubone and Rocknarrag. Creations tastefully designed by Madame Berthe Delamode. Dances arranged by Harley Quinn and Coollimbeina. Jests, jokes, jigs and jorums for the Wake lent from the properties of the late cemented Mr. T.M. Finnegan R.I.C.' (221.18–27). Joyce's mythic conception, reduced to a child's point of view, appears to involve the gigantism of Cecil B. DeMille and more strictly cinematic aspects of Chaplin and Griffith. The same might be said of *8½* with its overt and conscious exploration of the spectacle of gigantism present in much commercially produced media and its meditations on the film-maker as artist.

Fellini, like Joyce, wants to include the whole body of his previous film productions within the work that he is executing; consequently the title, *8½* (for up to this point in his career, Fellini had made seven and one-half pictures, including *The Temptation of Dr Antonio*, his contribution to a trio of films by different Italian directors, entitled *Boccaccio 70*). *8½* weaves together images from each of these earlier films, as well as images from his remembrance of his own life, going back to portrayals of early childhood life in Italian schools run by clerics, highly reminiscent of those Irish Catholic schools encountered by Joyce's Stephen in *A Portrait of the Artist as a Young Man*. Signs flock to Fellini from his own history, from his memory, from the world about him, and from a world of fantasy which he is in the process of assembling. It is precisely this dance of signs and symbols which haunts Guido throughout the film since he has to confront the problem of shaping this material into a film.

Guido's problem, therefore, is complexly involved with the process of film communication, for at the outset of *8½* he finds himself unable to begin making the film itself and, because of this block, cut off, from communicating with his family, friends, and other associates. His oldest friends (writers, cameramen, and other co-workers) experience difficulty in responding to his mood. Tensions exist with his producer and with film critics and journalists. A dream image consisting of fragmented images of a woman – young, innocent, barefoot, and dressed in white (incidentally reminiscent of the bird girl wading with her skirts tucked up in Joyce's *Portrait*) - keeps running through his mind, further hindering him from meaningful relationships with his wife, mistress, friends, and those women, such as his wife's friend Rosella, who people his memory and imagination. Fellini's film is basically concerned with exploring a spectrum of signs and symbols that radiate out beyond these immediate concerns to include them within the more general context of the realities of his everyday world: Rome, its society, its daily life.

The interweaving of images, rhythms, movements, sounds, and words in *8½* becomes part of the process of separating the elements of reality to provide for the possibility of new signs and symbols that will lead to an understanding of the dilemma in which Guido is enmeshed. Pirandello's 'theatre of the grotesque' as well as the *commedia dell'arte,* which influenced Pirandello, have had a considerable impact on Fellini. The 'escutcheon construction' (or, as it has been 'Englished,' 'mirror construction'), as Metz pointed out, is close to the way that Pirandello sets up tension between 'characters' and actors in *Six Characters in Search of an Author.* Here the device of a 'play within a play' closely parallels the escutcheon-like construction of Fellini's 'film within a film.'

Fellini intensifies Pirandello's commitment to the grotesque by making it a major means of communicating Guido's melancholia and his acute sense of alienation. Fellini's imaginary sense of his world as a puppet theatre is comparable to that which dominated the 'theatre of the grotesque,' except that he merges this grotesquerie with a sense of the bizarre and the baroque reminiscent of Kafka, Welles, and Céline. Such grotesque realism as a way of constructing the world of dream is one of the many links between Fellini and Joyce's Nighttown scene in the 'Circe' episode of *Ulysses,* or the entire anarchistic dreamscape of *Finnegans Wake* (e.g., the image of his innkeeper as a gigantic earwig). The blending of the comic, the erotic, and the grotesque manifests itself in bizarre scenes: for example, the apparently obscene rumba that the obese Saraghina dances for the young schoolboys on the beach.[26] In such scenes, the satirically grotesque treatment is not directed towards the earthiness of La Saraghina, but towards the priests and brothers who were responsible for young Guido's education. A farcical chase on the beach, accompanied by the same rumba music, deliberately manifests and magnifies the cleric's grotesque, animal-like characteristics.

Later, Guido in a daydream reminiscent of surrealist cinema assembles all the female figures who have moved through his life in a phantasmagoric harem dreamscape: his mother, his relatives, their housemaid, and La Saraghina; his wife and her sister; his actresses and mistresses. He casts his wife, Luisa, as first wife and dowdy, submissive overseer of this dream menage. This entire dream scene, which takes place in a farmhouse associated with his childhood, reflects back on his own failings that have emerged in the realistic scenes of *8½*; his own ambivalence about himself in the role of a director who manipulates actors and actresses; his having produced the conditions that have made Luisa stiff and armoured. This scene, like the 'Circe' episode in *Ulysses,* is a climactic fantasia which forces Guido to confront his Narcissism and in that process allows him to free his creative imagination by disassembling, assembling, and reassembling the signs that shape his memory. This scene cuts deeply into basic bodily experience and manifests suppressed 'polymorphous perversity,' because Guido's sensual as well as mental release is essential to his creating the waking phantasmagoria of the film itself.

The action moves from this harem scene to the denouement. There is duplex duplicity in this two-part conclusion: first, the spectacular press conference, a modern version of Trimalchio's feast, staged by Guido's producer, during which Guido panics, hides under the table, and confirms his artistic failure by his suicide; then follows the actual concluding episode, which begins with the disassembling of the set and ends with the actual realization of the film by using the same set to produce the circus-like parade and labyrinthine dance with which his film concludes. The *8½* set, as a tension between the mundane (the film world as reality) and the imaginary (the film as future or alternative world), reflects the dialectic of ambivalence in the film, thus shaping the film's resolution: the movement from Guido's imagined suicide at the press conference when he feels that the 'grandiosity,' the 'mythicality,' and the 'history' of the film he is making will only produce the practical banality of the everyday world of the journalists and critics, to the imaginary suicide being superseded when he allows the whole of his imaginary world to blend into his real world and his consciousness.

The elaborate set which Guido has built – a science fiction set of grandiose dimensions – and which figures prominently in a variety of scenes, is a many-storeyed tower, a machine-like maze of iron and steel, temporarily erected on a beach. (Fellini had long wanted to make a science fiction film and later expressed his great admiration for Kubrick's *2001*.) The final scene, which starts with a descent from this tower moves into a serpentine, maze-like dance that figures centrally in the film's conclusion. The labyrinth or maze underlines the interlacing or interweaving movement of Fellini's compositions; as well, it adapts rather effectively to the representation of the apparently fruitless complications of Guido's life in an estranged world. Guido's own process of composition as a director is maze-like or labyrinthine, as is Fellini's. The retracing of these mazes, as suggested in the epistemology of symbolist poetics, results in the unravelling of mental states.

Fellini's or Guido's consumers recreate a labyrinthine pattern in the process of remaking the film, which confirms the interdependence of communication and the network-like maze or rhizome that Eco describes when he contrasts the arboreality of the dictionary with the wandering network of the encyclopaedia. The motif by which the film is realized is the motif of the film itself: the imaginary wanderings of the film-maker which underline the encyclopaedic suggestivity of the regime of signs with which the film-maker works to produce the film. In the contemporary context, SF is basically encyclopaedic in intent and execution; so that the equating of the SF set with magic, light, and movement is a way of integrating the multitude of popular references into realizing a production whose consumption will be an act of communion and communication.

The image of the labyrinth as it relates to the artistic process is another way in which the creative practice of Fellini and Joyce compare, for Stephen Dedalus, the protagonist of *The Portrait of the Artist as a Young Man,* is named after the creator of the labyrinth and figures in the action both as a Daedalus and as an Icarus, the son of Daedalus, who was killed because his wings melted when he attempted to fly and approached too near to the sun. Fellini's highly explicit use in *Satyricon* of the labyrinth and the minotaur as the machines which restore Encolpius's ability to communicate with others reflects back on how the labyrinthine dance in *8½* becomes the symbol of Guido's rediscovery of his ability to communicate.

The labyrinth as symbol fascinated the *symbolistes,* especially Mallarmé, who said that the poem was a labyrinth sealed at both ends. Eliot's *Waste Land* is labyrinthine, and the minotaur is a central figure in Picasso's work, especially in the *Guernica* mentioned earlier. The labyrinth associated with the dance links physical movement to imaginary movement and movements of the mind, so that the act of consumption is a retracing of the act of production; but because of the root-like wanderings of the work, the retracing is the 'seim anew. Ordovico or viricordo' (*FW*215.23). The imaginary realization of Fellini's signs and mazes is a function of the interplay of light and movement with images and sounds.

For Fellini the fundamental element is light, the means by which the image manifests itself: 'the cinema is this – images. Light is my basic element. ... light comes even before the theme, even before the actors selected for the various roles. Light is really everything; it is substance, sentiment, style, description ... The image is expressed with light.'[27] Although image, sound, and movement are crucial elements in the grand finale of *8½*, light permeates the entire presentation, defining the relationship between all the other elements. Nino Rota's music is an accompaniment to a 'light show' where the magician and the film-maker are the masters of light and dark. Light is a kind of movement and clearly a crucial factor in Fellini's special signature: 'Style is light. Light comes before everything, even before the plot, the screenplay or the word ... Style is light, as in painting. Painting and cinema are closely connected. The film camera shows the distance between the film-maker and things, and helps to compose his style; although, with its movements, it acts rather as grammar does in writing, to regulate what is said.'[28] Fellini employs light in the rendition of space and movement in such a way as to constitute the very special use of the grey scale of colour which leads us to think of *8½* as a coloured film in black and white. That medium, composed of white, black, and tones of grey, assembles the dream space as well as the spatio-temporal association of Fellini with the material world: faces, bodies, machines, objects.

Since *Finnegans Wake* is centrally concerned with exploring the entire spectrum of communication through language, the interplay of light and the word, which has strong mythic and religious implications, permeates the dream as well. The *Wake*'s finale, just as *8½*'s, is centred on light. As dawn approaches, the dreamer dreams of light breaking through the stained-glass triptych of a chapel next to the River Liffey and directly across the street from his inn in Chapelizod. With the impending dawn, a debate on light, colour, and perception takes place between Saint Patrick and the Archdruid. This dream event concerns the lighting of the paschal candle during the Easter Vigil as well as the lighting of the Druidic fires at the spring festival. Their debate involves problems of chiaroscuro and colour, with the 'blackinwhitepaddynger' (612.18) opposing the 'sevenhued sept-coloured druidic philosopher' (611.6). A resolution is reached by noting the way that colour and chiaroscuro are reduced to white light by the rising sun, the spectral source of all differentiation, the source of the effect of the rainbow.

This association of light, word, and movement continues through to the conclusion of the *Wake*, for the entire work is a communication 'type by tope, letter from litter, word at ward, with sendence of sundance' (615.1–2). This draws attention to the problem of basic differentiations in density (on the part of communication through light, sound, image, and kinaesthesia) and in phonological, syntactic, and semantic contrasts (on the part of communication through the word). Fellini's practice, which emphasizes the differentiating importance of light, parallels Joyce's use of the complex differences made available by words. Both Fellini and Joyce shape their practice through a self-awareness of the particular mode(s) of communication which contribute to the nature of the construct that is produced. Light is a way of shaping difference, which assembles that filmic machine that results in a secularized communion through intensified communication. This is why Fellini's use of light and movement, like Joyce's use of words and sentences, is so crucial to his style.

8½'s dialectic of the mundane and the imaginary produces a poetic film that enhances and enables enriched communication. Fellini attributes such communication partly to the sacred aspect of the spectacle in the circus, the theatre, and the cinema. He argues, possibly erroneously, that the private world of television cannot achieve the same rapport. Dialectical movement, which is partly realized through the tension that develops between the white clown and the Auguste, is absolutely crucial to generating this possiblity for relatively undistorted communication. Fellini is engaged in creating a dialectic of destruction and discovery; just as Joyce's writing generates a dialectic of 'decomposition' and 'subsequent recombination.'

Fellini's social involvement, like Joyce's, comes about through the way his productions involve the erotic and the lower bodily parts – the restoration of a sense of 'sensuous form' achieved by stressing the importance of eros in the process of intersubjective communication. Therefore, the apparent lack of social concern in *8½* is actually a shifting of the social problem of the poetic to the place where a critical problem emerges today: the problem of evolving new ways of achieving communication by breaking through the barriers of the prosaic and banal, which have contributed to establishing a hegemony of the illusions of a one-dimensional society. It is a process to which even an avowedly apolitical artist such as Fellini can contribute.

By the conclusion of *8½*, the entire set of relationships involved in the making of a film and the problematic of the film-maker as culture hero – the myth of the *auteur* theory of film – have been re-examined. *8½* also confronts the theoretical problem of the psychological and sociological sources of the expressive and communicative signs directors use in making films. The conclusion implicitly exemplifies the complexity of these signs: the first version would result in Guido's death because of his defensive reaction to the reductionism of journalism, commercialism, and 'la mode'; the second, an alternative ending, is a critique which raises the question of the entire relationship between a director and his created world of production and consumption.

In *8½*, as in Joyce's *Wake*, the barrier between art and the people breaks down, so that here, too, the director's producers are also his consumers. This is achieved by a process of communication that permits the play of transversality throughout the entire work. Fellini's memory as well as the memory of his comic hero, Guido Anselmi, interweave images from various layers of personal history and from various temporal moments in the unfolding of the film. By recognizing the day-by-day complications of the context within which the director works, these images and memories can be permitted to interpenetrate the various levels of the film's escutcheon-like ('mirror') structure. Parts are embedded within parts, creating a constant tension as to what is real and what is imaginary; what is a matter of conscious awareness and what is a question of the unconscious.

Communication through the mediation of a productive process such as film becomes intense intersubjective communication only through the breaking down of preordained chains of association: the disruption of the flows of signification, which first made *8½* such an enigma. This is how

Fellini – who in the 1970s argued that the movements fostered by the 1960s generation were necessary – poetically generates an ecological activity which contributes to social change. Guido is seeking to construct a critique, the essence of which can be humane, and in which, in his comic assessment of those who give shape to his imaginary world, he can simultaneously accept their co-presence in his life and his co-presence in theirs. The clown-jester-magician figure becomes the very image of a negation which destroys in order to create. This is a counter strategy to the intellectualized cynicism of the critic, Carini, for whom it is better to destroy.

Guido's friend and mentor, Maurice the Magician, is an Auguste-type clown. Concerning such clowns Fellini comments, 'I might talk of Hegel and dialectics, and say that perhaps the Auguste is an image of the sub-proletariat: the hungry, the lame, the rejected, those capable of revolt perhaps but not of revolution.'[29] Fellini illustrates the role of his clowns by relating them to Lao Tse's satiric comment on an idealized education: 'If you make a thought, laugh at it.' The 'white clown' represents the 'idealized thought'; the 'Auguste' is the wild laughter of critique. This is why Maurice can disappear at the point when Guido himself becomes willing to be an Auguste; to adopt a point of view as communicator by becoming a sensuous participant-observer, rather than merely the abstract observer he has previously appeared to be. If the result is very circus-like, it is because Fellini feels that 'the cinema is very much like the circus,'[30] just as 'clowns ... are ambassadors of my calling.'[31]

16

Conclusion

One AI approach for modelling the activity of the CNS involves the idea of parallel processing: a number of individual computers each simultaneously handles a small bit of a problem for our neural networks. This nervous system functions more like the rambling network formed by the growth of a system of roots, instead of like the trees and grids designed by logicians. Parallel processing, therefore, suggests looking at society as a community of people forming collective assemblages, each participant of which might be thought to simulate the individual processor involved in parallel processing. This provides a contemporary restructuring of the image of the *urbus* as *corpus* – one of the central motifs of *Ulysses* and *Finnegans Wake*.

Since twentieth-century artists were fascinated by the new technologies and the problems they raised concerning relationships between art, communication, and expression, in their practice they anticipated the human sciences' later interest in structure and structural formations such as the arboreal (tree-like) and the rhizomic (root-like). It is not surprising, then, that some of the questions cognitive science was to explore later in the century had already intrigued many of the artists. Proust's and Joyce's writings anticipate many aspects of structuralism and post-structuralism as well as concepts about perception that are now of interest to cognitive scientists. Perhaps most significantly for the study of communication, their practice anticipated complex theories about the sign and about space, time, and memory.[1]

Cognitive scientists have clearly recognized the importance of the arts, especially twentieth-century art. In *The Society of Mind* Marvin Minsky opens his section on 'Default Assumptions' with:

Only by art can we get outside ourselves; instead of seeing only one world, our own, we see it under multiple forms, and as many as there are original artists, just so many worlds have we at our disposal.

– Marcel Proust

Minsky stresses the way in which the arts make 'things clearer than reality,' for they 'activate great networks of assumptions that already lie in the minds' of people to provide what Proust described as an 'optical instrument which ... offers to let the reader discover in himself what he would not have found' otherwise.[2] Joyce carries this further, for his work can properly be described as using a language of 'multiple roots,' for he himself speaks of his 'glossery which purveys aprioric roots for aposteriorious tongues' (*FW*83.11) and of how an inventory of the text produced by this writing 'would reveal a multiplicity of personalities inflicted on the documents or document' (107.24–5).

This world of social communication is an assemblage of multiplicities. The multiple nodes of the social network and people's nomadic movements among them replicate the nerves of the individual, so that there is a telling force to metaphors such as *the nerves of the city*. Different collectivities that occupy different neighbourhoods or sections experience the city in different ways, which they then integrate with prior experiences from their social and personal histories: class, financial situation, nationality, ethnic background. Joyce quite naturally opens the third and final part of *Ulysses* – the fusion of Bloom and Stephen – with an initial episode in which the dominant organ of the body (the corporate as well as the individual body) is the human nervous system.[3] Poetic actions provide the social world with multiplicities of probable embodiments, as Minsky has noted; this creates a tension with institutional structures, which thrive on limitations of such multiplicity by means of the maintenance of well-defined boundaries and the defence of their autonomy. This tension between culture and art is the essential tension underlying the desire for depth and relative lack of distortion in communication; for while new art can only exist within culture, it is always thrusting beyond culture by returning to the body and seeking extension of its limits.

As I was finishing the writing of this book, I read Michael Phillipson's perceptive and playful philosophical comedy *In Modernity's Wake: The Ameurunculus Letters*. In this medley of satire and theory, Ethelred Ameurunculus, the imaginary author of these imaginary letters, tells us that in interacting with Culture, Art (or poetry) 'offers us its *version* which is always a turning of culture's version against itself: it reverses culture.'[4] Just as the potential of communication must already exceed the culture (and the society of the moment), the poetic as the exploratory exuberance of communication (the ecology of sense) must go beyond the moment, beyond the mediated. This going-beyond results from that tension between the spirit and the lower parts which is marked by the comic. (It should be noted that: Ameurunculus = amour+uncul+culus; which appears to signify the love of that hook of the executioner that is dung or fundament.)

Poetic communication with its dependency on the generation of 'feelful thinkamalinks,' cannot develop in the absence of excess, as Bataille has argued;[5] whereas the objective of censorship – unaware of excess's vital role in regenerating communication – is to suppress the entire operation of those processes on which the exploratory exuberance of poetic communication depends. When a culture is confronted with the obvious embarrassment that can occur when many people do not wish to extend their dialogue beyond the limits of the present into the memory of the past and the unfolding of the future, the issue of censorship, or other forms of indirect suppression, arises.

Since changing potentials in communication accompany other processes of change, they may appear threatening. In extreme cases – such as Joyce's *Ulysses* in the 1920s, Makavéjev's *Sweet Movie* in the 1970s, or recent efforts to censor rock videos – the forces bringing about the direct censorship or indirect suppression become apparent. But there are obviously other cases in which the process works by concealment and indirection; by lack of opportunity or intimidation through control of the channels of communication. Because of these potential censorship problems, the ecological role of all the arts must be taken into consideration in any debate concerning issues of freedom of communication. Since the very processes involved in the ecology of sense naturally generate resistance, is there not a necessity to minimize the actual bureaucratic and legal barriers of direct or indirect censorship in the interests of the revivification of communication?

That censorship does direct itself towards the innovative communication of the arts is clear from the Roman Catholic Inquisition and the Index, which were both equally as suppressive of the work of Milton, Rousseau, Rabelais, and Giordano Bruno. Similarly, official Puritanism held Spenser, Shakespeare, and other poets and dramatists to be suspect. Today the Islamic world can place a death sentence on Salman Rushdie for having written *The Satanic Verses*. In spite of Christian religious institutions no longer having the same hegemonic status as in the past, the censorial activity has continued throughout our century – in fact, recently it has once again increased.

Edward de Grazia, in *Girls Lean Back Everywhere: The Law of Obscenity and the Assault on Genius*, has traced the history of state censorship in

England and the United States – a history that shows attempts to repress the writings of Joyce, Lawrence, Henry Miller, Edmund Wilson, Theodore Dreiser, Radclyffe Hall's *The Well of Loneliness* (an early, powerful novel about lesbianism), Allen Ginsberg, Lawrence Ferlinghetti, and many others. The last decade has seen a renewal of calls for suppression of works that could be deemed pornographic, or as counselling violence or hate, and even as promulgating points of view that might be considered offensive to some particular group. Legal restraint has been further reinforced by new uses of copyright, libel, and other civil laws.

What de Grazia means by the use of the somewhat questionable 'assault on genius' is the attack on innovative communication – a fact confirmed by the list of writers whose works have been the object of suppression. The same 'assault' occurs on all innovative cultural production. But the modernist experiment clearly shows that a dialogic and dialectical interaction is ecologically sounder than suppression, since it permits the communication system to cope with social and technological change. Suppression never is genuinely selective nor can it be legislated to be so, and the result is that a film-maker as important as Makavéjev can be indirectly suppressed and the mere threat of legal retaliation can prevent cultural production from coming to be. In the process, the poetic activity continues to be inhibited, in spite of social guarantees concerning redeeming merit and social value, as recent prosecutions of visual artists in Toronto (Eli Lange) and Cincinnati (Robert Motherwell) have illustrated.

If value questions have not seemed paramount in examining the poetic as an ecology of sense, it is primarily because the understanding of the poetic as intensive communication is a necessary prolegomenon to considering questions of value. Clearly the importance of the 'lower,' polymorphous bodily aspects to the opening up of communication – that place where, as Bateson brilliantly intuited, lewd jokes and poetic drama meet – indicates that the secularized communion which forms community must increasingly 'pitch its mansion in the place of excrement,' for that is where the very energies which create gaps and permit rambling pathways between breaks take place. Since this appears anathema to the orderliness of technocratic bureaucratization, it is difficult (as it always has been and always will be) to achieve the goals within the limits of established social institutions. If Joyce were a socialist anarchist throughout his life, it is because some measure of semiotic anarchism is essential to the regeneration of communication.

These questions ought not to be far from questions of media analysis, policy analysis, or the analysis of culture and technology. The difficulty in accomplishing this goal is partly a question of the complex trans-diciplinary issues involved, but it is largely a question of how professions strongly grounded in the workings of society deal with the issue that while *the poetic operates within culture*, it only succeeds as it goes *beyond* culture, *exceeds the limits of* culture. The poetic regenerates culture, as the culture stabilizes the poetic to create momentary (at least in pan-historical terms) intelligibility. If Maoism had really been true to the principle of 'Let a thousand flowers bloom,' it would have become the hub of energy for the poetic, rather than the producer of propagandistic posters that parodied Coca-Cola and Phillip Morris ads or Marxist historical films that parodied Eisenstein, Cecil B. deMille, and *Gone with the Wind*.

The tendency to scientize all progress often leads us to disregard the importance of the heuristic power of the poetic in what comes to be. Before advertising became a fully acceptable object of research to social theory and the basic (i.e., non-applied) social sciences and before it had sensitized itself to its reciprocal relationship with the arts, it had already been probed by artists, writers, critics, and theorists (Wyndham Lewis, Leavis, McLuhan, Barthes, Lem). Both the semiotic and content-analysis approaches to advertising (as outlined by William Leiss, Steve Klein, and Sut Jhally) are rooted in humanistic approaches for studying language and the arts that derived from philology, literature, and linguistics. (It is worth noting that one of the fathers of official U.S. communication studies was Wilbur Schramm, who originally was an English professor, while Marshall McLuhan, another English professor, launched Canadian interest in communication and Raymond Williams, yet another, British communication studies.)

The poet qua poet provides an 'epistemological' model. The poet's role is not elitist but 'charismatic.' Marked by making a model and possessing the mastery of a discipline, the poet can be wrong or even intentionally evil; but well-crafted error is insightful. There is a specific ecological importance to innovative cultural productions which are committedly poetic. That such commitment may be ultimately undefinable arises in the cultural attitudes of such groups as the Balinese, who claim they have no art but assert the principle that it is necessary to do everything well. Since life itself is expressive and communicable, all life must be guided by the poetic; for quite literally, people produce and reproduce themselves. When the poetic is so conceived, it is necessary to recognize that potentially everyone is a poet.

To live in common with other people makes the exploratory exfoliation of modes of communication necessary. Even in a relatively (since there is no possibility of an absolute homeostasis) stable-state society such as Bali, there is the dynamic movement of exploratory poetic activity for, as Bateson has demonstrated, the Balinese have achieved a plateau of 'intensive stabilization' that has to be constantly maintained by a controlled, yet dynamic, transgressive intensity. One major theory promulgated by artists about the function of poetry in the twentieth century is that modern poetry involves a re-evaluation of the historical sense of the poetic as an art of assembling or making: imaginary engineering.

The poetic, even in Aristotle's conception, imitated nature *sua operatione*,[6] reflecting that evolutionary Mind-Nature bond that is central to an ecological conception of communication. Works of art which are avowedly against nature (like certain contemporary movements) still must work within nature. The poet is an engineer because he works in tandem with nature; creating imaginary worlds by developing productive processes that are parallel to those of the natural world. The poetic is ecological knowledge which 'opens up' and liberates by generating forms of communication and understanding for comprehending society and people's physical, psychological, and cultural environment.

Poetry, 'dancing what can only be danced,' generates a wild semiology which implicates that wild sociology that the social theorist John O'Neill has so aptly described: 'In practice wild sociology achieves a return to things that is the direction of poetry. All of modern thought addresses nature's body, bringing reason to its sense through the recognition of the primacy of perceptual knowledge ... Moreover, this poetry is in keeping with the viewpoint of modern science, provided that in both cases we properly understand that the very notion of viewpoint in no way involves a fall into subjectivism and relativism.'[7] If Carpenter, in launching *Explorations* in 1953 with McLuhan, could read a novel such as *Ulysses* partly as urban social and ethnological theory, O'Neill twenty-five years later as a critical phenomenologist is able to set forth a theory of 'wild' sociology that is socially and scientifically grounded as poetic theory.

This 'wild' sociology is based on understanding the communicative process as a 'making sense.' Since growth and development are themselves radical processes, communication is a radical concept, part of the life-producing processes of humans in nature. Nietzsche makes one of the strongest modern statements about art as an ecology of sense when, in *The Will to Power*, he ascribes to art a privileged role with respect to communication as communion. Observing that 'all art exercises the power of suggestion over the muscles and the senses which in the artistic temperament are originally active,' he proclaims that a work of art 'tonically, inflames desire ... excites all the more subtle recollections of intoxication.' He goes on to condemn the role of 'the layman,' for he asserts that what we have called the *poetic* 'speaks only to artists – [for] it speaks to this kind of a subtle flexibility of the body.'

There is a special memory that penetrates such states: a distant transitory world of sensations comes back, which negates ugliness and dismisses the bluntness of logic: 'The aesthetic state possesses a superabundance of *means of communication*, together with an extreme receptivity for stimuli and signs. It constitutes the high point of communication [communion] and transmission between living creatures – it is the source of languages. This is where languages originate: the languages of tone as well as the languages of gestures and glances. The more complete phenomenon is always the beginning: our faculties are subtilised out of more complete faculties. But even today one still hears with one's muscles, one even reads with one's muscles' (emphasis added).[8] Dewey's theories concerning 'art as experience' echo Nietzsche's strong insistence on the poetic (i.e., 'the aesthetic state') as 'a high point of communication [communion]' between people and as the neuro-muscular source of all languages – tone, gesture, and glances – for the world is attended to, listened to, and deciphered by the neuro-muscular system.

As the basis of any artistic code, *convention*, an intrinsic aspect of the mature arts (as languages), 'is the condition of great art, *not* an obstacle.' That which marks the differences, as convention certainly does, makes art's contribution to the communication process possible: 'Every enhancement of life enhances man's power of communication, as well as his power of understanding. Empathy with the souls of others is originally nothing moral, but a physiological susceptibility to suggestion: "sympathy" or what is called "altruism" is merely a product of that psychomotor rapport which is reckoned a part of spirituality ... One never communicates thoughts: one communicates movements, mimics signs, which we then trace back to thoughts.'[9] This interpretation of the artistic or poetic state is ecological, for it suggests that there is an interdependence within society in shaping the means of communication; for those who possess 'more complete' faculties share with others the 'subtilised' forms produced by their richer capabilities.[10] That sharing, though, as Joyce realized, comes about only because the artist's consumers are also the artist's producers.

The language of tones, gestures, and movement, and the mimicry of signs, are continuously made more subtle by the poetic experience through a process which is fundamentally physiological and materialistic. The poetic's ecological function accompanies its communication of excess; yet in that very process, a newer more 'subtilised' communication challenges the current everyday communication. This is neither a vertical nor hierarchical relationship, for this 'subtilised' communication operates diagonally or obliquely – transversally – segmenting and fragmenting everyday communication in the way a Schwitters collage, a Duchamp assemblage, or a Lichtenstein parody confronts the everyday expression of mass production of words, images, and things.

The relation frequently noted between advertising and art, especially modernist or avant-garde art, is then explicable because of the role that art plays in the evolution of communication and the generation of languages. If advertising eventually tries to encompass that which challenges it, then reciprocally, future artistic works arise to confront these new 'languages,' seeing through and breaking through their constraints and limitations. This innovative art is frequently not official art, for it can equally as well result from the creative excess of the transgressive expressions of everyday life, such as in *Doonesbury*, reggae, or the unsung tale-telling of a subculture. The poetic imposes value on the social by being outside or going beyond, forming a community based on the body and its primacy; for the poetic is an infinite assemblage, like Spinoza's intuition of the relation of body and soul, where the body's indivisibility from the soul involves a body which communicates through relations and intensities.[11]

Communication is a process of becoming. The poetic-dramatic theory of communication sees communication as a social *praxis*; poetic communication is an eco-social praxis in which the production of ways of coping with 'feelfully' thinking about stability and change is central. The many exhibits explored in this book illustrate how this complex sign-generating activity (morphogenesis) is a necessary, though not sufficient, requirement to bring about more fruitful and productive processes of change. Quite frequently, the poetic activity as a praxis that implies a theoretical orientation precedes the intellectual construction and rational demonstration of theory. Joyce's later writings, Klee's paintings, and Welles's cinema are extremely strong instances of works implying major theoretical orientations.

Since communication is a social practice, there are obviously degrees of intensity of communication, as Nietzsche recognized. An ad sequence communicates, but it does not serve primarily or extensively to replenish the communicative potential of society. While such advertising may indirectly serve as a way of transmitting those revivifying signs produced by others, to the extent that it succeeds, it has to that degree undermined its own primary motives. Since advertising has to play with and distort desire, it is involved in the tricky game of invoking desire and then repressing or controlling it. The success of social practice is finally measured in part by the degree to which the process of communication involves a yearning for and an achievement of that enriched communication which Nietzsche talks about – and that Mead, Dewey, and Burke identified as a secularized communion.

Any poetry, even the poetry of bourgeois art, exists as a radical presentness; a de-negation of finalities which is the actualization of desire no longer relegated to a delusive future liberation. Advertising, as exemplified in our discussion, tries specifically to seduce desire by establishing constricting limits within which it must operate, thus preventing it from pursuing the vocation of exploding the status quo. The poetic-dramatic theory of communication marks out that small bit of space and moment of time within which, through its social practice, the actualization of desire overflows the narrow communication channels imposed by the code of the status quo. Still, the processes of the poetic and of communication are processes of becoming; a becoming that is allied to memory and to the future, for its very movement, implicit in the poetic act, precludes the arresting of the present. The artistic moment has always been that illusory presence which has already happened and is still to happen.

Memory, regarded as a process forming the future, is essential to the social bond of communication. Those gaps and breaks that characterize the functioning of memory and take us beyond what is expected are necessary to achieve Joyce's 'flash from a future'[12] by generating 'feelful thinkamalinks.' Joyce's dream, by placing memory at its centre, is still a drama of liberation, not from the human, but from that which inhibits the realization of the human. The para-humanism of *Finnegans Wake* is based on people's true humanity emerging from their discovery that the truly human is neither ethnocentric in the interest of some racial group, socio-centric in the interests of some class, nor anthropocentric in the interest of human domination.

Memory embraces a remembered and retraced 'ancient legacy of the past' as well as a retracing of the lived and living experience of the person in the process of becoming – which may include some or all of becoming human, becoming animal, becoming imaginary, or becoming an engineer. Deleuze has connected the processes of becoming and memory within living and lived experience; but this is a living and lived experience which itself includes a reconstruction, an assemblage, of the remote past as well as of the immediate past of the living present. Modernity did not reject memory, as structuralism rejected the privilege of the diachronic. Postmodernism reasserted the role of memory, as Derrida's aphorism indicates: 'To deconstruct is to do memory work.' Contemporary communication theory is grounded on memory and history as distinct, yet interrelated, concepts. That key section about forgetting and remembering in the Joycean 'vicociclometer,' examined in detail earlier, which parallels the making of works of art within the dream action to the cooking, eating, and digesting of eggs, clearly asserts that a deconstructive and accompanying reconstructive process is essential to transforming the 'heroticisms, catastrophes and eccentricities' through the 'ancient legacy of the past' into what 'may be there for you' (*FW*614.35–615.8).

The historical association of the art of memory with alchemy and occultism forcefully emphasized its potentially transgressive role and its role in the decomposition and recombination involved in producing the poetic work. Yates, speaking of how Bruno's 'art of memory is a magical art, a Hermetic art,' suggests that 'the Hermetic experience of reflecting the universe in the mind is ... at the root of Renaissance magic memory, in which the classical mnemonic with places and images is now understood, or applied, as a method of achieving this experience by imprinting archetypal, or magically activated, images on the memory. By using magical or talismanic images as memory-images, the Magus hoped to acquire universal knowledge, and also powers, obtaining through magical organisation of the imagination a magically powerful personality, tuned in, as it were, to the powers of the cosmos.'[13] The hermetic transmission of the classical art of memory underlines that art's orientation to the future, for the magical power is a power to change what comes to be. In this way, the traditional art of memory persisted through an epoch of Cartesianism by its association with the underground world of the occult and the alchemical, emerging in modernity as a corollary of communication with the unconscious, thus becoming inextricably intertwined with the poetics of modernism.

Joyce's uniting memory and evolution – the unfolding of the future – is Viconian in part, which is why there are fewer apparent direct references than might be expected in the *Wake* to Darwin, evolution, and the *The Origin of Species*. Joyce construes Vico's theory of history, not as cyclical in the strictest sense, but as producing a helical movement in which the 'seim anew' (*FW*215.23) represents a progress that arises from the memory of history. In constructing his poetic dream and incorporating within it a philosophy of becoming that transforms the historical sense of time, Joyce sensed that past time and future time can be comprehended, while present time can never be fully comprehended, since it is instantly moving into the future away from the past.[14]

At the conclusion of the *Wake*, memory unites with evolutionary values in the new dawning of society that accompanies the coming forth of day. Communion is necessary if memory is to combine with the making of sense, and communion can only be achieved through those 'feelful thinkamalinks' – the centrality of the body and the participation of people's bodies with nature's body, the 'world's body' – in the processes of communication. So memory encounters the future only in that arrested moment which is time present – the here and now. Joyce and most other modernists again and again stress this doctrine of arrest. Joyce argued that the comic effect could only be realized in such moments of arrest; for the shock of the comic took the participant out of time for a moment in the same sense that a communion is achieved only as that 'moment out of time.' Benjamin has spoken of this in 'Theses on the Philosophy of History' as the Messianic moment: to articulate the past historically does not mean to recognize it '"the way it really was" (Ranke). It means to seize hold of a memory as it flashes up at the moment of danger ... In every era the attempt must be made anew to wrest tradition away from a conformism that is about to overpower it. The Messiah comes not only as the redeemer, he comes as the subduer of Antichrist.'[15] The moment in and out of time, in which memory encounters the future, associates memory with that special shock of the poetic through which it achieves its morphogenesis.

Central to that *architectonic* function – the machinic assemblage which opens up a secular communion, a collective assemblage constructed by the artist – is that catharsis produced by genuine shock or surprise (emphasized by Burke in *Language as Symbolic Action)*. The cathartic transcends and re-evaluates the world of everyday life. Intensely poetic actions (e.g., *8½*) perform such a cathartic function most powerfully and profoundly. John Fekete, in *The Critical Twilight,* a study of McLuhan, Frye, and the New Criticism, explains Lukács's view of the relation between shock and catharsis, for 'art, the argument goes, is – in each work – both the *memory of mankind* (concentrating in itself an essential step of human historical development) and the (always *sensible*) *self-consciousness of humanity* (blending acutely concentrated subjectivity and objectivity, and expressing in the substance of the art *object* the substance of the generic essence within the *subject*).'[16]

Lukács conceives the Romantic suspension of disbelief as a suspending of the actuality of everyday life by the person who experiences the work of art, just as the one who made it does. Fekete explains how: 'This breaks through his organized fetishized world picture. The generic value hierarchy (organized from the point of view of human development and destiny) that is embodied in the formally closed "world" of art collides with the fetishes of the everyday world. A question is posed as to how human is the world (of the work and of the receiver's daily life)? This elicits a shock (which Lukács calls *catharsis,* generalizing that category beyond its classical restriction to tragedy).'[17] Here the historical and the sensible, memory and consciousness, create a cultural practice which breaks through the objectification of the everyday world. The shock derived through the co-presence of memory and becoming, which occurs from the dynamiting of that particular world by the artwork, transversally interrelates aesthetics and ethics. Lukács demonstrates how 'the (defetishizing) social function of art flows ... precisely from the specific formal objectivity (aesthetic integrity) of the work.'

The extent and impact of catharsis measure its depth and intensity. Catharsis, as conceived by Plato in the *Sophist*, is a sorting process which permits learning by eliminating (i.e., purging) ignorance – a sorting in which the new is separated from the old; the interior is confronted by the exterior.[18] Aristotle gave a medical and therapeutic turn to the concept in the *Politics*, since there is a relationship between ethical or intellectual purgation and medicinal purgation, if that which is purged is an embodied person. This carries the poetic process into the area of purgation and disposal, of the elimination of human wastes and the disposal of intellectual and emotional garbage. Rabelais's grotesqueries, Joyce's cleansing of the stables, Picasso's vision of aerial bombardment, and Makavéjev's excesses in *Sweet Movie* relate immediately to this value of purgation and disposal. Burke's explorations of the body's underworld in his chapters on the 'Thinking of the Body' and 'Somnia ad Urinandum' in *Language as Symbolic Action* establish art's relevance to the humbler excretory parts of the body and examine the flow of words as a diuresis:[19] for Eros, as the motivator of communication, has 'pitched his mansion in the place of excrement.'[20]

People's bodies and the social body, incarnating the roots of remembering in the future and that which is remembered, prepare the ground for that cathartic shock which of necessity is intricately interwoven with the work of memory and its inescapable involvement with the body/mind or body/soul, where, as in Spinoza, the body is inseparable from the compound.[21] Catharsis in and of itself constitutes a social value of the poetic, for it unveils the interface within the social unconscious of the personal psyche and the unarticulated or unspoken that constitutes the social unconscious. The effect of this purgation is to make for revivified communication that is more flexible and responsive to needs. Through the intersection of memory and the moment of assemblage, the poetic explodes the linear progress of time and establishes a spatio-temporal node in history (the arrested moment of its execution) which makes it available for people to experience in the future, directly and/or indirectly through its effects on communication. A further potentiality exists for the poetic act to become a conscious social critique (e.g., Brecht's drama, Godard's films, Joyce's epics, or Rauschenberg's paintings).

The poetic act, since it depends on transgressive activity and since its very excess overflows the moment of its inception, is always executed outside or beyond society (even when its agent may firmly wish to be within the limits of society). Being outside society does not mean that it is not defined by the society in which it arises, but that in arising it opens up possibilities for feelfully thinking about other life-worlds and at the very least provides modes of expression for exposing the ambivalences of the world of the present. As such, the poetic act represents an anarchic moment that to a greater or lesser extent challenges society. Whether through an excessive 'rage for order,' to which the poetry of Wallace Stevens spoke so eloquently, or the 'rage for disorder' of Charlie Chaplin, its very need to go beyond the everyday expressiveness of the world breaks through. That is why the pun as *breakthrough through breakdown* is such a haunting archetype of the poetic, arousing simultaneously contempt and admiration.

Poetry's major social role emerges from the role it plays in contributing to the social dialogue – in its participation in secular communion; the remembrances of the moment of its inception. Here art provides the changes in the regime of signs needed to permit heretofore prohibited dialogue. Heinrich Böll's *The Lost Honor of Katarina Blum: How Violence Develops and Where It Can Lead* produces ways of speaking with feeling about the ambivalence of a free press; Duchamp's machinic devices unleash images to be invoked in coming to understand the processes of mechanization and the accompanying regimentation of liberation; Makavéjev's scatalogical movie about sweetness provides new modes of exploring manipulative rhetoric and propaganda; Leni Riefenstahl's infamous film *Triumph of the Will* exposes the sentimental poetry that shapes the seductive aspects of the life-world produced by fascism.

Through a complex and multifarious process, the poetic insinuates itself within the processes of dialogue and discourse: juxtaposition of works of art; works of art inviting criticism and other modes of talk; works of art shaping the suppleness of the language to cope with states of feeling confronted by social and technological change; works of art opening up new ways of thinking (imagining) the world as a way of confronting the future; finally works of art becoming part of the language by which rational discourse invokes the world of 'feelful thinkamalinks.' The social functions of art are no more an accidental aspect of the social dialogue than the fact that art always communicates is an accidental aspect of poetic expressive activity. Its erotic function links it to the social aspect of people's life-worlds; for in the very pleasure of playing with expression in and for itself lies the beginning of the social function of art. Eros is the inescapable foundation of communication. Since it is recognized that eros is an essential participant for achieving that relatively undistorted communication necessary to making sense of the world, then the analysis of sign and symbol and the processes of interpretation becomes a key aspect of the ecological relationship between Mind and Nature. Joycean wordplay is a fundamental strategy for establishing these networks, since it ties together the problematic of the psychoanalytic and the social unconscious; the problematic of the polysemy of signs; the poetic-metaphoric basis of human communication; and the 'joycing' characteristic of the contemporary evolution of the arts.

Exploring the importance of minimal elements in the modern arts leads to extending the concept of *pun as perspective by incongruity* to produce a poetic and metaphoric basis for the dramatic action of all of the traditional and emerging arts, as Burke anticipated. Word, image, sound, and gesture have led to a way of examining Joyce's insistence on text, code, and sign which, unlike the reverberating ambiguities of *symbolisme*, operates within an historical context and moves between memory and prophecy. The relevance of Joyce's poetics for understanding this interrelationship within the community of signs should now be apparent, for in its very concentrated intensity, it reveals how poetic cultural productions are comprehensible as intensifications and transformations of everyday life, which by a 'commodius vicus of recirculation' return to everyday life to enrich communication and provide the basis for the ecology of sense.

Contemporary hallucinatory, oneiric, or surrealistic film, like that of Fellini or Makavéjev, pertains to these very same concerns and exhibits the same complexities of human communication that Joyce reveals in that penultimate vision, as day dawns in *Finnegans Wake*, where the dreamer reflects on forgetting and remembering, decomposition and recombination, present catastrophes and ancient legacies. Fellini as well as Joyce spans this gap between processes of memory and the complexity of that labyrinthine *semiosis* which constitutes human communication. Makavéjev, interpreting the processes of history and the Utopian vision of the future, particularly reveals the tortuous, nomadic, root-like network between sex, eros, and transubstantiation and the banal material of cliché, the distorted communication of alienation, and the deliberately manipulative commodified life in advertising and propaganda. The theoretic nucleus for understanding the poetic of communication through artistic practice is made manifest by 'rereading' Joyce (the ante-post-modern), who provides such a depth of insight into the ecology of sense. Rereading Joyce after the 1960s redeems the vision that McLuhan had perceived in radical modernism, but suppressed in the interests of preserving a religious conservatism.

The heart of the Joycean sense of prophecy and the future-directedness of the poetic, which in the 'Cyclops' and 'Circe' episodes of *Ulysses* is associated with Bloom as prophet and with his comic visions of the new 'Bloomusalem,' materializes in *Finnegans Wake* through the projective nature of the dream and the act of awakening. 'Wait till Finnegan Wakes' is the Joycean refrain. In the opening of the last book of *Finnegans Wake*, dreaming is directly associated with the process of becoming: 'The untireties of livesliving being the one substrance of a streamsbecoming' (597.8–9). The dialectic of dream and waking weaves the web of a story, 'Totalled in toldteld and teldtold in tittletell tattle,' because 'graced be Gad and all giddy gadgets, in whose words were the beginnings ... feeling aslip and wauking up, so an, so farth' (597.10–11). As day comes in 'A shaft of shivery in the act, anilancinant' (597.24), with the 'sleeper awakening,' there is a 'flash from a future of maybe mahamayability through the windr of a wondr in a wildr is a weltr as a wirbl of a warbl is a world' (597.29).

Such passages link the whole process of talk and talk about modes of communication and expression to the process of dreaming and to discovery – the awakening – through that grace (or transgression!) beyond the reach of art, 'in whose words were the beginnings' (597.10). Such grace, like the 'shaft of shivery in the act,' is related to the eros of the creative goddess of Tantric yoga, Mahaya, in an intimation of the future 'a flash from a future of maybe mahamayability' (597.28). The art of visibilities, of light, has come full circle to that point where it can be seen as an act of achieving social intelligibility. Awakening, like discovery in the poetic-dramatic act, is an intimation of the future based on a coming-to-understand the context of the social and psychoanalytic unconscious as it manifests itself in the present.

Joyce's work is certainly not the only way of discovering a theory of communication in practice; but it is a particularly important way, since it is 'acomedy of letters' that recognizes the centrality of biological, psychological, social, and cultural interpretations which are supposed to be brought to light in the 'dancing of an attitude' (whether in dance, drama, poetry) and then later become an intrinsic part of reflection for human communication. This is not exclusively rooted in the human sex act; for Joyce insists on rooting it in the erotic nature of human life. He does not envision an emergence into a new tribalism, but instead a reintegration passing beyond the theocentric and anthropocentric and therefore once again being able to understand the essential wisdom of ancient mystery in the light of a newly civilized world.

This exploration of the ecology of sense begins the path to understanding the social role of the arts in terms of the vital contribution that they perform to permit people to make sense of their world. Communication depends on everyday social life and is intrinsically involved with the economic and political goals of people in society. Yet any view which fails to appreciate the reciprocal importance of the making of metaphors and the understanding of economic and political goals ultimately fails to achieve an understanding of how humans do communicate and that language, while central and vital to such communication, is an aspect of a multiplicity of communicative modes which are constantly in interaction.

While social, political, and economic goals place a limit on what signs evolve for communicative use, the metaphors and poetic visions in which new signs are produced of necessity contribute part of the process of questioning which leads to change. In the movements which constituted the modern arts, Joyce comprehended the broader global importance of their metaphorical inventiveness, their cathartic function, and their poetic vision as the prolegomena to any ecological vision which could lead to a future. It is necessary that communication theorists fully recognize the centrality of the profound insights that Burke had when he demonstrated the fundamental dramatistic base connecting art and communication and once again recognize the crucial contributions that art, literature, and poetics can make to the understanding of their subject. Attention to the role of the Dionysian wisdom of the body in the processes of human communication and how it generates the very basis of our theories and interpretations must become an intrinsic aspect of our understanding of human communication. The poetic, whether achieved in the give and take of everyday life or crafted by artists, must assume its appropriate role as the means of understanding the morphogenetic aspects of human communication.

Notes

Introduction

1 In the mid-1980s, the science fiction novelist William Gibson first identified the emergence of cyberspace as the most recent moment in the development of electro-mechanical communications, telematics, and virtual reality. Cyberspace, as Gibson saw it, is the simultaneous experience of time, space, and the flow of multidimensional, pan-sensory data: 'All the data in the world stacked up like one big neon city, so you could cruise around and have a kind of grip on it, visually anyway, because if you didn't, it was too complicated, trying to find your way to the particular piece of data you needed. Iconics, Gentry called that' (William Gibson, *Mona Lisa Overdrive*, 16).

1: The Poetic Body in the New Culture of Time and Space

1 Gertrude Stein, *Picasso*, 49–50. See also Stephen Kern, *The Culture of Time and Space 1880–1918*, 244.
2 James Joyce to Harriet Shaw Weaver (28 May 1929), *Letters*, 1:281.
3 See 'The Work of Art in the Age of Mechanical Reproduction,' in Walter Benjamin, *Iluminations*, 219–53.
4 Maurice Horn, ed., *The World Encyclopedia of Comics*, 245
5 Joyce told his friend Eugene Jolas, the surrealist editor of *transition*, which published parts of *Work in Progress* (the working title of *Finnegans Wake*): 'Really it is not I who am writing this crazy book ... but you, and that man over there and the girl at the next table' (Jolas, 'My Friend James Joyce,' 13).
6 The early issues of the seminal *Communications* listed the publisher as 'Le Centre d'Etudes Transdisciplinaire: Sociologies, Anthropologie, Sémiologies,' a branch of Section VI of L'Ecole Pratique, directed by Georges Friedmann. Later

issues listed the publisher as 'Le Centre d'Etudes des Communications de Masse,' with the same section and director. Roland Barthes was listed as one of the five members of the editorial committee for both the early and later issues. Barthes, Baudrillard, Todorov, Kristeva, and Metz were among those who published in *Communications.*

7 Kenneth Burke's *Permanence and Change,* which was originally to be entitled 'Treatise on Communication,' written during 1932–3, was first published in 1935 (Burke, *Permanence and Change,* xxx, xlviii).

8 See S.T. Coleridge, 'On Poesy or Art,' in *Biographia Literaria,* 2:253–63.

9 Friedrich Nietzsche, *The Portable Nietzsche,* 672–3. This appears both in *Nietzsche contra Wagner* (1888), which is a pastiche of segments from other works, and in *Beyond Good and Evil* (1886), where it first appeared.

10 In his early work, he used the terms 'vivisection' and 'epiphany.' For a full discussion, see chapter 4.

11 Michael Phillipson, *In Modernity's Wake: The Ameurunculus Letters,* 15–17. Before reading Phillipson, I had spoken of Joyce in a similarly comic and ironic sense as 'ante-pre-post-modern.' For a satiric, yet brilliantly theoretic discussion of the problem, see Phillipson, 12–27 and 127.

12 'Machinic' is used here very deliberately as distinct from 'mechanical.' See Gilles Deleuze and Claire Parnet, *Dialogues,* 70–1, where Deleuze discusses the difference between the machine and the 'machinic' in contradistinction to the mechanical.

13 For a fuller discussion of Joyce and these themes, see Donald F. Theall, 'James Joyce: Literary Engineer,' 11–27; Donald and Joan Theall, 'Marshall McLuhan and James Joyce,' 60–1; and Donald F. Theall, 'The Hieroglyphs of Engined Egypsians: Machines, Media and Modes of Communication in *Finnegans Wake,*' 129–52.

14 'Jousstly' refers to Jousse, whose writings on gesture Joyce had read. This is first discussed at length in David Hayman, *Joyce et Mallarmé,* 1:160–1 (cited in James Atherton, *Books at the Wake,* 177).

15 'Delivery is often styled action. But the first name is derived from the voice, the second from gesture. For Cicero in one passage speaks of action as being a form of speech, and in another as being a kind of physical eloquence' (Quintilian, *Insitutio Oratorio,* trans. H.E. Bulter, XI, iii, 4:243). For Demosthenes, see ibid., 245.

16 – There should be an art of gesture, said Stephen one night to Cranly.

– Yes?

– Of course I don't mean art of gesture in the sense that the elocution professor understands the word. For him a gesture is an emphasis. I mean a rhythm. You know the song 'Come unto these yellow sands'?

– No.

– This is it, said the youth making a graceful anapaestic gesture with each arm. That's the rhythm, do you see? (James Joyce, *Stephen Hero*, 184)

The passage quoted above from *Finnegans Wake* (see note 14) continues: 'His hearing is in-doubting just as my seeing is onbelieving. So dactylise him up to blankpoint and let him blink for himself where you speak the best ticklish. You'll feel what I mean' (468.15–17).

17 Gregory Bateson, *Steps*, 137

18 Alan Ross Macdougall, *Isadora*, 218 (quoting a statement by Duncan to the Chicago press in October 1922)

19 Walter Benjamin, *Understanding Brecht*, 3

20 Ibid., 3, 19

21 Siegfried Giedion, *The Eternal Present*, 117

22 Theall and Theall, 'Marshall McLuhan and James Joyce: Beyond Media,' 54–5

23 Kenneth Clark, *The Nude*

24 Giambattista Vico, *The New Science of ...*, §401. Cf. his axiom 'Mutes make themselves understood by gestures or objects that have natural relations with the ideas they wish to signify' (§225).

25 Georges Bataille, *Inner Experience*, xxxiii

26 Coleridge, *Biographia Literaria*, 2:253–63

27 T.S. Eliot, 'Lettre d'Angleterre,' 620–2

2: The Micro as the Medium and the Message

1 Donald F. Theall, 'Beyond the Orality/Literary Dichotomy: James Joyce and the Pre-History of Cyberspace,' 31. This argument is developed throughout *The Medium Is the Rear View Mirror: Understanding McLuhan*.

2 Jorge Luis Borges, *Other Inquisitions, 1937–1952*, 6–9

3 Stuart Brand, *The Media Lab*

4 Marshall McLuhan to Robert J. Leuver, *Letters*, 385

5 James Carey, *Culture as Communication*; Walter Ong, *Orality and Literacy: The Technologizing of the Word*

6 It should be noted that the first concept for a telegraph was proposed in 1753. Volta's battery in 1800 made it more practical, so that the first telegraph based on that concept was designed by Francisco Silva in 1804. Cooke and Wheatstone based their patent on an 1832 invention of Baron Schilling. By 1855 David Hughes developed a printing telegraph. See Trevor Williams, *History of Invention*, 233. Morse's code introduced a binary system to telegraphy.

7 'Compunication' is a coinage to indicate the marriage between computers and telecommunications that enables the creation of the Matrix (i.e., the informa-

tion highway). 'Chaosmos' is a term borrowed from Joyce's *Finnegans Wake* to stress the chaotic theory on which the cosmos and hence the Matrix itself is grounded (see *FW*118.21). 'Telematic' is a more common term, but it does not in its morphology remind the reader of the linking of CPUs (central processing units) through telecommunications.

8 Sergei Eisenstein, *Film Sense*, 69–109. Cf. Sergei Eisenstein, *Film Form*, 255.

9 'Notoriously, it is the visual technique of a Picasso, the literary technique of James Joyce' (Marshall McLuhan, *The Mechanical Bride: Folklore of Industrial Man*, 3).

10 André Bazin, 'The Originality of Welles as a Director,' 128–9

11 John Fekete, *The Critical Twlight*, 155

12 All of these figures are specifically mentioned or alluded to in the *Wake*. The works of Swift, Sterne, and Wyndham Lewis are all recognized as 'structural books.'

13 Giambattista Vico, *The New Science of ...*, §363

14 Herbert Marcuse, *Eros and Civilization*, 166

15 See, for example, Aristotle, *Poetics*, 1448b.

16 Gregory Bateson, *Steps*, 222–4. See also 177–93.

17 Ibid., 448–60

18 Rosalind Krauss, *The Originality of the Avant-Garde and Other Modernist Myths*, 43–84

19 For example, Bakhtin's analysis of Rabelais's style in *Rabelais and His World*

20 Umberto Eco, *Semiotics and the Philosophy of Language*, 162–3. The entire chapter, 'Symbol,' 130–63, is relevant to this point.

21 Gilles Deleuze and Felix Guattari, *A Thousand Plateaus*, 69–70

22 Malcolm Lowry to Jonathan Cape, 2 Jan. 1946, *Selected Letters*, 66

23 Ibid.

24 'For if a work of art communicates with a public, and even gives rise to that public, if it communicates with the other works of the same artist, and gives rise to works to come, it is always within this dimension of transversality, in which unity and totality are established for themselves, without unifying or totalizing objects or subjects' (Gilles Deleuze, *Proust and Signs*, 149–50).

25 Gilles Deleuze and Felix Guattari, *Anti-Oediupus*, 318–19

26 ' ... on ne va pas des sons aux images et des images au sens: on s'installe «d'emblée» dans le sens' (Gilles Deleuze, *Logique du sens*, 41; my translation in text).

3: From Sense to Nonsense

1 Gödel's theorem (1931) of incompleteness or undecidability demonstrated the

impossibility of proving the consistency of a formal system that contains the arithmetic of natural numbers. This meants that it is not possible to construct a unitary deductive system in which all mathematical truths can be deduced. The theorem states that in any formal system which contains the arithmetic of natural numbers there is a formula which, if the system is consistent, can neither be proved nor disproved, neither it nor its negation being deducible from axioms (Alan Bullock et al., eds, *The Fontana Dictionary of Modern Thought*). For a full discussion of the theorem and its implications, see E. Negal and J.R. Newman, *Gödel's Proof*. Disciples of Bateson working with Paul Watzlawick discuss the theorem in relation to communication, computers, and its status as the ultimate contemporary paradox in Paul Watzlawick et al., *Pragmatics of Human Communication*, 268–70.

2 Georges Pitcher, 'Wittgenstein, Nonsense and Lewis Carroll,' in Lewis Carroll, *Norton Critical Edition of Alice in Wonderland*, 387–402
3 Ovid, *Metamorphoses*, 8:155–262
4 Francis Bacon, 'Wisdom of the Ancients,' in *The Essays, or Counsels Civil and Moral of Francis Bacon*
5 Gilles Deleuze, *Logique du sens*, 36–41
6 John Dewey, *Democracy and Education*, 5–6
7 John Dewey, *Art as Experience*, 105
8 Ibid., 244
9 John Dewey, *Experience and Nature*, 392
10 Ibid., 389
11 Karl Marx, *The Economic and Philosophic Manuscripts*, 140–1
12 Dewey, *Art as Experience*, 22
13 Dewey, *Experience and Nature*, 261
14 W.B. Yeats, 'Word for Music Perhaps' [Poem VI], in *The Collected Poems*, 294–5
15 Mikhail Bakhtin, *The Dialogic Imagination*, 63–8
16 Mikhail Bakhtin, *Rabelais and His World*, 423
17 Bakhtin (in ibid., 317–39) has an extended discussion of each of these phęnomena. The phrase 'body without organs' is borrowed from Deleuze but is consistent with Bakhtin's description.
18 Ezra Pound, 'Paris Letter,' *Dial*, 72.6 (June 1922); reprinted in *The Literary Essays of Ezra Pound*, 405
19 James Joyce to Harriet Shaw Weaver, 31 May 1927, in *Letters*, 255
20 Bakhtin, *Rabelais*, 46. See comments on two kinds of modern revivals of grotesque.
21 Kenneth Burke, *Language as Symbolic Action*, 308–43, 419–21, 469–79
22 Bakhtin, *Dialogic Imagination*, 21

23 'The tasks above are as the flasks below, saith the emerald canticle of Hermes and all's loth and pleasestir, are we told, on excellent inkbottle authority, solarsystemised, seriolcosmically, in a more and more almightily expanding universe under one, there is rhymeless reason to believe, original sun' (*FW*263.21–7).

24 Cf. Bakhtin, *Rabelais*, 58, where Rabelais's work is described as 'an encyclopedia of folk culture.' Joyce's encyclopaedic *Wake* can be considered as an encyclopaedia of 'the everyday world of post-industrial peoples' – ads, comics, pulps, TV, radio, sporting news, racing forms, gadgets, etc.

25 Stephen Toulmin, *The Return to Cosmology: Postmodern Science and the Theology of Nature*, 201–75

26 Morris Berman, *The Re-enchantment of the World*. See particularly the discussions of Bateson: 211–33, and 272–6.

27 Bakhtin, *Rabelais*, 7

28 It is interesting to note how the semiologist Umberto Eco, who is also a medievalist and a critic and scholar of Joyce, gained popular recognition for *The Name of the Rose*, which (using the populist Franciscan tradition) is able to encompass much of the carnivalesque, thus creating a considerable contemporary appeal.

29 'In grotesque realism and in Rabelais' work ... excrement was conceived as an essential element in the life of the body and of the earth in the struggle against death. It was part of man's vivid awareness of his materiality, of his bodily nature, closely related to the life of the earth' (Bakhtin, *Rabelais*, 224).

30 Ibid., 25–6

31 Ibid., 341

32 Federico Fellini, *Juliet of the Spirits*, 50

33 Giambattista Vico, *The New Science of* ..., 70. See also John O'Neill's remarks on this passage in *Five Bodies*, chapter 2, 'The World's Body.'

34 Vico, *The New Science of* ..., 108 [§384]

35 Ibid., 280 [§819]

36 See, for example, the discussion on language in section 5 of Joyce's *Portrait of the Artist as a Young Man*.

37 Cf: 'Furthermore, the sources of all poetic locution are found to be two: poverty of language and necessity to explain and make oneself understood' (Vico, *The New Science of* ..., 19 [§34]).

38 Blood is named as the dominant organ in the both the structural charts that Joyce gave to Linati and to Gilbert. Though it is an unusual usage, he apparently considered the circulatory system to be an 'organ' on the grounds that it was part of an animal that formed a structural and functional unit.

4: The Joyce Era

1 Richard Ellmann and Charles Feidelson, *The Modern Tradition*, 679
2 Ibid., 681
3 T.S. Eliot, *Selected Essays*, 341
4 T.S. Eliot, 'Talk on Dante'
5 This ambiguous construction is meant to indicate the existence of two sets of plans, which are discussed and illustrated in Richard Ellmann, *Ulysses on the Liffey*.
6 Frank Budgen, *James Joyce and the Making of Ulysses*, 92. As David Hayman says: 'There is not real reason to doubt that, though he clearly perfected and enlarged the technique, Joyce derived it most directly from Dujardin's novelette' (*Ulysses: The Mechanics of Meaning*, 69).
7 Anthony Giddens, *The Constitution of Society*, 41–5
8 Gregory Bateson, *Steps*, 135–6
9 Richard Ellmann, *James Joyce*, 527–8
10 'To create the dynamic laughter of *Ulysses* and especially *Finnegans Wake*, he had to move beyond his earlier static concept of comedy, expressed in these youthful Pola note-books, and the route by which to do so was opened up to him by his reading of Ben Jonson's works in the Sorbonne Library in Paris. Jonson, like Joyce, stressed the priority of the comic and exemplified a dynamic use of the comic in his dramas' (James Joyce, *The Critical Writing of*, 144).
11 *Comic Cuts* was one of two great comic papers founded in 1890 that lasted until 1953. 'Ally Sloper's Half-Holiday,' the first regular comic in the modern sense, which first appeared on 3 May 1884, contributed much to the format of *Comic Cuts*.
12 Gilles Deleuze and Felix Guattari, *Anti-Oedipus*, 315–9
13 Hugh D. Duncan, *Communication and Social Order*, 413–30
14 See Roland Barthes, *Mythologies*, and Marshall McLuhan, *The Mechanical Bride: Folklore of Industrial Man*, which in pioneering the technique perhaps went furthest in trying to develop it artistically so as to embrace the complexities of contradictions. This accounts for McLuhan's symbolist-cubist layout in his presentation in *The Bride*.
15 Eugene Jolas, 'My Friend James Joyce,' 13
16 James Joyce, *Stephen Hero*, 186
17 The Joycean epiphany dramatizes the commonplace, transforming it by a radiant or clarifying illumination. Joyce's awareness of this phenomenon predates the surrealists and even the Dadaists, for he began collecting epiphanies in the first decade of this century. He explained his conception of an epiphany in *Stephen Hero* (the early manuscript draft of *A Portrait of the*

Artist as a Young Man): 'This triviality (an overheard conversation) made him think of collecting many such moments together in a book of epiphanies. By an epiphany he meant a sudden spiritual manifestation, whether in the vulgarity of speech or of gesture or in a memorable phase of the mind itself. He believed it was for the man of letters to record these epiphanies with extreme care, seeing that they themselves are the most delicate and evanescent of moments. He told Cranly that the clock of the Ballast Office was capable of an epiphany' (211).

Joyce chose the term 'epiphany' deliberately and continued to refer to it throughout his works. The Greek term 'epiphany' had referred to a manifestation of a deity; the Christian feast of the Epiphany (January 6th, the twelfth day after Christmas) celebrates the first manifestation of the newly Incarnated God to the faithful through the visit of the Magi. Joyce's adoption of the term is a conscious secularization of the Christian concept, suggesting that any object or event under the proper circumstances can become a privileged representation of a 'life force' – the energy of nature or human nature manifesting itself through the everyday object or event. This borrowing of the term 'epiphany' from the name of a feast in Christian liturgy reinforces the conscious secularization of the sacred that permeates Joyce's treatment of the signs of everyday life, a practice typical of modern art. Joyce's profane gesture upon the publication of *Finnegans Wake* (on 2 February 1939 – the Feast of Candlemas – his fifty-fifth birthday) is both a confirmation of such activity and a prime example of an epiphany. While cutting his birthday cake, he spoke the words for the consecration of the Eucharist in the Mass, an act deliberately designed to have serious implications for future interpretation of his work, for his is a book which secularizes the sacramental sensibility as a way of maintaining communication, communion, and community in a world where God is dead and man is no longer the centre of the universe. This action constitutes a mini-drama which is a significant gloss on the work – susceptible of interminable interpretation, just as his works themselves. Calling such a phenomenon an epiphany clearly recognizes that this technique is dramatic, for the feast of the Epiphany is a dramatic re-presentation of the Incarnation. It also recognizes that the technique is an aspect of social communication, for Joyce is producing an intricate message about the cultural import of his work. Epiphany whether in actions or in words, which themselves are actions, is one of the chief means by which he produces works to be 'read' by 'projective readers.'

18 I consider the inquisition of the sleeping Yawn to be the climax of the *Wake*, with the two chapters that follow providing the dénouement and conclusion. I take the conclusion to be the awakening of HCE and the final version of ALP's letter followed by ALP's epilogic monologue (echoing Molly's in *Ulysses*).

19 Bataille stresses the importance of communication and laughter in *Inner Ex-*

perience. Pound's interest in communication is well illustrated in *The ABC of Reading*.

20 Ezra Pound, *Ernest Fenollosa: The Chinese Written Character as a Medium for Poetry with the Offset Edition of the Pivot*, 53–96 See also Sergei Eisenstein, *Film Sense*, 28–45; Peter Stallybrass and Allon White, *The Politics and Poetics of Transgression*, 5.

21 See Rosalind E. Krauss, *The Originality of the Avant-Garde and Other Modernist Myths* 43–85.

22 The allusions bringing together Pope and Pound are quite intentional. Read in the context of the satire of such works as *The Dunciad* or *The Epistle to Dr Arbuthnot*, Pope's oft-quoted lines from his *Essay on Criticism* take on their own ambivalence:

Great Wits sometimes may gloriously offend,
And rise to Faults true Criticks dare not mend;
From vulgar Bounds with brave Disorder part,
And snatch a Grace beyond the Reach of Art (152–5)

Pope's hyper-conscious neo-Augustan awareness of the 'limits' of art and the 'rage for order' made him also acutely aware to the role of transgressing the rules, exceeding the limits. Incidentally, in the late sixteenth century, George Puttenham spoke of the 'figures of speech' as 'transgressions of speech' and actually illustrated the use of metaphor by a metaphor involving implications of sexual transgression. The phrase 'Make it new' comes from Ezra Pound, who in addition to using it as an epigram for the work of the artist (supposedly based on Confucius), made it the title of a key collection of essays – *Make It New*.

23 Walter Benjamin, *Illuminations*, 167

24 Walter Benjamin, *Charles Baudelaire: A Lyric Poet in the Era of High Capitalism*, 110–1

25 See ibid., 131–2.

26 Ezra Pound, *The ABC of Reading*, 81. McLuhan spoke of the artist as 'an early warning system.'

27 Aristotle, *Poetics*, xxiv.10, in *Aristotle's Theory of Poetry and Fine Art*, ed. and trans. S.H. Butcher, 95

28 Desiderius Erasmus, *The Praise of Folly*, xiv–xv

29 Michel Foucault, *The Order of Things: An Archeology of the Human Sciences*, 3–16

30 Paul Valéry, 'Introduction to the Method of Leonardo da Vinci,' in *Paul Valéry: An Anthology*, 33–94

31 See, for example, Stewart Brand, *The Media Lab*; and Michael Benedikt, ed., *Cyberspace*.

32 The term 'paraliterature' is used to suggest the continuity of poetry from oral

and printed literature to the complex productions of film, television, and computerized media. In the early 1970s at a symposium in Montreal with Marc Angenot and Darko Suvin, I coined the terms 'para-aesthetic' and 'parapoetic' to more properly cover the full spectrum of cultural production, but I now use 'multimedia paraliterature,' since the term has become familiar. It appears to have been used first in France in 1970. Paraliterature here is used in a sense of 'beyond literature.' It also embraces the contextual proliferation which is naturally part of the multimedia-paraliterature complex: productions in different modalities (e.g., comics, animated films, talking books, etc.), fanzines, hot lines, clubs, etc. For a discussion of the whole thrust of going 'beyond media,' which this really implies, see Donald Theall and Joan Theall, 'Marshall McLuhan and James Joyce: Beyond Media.' To put the problem in context, note the ambivalence of the prefix 'para-.' The *Oxford English Dictionary* contains the following entry: 'As a preposition Greek *para-* had the sense "by the side of, beside" whence "alongside of, by, past, beyond, etc." In composition it had the same senses, with such cognate adverbial ones as "to one side, amiss, faulty, irregular, distorted, wrong," also expressing subsidiary relations, alteration, perversion, stimulation.'

This introduction is followed by two sets of entries, one from natural history and anatomy, where 'para-' is used in the sense 'beside or near or standing in some subsidiary relation to,' and another from chemistry, where it is placed before the name of substances which are supposed to have been modifications of other substances, such as 'paraformaldehyde.' This is interesting, for many of the examples of the various genras that might be classified as paraliterary appear to be parallel to the literary (e.g., utopian science fiction or Le Guin's *The Dispossessed*); some may go beyond literature in their explorations, such as some of the work of Brian Aldiss or Stanislaw Lem, though most of the examples are generally seen to be subsidiary to literature or literature gone amiss, such as novels by Dean Koontz; some finally may seem almost to be outside of literature (beyond the bounds) like Hienlein's *Stranger in a Strange Land* (beyond because of the peculiar breakdown between imagination and execution that marks a work of this kind). Similar examples could be brought forth from other genres, even comic strips. *Popo*, it is arguable, and in a different way, *Krazy Kat*, are flirting with the activity of extending the bounds of literature and certainly are strong examples of paraliterature, though naturally such conceptions when related to literature will certainly still strike many as a 'perversion' or 'distortion' of a serious kind. It is important, however, that many scholars of literature, art, and cultural theory now suddenly want to give a name to such activities, which I have here labelled multimedia paraliterature and/or para-artistic or parapoetic, in order to make them part of a continuum of cultural production along with the literary and the traditionally artistic. It is also crucial that we be aware that these and similar names which seem to be gaining popularity are susceptible of rather ambivalent interpretations, making them attractive to different people for different reasons.

33 Wyndham Lewis, *Time and Western Man*. This work contains Lewis's most extensive critique and discussion of Bergson.

34 Marshall McLuhan, *Letters*, 505

5: The Book, the Press, Eisenstein, and Joyce

1 See Mikhail Bakhtin, *The Dialogic Imagination*, 275–94

2 James Joyce, *Ulysses: A Critical and Synoptic Edition*, 7.1–2. The episode opens with the headline. 'IN THE HEART OF THE HIBERNIAN METROPOLIS.'

3 Joyce's spelling for the term 'enthymatic'

4 From the Linati and Gorman-Gilbert appendix in Richard Ellmann, *Ulysses on the Liffey*, following p. 187

5 Joyce, *Ulysses*, 7.6–101

6 Roland Barthes, *The Semiotic Challenge*, 64 (originally composed during 1964–5 and published in *Communications*)

7 This is not to preclude relating this phrase to the action of the Crucifixion, that action itself being a dramatic communication. For a full discussion of print and other communication technologies in Joyce's work, see Donald F. Theall, 'Hieroglyphs of Engined Egypsians.'

8 Ezra Pound, *ABC of Reading*, 29

9 Marshall McLuhan, *The Interior Landscape: The Literary Criticism of Marshall McLuhan 1943/1962*, 5–21

10 Stéphane Mallarmé, *Oeuvres complètes*, 376. From the section of 'Quant au livre' (As regards the book) entitled 'Etalages' (Shop windows). This is quoted and discussed in McLuhan, *The Literary Criticism of*, 13–15.

11 Walter Benjamin, *Understanding Brecht*, 89

12 Ibid., 90

13 Ibid., 93

14 Ronald Gottesman, ed., *Focus on Citizen Kane*, 128–9

15 George Perry and Alan Aldridge, *The Penguin Book of Comics*, 254

16 Jean-Luc Godard, *Godard on Godard*, 239

17 Ibid., 139

18 Sergei Eisenstein, *Film Sense*, 5–6

19 Sergei Eisenstein, *Film Form*, 104

20 Ibid., 84
21 Ibid., 184–6, 250
22 Ibid., 28
23 Ibid., 35n
24 Ibid., 195–255
25 Laszlo Moholy-Nagy, *Vision in Motion*, 349. He actually quotes an earlier version from *Work in Progress*, which had 'panaroma of all fores of speaches.' Hence his list of things to touch and feel includes: 'peaches, speeches and species.' (In my text, I have substituted 'flores,' 'peach,' and 'speech.')
26 Ibid., 350
27 Ibid.
28 Eisenstein, *Film Form*, 184–5
29 Stewart Brand, *The Media Lab*, 141

6: Beyond Media

1 Marshall McLuhan, *Letters* 305
2 Marshall McLuhan, *Understanding Media*, 26
3 Jürgen Ruesch and Gregory Batson, *Communication*, 276–82
4 Paul Heyer, *Communications and History*, 168
5 McLuhan's PhD thesis, 'The Place of Thomas Nashe in the Learning of His Time,' was accepted by Cambridge in 1943. For a brief description of this work, which contextualized Nashe's quarrel with Gabriel Harvey in a history of the trivium (grammar, logic, and rhetoric) from Greece and Rome through the Middle Ages to the Renaissance, see Marshall McLuhan, *Letters*, 103n.
McLuhan's thesis circulated privately among many key figures in literary theory and criticism including W.K. Wimsatt, Jr, Cleanth Brooks, Hugh Kenner, Walter Ong, and others. Extensive use is made of the thesis material in sections of Brooks and Wimsatt's *Literary Criticism: A Short History*. There are clear influences in the writings of Ong and Kenner as well. It should be noted that McLuhan's work in this area predated such important subsequent studies as George Williamson's *The Senecan Amble* and also predated the intense contemporary interest in rhetoric among literary theorists and communication scholars, especially in the field of speech communication.
6 Joshua Meyrowitz, *No Sense of Place*; and 'Medium Theory,' in David Crowley and David Mitchell, eds, *Communication Theory Today*, 50–77
7 I coined this term when writing about McLuhan in *The Medium Is the Rear View Mirror*, 239–41
8 Raymond Williams , *Keywords*, 20
9 Ibid., 203

10 Crowley and Mitchell, 'Communication in a Post–Mass Media World,' in Crowley and Mitchell, *Communication Theory Today*, 1–24

11 Marshall McLuhan and Wilfred Watson, *From Cliché to Archetype*, 21

12 Marshall McLuhan and Eric McLuhan, *Laws of Media*, 93–4. It should be noted that in the introduction Eric McLuhan expresses some uneasiness about the title, suggesting it should probably have been 'The New Science: Laws of Media.' 'Media' clearly by this point is virtually synonymous with 'technology' in the broad sense of tool-making that can encompass virtually any artefact, from computers to the trivium and from wine to scientific laws. This is not the place for a full critique of this book, but it does show dramatically the problems in dealing with the concept of 'medium.'

13 Elizabeth Eisenstein, *The Printing Press as an Agent of Change*, 34–41; Carolyn Marvin, *When Old Technologies Were New*. See also, Heyer, *Communications and History*, 164–5. He points out how neither Eisenstein nor McLuhan respected one another's work and how Eisenstein only grudgingly admits any debt to McLuhan.

14 Innis's correspondence clearly shows that he had been influenced by Havelock, even though Havelock's major work did not appear in print until the 1960s. For a discussion of the issue, see Graeme Patterson, *History and Communications*, 64–9. See also Eric Havelock, *The Muse Learns to Write*, 16. Havelock recognizes Milman Parry's influence on his work. Parry's papers, which appeared in the late 1920s and early 1930s were edited by his son: A. Milman Parry (*The Making of Homeric Verse*). The question of orality and its background have been discussed in Walter Ong, *Orality and Literacy*, 16–31. The anthropologist Jack Goody extended the work on orality to non-Western and aboriginal cultures (e.g., Jack Goody, *The Logic of Writing and the Organization of Society*). This is discussed in Heyer, *Communications and History*, 160–4.

15 Cf. Derrida's later analysis and critique of Rousseau and orality in *Of Grammatology*.

16 Harold Innis, *The Idea File*, vii–viii. See also Donald F. Theall, 'Explorations in Communications since Innis.'

17 *Leonardo*, the art journal which pioneered theoretical and practical discussion of the evolving relationship between art and technology, is an excellent source for information on what has been and will be happening.

18 Jürgen Habermas, *The Theory of Communicative Action*, 2:390–1

19 The selection of 'production' for cultural assemblages, rather than 'object,' is intentional and deliberate. A cultural production is not fully realized until there are those who participate in the production. This is as true of e-mail communication by computer networks as it is of a book or a film. Since the

creator, of necessity, loses herself in the act of creation, the participant necessarily loses himself in the act of reception. The production is, therefore, always being reassembled, but this reassemblage does not imply that there is no shared experience between the sender (creator) and receiver (participant, audience, or recreator).

20 Umberto Eco, *Semiotics and the Philosophy of Language*, 21–4, 291–307

21 Herbert Marcuse, *The Aesthetic Dimension*, especially 1–21

22 Jean Baudrillard, *Ecstasy of Communication*, 12

23 Ibid.

24 Dell Hymes, review of *Language as Symbolic Action*, by Kenneth Burke, in *Foundations in Sociolinguistics*, 135–41. Originally published in *Language* 44, no. 3 (1968), 664–9

7: The Comic, Wit, and Laughter

1 James Joyce, *Letters*, I:606

2 Frank Budgen, 'James Joyce,' in Sean Givens, ed., *James Joyce*, 24

3 Puns, like metaphor, are first discussed in classical rhetorical treatises such as those of Aristotle, Quintilian, Cicero, and the *Rhetorica ad Herennium*. In the *ad Herennium* three subcategories of the pun are described in different places: *traductio* (IV. xiv. 20), *adnominatio* (or *paronomasia*) (IV.xxi.29–xxiii.32), and *significatio* (IV.liv.67–8). The first refers to the use of the same word in different connotations or a balancing of homonyms; the second to repetition of a word with the addition of suffixes or prefixes, or the transposition of letters or sounds (the play with various 'sense'-related words produce such figures); the third is what is most usually involved in modern puns, including the *double entendre*. The feature that unites all of the variety of subcategories of a pun discussed in the history of rhetoric is a similarity of sound and a disparity of meaning which force a shift or transfer of meaning, either for rhetorical emphasis or for other more semantic functions.

4 Sigmund Freud, *The Basic Writings*, 653–6. Freud sees the pun as a subset of what he describes as '*Witz*.' Historically, 'wit' is the more appropriate term (see, for example, Pope's *Essay on Criticism*), but I am using pun in its broader sense, as usage has developed, which permits it to be a synonym for what Freud or Bergson would call wit. I appreciate that for Freud '*witz*' is closer to 'joke,' but his usage belies this limitation.

5 Kenneth Burke, *A Grammar of Motives and a Rhetoric of Motives*, 834

6 Kenneth Burke, *Permanence and Change: An Anatomy of Purpose*, 113

7 Ibid., 113–14. While first published in 1935, Burke has stated that *Permanence and Change* was written during 1932–3.

8 The phoenix refers to the mythical bird that rises out of its own ashes; 'secular' plays on Milton's having used the phrase 'secular bird' for the phoenix in *Samson Agonistes* (1699–1707).
9 Henri Bergson, *Laughter: An Essay on the Meaning of the Comic*, 105–6
10 'En-twin-ning' because Shem and Shaun, the two brothers, are twins.
11 See the entry on 'montage' in Alan Bullock et al., eds, *The Fontana Dictionary of Modern Thought*, 546.
12 Note this extension of usage throughout McLuhan, beginning with *The Mechanical Bride*. It becomes a central principle in *Understanding Media*.
13 Stanley Mitchell, Introduction, to *Understanding Brecht*, by Walter Benjamin, xiii
14 Benjamin, *Understanding Brecht*, 6
15 Walter Benjamin, *Illuminations*, 130–1
16 Jean Baudrillard, *The Ecstasy of Communication*, 84
17 In Deleuze's sense of machinic as opposed to mechanistic or mechanical. See, for example, Gilles Deleuze and Felix Guattari, *A Thousand Plateaus*, 88–90.
18 Roland Barthes, *Mythologies*, 89. In choosing this example, I am conscious of Baudrillard's using it critically to illustrate his point about wit today. The analysis implicitly refutes Baudrillard by insisting on the historical background of ambivalence.
19 Barthes, *Mythologies*, 90
20 See Paul Ricoeur, *The Conflict of Interpretation: Essays in Hermeneutics*, 66.
21 Donald F. Theall, *The Medium Is the Rear View Mirror: Understanding McLuhan*, 149
22 See remarks by Michael Phillipson in the concluding chapter of his *In Modernity's Wake: The Ameurunculus Letters*.
23 Georges Bataille, *Inner Experience*, 94 5
24 Ibid., 97–8
25 Phillipson, *In Modernity's Wake*, 101–2
26 Raymond Williams, *Television: Technology and Cultural Form*, 86–92
27 Jürgen Habermas, *Theory of Communicative Action*, 2:390
28 Walter J. Ong, 'Wit and Mystery: A Revaluation in Medieval Hymnody'

8: A Dramatic Theory of Communication

1 Paul Ricoeur, 'The Model of the Text: Meaningful Action Considered as a Text'
2 Kenneth Burke, *A Grammar of Motives and a Rhetoric of Motives*, xviii ff
3 Erving Goffman, *The Presentation of Self in Everyday Life*, 240–1

4 Kenneth Burke, 'Dramatism,' in *The Encylopedia of the Social Sciences* 7 (1968), 445–51. See also Kenneth Burke, *Permanence and Change*, 274–94.
5 Kenneth Burke, *The Philosophy of Literary Form: Studies in Symbolic Action*, 59–61
6 Gilles Deleuze and Felix Guattari, *Anti-Oedipus: Capitalism and Schizophrenia*, 316–18. On becoming, see Gilles Deleuze and Felix Guattari, *A Thousand Plateaus: Capitalism and Schizophrenia*, 239–53.
7 Burke, *Permanence and Change*, xlviii
8 Burke, *Philosophy of Literary Form*, 262
9 Kenneth Burke, 'The Poetic Motive,' 63
10 Burke, *Permanence and Change*, 269–70
11 'The electric light is pure information. It is a medium without a message' (Marshall McLuhan, *Understanding Media: The Extensions of Man*, 8).
12 William S. Wilson, 'Dan Flavin: Fiat Lux,' 148
13 Walter Benjamin, *Illuminations*, 252–3. See also Sigfried Kracauer, *From Caligari to Hitler: A Psychological History of German Film*.
14 Roland Barthes, *The Semiotic Challenge*, 50
15 Roland Barthes, 'The Old Rhetoric: An Aide-Memoire,' in *The Semiotic Challenge*, 50 (originally published in *Communications* [1970])
16 Burke, *Permanance and Change*, lvi
17 Roland Barthes, *The Eiffel Tower: And Other Mythologies*, 4
18 Burke, 'The Poetic Motive,' 54–60. It is tempting to think of this in terms of the image of a cat because of such ancient associations as the Old Irish poem about the hermit and his cat which Samuel Barber set to music.
19 Aristotle, *Physics*, 2.194 a.21
20 James Joyce , *Critical Writings*, 145
21 Theodor Adorno, *Aesthetic Theory*, 173–96; see especially 176–9.
22 Ibid., 7
23 Umberto Eco in *The Open Work*, 43–83, explores this subject in a discussion of considerable detail, which is limited only by the fact that it was originally published in 1962. Eco returns to the theme in his *A Theory of Semiotics*, where he specifically speaks about the 'monoplanar' aspect of information theory (see 40ff). He returns to the more complex issues on page 140, where he argues that it is correct to speak about the 'information of the message' as well. A good coverage of other contributions to the discussion can be found in *The Open Work*. It should be noted, however, that Eco's use of the term 'poetic' varies from mine.
24 Roman Jakobson 'Closing Statement: Linguistics and Poetics'
25 Leonard B. Meyer, *Emotion and Meaning in Music*, 43–82

26 E.H . Gombrich, *Art and Illusion: A Study in the Psychology of Pictorial Representation*

27 Gregory Bateson *Steps,* 222

28 Ibid., 203

29 Ibid., 179–80. The message 'This is play,' by which one animal signals to another of the same species that a simulated attack is not a real fight, is Bateson's archetype for all of these forms. In a message such as 'This is play,' paradox is doubly present both in the metalanguage within which the signs are exchanged and in the attitude which the audience adopts both as participant and observer.

30 Bateson, *Steps,* 137

31 Ibid., 145

32 Ibid., 464

33 Ibid.

34 By constructing a meta-level theory of communication and learning, Bateson explains the process by which people learn about their processes of communication. He had already noted that animals are able to communicate to one another messages such as 'This is play.' For example, when two cats encounter one another and start fighting, both participants can distinguish the difference between a real territorial fight and a playful mock battle. Those cats have communicated about communication, a process which Bateson called meta-communication. People also meta-communicate, though in far more complex ways. In addition to carrying on meta-communication, people also can communicate about meta-communication, just the way Bateson speaks about the communication of the message 'This is play' between the cats. This is a level of meta-meta-communication or, to put it in our terms, talk about meta-communications.

35 It is interesting to note that Deleuze and Guattari adopted the term 'plateau' from Bateson. On two occasions, the source of the term is stressed by them. See Deleuze and Guattari, *A Thousand Plateaus,* 20–1, 158, and the accompanying notes.

36 Some terminology throughout this section has been taken from Gilles Deleuze and Claire Parnet, *Dialogues,* (e.g., 98); and Deleuze and Guattari, *A Thousand Plateaus* (e.g., 21–2).

37 Paul Klee, Plate 19, in Norbert Lynton, *Klee,* 41

9: Communication and Comedy

1 For a discussion of incongruity and the phrase 'perspective by incongruity,' see Kenneth Burke, *Permanence and Change,* part 2 ('Perspective by Incongruity') 71–168.

2 Kenneth Burke, *A Grammar of Motives and a Rhetoric of Motives*, 834n
3 It should be noted that Joyce did not read any of Lewis Carroll's writings before he began composing *Work in Progress*. The same is also true of Rabelais's *Gargantua*. Joyce was led to read these works by comments others made about the language of *Work In Progress* (the working title of *Finnegans Wake*).
4 Gilles Deleuze and Felix Guattari, *Anti-Oedipus*, 316–8
5 Ibid., 276
6 Gregory Bateson, *Steps*, 136–8
7 James Joyce, *Critical Writings*, 145
8 Ibid., 144
9 See Gilles Deleuze, *Proust and Signs*, 133–43.
10 It should perhaps be noted that Strangelove's Germanic pronunciation in his use of 'mineshaft' (Ger. *mein schaft* = my shaft or spear, etc.) is a pun carrying obvious sexual connotations.
11 Georges Bataille, *Inner Experience*, 24
12 Ibid., 95
13 Ibid., 26–7
14 For example: H.D. Duncan, *Communication and Social Order*
15 Kenneth Burke, Introduction, *Attitudes toward History*, iii
16 Ibid., 170–1
17 Ibid., 172
18 Mikhail Bakhtin, *Rabelais*, 436, quoting Marx and Engels, *Collected Works*, I:418
19 Burke, *Attitudes*, 173
20 Kenneth Burke, 'The Poetic Motive,' 63
21 Burke, *Attitudes*, 173
22 Ibid., 237
23 Ibid., 171
24 Kenneth Burke, *Counter-Statement*, 215
25 Burke, *Attitudes*, 167
26 Ibid., iii
27 Ibid., 150
28 Kenneth Burke, *Language as Symbolic Action*, 20
29 Wyndham Lewis, 'The Meaning of the Wild Body,' in *The Complete Wild Body*, 158
30 Lewis, *Complete Wild Body*, 151
31 Paul Valéry, *The Outlook for Intelligence*, 81
32 Deleuze and Guattari, *Anti-Oedipus*, 317
33 See chapter 1, pp. 8–9.

10: Tactility and the Intersensory

1 Gregory Bateson, *Steps*, 137
2 Paul Valéry, 'Dance and the Soul,' in *Paul Valéry: An Anthology*, 295–6
3 Ibid., 321
4 W.B. Yeats, *The Collected Poems*, 244–5
5 Ezra Pound, *The ABC of Reading*, 63
6 Kenneth Burke, *The Philosophy of Literary Form*, 9
7 Bateson, *Steps*, 135–6
8 Georges Bataille, *Vision of Excess*, 20–1
9 Ibid., 23
10 George Puttenham, *The Arte of English Poesie*, 154–5, 262
11 Ibid., 196
12 Marshall McLuhan and Quentin Fiore, *The Medium Is the Massage*, 90–1; Marshall McLuhan, *Understanding Media*, 327
13 Gerard Manley Hopkins, 'God's Grandeur' [Poem 31], in *Poems*, 70
14 McLuhan and Fiore, *The Medium Is the Massage*, 90–1

11: Electro-Mechanization and the Global City

1 Richard Ellmann, *Ulysses on the Liffey*, 186–8
2 Since in 1904 Easter was April 3, the action of *Ulysses* takes place in the Octave of the Feast of the Sacred Heart of Jesus, that feast itself being within the Octave of Corpus Christi, so that the action takes place in the extended Corpus Christi season. As I was completing this work, a book had just been announced which will show the relevance of the Octave of the Sacred Heart to the action of *Ulysses*; but it had always been apparent that the action of *Ulysses* has obvious liturgical references to the heart and body of Christ.
3 Raymond Williams, *The Country and the City*, especially 236–47 and 272–88
4 Raymond Williams, *Television: Technology and Cultural Form*, 27
5 Ibid., 26
6 Sergei Eisenstein, *Film Sense*, 98
7 The passage from Eisenstein quoted immediately above continues: Particularly noticeable here is that characteristic pointed out by Guilleré, namely, the absence of perspective.

All sense of perspective and of realistic depth is washed away by a nocturnal sea of electric advertising. Far and near, small (in the *foreground*) and large (in the *background*), soaring aloft and dying away, racing and circling, bursting and vanishing – these lights tend to abolish all sense of real space, finally melting into a single plane of coloured light points and neon lines moving over a surface of black velvet sky. It was thus that people used to picture stars – as glittering nails hammered into the sky!

Headlights on speeding cars, highlights on receding rails, shimmering reflections on the wet pavements – all muddled in puddles that destroy our sense of direction (which is top? which is bottom?), supplementing the mirage above with a mirage beneath us, and rushing between these two worlds of electric signs, we see them no longer as a single place, but as a system of theatre wings, suspended in the air, through which the night flood of traffic lights is streaming. (Ibid., 98–9)

8 James Joyce to Frank Budgen [July 1939], *Letters*, I:406. This passage of the letter is misquoted in Grace Eckley, *Children's Lore in 'Finnegans Wake,'* 183.

9 Cf. T.S. Eliot's early poem 'The Boston Evening Transcript,' in *Collected Poems: 1909–1935*, 32.

10 John Bishop, *Joyce's Book of the Dark*, 274–9. See also Donald F. Theall, 'The Hieroglyphs of Engined Egypsians.'

11 Umberto Eco, *The Role of the Reader*, 46–86. It is interesting to note that Eco's commercially successful novel *The Name of the Rose* (later made into a film) is a reflexive twentieth-century re-creation of the impact of communication and transportation technologies on the later Middle Ages during which the role of the monastic communities in the preservation, development, and dissemination of knowledge bears some resemblance to contemporary functions of information networks, since the library and the scribe were the state of the art for the information storage and retrieval of the medieval world. Eco's interest in the library should be compared with that of Borges.

12 See Joshua Meyrowitz, *No Sense of Place*; and his 'Medium Theory,' in David Crowley and David Mitchell, eds, *Communication Theory Today*, 50–77.

13 Roland McHugh, *Annotations to 'Finnegans Wake,'* 378

14 These come together in Homer and the Greek tradition, the tradition of medieval romance, Chaucer's *Canterbury Tales*, and in the banquet and symposia.

15 'Today with electronics we have discovered we live in a global village, and the job is to create a global *city*, as centre for the village margins. The parameters of this task are by no means positional. With electronics any marginal area can become centre, and marginal experiences can be had at any centre. Perhaps the city needed to coordinate and concert the distracted sense programs of our global village will have to be built by computers in the way in which a big airport has to coordinate multiple flights' (McLuhan, *Letters*, 78).

16 James Joyce to Harriet Shaw Weaver [postcard, 16 April 1927], *Letters* I:251

17 Gilles Deleuze, *Proust*, 91

18 'In the meantime ... I am preparing for it by pulling down more earthwork.

The gangs are now hammering on all sides. It is a bewildering business. I want to do as much as I can before the execution. Complications to the right of me, complications to the left of me, complex on the page before me, perplex in the pen beside me, duplex in the meandering eyes of me, stuplex on the face that reads me. And from time to time I lie back and listen to my hair growing white' (James Joyce to Harriet Shaw Weaver [16 Nov. 1924], *Letters*, 1:222).

19 Roland Barthes, *Critical Essays*, 214

20 Ibid., 216

21 Ibid., 217–18

22 Walter Gropius, *Scope of Total Architecture*, 23

23 Ibid., 24–5

24 Arnold Schönberg, *Style and Idea*, 107

25 Sergei Eisenstein, *Film Form*, 31

26 Henri Foçillon, *Life of Forms in Art*. Foçillon is considered by Herbert Read to be one of the four major contemporary masters of artistic theory.

27 See Douglas Hofstadter, *Gödel, Escher, Bach: An Eternal Golden Braid.*

28 Foçillon, *Life of Forms*, 18

29 Curt Sachs, *The World History of the Dance*, 151 (see 151–5 for the serpentine or labyrinthine dance). See Robert Graves, *The White Goddess*, 89, 269, for the *troia* game. Graves quotes Homer on the subject of the dance and the labyrinth: 'Daedalus in Cnossos once contrived / A dancing-floor for fair-headed Ariadne.'

30 Foçillon, *Life of Forms*, 18

31 Emile Mâle, *L'Art religieux de la fin du Moyen-Age en France*

32 Rhizome-like networks are those that are imposed in closing gaps that break up flows and inscribe the body-without-organs so as to create a labyrinthine structure, using an image that Eco attributes to his net or network: 'a net is an unlimited territory.' See Umberto Eco, *Semiotics and the Philosophy of Language*, 81. It should be noted that Eco (p. 80) points out that the German word for maze is *Irrgärten* or *Irrweg* (cf. Joyce's Earwicker = earwig). Eco also notes the relationship to Deleuze's rhizome (see Gilles Deleuze and Felix Guattari, *A Thousand Plateaus*). Furthermore, the other sense of a maze can well coexist with the notion of a net; in fact, it does so in Gothic and modern modes.

33 Marshall McLuhan, *The Interior Landscape: The Literary Criticism of Marshall McLuhan 1943–1962*, 20. See the discussion of Lewis Carroll in Gilles Deleuze, *Logique du sens*. Esoteric and portmanteau words force the reader to retrace the semiotic series from which Carroll's nonsense arises.

34 Stéphane Mallarmé, *Oeuvres complètes*, 885–1139. Mallarmé's *Les Mots anglais* and *Thèmes anglais* show his detailed professional linguistic interest in

English. The importance of linguistics in Mallarmé's poetic is made abundantly clear in Julia Kristeva, *La Révolution du langage poétique.*

35 Eco, *Semiotics and the Philosophy of Language,* 187. He goes on to point out that 'it is not by chance or by deliberate unfaithfulness that, in the 1960's, so-called post-structuralists simply started from the model of the code and of the linguistic sign to find out, beyond or beneath that rule and the organization, the "whirl," the difference, the *béance.*'

12: Memory

1 Francis Bacon, *The Advancement of Learning,* 83
2 Marvin Minsky, *The Society of Mind,* 89, 153–8
3 Gilles Deleuze and Felix Guattari, *Thousand Plateaus,* 16
4 Umberto Eco, 'Dictionary vs. Encyclopedia,' in *Semiotics and the Philosophy of Language,* 46–56
5 Deleuze and Guatarri, *Thousand Plateaus,* 294
6 Ibid., 298. While Deleuze's theory of memory is suggestive, there are obviously differences between his account and the Viconian conception of memory as imagination. While Deleuze may be right in suggesting all memory systems are arborescent, the operation of memory itself in the act of assembling or constructing of necessity becomes rhizomic as Deleuze's own analysis suggests in assigning becoming the role of *anti-memory.*
7 Robert Henry, 'Horizontally Oriented Rotating Kinetic Painting,' in *Kinetic Art Theory and Practice: Selections from the journal 'Leonardo,'* 12
8 Gyorgy Kepes, *Language of Vision,* 200
9 Eric Havelock, *The Muse Learns to Write,* 111–12. The problems are discussed at length in Eric Havelock, *Preface to Plato,* especially 40–1 and note 17
10 For example, Jacques Derrida, *Of Grammatology,* trans. G.C. Spivak
11 Lorraine Weir, 'The Choreography of Gesture: Marcel Jousse and *Finnegans Wake*'; and *Writing Joyce,* 37–8, 50–6, 73, 85
12 Frances Yates, *The Art of Memory,* 22; quoting Quintilian, XI, ii, 18
13 Ibid., quoting Quintilian, XI, ii, 20
14 Frances Yates's various writings trace in detail the significance of the history of the' art of memory' and its interrelationships with Bruno, alchemy, Rosicrucianism, and the occultisms of the Renaissance. Her writings form a key series of works for an understanding of the later Joyce. Yates was initially interested in the writings of Giordano Bruno, a figure who appears prominently in *Finnegans Wake* and who had fascinated Joyce all his life. Her attempts to understand Bruno led her to study the classical conceptions of the art of memory and their transmission through the Middle Ages to the Renais-

sance. The theory of memory that she develops will be referred to a number of times in this work. The arts of memory were chiefly preserved in the Renaissance by participants in the occult tradition that Yates traced in a series of books, including *The Rosicrucian Enlightenment* and *The Occult Philosophy in the Elizabethan Age*. She sees Bruno's work as intimately linked with alchemy and the occult philosophy. It is apparent that Joyce touches on many of these themes, including Bruno, the arts of memory, and the occult tradition. Bruno's writings have long been recognized as of major importance. See, for example, James Atherton, *Books at the Wake*, 36–7.

15 Leonard Bloomfield, whose seminal book, *Language*, dominated American linguistic theory until the rise of Noam Chomsky, is generally credited with being the 'father of structural linguistics' and therefore of linguistic structuralism. Bloomfield and his followers acknowledged the debt of his work to the seminal lectures of Ferdinand de Saussure in the early twentieth century. Subsequent to the writings of Claude Lévi-Strauss and the rise of structuralism in France, de Saussure, who had called his theory a semiotics, became recognized as the 'father of structuralism.' De Saussure's work was first published in 1915 in Geneva. Joyce finished *Ulysses* and started writing *Finnegans Wake* prior to Bloomfield's initial publication of *Language* (1933). Jonathan Culler in *Structuralist Poetics* discusses the importance of de Saussure's discussions of the sign and semiotics. The point is that structuralist elements in Joyce's work predate the beginnings of de Saussure's impact on structuralism.

Intimations of both linguistic structuralism and the later anthropological structuralism are present in Joyce's work. Linguistic structuralism is implicit in the way he designs his language, which must be read simultaneously by eye and ear. Minimal phonological contrasts are crucially important, as John Bishop has demonstrated, for in creating his language Joyce undertakes a diachronically sensitive reading of the history of phonology. Anthropological structuralism is involved in Joyce's play with kinship and family structure and in his way of building tales within tales to undermine traditional narrative.

16 See R.H. Robins, *Ancient and Medieval Grammatical Theory*; and C.K. Ogden and I.A. Richards, *The Meaning of Meaning*, Appendix D, 'Some Moderns' [C.S. Peirce], 279–90. Originally published in 1923, the eighth edition of *The Meaning of Meaning* incoporates articles published during 1923–46. The publication predated Joyce's writing of *Finnegans Wake*. Joyce, it has been noted, once wished Ogden to write an article on the *Wake*, and Ogden was also involved in the recording of Joyce reading the Anna Livia Plurabelle section of the *Wake*.

17 See Ezra Pound, *Guide to Kulchur*, 73–5, 233–4; and Murray Schaeffer, 'Ezra

Pound and Music.' Schaeffer emphasizes the relation of Pound's notion of a Great Bass to providing a 'basis.'

18 I use 'compunications' here rather then terms like 'infomatics' or 'telematics' to emphasize the marrriage of telecommunications and microprocessors, since it dramatizes the link between communication, electrocommunication, and data and text processing.

19 Yates, *The Art of Memory*, 129–72, 320–68

20 Cf. Joyce's description in *A Portrait of the Artist as a Young Man*, part 4: 'Like a scene on some vague arras, old as man's weariness, the image of the seventh city of christendom was visible to him across the timeless air, no older nor more weary nor less patient of subjection than in the days of the thing-mote' (quoted in Roland McHugh, *Annotations to Finnegans Wake*, 53).

21 It may be of interest that the phrase is taken from the mechanical theosophy of Yeats's *A Vision*, a work which is in part Yeats's philosophy of artistic communication.

22 S.T. Coleridge, *Biographia Literaria*, 202

23 John Bishop, *Joyce's Book of the Dark: Finnegans Wake*, 174–215

24 Paul Watzlawick et al, *The Pragmatics of Human Communication*, 37–42, 76, 82–3, 154–86. Furthermore, Watzlawick uses *Finnegans Wake* In *How Real Is Real.*

25 Gregory Bateson, *Steps to an Ecology of Mind*, 222

26 Ibid., 177ff

27 Ibid., 461–2

28 Ibid., 154

29 Anthony Wilden, *System and Structure: Essays in Communication and Exchange*, 398

30 Bateson, *Steps*, 137

31 Ibid., 145

32 Ibid., 193

33 Deleuze and Guattari, *Thousand Plateaus*, 352–3

34 Bateson, *Steps*, 129

35 Alexander Pope, *Pastoral Poetry and Essay on Criticism*, 257–8

36 Following the theory of Multiple Intelligences as outlined in Howard Gardner, *Frames of Mind.*

13: History of the Poetic

1 Donald F. Theall, 'Traditional Satire in Eliot's *Coriolan*'

2 Norbert Lynton, *Klee*, 42

3 Cf. Gilles Deleuze and Felix Guattari, *A Thousand Plateaus*, 310ff

4 Ibid., 346

5 Stephen Kern, *The Culture of Time and Space 1880–1918*, 302–4, 312
6 John Bishop, *Joyce's Book of the Dark: Finnegans Wake*, 184
7 The root **mei* (change, move, go; with derivatives referring to the exchange of goods and services in society as regulated by custom or law) provides an example, being present in permeate, commute, transmute, common, communication, communism, communion, mutate, remunerate, municipal, migrate, etc., and providing such examples as MUTUOMORPHOMUTATION (FW, 281.R1), mutualiter (247.2), mutuurity (230.14), *mutatis* (508.23), *mutatus* (60.33), Mutantini (238.23), munificent (261.21), communionistically (453.32), communial (600.34), commulion (380.10), and commulium (498.30).
8 Bishop, *Joyce's Book of the Dark*, 210
9 Karl Marx, *Capital: A Critique of Political Economy*, 1:372 n3
10 Antonio Gramsci, *Selections from Cultural Writings*, 364
11 George Puttenham, *The Arte of English Poesie*, 84–108
12 G. Gregory Smith, ed., *Elizabethan Critical Essays*, I:87–134. Spenser's *Preface to the Shepheards Calender* is dedicated to Harvey and continues the discussion of the theme of the standardization of metrics, language, etc.
13 Marshall McLuhan, *The Gutenberg Galaxy*, 259–63
14 Lucien Goldmann, *Le Dieu cache*
15 Charles Williams, *Reason and Beauty in the Poetic Mind*. 45–7, 172
16 Norman Ault, *New Light on Pope*, 222–4
17 Innis discusses the situation among printers and journalists in the eighteenth century in *Changing Concepts of Time*.
18 Martinus Scriblerus, ΠΕΡΙ ΒΑΘΟΥΣ: *or, Of the Art of Sinking in Poetry*, in Alexander Pope, *Selected Poetry and Prose*, 354
19 Pope, *Selected Poetry and Prose*, 349–50
20 Pope, *The Dunciad*, 49
21 References are to the Twickenham edition of *The Dunciad*, cited above.
22 McLuhan, *The Gutenberg Galaxy*, 261
23 Paul Heyer, *Communications and History*, 14, 35; and Jacques Derrida, *Of Grammatology*, 75–81
24 When to the sessions of sweet silent thought
I summon up remembrance of things past,
I sigh the lack of many a thing I sought
And with old woes new wail my dear time's waste. (Sonnet 30)
25 E.H. Gombrich, *Art and Illusion*, 242–59
26 Frances Yates, *The Art of Memory*, 95
27 Mikhail Bakhtin, *Rabelais and His World*, 34
28 For further discussion, see Donald F. Theall, 'James Joyce: Literary Engineer'; and Donald F. Theall, 'The Hieroglyphs of Engined Egypsians: Machines, Media and Modes of Communication in *Finnegans Wake*,' 129–52.

14: High Decibel Dialogue of the Electronic Fairground

1 For example: 'Childs will be wilds. 'Twastold. And vamp, vamp, vamp, the girls are merchand' (246.21–3). A whole group of such references between 232.27–36 and 233.1–4 are associated with the role of the wireless in the sinking of the *Titanic*: 'Now a dash to her dot! Old cocker, young crowy, sifadda, sosson. A bran new, speedhount, outstripperous on the wind. Like a waft to wingweary one or a sos to a coastguard. For ... in appreciable less time than it takes a glaciator to submerger an Atlangthis, was he again, agob, before the trembly ones, a spark's gap off, doubledasguesched ... The smartest vessel you could find ... '

2 Marshall McLuhan, *Understanding Media*, 53

3 Ibid., 241

4 See Garry Leonard and Jennifer Wicke, guest editors, special issue on 'Joyce and Advertising,' *James Joyce Quarterly*, 30.4 (Summer 1993) and 31.1 (Fall 1993).

5 Wyndham Lewis, *Time and Western Man*, 91–130. The tendency of Joyce's analysis was grasped earlier by Lewis, who in *Time and Western Man* (before Joyce's *Work in Progress* had really started appearing) turned his critique of the time sense in modern philosophy, culture, and society toward, such phenomena as the Chaplinesque movie, the popular novel (like *Gentlemen Prefer Blondes*, by Anita Loos), and the length of women's skirts, interrelating these phenomena with contemporary music, the Bolshoi Ballet, and the writings of Joyce, Gertrude Stein, and Henri Bergson. It could be argued that, like some of Walter Benjamin's even more sensitive works, this was an anticipation of much of the work of McLuhan and of many recent semioticians, especially Roland Barthes; though, naturally, Lewis and Benjamin lack the systematization that has been introduced by the semiotic and structuralist movements.

6 Lucy Lippard, *Pop Art*, 13–20. The roots and history of 'Pop' are a complex and controversial subject, as Lippard's history clearly demonstrates.

7 Gilles Deleuze and Felix Guattari, *Anti-Oedipus*, 51–68

8 Dušan Makavéjev, *WR: Mysteries of the Organism*, 16

9 Dušan Makavéjev, *Sweet Movie*, [original screen play], xv

10 Ibid., vii

11 Makavéjev, *WR*, 17–18

12 Jean-Luc Godard, *Godard on Godard*, 242

13 Makavéjev, *WR*, 21–2

14 Dušan Makavéjev, *Sweet Movie: Un film de Dušan Makavéjev*, [9]

15 Makavéjev, *Sweet Movie: Un film*, [20]

16 Makavéjev, *Sweet Movie* [the movie]

17 Makavéjev, *Sweet Movie* [original screen play], 47

15: The Ambivalence of the Poetic as Critique

1 Darko Suvin, *Metamorphoses of Science Fiction: On the Poetics and History of a Literary Genre*
2 Stephen Kern, *The Culture of Time and Space 1880–1918*, 212–13
3 Ibid., 69, 333n18
4 Suvin, *Metamorphoses of Science Fiction*, 149
5 William Gibson, *Neuromancer*, 51
6 Ibid., 55
7 Ibid., 105
8 William Gibson, *Mona Lisa Overdrive*, 48–9
9 Kevin Kelly, 'Cyberpunk Era,' 84–5
10 Ibid., 81
11 Gibson, *Mona Lisa Overdrive*, 49
12 Kelly ('Cyberpunk Era,' 78) credits Timothy Leary with the phrase.
13 Gibson, *Mona Lisa*, 16
14 Stanislaw Lem, *Futurological Congress*, 72
15 Ibid., 105–6
16 Ibid., 108
17 Ibid.
18 Federico Fellini, *Juliet of the Spirits*, 50
19 Federico Fellini, *Fellini on Fellini*, 54
20 Ibid., 123–4
21 Ibid., 54
22 Ibid., 153–4
23 Curt Sachs, *World History of the Dance*, 55
24 Gregory Bateson, *Steps*, 137
25 Christian Metz, *Film Language: A Semiotics of the Cinema*, 230
26 It might be noted that Joyce described the dance pattern of the *Wake* as 'the scheme is like your rumba round me garden' (309.7).
27 Federico Fellini, *Essays in Criticism*, 14
28 Fellini, *Fellini on Fellini*, 165
29 Ibid., 125
30 Ibid., 98
31 Ibid., 119

16: Conclusion

1 For example, Michael Phillipson, *In Modernity's Wake*; Gilles Deleuze, *Proust*

and Signs; Derek Attridge and Daniel Ferrer, eds, *Post-structuralist Joyce*.

2 Marvin Minsky, *The Society of Mind*, 247

3 In fact, according to the outline he gave Linati, his last four episodes focus on the following parts of the body: skeletal structure, nerves, juices, and fat.

4 Phillipson, *In Modernity's Wake*, 99

5 Georges Bataille, *Inner Experience*, 10–12

6 The youthful Joyce stressed this fact in his interpretation of Aristotle, as previously discussed; but also in the *Physics* Aristotle asserts that art imitates nature in its operation. Admittedly, there is an ambivalence in his treatment of *mimesis*, but the strong stress on reproduction and reflection – in the sense of a mirror – comes from Aristotle's interpreters rather than from Aristotle himself.

7 John O'Neill, *Making Sense Together: An Introduction to Wild Sociology*, 23

8 Friedrich Nietzsche, *The Will to Power*, 427–8 (809)

9 Ibid., 428 (809)

10 Ibid.

11 Gilles Deleuze and Claire Parnet, *Dialogues*, 60–2

12 'Where did thots come from? It is infinitesimally fevers, resty fever, risy fever, a coranto of aria, sleeper awakening, in the smalls of one's back presentiment, gip, and again, geip, a flash from a future of maybe mahamayability through the windr of a wondr in a wildr is a weltr as a wirbl of a warbl is a world' (*FW*, 597.25–9).

13 Frances Yates, *The Art of Memory*, 191–2

14 A comic foil that enunciated a popularized rendition of the problem is provided by J.W. Dunne, *Experiment with Time*.

15 Walter Benjamin, 'Theses on the Philosophy of History,' in *Illuminations*, 257

16 John Fekete, *The Critical Twilight*, 225

17 Ibid.

18 Aristotle, *Politics*, ed. Franz Susemihl and R.D. Hichs, 647–8. In the *Sophist* Plato uses catharsis in an educational context where it involves the purging of ignorance, that is, the separation of truth from error. Susemihl argues that his is distinct from Aristotle's medically based idea of purgation. But there is a way in which the physical purging of the body and the act of separating the wanted from the unwanted can be co-present in the same concept.

19 Kenneth Burke, *Language as Symbolic Action*, 345–9

20 W.B. Yeats, 'Crazy Jane and the Bishop,' in *Collected Poems*

21 See Deleuze and Parnet, *Dialogues*, 59–62; and Gilles Deleuze, *Spinoza*, 86–92.

Bibliography

Adorno, Theodor. *Aesthetic Theory*. Ed. Gretel Adorno and Rolf Tiedemann. Trans. C. Lehnhardt. London: Routledge and Kegan Paul 1984

Aristotle. *Aristotle's Theory of Poetry and Fine Art*. Trans. S.H. Butcher. 4th ed. New York: Dover Publications 1951

– *Basic Works*. Ed. Richard McKeon. New York: Random House 1941

– *On Poetry and Style*. Trans. G.M.A. Grube. Library of Liberal Arts. New York: Bobbs-Merrill 1958

– *Politics*. Ed. Franz Susemihl and R.D. Hichs. London: Macmillan 1894

Atherton, James S. *The Books at the Wake: A Study of Literary Allusions in 'Finnegans Wake.'* London: Faber and Faber 1959

Attridge, Derek, and Daniel Ferrer, eds. *Post-Structuralist Joyce: Essays from the French*. London: Cambridge University Press 1984

Ault, Norman. *New Light on Pope*. London: Methuen 1949

Bacon, Francis. *The Advancement of Learning*. London: J.M. Dent and Sons 1950

– 'Wisdom of the Ancients.' In *The Essays, or Counsels Civil and Moral of Francis Bacon*. N.p.: Homewood Publishing Co. [1883]

Bakhtin, Mikhail. *The Dialogic Imagination*. Ed. Michael Holquist. Trans. Caryl Emerson and Michael Holquist. Vol. 1 of University of Texas Press Slavic Series. Austin: University of Texas Press 1981

– *Rabelais and His World*. Trans. Helene Iswolsky. Cambridge, Mass.: MIT Press 1968

Barthes, Roland. *Critical Essays*. Trans. Richard Howard. Evanston, Ill.: Northwestern University Press 1972

– *The Eiffel Tower: And Other Mythologies*. Trans. Richard Howard. New York: Hill and Wang 1979

– *Mythologies*. Trans. Annette Lavers. Frogmore, St Albans, Herts: Paladin 1973

– *The Semiotic Challenge*. Trans. Richard Howard. New York: Hill and Wang 1988

Bataille, Georges. *Documents*. In *Oeuvres complètes*. Paris: Gallimard 1970
– *L'Erotisme: Death and Sensuality*. Trans. Mary Dalwod. San Francisco: City Lights Books 1986
– *Histoire de l'oeil*. Paris: J.J. Pauvert 1967
– *Inner Experience*. Trans. Leslie Anne Boldt. SUNY Intersections Series: Philosophy and Critical Theory. Albany: State University of New York Press 1988
– *Visions of Excess: Selected Writings 1927–1939*. Ed. Alan Stoekl. Trans. Alan Stoekl, Carl R. Lovitt, and Donald M. Leslie, Jr. Theory and History of Literature Series, vol. 14. Minneapolis: University of Minnesota Press 1985
Bateson, Gregory. *Steps to an Ecology of Mind*. New York: Ballantine 1972
Baudrillard, Jean. *The Ecstasy of Communication*. Ed. Sylvere Lorringer. Trans. Bernard Schutze and Caroline Schutze. Semiotexte Foreign Agents Series. New York: Columbia University Press 1988
Bazin, André. 'The Originality of Welles as a Director.' In *Focus on Citizen Kane*. Ed. Ronald Gottesman. Englewood Cliffs, N.J.: Prentice-Hall 1971
– *Orson Welles*. Trans. Jonathan Rosenbaum. New York: Harper and Row 1978
Benedikt, Michael, ed. *Cyberspace: First Steps*. Cambridge, Mass.: MIT Press 1992
Benjamin, Walter. *Charles Baudelaire: A Lyric Poet in the Era of High Capitalism*. Trans. Harry Zohn. London: NLB 1973
– *Illuminations*. Ed. Hannah Arendt. Trans. Harry Zohn. New York: Harcourt Brace and World 1968
– *Understanding Brecht*. Trans. Anna Bostock. London: NLB 1973
Bergson, Henri. *Laughter: An Essay on the Meaning of the Comic*. New York: Macmillan 1911
Berman, Morris. *The Re-enchantment of the World*. Toronto: Bantam 1984
Bishop, John. *Joyce's Book of the Dark: 'Finnegans Wake.'* Madison: University of Wisconsin Press 1986
Borges, Jorge Luis. *Other Inquisitions, 1937–1952*. Trans. Ruth L.C. Simms. 1964; rpt, New York: Simon and Schuster 1968
Brand, Stewart. *The Media Lab*. New York: Viking 1987
Brooks, Cleanth, and W.K. Wimsatt, Jr. *Literary Criticism: A Short History*. New York: Knopf 1957
Budgen, Frank. *James Joyce and the Making of 'Ulysses.'* Bloomington: Indiana University Press 1960
Bullock, Alan, et al., eds. *The Fontana Dictionary of Modern Thought*. London: Fontana 1977
Burke, Kenneth. *Attitudes toward History*. 1937; rev. 2d ed., 1959; rpt, New York: Hermes 1961

– *Counter-Statement*. New York: Harcourt Brace 1931
– *A Grammar of Motives and a Rhetoric of Motives*. Cleveland: World Publishing Co. 1962
– *Language as Symbolic Action: Essays on Life, Literature, and Method*. Berkeley: University of California Press 1968
– *Permanence and Change: An Anatomy of Purpose*. Indianapolis: Bobb-Merrill Co. 1965
– *The Philosophy of Literary Form: Studies in Symbolic Action*. New York: Vintage 1957
– 'The Poetic Motive.' *Hudson Review* 2 (1958–9), 54–63
Carey, James. *Communication as Culture: Essays on Media and Society*. Boston: Unwin Hyman 1989
Carroll, Lewis. *Norton Critical Edition of Alice in Wonderland*. Ed. Donald J. Gray. New York: W.W. Norton 1971
[Cicero?] *Ad Herennium de Ratione Dicendi (Rhetorica ad Herennium)*. Vol. 1. Trans. Harry Caplan. Loeb Classical Library. 1954; rpt, Cambridge, Mass.: Harvard University Press 1977
Clark, Kenneth. *The Nude: A Study in Ideal Form*. Garden City, NY: Doubleday 1959
Colerdige, Samuel Taylor. *Biographia Literaria*. Ed. J. Shawcross. Oxford Standard Authors. London: Oxford University Press 1907
Crowley, David, and David Mitchell, eds. *Communication Theory Today*. Stanford: Stanford University Press 1994
de Grazia, Edward. *Girls Lean Back Everywhere: The Law of Obscenity and the Assault on Genius*. New York: Random House 1992
Deleuze, Gilles. *Foucault*. Ed. and trans. Sean Hand. Minneapolis: University of Minnesota Press 1988
– *The Logic of Sense*. Ed. Constantin V. Boundas. Trans. Mark Lester. New York: Columbia University Press 1990
– *Logique du sens*. Paris: Éditions de Minuit 1969
– *Proust and Signs*. Trans. Richard Howard. New York: George Braziller 1972
– *Spinoza: Practical Philosophy*. Trans. Robert Hurley. San Francisco: City Lights Books 1988
Deleuze, Gilles, and Felix Guattari. *A Thousand Plateaus: Capitalism and Schizophrenia*. Trans. and Foreword, Brian Massumi. Minneapolis: University of Minnesota Press 1987
– *Anti-Oedipus: Capitalism and Schizophrenia*. Trans. Robert Hurley, Mark Seem, and Helen R. Lane. New York: Viking 1977
Deleuze, Gilles, and Claire Parnet. *Dialogues*. Trans. Hugh Tomlinson and Barbara Habberjam. New York: Columbia University Press 1987

Denney, Reuel. *The Astonished Muse*. Introd. David Riesman. New York: Grosset and Dunlap 1964
Derrida, Jacques. *Of Grammatology*. Trans. Gayatri Chakravorty Spivak. Baltimore: Johns Hopkins University Press 1976
Dewey, John. *Art as Experience*. New York: G.P. Putnam 1958
– *Democracy and Education*. New York: Free Press 1966
– *Experience and Nature*. New York: Dover 1958
Duncan, H.D. *Communication and Social Order*. London: Oxford University Press 1962
Dunne, J.W. *Experiment with Time*. 5th rev. ed., 1927; rpt, London: Faber and Faber 1938
Eckley, Grace. *Children's Lore in 'Finnegans Wake.'* Syracuse: Syracuse University Press 1985
Eco, Umberto. *The Open Work*. Trans. Anna Cancogni. Cambridge, Mass.: Harvard University Press 1989
– *The Role of the Reader*. Bloomington: Indiana University Press 1984
– *Semiotics and the Philosophy of Language*. Bloomington: Indiana University Press 1984
– *A Theory of Semiotics*. Bloomington: Indiana University Press 1976
– *Travels In Hyper-Reality*. Trans. William Weaver. New York: Harcourt Brace Jovanovich 1986
Eisenstein, Elizabeth. *The Printing Press as an Agent of Change*. Cambridge: Cambridge University Press 1979
Eisenstein, Sergei. *Film Form*. Ed. and trans. Jay Leyda. New York: Harcourt Brace 1949
– *Film Sense*. Ed. and trans. Jay Leyda. New York: Harcourt Brace 1947
Eliot, T.S. *Collected Poems: 1909–1935*. New York: Harcourt, Brace 1936
– 'Lettre d'Angleterre.' *Nouvelle Revue Française* (1923)
– *Selected Essays*. New York: Harcourt, Brace 1932
– 'A Talk on Dante.' In *Selected Prose*. Ed. John Hayward. Harmondsworth: Penguin 1953
– 'Ulysses: Order and Myth.' *Dial* (Nov 1923). Reprinted in *Criticism: The Foundations of Modern Literary Judgment*. Ed. Mark Schorer et al. New York: Harcourt, Brace 1948, 269–71
Ellmann, Richard. *James Joyce*. Rev. ed. Oxford: Oxford University Press 1982
– *Ulysses on the Liffey*. New York: Oxford University Press 1973
Ellmann, Richard, and Charles Feidelson. *The Modern Tradition*. New York: Oxford University Press 1965
Erasmus, Desiderius. *The Praise of Folly*. Trans. H.H. Hudson. Princeton: Princeton University Press 1941

Fekete, John. *The Critical Twilight*. London: Routledge and Kegan Paul 1977

Fellini, Federico. *Essays in Criticism*. Ed. Peter Bordanella. New York: Oxford University Press 1978

– *Fellini on Fellini*. Trans. Isabel Quigley. N.p.: Delacorte Press/ Seymour Lawrence 1976

– *Juliet of the Spirits*. Ed. Tullio Kezich. Trans. Howard Greenfeld. New York: Ballentine Books 1966

Foçillon, Henri. *Life of Forms in Art*. 2d ed. Ed. and trans. Charles Beecher Hogan, George Kubler, and S.E. Laison, Jr. New York: Wittenborn, Schultz 1948

Foucault, Michel. *The Order of Things: An Archeology of the Human Sciences*. New York: Vintage Books 1973

Freud, Sigmund. *The Basic Writings*. Ed. and trans. A.A. Brill. New York: Random House 1938

Gardner, Howard. *Frames of Mind: The Theory of Multiple Intelligences*. New York: Basic Books 1983

Gibson, William. *Mona Lisa Overdrive*. New York: Bantam 1988

– *Neuromancer*. New York: Ace 1984

Giddens, Anthony. *The Constitution of Society: Outline of the Theory of Structuration*. Berkeley: University of California Press 1984

Giedion, Siegfried. *The Eternal Present: The Beginnings of Art*. Bollingen Series 35.6.1. New York: Pantheon 1962

Givens, Sean, ed. *James Joyce: Two Decades of Criticism*. New York: Vanguard 1948

Godard, Jean-Luc. *Godard on Godard*. Ed. and trans. Tom Milne. London: Secker and Warburg 1972

Goffman, Erving. *The Presentation of Self in Everyday Life*. Garden City, NY: Doubleday 1959

Goldmann, Lucien. *Le Dieu caché*. Paris: Gallimard 1959

Gombrich, E.H. *Art and Illusion: A Study in the Psychology of Pictorial Representation*. Bollingen Series 35.5 New York: Pantheon 1960

Goody, Jack. *The Logic of Writing and the Organization of Society*. Cambridge: Cambridge University Press 1986

Gottesman, Ronald, ed. *Focus on Citizen Kane*. Englewood Cliffs, NJ: Prentice Hall 1971

Gramsci, Antonio. *Selections from Cultural Writings*. Ed. David Forgacs and Geoffrey Nowell-Smith. Trans. William Boelhower. Cambridge, Mass.: Harvard University Press 1985

Graves, Robert. *The White Goddess: A Historical Grammar of Poetic Myth*. New York: Creative Age Press 1948

Gropius, Walter. *Scope of Total Architecture*. New York: Collier 1962

Habermas, Jürgen. *Lifeworld and System: A Critique of Functionalist Reason*. Vol. 2 of *The Theory of Communicative Action*. Trans. Thomas McCarthy. Boston: Beacon 1987

– *The Philosophical Discourse of Modernity*. Trans. Frederick Lawrence. Cambridge, Mass.: MIT Press 1987

– *Reason and the Rationalization of Society*. Vol. 1 of *The Theory of Communicative Action*. Trans. Thomas McCarthy. Boston: Beacon 1984

Havelock, Eric. *The Muse Learns to Write*. New Haven: Yale University Press 1986

– *Preface to Plato*. Cambridge, Mass.: Harvard University Press 1963

Hayman, David. *Ulysses: The Mechanics of Meaning*. Englewood Cliffs, NJ: Prentice Hall 1970

Henry, Robert. 'Horizontally Oriented Rotating Kinetic Painting.' In *Kinetic Art: Theory and Practice: Selections from the Journal 'Leonardo.'* Ed. Frank J. Malina. New York: Dover 1974, 11–22. Originally published in *Leonardo* 2 (Summer 1969), 239–50

Heyer, Paul. *Communications and History: Theories of Media, Knowledge and Civilization*. New York: Greenwood Press 1988

Hofstadter, Douglas. *Gödel, Escher, Bach: An Eternal Golden Braid*. New York: Basic Books 1979

Hopkins, Gerard Manley. *Poems*. Ed. W.H. Gardner. New York: Oxford University Press 1948

Horn, Maurice, ed. *The World Encyclopedia of Comics*. New York: Chelsea House 1976

Hymes, Dell H. 'The Contribution of Poetics to Sociolinguistic Research.' Review of *Language as Symbolic Action*, by Kenneth Burke. In *Foundations in Sociolinguistics: An Ethnographic Approach*. London: Tavistock Publications 1977, 135–41. Originally published in *Language* 44.3 (1968), 664–9

Innis, Harold. *Changing Concepts of Time*. Toronto: University of Toronto Press 1952

– *The Idea File*. Ed. William Christian. Toronto: University of Toronto Press 1980

Jakobson, Roman. 'Closing Statement: Linguistics and Poetics.' In *Style and Language*. Ed. Thomas Sebeok. New York: John Wiley and Sons 1960, 360–77

Jolas, Eugene. 'My Friend James Joyce.' In *James Joyce: Two Decades of Criticism*. Ed. Seon Givens. New York: Vanguard 1948, 3–18. Originally published in *Partisan Review* (March-April 1941)

Joyce, James. *The Critical Writings*. Ed. Ellsworth Mason and Richard Ellmann. New York: Viking 1959

– *Finnegans Wake*. 1939; rpt, New York: Viking 1960

– *Letters*. Vol. 1. Ed. Stuart Gilbert. New York: Viking 1957

– *Stephen Hero*. Ed. Theodore Spence, John J. Slocum, and Herbert Cahoon. New York: New Directions 1955

– *Ulysses: A Critical and Synoptic Edition*. Ed. Hans Walter Gabler et al. 3 vols. New York: Garland Publishing 1986

Kelly, Kevin. 'Cyberpunk Era.' *Whole Earth Catalogue* 63 (Summer 1989)

Kepes, Gyorgy. *Language of Vision*. Chicago: Paul Theobald 1951

Kern, Stephen. *The Culture of Time and Space 1880–1918*. Cambridge, Mass.: Harvard University Press 1983

Kracauer, Sigfried. *From Caligari to Hitler: A Psychological History of German Film*. Princeton: Princeton University Press 1947

Krauss, Rosalind E. *The Originality of the Avant-Garde and Other Modernist Myths*. Cambridge, Mass.: MIT Press 1986

Kristeva, Julia. *La Révolution du langage poétique*. Paris: Editions du Seuil 1974

Lem, Stanislaw. *The Cyberiad: Fables for the Cybernetic Age*. Trans. Michael Kandel. New York: Seabury Press 1974

– *The Futurological Congress*. Trans. Michael Kandel 1974; rpt, New York: Avon Books 1976

Leonard, Garry, and Jennifer Wicke, eds. Special issue on 'Joyce and Advertising.' *James Joyce Quarterly* 30.4 (Summer 1993) and 31.1 (Fall 1993)

Lewis, Wyndham. *Childermas*. 1928; rpt, London: Jupiter Books / John Calder 1965

– *The Complete Wild Body*. Ed. Bernard Lafourcade. Santa Barbara, Calif.: Black Sparrow Press 1982

– *Men without Art*. Ed. Seamus Cooney. Santa Rosa, Calif.: Black Sparrow Press 1987

– *Time and Western Man*. London: Chatto and Windus 1927

Lippard, Lucy. *Pop Art*. New York: Praeger 1966

Lowry, Malcolm. *Selected Letters*. Ed. Harvey Breit and Margerie Bonner Lowry. New York: J.B. Lippincott 1965

Lynton, Norbert. *Klee*. London: Spring Books 1964

Macdougall, Alan Ross. *Isadora: A Revolutionary in Art and Love*. New York: Thomas Nelson 1970

Makavéjev, Dušan. Sweet Movie: *Un film de Dušan Makavéjev*. N.p.: Vincent Malle, n.d. [1974]

– *WR: Mysteries of the Organism*. New York: Avon 1972

Makavéjev, Dušan, and Martin Melina. *Sweet Movie*. From an original screenplay. Paris: V.M. Productions [1974]

Mâle, Emile. *L'Art religieux de la fin du Moyen-Age en France*. Paris 1922

Malina, Frank, ed. *Kinetic Art: Theory and Practice*. New York: Dover 1974

Mallarmé, Stéphane. *Oeuvres complètes*. Ed. Henri Mondor and G. Jean Aubray. Bibiliotheque de la Pleiade, vol. 65. Paris: NRF 1945

Marcuse, Herbert. *The Aesthetic Dimension: Toward a Critique of Marxist Aesthetics*. Trans. Herbert Marcuse and Erica Sherover. Boston: Beacon 1978

– *Eros and Civilization*. New York: Random House 1955

Marvin, Carolyn. *When Old Technologies Were New: Thinking about Electric Communication in the Late Nineteenth Century*. New York: Oxford University Press 1988

Marx, Karl. *Capital: A Critique of Political Economy*. Ed. Frederick Engels. Trans. Samuel Moore and Edward Aveling. New York: International Publishers 1967

– *The Economic and Philosophic Manuscripts*. New York: International Publishers 1964

McHugh, Roland. *Annotations to 'Finnegans Wake.'* Baltimore: Johns Hopkins University Press 1980

McLuhan, Marshall. *The Gutenberg Galaxy*. Toronto: University of Toronto Press 1962

– *The Interior Landscape: The Literary Criticism of Marshall McLuhan 1943–1962*. Ed. Eugene McNamara. New York: McGraw-Hill 1969

– *The Letters of Marshall McLuhan*. Ed. Matie Molinaro, Corinne McLuhan, and William Toye. Toronto: Oxford University Press 1987

– *The Mechanical Bride: Folklore of Industrial Man*. Boston: Beacon 1967

– *Understanding Media: The Extensions of Man*. New York: McGraw-Hill 1964

McLuhan, Marshall, and Quentin Fiore. *The Medium Is the Massage*. New York: Random House 1967

McLuhan, Marshall, and Eric McLuhan. *Laws of Media: The New Science*. Toronto: University of Toronto Press 1988

McLuhan, Marshall, and Harley Parker. *Through the Vanishing Point: Space in Poetry and Painting*. New York: Harper and Row 1968

McLuhan, Marshall, and Wilfred Watson. *From Cliché to Archetype*. New York: Viking 1970

Metz, Christian. *Film Language: A Semiotics of the Cinema*. New York: Oxford University Press 1974

Meyer, Leonard B. *Emotion and Meaning in Music*. Chicago: University of Chicago Press 1956

Meyrowitz, Joshua. *No Sense of Place*. New York: Oxford University Press 1985

Minsky, Marvin. *The Society of Mind*. New York: Simon and Schuster 1986

Mitchell, Donald. *The Language of Modern Music*. London: Faber and Faber 1963

Moholy-Nagy, Laszlo. *Vision in Motion*. New York: Paul Theobald 1947

Negal, E., and J.R. Newman. *Gödel's Proof*. New York: New York University Press 1960

Nietzsche, Friedrich. *The Portable Nietzsche*. Ed. and trans. Walter Kaufmann. Viking Portable. New York: Viking 1982

– *The Will to Power*. Trans. Walter Kaufman and R.J. Hollingdale. New York: Random House 1967

O'Neill, John. *Five Bodies: The Human Shape of Modern Society*. Ithaca, NY: Cornell University Press 1985

– *Making Sense Together: An Introduction to Wild Sociology*. New York: Harper and Row 1974

Ogden, C.K., and I.A. Richards. *The Meaning of Meaning: A Study of The Influence of Language upon Thought and of The Science of Symbolism*. 8th ed. New York: Harcourt Brace 1947

Ong, Walter. *Orality and Literacy: The Technologizing of the Word*. London: Methuen 1982

– 'Wit and Mystery: A Revaluation in Medieval Hymnody.' *Speculum* 22 (1947), 307–27

Ovid. *Metamorphoses*. Trans. Frank Justus Miller. 2 vols. Loeb Classical Library. New York: G.P. Putnam's Sons 1916

Ozenfant, [Amédée]. *Foundations of Modern Art*. Trans John Rodker. Rev. ed. New York: Dover 1952

Parry , Milman. *The Making of Homeric Verse*. Ed. and trans. A.M. Parry. Oxford: Clarendon Press 1971

Patterson, Graeme. *History and Communications: Harold Innis, Marshall McLuhan, the Interpretation of History*. Toronto: University of Toronto Press 1990

Perry, George, and Alan Aldridge. *The Penguin Book of Comics*. London: Penguin 1971

Perry, Ted. *Filmguide to '8½.'* Bloomington: Indiana University Press 1975

Phillipson, Michael. *In Modernity's Wake: The Ameurunculus Letters*. New York: Routledge 1989

Poe, Edgar Allan. 'The Philosophy of Composition.' In *The Complete Works of Edgar Allan Poe*. New York: Ams Press 1965

Pope, Alexander. *The Dunciad*. Ed. James Sutherland. Twickenham edition, Vol 5. London: Methuen 1953

– *Pastoral Poetry and Essay on Criticism*. Ed. E. Audra and Aubrey Williams. Twickenham edition, vol. 1. London: Methuen 1961

– *Selected Poetry and Prose*. Ed. W.K. Wimsatt, Jr. New York: Holt, Rinehart 1961

Pound, Ezra. *The ABC of Reading*. Norfolk, Conn.: New Directions n.d.

– *Ernest Fenollosa: The Chinese Written Character as a Medium for Poetry with the Offset Edition of the Pivot*. Washington, D.C.: Square $ Series, n.d. [1951]

– *Guide to Kulchur*. London: Faber and Faber 1938

– *The Literary Essays of Ezra Pound*. Ed. T.S. Eliot. London: Faber and Faber 1954

Puttenham, George. *The Arte of English Poesie*. Ed. Gladys Doidge Willcock and Alice Walker. 1589; rpt, London: Cambridge University Press 1936
Quintilian. *Institutio Oratoria*. Trans. H.E. Butler. Loeb Classical Library. 4 vols. 1921–2; rpt, Cambridge, Mass.: Harvard University Press 1953
Rabelais, François. *The Histories of Gargantua and Pantagruel*. Trans. J.M. Cohen. Montreal: Penguin 1955
Ricoeur, Paul. *The Conflict of Interpretations: Essays in Hermeneutics*. Ed. Don Ihde. Evanston, Ill.: Northwestern University Press 1974
– 'The Model of the Text: Meaningful Action Considered as a Text.' *Social Research* 38.3 (Autumn 1971), 529–62
Robins, R.H. *Ancient and Medieval Grammatical Theory*. London: Bell & Sons 1951
Ruesch, Jürgen, and Gregory Bateson. *Communication: The Social Matrix of Psychiatry*. New York: Norton 1951
Sachs, Curt. *The World History of the Dance*. Trans. Bessie Schonberg. New York: W.W. Norton 1963
Schaeffer, Murray. 'Ezra Pound and Music.' *Canadian Music Journal* 5 (Summer 1961), 15–43
Schönberg, Arnold. *Style and Idea*. London 1951
Sebeok, Thomas, ed. *Style in Language*. New York: John Wiley and Sons 1960
Seldes, Gilbert. *The Seven Lively Arts*. New York: The Sagamore Press 1957
Smith, G. Gregory, ed. *Elizabethan Critical Essays*. 2 vols. 1904; rpt, New York: Oxford University Press 1959
Stallybrass, Peter, and Allon White. *The Politics and Poetics of Transgression*. Ithaca, NY: Cornell University Press 1986
Stein, Gertrude. *Picasso*. New York: Scribners Sons 1939
Suvin, Darko. *Metamorphoses of Science Fiction: On the Poetics and History of a Literary Genre*. New Haven: Yale University Press 1979
Theall, Donald F. 'Beyond the Orality/Literary Dichotomy: James Joyce and the Pre-History of Cyberspace.' *Post Modern Culture* 23 (May 1992) [an electronic journal; available by gopher: //jefferson.village.virgina.EDU/O/pubs/pmc/issue.592/theall.592]
– 'Exploration in Communications since Innis.' In *Culture, Communication and Dependency: The Tradition of H.A. Innis*. Ed. William H. Melody, Liora R. Salter, and Paul Heyer. Norwood, NJ: Ablex Publishing Corp 1981, 225–34
– 'The Hieroglyphs of Engined Egypsians: Machines, Media and Modes of Communication in *Finnegans Wake*.' In *Joyce Studies Annual 1991*. Ed. Thomas F. Staley. Austin: University of Texas Press 1991, 129–76
– 'James Joyce: Literary Engineer.' In *Literature and Ethics: Essays Presented to*

A.E. Malloch. Ed. Gary Wihl and David Williams. Kingston and Montreal: McGill-Queen's University Press 1988, 11–26

– *The Medium Is the Rear View Mirror: Understanding McLuhan*. Montreal: McGill-Queen's University Press 1971

– 'Traditional Satire in Eliot's *Coriolan*.' *Accent* 11 (Autumn 1951), 194–206

Theall, Donald, and Joan Theall. 'Marshall McLuhan and James Joyce: Beyond Media.' *Canadian Journal of Communication* 14.4–5 (Dec. 1989), 46–66

Toulmin, Stephen. *The Return to Cosmology: Postmodern Science and the Theology of Nature*. Berkeley: University of California Press 1982

Valéry, Paul. *The Outlook for Intelligence*. Trans. Denise Folliot and Jackson Matthews. Bollingen Library / Harper Torchbooks. New York: Harper 1962

– *Paul Valéry: An Anthology*. Ed. and introd. James R. Lawler. Bollingen Series 45. Princeton: Princeton University Press 1977

Vico, Giambattista. *The New Science of ...* Trans. T.G. Bergin and M.H. Fisch. Ithaca, NY: Cornell University Press 1948

Watzlawick, Paul. *How Real Is Real? Confusion, Disinformation, Communication*. New York: Random House 1976

– et al. *The Pragmatics of Human Communication: A Study of Interactional Patterns, Pathologies and Paradoxes*. New York: Norton 1967

Weir, Lorraine. 'The Choreography of Gesture: Marcel Jousse and *Finnegans Wake*.' *James Joyce Quarterly* 14.3 (Spring 1977), 313–25

– *Writing Joyce: A Semiotics of the Joyce System*. Bloomington: Indiana University Press 1989

Wiener, Norbert. *Cybernetics: Or Control and Communication in the Animal and the Machine*. 1948; rpt, Cambridge, Mass.: MIT Press 1961

Wilden, Anthony. *System and Structure: Essays in Communication and Exchange*. London: Tavistock 1972

Williams, Aubrey. *Pope's 'Dunciad.'* London: Methuen 1955

Williams, Charles. *Reason and Beauty in the Poetic Mind*. Oxford: Oxford University Press 1933

Williams, Raymond. *The Country and the City*. Oxford: Oxford University Press 1973

– *Keywords: A Vocabulary of Culture and Society*. London: Fontana (Flamingo Paperback) 1983

– *Television: Technology and Cultural Form*. London: Fontana/Collins 1974

Williams, Trevor. *History of Invention*. New York: Facts on File 1987

Williamson, George. *The Senecan Amble: A Study in Prose Form from Bacon to Collier*. London: Faber and Faber 1951

Wilson, William S. 'Dan Flavin: Fiat Lux.' In *Light in Art*. Ed. Thomas B. Hess and John Ashbery. Art News Series. New York: Macmillan (Collier Books) 1971, 137–49

Wordsworth, William. *The Poetical Works*. Ed. Thomas Hutchinson; rev. by Ernest de Selincourt. London: Oxford University Press 1950

Yates, Frances Amelia. *The Art of Memory*. Chicago: University of Chicago Press 1974

– *Giordano Bruno and the Hermetic Tradition*. 1964; rpt, Chicago: University of Chicago Press 1982

– *The Occult Philosophy in the Elizabethan Age*. London: Routledge and Kegan Paul 1979

– *The Rosicrucian Enlightenment*. Boston: Routledge and Kegan Paul 1972

Yeats, W.B. *The Autobiography of William Butler Yeats*. London: Macmillan 1953

– *The Collected Poems*. London: Macmillan 1950

Index

www.ingramcontent.com/pod-product-compliance
Lightning Source LLC
LaVergne TN
LVHW010448080826
844660LV00027B/1231

* 9 7 8 1 4 8 7 5 8 5 0 4 4 *